STRINDBERG

Eight Famous Plays

AUGUST STRINDBERG
(1902)

AUGUST STRINDBERG

Eight Famous Plays

TRANSLATED BY

EDWIN BJÖRKMAN and N. ERICHSEN

WITH AN INTRODUCTION BY ALAN HARRIS

GERALD DUCKWORTH & CO., LTD.

3 HENRIETTA ST, LONDON, W.C.2

PRINTED IN ENGLAND BY
COMPTON PRINTING LTD
LONDON AND AYLESBURY

CONTENTS

All the above plays are in the authorised translation by EDWIN
BJÖRKMAN, *except "The Father," translated by* N. ERICHSEN.

INTRODUCTION

Odi et amo. Quare id faciam fortasse requiris.
Nescio, sed fieri sentio et excrucior.

In literature too, as in politics, it is harder (other things being equal) for the small nation to make itself heard in the world, and in proportion to its peripheral position, to the narrow diffusion, peculiarity, and difficulty of the language, its productions will be handicapped in attaining international currency. If, then, the one figure in Swedish literature of whom no man of literary pretensions could afford to confess total ignorance is Strindberg, that is no reflection on the merits of Swedish literature as a whole but rather a tribute to Strindberg's extraordinary qualities. Even so, it is only a section of his work that has thus imposed itself. He was an extremely productive writer in many fields: poet, journalist, social critic, historical and "regional" novelist as well as dramatist (not to mention his painting); but the Strindberg with whom the world is mainly concerned is the writer of a dozen or so plays, and among these it is the domestic dramas which spring first to the mind at the mention of his name, and on which his wider fame principally rests.

In them he had the advantage of an inexhaustible, a never-palling theme, the basic relations of the *couple humain*, to the treatment of which he brought the combination of penetrating insight and freedom from taboos that marks him. His speciality is the uncovering of " that yawning abyss which is called the human heart," as one of his characters calls it, and in that task, like Dostoyevsky, with whom he is in some respects comparable, he seems to reach a point where imaginative literature can only hand over to psycho-analysis.

Indeed the first approach to his best-known work is apt to produce the same nightmare feeling as the first approach to psychoanalytical doctrine; but after a time we realise that these people are simply saying the things we all at times feel but normally

7

refrain from saying or even fully admitting to our consciousness. In the story of his own childhood, *The Son of a Servant*, Strindberg relates how at the death-bed of his mother, to whom he was devoted, his mind dwelt on the gold ring he was to inherit from her, and how he afterwards reproached himself; but later experience taught him, he says, "that the brain is a strange thing which goes its own way and that there is a great similarity among men in the double life which they lead, the outward and the inward, the life of speech and the life of thought." It is the normally suppressed, but not abnormal, life of thought breaking out into speech that gives *The Father* and *The Dance of Death* their peculiar horror, and, incidentally, makes the conventions of polite society, so easily assailable from many sides, suddenly seem infinitely precious.

Strindberg himself felt them to be so. He is full of admiration for the ideal seemly life of the upper classes, so different from his own, in which, to judge from all accounts, the gloves were off almost as constantly as in those two plays. In *The Thunderstorm*, one of the latest, which deals with his last marriage, the ex-husband says: "Neither of us believed that the relationship would last, because we unmasked at once, and gave free vent to our antipathies," and it is his own admiration of the opposite way of life that Louise is expressing when she says: "I love the quiet and whatever is dignified, graceful, and measured—with nobody blurting out things and all thinking it a duty to overlook the less pleasant features of daily life." Such identification of a dramatist's own views and feelings with his characters' is notoriously rash as a rule, but Strindberg's passion for self-revelation, carried to the pitch of exhibitionism, makes it possible to check the parallel at innumerable points and to see how deeply and continuously his work is consubstantial with his life.

Much in that life, with its background of drink, penury, and constant odds with society, suggests some Dostoyevsky character paradoxically endowed with an excellent constitution and a capacity for hard, and even regular, work. With his extraordinary power of introspection and self-analysis (ever one of the primary tools of the psychologist), Strindberg had but to look steadily into himself to find a whole text-book of psycho-analysis.

Megalomania, over-compensating arrogance, masochistic tendencies, mother-fixation, agoraphobia, the habitual projection of his
own hostile impulses in wild accusations against the partner, perse-
cution-mania—the full catalogue would be endless, and his whole
personality often seems barely held together in an equilibrium
always precarious and for at least one long period upset altogether.
The kinship between genius and madness is proverbial, but not
even Nietzsche provides quite such an example of a life-long and
fruitful partnership between them.

Though the very vividness and power with which he depicts
the humiliations and frustrations of his childhood in *The Son of
a Servant* bring home to us how far they were either the common
lot of childhood or the result of his own extremely difficult
character—it is impossible not to have some sympathy with his
repressors—the Strindberg home, with all possible deductions
made, cannot be described as anything but unsatisfactory. His
father, a shipping agent, whom he calls "an aristocrat by birth
and education," had formed a connection with a woman socially
much beneath him and only regularised it just before the birth, on
22nd January, 1849, in Stockholm, of August, their fourth but
by no means last child, and at about the same time as his bank-
ruptcy, in consequence of which August's early years were spent
in slum-like squalor and overcrowding. As time went on, the
family's fortunes were to some extent repaired, but they never
seem to have run to adequate clothes or pocket-money for the boy,
nor did matters improve when his mother died and his father
married the young housekeeper.

Like Wells, Strindberg was convinced that the circumstances
of his upbringing had maimed him for life, but mentally not
physically: it was for his "weak character," as manifested in the
subsequent failures and disorders of his life, that he blamed his
early environment, which also helps to account for the intensity
of his preoccupation with Class. He was obsessed by the feeling
of having a foot in each camp and being at home in neither: his
mother's "slave blood" made him side with the underdog, but as
his father's son he felt that the "splendour of the upper class"
was his natural element.

From the latter point of view his first steps in the world were anything but auspicious.   After being moved from school to school he became a student at Upsala in 1867; but his studies were constantly interrupted either through poverty, which made it necessary for him to pay his way by odd teaching jobs, or his own wayward and rebellious nature, which would submit to no authority, and though he interested himself in a great variety of subjects he never succeeded in getting a degree.   One of these interruptions was caused by a sudden fancy to go on the stage. The venture was a fiasco but not an entirely useless one, for soon afterwards he had two plays accepted by the Theatre Royal in Stockholm.   Neither succeeded, but one of them, *The Outlaw,* attracted the attention of the King, Charles XV, who offered him a small pension.   That, too, proved a fiasco with the King's death, if not before; and after his final failure at Upsala he drifted wretchedly from one journalistic job in Stockholm to another, his bitterness aggravated by the rejection of his first important piece of work, the play *Master Olaf,* till he finally reached what seemed a safe haven in the Royal Library, where he was appointed Assistant Librarian in 1874.   Characteristically, neither time nor subsequent success ever cast a softer light over the memory of those struggles, and Strindberg remained a resolute debunker of Youth.   " Do you find it enviable to be young? " asks the Stranger (Strindberg's mouthpiece) in *After the Fire,* and when the Youth answers that he does not, he goes on: " No, youth is not its own master; it never has any money, and has to take its food out of other hands; it is not permitted to speak when company is present, but is treated as an idiot; and as it cannot marry, it has to ogle other people's wives, which leads to all sorts of dangerous consequences.   Youth—humbug! "

For Strindberg, the Royal Library only afforded a short interlude of calm, in which he achieved the beginnings of a reputation as a man of learning, before he met his fate in the shape of Siri, the wife of Baron Wrangel, an officer in the Guards.   Strindberg has told the story of their relationship, which was in every sense the central experience of his life and in which he explored the whole heaven and hell of love, in the *Confession of a Fool,* with a combination of mud-slinging and self-exposure than can scarcely have been surpassed.   After a strange initial period of triangular friendship, which ended in their becoming lovers, the Baron obtained a divorce in 1876 and they married next year. Siri now realised an old ambition by going on the stage, where she had a moderate success, while Strindberg scored his first real hit with his novel *The Red Room*. In the next few years the ups and downs of his reputation were matched by his fluctuations between love and hatred of Siri.

By 1883 things had become so uncomfortable in Sweden that he decided to live abroad, which meant giving up the Library and with it his only source of regular income; but their relations did not improve in exile, and after a few more years of mutual torment they were divorced in 1891. As so often, the writer's personal disaster was the world's gain, for out of it came, not merely *Married* (for which Strindberg was prosecuted in Sweden) and the *Confession of a Fool*, but the plays of 1887–8, in some ways the peak of his achievement, of which *Miss Julia* and *The Father* appear in this selection.

Many of their quarrels belong to the ordinary small change of married unhappiness, but certain features of the situation, as reflected in both the plays and the story, stand out as specially characteristic of Strindberg. First, the " kick " he got from the difference in their social position: as he put it, " the son of the people had conquered the white skin." This, at least as much as the lewd, seducing female, is the theme of *Miss Julia*, where the daughter of an aristocratic house, on midsummer night, leads her father's valet on till the inevitable happens, and next morning, when she realises the position thus created, kills herself. The play is saturated with class feeling and Strindberg certainly saw himself in the valet, the coming gentleman by virtue of his energy and ability, as against the " degenerate " aristocrat. That Jean is not more attractively portrayed is typical of Strindberg's over-riding honesty; for it is clear from his preface—in which he also discusses his aims and methods as a Naturalist playwright—that he did not intend us to waste much sympathy on Julia. The response of the Swedish working-class audience which cheered the fall of the aristocrat and the triumph of the worker, bizarre as it seems, was probably not so very far removed from the author's intentions at the time he wrote the play. But while he makes

Julia's dominant traits masculinity, his special aversion in women, and lewdness, he also emphasises her splendid physique and her fine aristocratic sense of honour which he cannot but admire, however certain he may be that Evolution is on the side of the Jeans. It really seems that he thought it a proof of her degeneracy that she had strong passions and usurped the "man's privilege" of showing it.   For Julia is also Siri, and perhaps the most repellent thing in the *Confession of a Fool* is the way Strindberg flings back in Siri's face the frankness with which she had shown him that she loved him.   By the time he gets to the divorce he already sees himself as the poor weak male in Messalina's toils, and from there it was not far to the final phase, in which he tormented her with incessant accusations of immoral conduct, including homosexuality (to which his reactions were entirely those of the common man, except that he did not mind mentioning it) and, like the Captain in *The Father*, drove himself to distraction with fantastic doubts about the paternity of their children.

It is in this play that his views of Women and Marriage—or, what is much the same thing, his deductions from his experience with Siri—find their ultimate expression.   Married life is depicted as a perpetual war to the knife: *femina viro lupa*.   Laura, the wife, is a fiend, hardly credible as a whole in retrospect; yet the play succeeds, because in each successive episode or touch he hits the nail on the head with such terrible precision, though we may tell ourselves afterwards that the entire conception is that of a man scarcely sane.   But what raises the play to greatness is those moments where Strindberg rises for an instant above his own frantic rancour and sums up the whole tragedy of life in a few words of sublime fairness—when, for instance, the Nurse says of the two of them: "My God, why should two people torment the life out of one another; two people who are otherwise so good and wish all others well. . . ."   Or when the Captain himself says to Laura: "Think how beautiful life was, and what it is now.   You did not wish to have it so, and neither did I, and yet it happened.   What then rules our life?"

In a later play, *The Link*, he recalls the actual divorce proceedings.   The parties begin with admirable resolutions to avoid all recrimination, but as the case proceeds, they gradually provoke each other into bringing all the skeletons out of the domestic cupboard, some of which correspond so closely with the *Confession of a Fool* that the play may be regarded as giving an epitome of the later stages of the marriage. " It is horrible," says the Judge when it is all over, " to see two persons who have loved trying to ruin each other. It is like being in a slaughter-house.

PASTOR. Well, that is love, Judge.

JUDGE. What then is hatred?

PASTOR. It is the lining of the coat."

Even after this, no one with a just view of the place of reason in human life will be surprised to learn that within two years of his divorce hope was triumphing over experience. Again it was a " white-skin " that he fell for, half his age this time and bemused with romantic notions of playing good angel to Fate-crossed Genius. She was Freda Uhl, daughter of an Austrian *Hofrat* but living an independent literary life in Berlin, where Strindberg had found a momentary refuge. After a courtship that would have frightened off anyone not utterly infatuated, she married him, in defiance of all the omens, in 1893. The past repeated itself, but at an accelerated pace, and they separated after only about eighteen months of nomadic bedlam. Strindberg stayed on in Paris, where they were last together and where several of his plays, among them *The Father*, were staged about that time; but he had recently spent an increasing amount of his time dabbling in the natural sciences and now cared for nothing but the theories which, with insane arrogance, he pitted against orthodox scientific doctrine. It was a symptom of the mental derangement which had long been the only explanation of his conduct and was now moving to its climax, where crazy chemical experiments combined with Swedenborgian speculations to form the nightmare life, dominated by delusions of persecution, which he has described with his usual precision in *Inferno*.

In *Marriage with Genius*, where Freda tells the whole fantastic story of their relations, she records that in the long discourse about himself which so dazzled her at their first meeting, after telling her that she was the woman he had so long been looking for, etc. etc., he went on: " For you—or her whom you recall to me. We are all in quest of her, our mother. I imagine I shall always remain tied to mine." It is indeed one of his recurrent themes, and now in his distraction he actually took refuge with Freda's mother, a religious woman with Swedenborgian leanings herself, who, with her sister, did her best to nurse him back to mental health but had to give it up in the end. Strindberg returned to Sweden, where he recovered, more or less, and finally settling in Stockholm, began once more to write plays.

The crisis had brought a definite break with his former positivism and he emerged from it with a firm belief in the supernatural and a vague religiosity which are both reflected in the new vein of mystical symbolism that tempers the old psychological realism in the plays of this period: *To Damascus*, in which he " worked off " his second marriage, *Advent, Easter, There are Crimes and Crimes*. The last-named starts as a representation of a vampire woman contrasted with a Madonna type, and develops into a study in the sense of guilt which makes people punish themselves with a severity beyond all reason. " There are crimes not mentioned in the criminal code," says one of the characters, " for they have to be punished by ourselves, and no judge could be more severe than we are against our own selves"—or as Freudians would say, our super-egos are against our egos; and curiously enough, the crimes in this case are those very death-wishes to which Freud gives so large a place in normal life.

The old savagery bursts out again in *The Dance of Death*, which outdoes *The Father* in horror in that now both the antagonists in the marriage-duel are monsters; but even here the figure of Kurt introduces a slightly less unrelenting note and *The Father* has nothing in it like the episode of Allan and Judith, which forms a sort of sub-plot in the second part and almost succeeds in transfiguring it by its poignancy and beauty. In these years, Strindberg also returned to the field of historical drama, which he had abandoned since the ill fortunes of *Master Olaf*, and produced a cycle of plays from Swedish history—represented in this selection by *Gustavus Vasa*—which did much to consolidate his reputation in his own country.

In this latest phase of his career he had withdrawn almost entirely from the world, but he still clung to hopes of domestic happiness, and Harriet Bosse, a Norwegian actress who had scored a great success in his *Easter*, finally accepted him, in somewhat the same spirit as Freda Uhl had done.   The marriage, which took place in 1901, was no more successful than its predecessors and they parted three years later.   Even that lesson was not enough for Strindberg; but Fanny Falkner, seeing the direction of all the footsteps near that cave, drew back in time.   She was an actress at August Falk's "little" theatre, for which Strindberg, having managed to capture it for the exclusive production of his own work, wrote a series of "chamber-plays," including *The Thunderstorm*, *After the Fire*, and *The Spook Sonata*.   The first two are kept reasonably close to earth by the material in them from Strindberg's own life; in *The Spook Sonata*, for all its realism of detail, symbolism gets the upper hand, so that, as with the second part of *Faust*, it is useless to ask what it "means" and each man must make what he can of it.   One of the ideas behind it may be the familiar one of stripping the façade that keeps the skeletons out of sight in "respectable" life, carried to its extreme point when the unmasker, Hummel, is himself unmasked.

Strindberg died, clasping a Bible, on 14th May, 1912, shortly after his 63rd birthday had been celebrated through all Sweden.   In these closing years, the mists of detraction, for which his own outrageous deeds, both literary and personal, were so largely responsible, had cleared away at last, leaving him secure on his pedestal to enjoy a fame no longer equivocal.   The final recognition by his own countrymen had been slow in coming, but they had much to forgive and forget.

In this sketch of certain phases in Strindberg's career no attempt has been or could be made to do justice either to his life or his work as a whole.   Its modest purpose was to throw a little light on the genesis of certain works in virtue of which he is a name of power to the Western world, the representative man of an attitude to life which will never be out-dated so long as the human predicament remains what it is.   "It's horrible," says Ericson in *After the Fire*, "don't you find life horrible?" "Yes," answers the Stranger, "horrible beyond all description."

ALAN HARRIS.

THE LINK

A TRAGEDY IN ONE ACT

1897

CHARACTERS

The Judge, 27 *years*
The Pastor, 60 *years*
The Baron, 42 *years*
The Baroness, 40 *years*
Alexander Eklund
Emmanuel Wickberg
Carl Johan Sjöberg
Eric Otto Boman
Ärenfrid Söderberg
Olof Andersson of Wik
Carl Peter Andersson of } *Jurors*
    Berga
Axel Wallin
Anders Eric Ruth
Swen Oscar Erlin
August Alexander Vass
Ludwig Östman
The Clerk of the Court
The Sheriff
The Constable
The Lawyer
Alexandersson, *a farmer*
Alma Jonsson, *a servant girl*
The Milkmaid
The Farm Hand
Spectators

THE LINK

A court-room. Door and windows in the background. Through the windows are seen the churchyard and the bell-tower. Door on the right. On the left, the desk of the judge on a platform. The front side of the desk is decorated in gold, with the judicial emblems of the sword and the scales. On both sides of the desk are placed chairs and small tables for the twelve jurors. In the centre of the room, benches for the spectators. Along the sides of the room are cupboards built into the walls. On the doors of these are posted court notices and schedules of market tolls.

SCENE I

The SHERIFF *and the* CONSTABLE.

THE SHERIFF. Did you ever see such a lot of people at the summer sessions before?

THE CONSTABLE. Not in fifteen years, or since we had the big murder at Alder Lake.

SHERIFF. Well, this story here is almost as good as a double parricide. That the Baron and the Baroness are going to separate is scandal enough, but when on top of it the families take to wrangling about properties and estates, then it's easy to see that there's going to be a hot time. The only thing wanting now is that they get to fighting over the child, too, and then King Solomon himself can't tell what's right.

CONSTABLE. What is there behind this case anyhow? Some say this and some say that, but the blame ought to rest on somebody?

SHERIFF. I don't know about that. Sometimes it is nobody's fault when two quarrel, and then again one alone is to blame for the quarrel of two. Now take my old shrew, for instance, she's running around at home scolding for dear life all by herself when I am away, they tell me. Besides, this is not just a quarrel, but a full-fledged criminal case, and in most such one party is complainant, or the one that has been wronged, and the other is defendant, or the one that has committed the crime. But in this case it is not easy to tell who is guilty, for both parties are at once complainants and defendants.

CONSTABLE. Well, well, queer things do happen these days. It's as if the women had gone crazy. My old one has spells when she says that I should bear children also, if there was any justice in things—just as if the Lord didn't know how he made his own creatures. And then I get long rigmaroles about her being human also, just as if I didn't know that before, or had said anything to the contrary; and of her being tired of acting as my servant girl, when, for a fact, I am not much better than her hired man.

SHERIFF. So-o. So you have got that kind of plague in your house too. Mine reads a paper she gets at the manor, and then she tells me as something wonderful, one day, that some farmer's lass has turned mason, and the next that an old woman has set upon and beaten her sick husband. I cannot quite get at what's the meaning of it all, but it looks most as if she was mad at me for being a man.

CONSTABLE. Mighty queer, that's what it is. [*Offers snuff.*] Fine weather we're having. The rye is standing as thick as the hairs in a fox fell, and we got over the black frosts without a hitch.

SHERIFF. There is nothing of mine growing, and good years are bad for me: no executions and no auctions. Do you know anything about the new judge who is going to hold court to-day?

CONSTABLE. Not much, but I understand he's a youngster who has just got his appointment and is going to sit for the first time now——

SHERIFF. And they say he is religious. Hm!

CONSTABLE. Hm-hm!— They're taking an awful time over the church services this year.

SHERIFF. [*Puts a big Bible on the judge's desk and a smaller one on each one of the jurors' tables.*] It cannot be long till they're done now, for they have been at it most of an hour.

CONSTABLE. He's a wonder at preaching, is the Pastor, once

he gets going. [*Pause.*] Are the parties to put in a personal appearance?

SHERIFF. Both of them, so I guess we'll have some scrapping—— [*The bell in the tower begins to ring.*] There, now they're done—— Just give the tables a wiping, and I think we are ready to start.

CONSTABLE. And there's ink in all the wells?

SCENE II

The BARON *and the* BARONESS *enter.*

BARON. [*In a low voice to the* BARONESS.] Then, before we part for a year, we are perfectly agreed on all points. First, no recriminations in court?

BARONESS. Do you think I would care to lay open the intimate details of our common life before a lot of curious peasants?

BARON. So much the better! And further: you keep the child during the year of separation, provided it may visit me when I do so desire, and provided it is educated in accordance with the principles laid down by me and approved by you?

BARONESS. Exactly!

BARON. And out of the income from the estate I give you three thousand crowns during the year of separation?

BARONESS. Agreed.

BARON. Then I have nothing more to add, but ask only to bid you good-bye. Why we part is known only to you and me, and for the sake of our son no one else must know it. But for his sake I beg you also: start no fight, lest we be goaded into soiling the names of his parents. It is more than likely, anyhow, that life in its cruelty will make him suffer for our divorce.

BARONESS. I don't care to fight as long as I may keep my child.

BARON. Let us then concentrate our attention on the child's welfare and forget what has happened between us. And remember another thing: if we fight about the child and question each other's fitness to take care of it, the judge may take it away from both of us and put it with some of those religious people who will bring it up in hatred and contempt for its parents.

BARONESS.   That's impossible!

BARON.   Such, my dear, is the law.

BARONESS.   It is a stupid law.

BARON.   Maybe, but it holds; and for you no less than for others.

BARONESS.   It is unnatural!   And I should never submit to it.

BARON.   You don't have to, as we have decided to raise no objections against each other.   We have never agreed before, but on this one point we are at one, are we not: to part without any kind of hostility?   [*To the* SHERIFF.]   Could the Baroness be permitted to wait in that room over there?

SHERIFF.   Certainly, walk right in.

The BARON *escorts the* BARONESS *to the door on the right and leaves then himself through the door in the background.*

SCENE III

The SHERIFF.   *The* CONSTABLE.   *The* LAWYER.   ALMA
JONSSON.   *The* MILKMAID.   *The* FARM HAND.

LAWYER.   [*To* ALMA JONSSON.]   Look here, my girl: that you have stolen, I don't doubt for a moment; but as your master has no witnesses to it, you are not guilty. But as your master has called you a thief in the presence of two witnesses, he is guilty of slander.   And now you are complainant and he defendant. Remember this one thing: the first duty of a criminal is—to deny!

ALMA JONSSON.   But please, sir, didn't you just say I was no criminal, and master was?

LAWYER.   You are a criminal because you have committed a theft, but as you have called for a lawyer, it is my unmistakable duty to clear you and convict your master.   Therefore, and for the last time: deny!   [*To the witnesses.*]   And as to the witnesses. what are they going to testify?   Listen: a good witness sticks to the case.   Now you must bear in mind that the question is not whether Alma has stolen anything or not, but only whether Alexandersson said that she had stolen.   For, mark you, he has no right to prove his assertions, but we have.   Why it should be so, the devil only knows!   But that's none of your business.   Therefore: keep your tongues straight and your fingers on the Bible!

MILKMAID. Lord, but I'm that scared, for I don't know what I'm going to say!

FARM HAND. You say as I do, and then you won't be lying.

SCENE IV

The JUDGE *and the* PASTOR *enter.*

JUDGE. Permit me to thank you for the sermon, Pastor.

PASTOR. Oh, don't mention it, Judge.

JUDGE. Yes—for, as you know, this is my first court. To tell the truth, I have felt some fear of this career, into which I have been thrown almost against my will. For one thing, the laws are so imperfect, the judicial practices so uncertain, and human nature so full of falsehood and dissimulation, that I have often wondered how a judge could dare to express any definite opinion at all. And to-day you have revived all my old fears.

PASTOR. To be conscientious is a duty, of course, but to be sentimental about it won't do. And as everything else on this earth is imperfect, there is no reason why we should expect judges and judgments to be perfect.

JUDGE. That may be, but it does not prevent me from harbouring a sense of tremendous responsibility, as I have men's fates in my hand, and a word spoken by me may show its effects through generations. I am especially thinking of this separation suit started by the Baron and his wife, and I have to ask you— you who have administered the two prescribed warnings before the Vestry Board—what is your view concerning their mutual relations and relative guilt?

PASTOR. In other words, Judge, you would either put me in your own place or base your decision on my testimony. And all I can do is to refer you to the minutes of the Board.

JUDGE. Yes, the minutes— I know them. But it is just what does not appear in the minutes that I need to know.

PASTOR. What charges the couple made against each other at the private hearings must be my secret. And besides, how can I know who told the truth and who lied? I have to tell you what

I told them: there is no reason why I should believe more in one
than in the other.

JUDGE.   But were you not able to form some kind of opinion
in the matter during the hearings?

PASTOR.   When I heard one, I formed one opinion, and
another when I was hearing the other.   In a word: I have no
settled view in this question.

JUDGE.   But I am to express a definite view— I, who know
nothing at all.

PASTOR.   That is the heavy task of the judge, which I could
never undertake.

JUDGE.   But there are witnesses to be heard?   Evidence to be
obtained?

PASTOR.   No, they are not accusing each other in public.   And
furthermore: two false witnesses will furnish sufficient proof,
and a perjurer will do just as well.   Do you think I would base my
judgment on servant gossip, on the loose-tongued chatter of en-
vious neighbours, or on the spiteful partisanship of relatives?

JUDGE.   You are a terrible sceptic, Pastor.

PASTOR.   Well, one gets to be so after sixty, and particularly
after having tended souls for forty years.   The habit of lying
clings like original sin, and I believe that all men lie.   As children we lie out of fear; as grown-ups, out of interest, need,
instinct for self-preservation; and I have known those who lied
out of sheer kindliness.   In the present case, and in so far as this
married couple is concerned, I fear you will find it very hard to
figure out who has told most of the truth, and all I can do is to
warn you against being caught in the snares set by preconceived
opinions.   You were married not long ago yourself, and you are
still under the spell of the young woman's witchery.   For this
reason you may easily become prejudiced in favour of a young
and charming lady, who is an unhappy wife and a mother besides.
On the other hand, you have also recently become a father, and
as such you cannot escape being moved by the impending separation of the father from his child.   Beware of sympathy with either
side, for sympathy with one is cruelty to the other.

JUDGE.   One thing will make my task more easy at least, and
that is their mutual agreement on the principal points.

PASTOR. Don't rely too much on that, for it is what they all say. And when they appear in court, the smouldering fire breaks into open flames. In this case a tiny spark will be enough to start a conflagration. Here comes the jury. Well, good-bye for a while! I stay, although I shall not be seen.

SCENE V

The TWELVE JURORS *enter. The* SHERIFF *rings a bell from the open doorway in the background. The members of the Court take their seats.* SPECTATORS *pour into the room.*

JUDGE. With a reminder of the provisions in Chapter Eleven, Sections Five, Six, and Eight, of the Criminal Code, as to the peace and order that must be maintained in Court, I hereby declare the proceedings of the Court opened. [*Whispers to the* CLERK OF THE COURT; *then*] Will the newly chosen jury please take the oath.

JURORS. [*Rise, each one putting the fingers of one hand on the Bible in front of him; then they speak in unison except when their names are being read out*]

I, Alexander Eklund;
I, Emmanuel Wickberg;
I, Carl Johan Sjöberg;
I, Eric Otto Boman;
I, Ärenfrid Söderberg;
I, Olof Andersson of Wik;
I, Carl Peter Andersson of Berga;
I, Axel Wallin;
I, Anders Eric Ruth;
I, Swen Oscar Erlin;
I, August Alexander Vass;
I, Ludwig Östman;

[*all at once, keeping time and speaking with low voices in a low pitch*] promise and swear by God and His Holy Gospel, that I will and shall, according to my best reason and conscience, judge rightly in all cases, no less for the poor than for the rich, and decide in accordance with the law of God and that of this country, as well as its legal statutes: [*in a higher pitch and with raised voices*] never tamper with the law or further any wrong, for the sake of either kinship by blood, kinship by marriage, friendship, envy, ill-will, or fear; nor for the sake of bribe or gift or any other cause, under any form whatsoever: and not make him responsible who has no guilt, or set him free who is guilty. [*Raising their voices still further.*]   Neither before judgment nor afterward, neither to parties in court nor to others, am I to discover such counsel as may be taken by the Court behind closed doors. All this I will and shall faithfully keep as an honest and upright judge, without fell deceit or design— [*Pause.*] So help God my life and soul!   [*The* JURORS *sit down.*

JUDGE.   [*To the* SHERIFF.]   Call the case of Alma Jonsson against the farmer Alexandersson.

SCENE VI

Enter the LAWYER, ALEXANDERSSON, ALMA JONSSON, *the* MILKMAID, *the* FARM HAND.

SHERIFF.   [*Calls out.*]   The servant girl Alma Jonsson and the farmer Alexandersson.

LAWYER.   I wish to present my power of attorney for the complainant.

JUDGE.   [*Examines the submitted document; then*]   The servant girl Alma Jonsson has had writ served on her former master, Alexandersson, bringing charges under Chapter Sixteen, Section Eight, of the Criminal Code, providing for imprisonment of not more than six months, or a fine, because Alexandersson has called her a thief without supporting his accusation or making legal charges.   What have you to say, Alexandersson?

ALEXANDERSSON.   I called her a thief because I caught her stealing.

JUDGE.   Have you witnesses to her theft?

ALEXANDERSSON.   No, as luck would have it, there's no witnesses, for I mostly go about by myself.

JUDGE.   Why did you not make a charge against her?

ALEXANDERSSON.   Well, I never go to court.   And then it

isn't the usage among us masters to prosecute household thefts, partly because there are so many of 'em, and partly because we don't like to spoil a servant's whole future.

JUDGE. Alma Jonsson, what have you to say in answer to this?

ALMA JONSSON. Ya-es——

LAWYER. You keep quiet! Alma Jonsson, who is not a defendant in this case, but the complainant, asks to have her witnesses heard in order that she may prove the slander uttered against her by Alexandersson.

JUDGE. As Alexandersson has admitted the slander, I shall ask for no witnesses. On the other hand, it is of importance for me to know whether Alma Jonsson be guilty of the offence mentioned, for if Alexandersson had reasonable grounds for his utterance, this will be held a mitigating circumstance when sentence is passed.

LAWYER. I must take exception to the statement made by the Court, for by Chapter Sixteen, Section Thirteen, of the Criminal Code, one charged with slander is denied the right to bring evidence as to the truth of his defamation.

JUDGE. Parties, witnesses, and spectators will retire so that the Court may consider the case.

[*All go out except the members of the Court.*

SCENE VII

THE COURT.

JUDGE. Is Alexandersson an honest and reliable man?

ALL THE JURORS. Alexandersson is a reliable man.

JUDGE. Is Alma Jonsson known as an honest servant?

ERIC OTTO BOMAN. I had to discharge Alma Jonsson last year for petty thievery.

JUDGE. And nevertheless I have now to fine Alexandersson. There is no way out of it. Is he poor?

LUDWIG ÖSTMAN. He's behind with his Crown taxes, and his crop failed last year. So I guess the fine will be more than he can carry.

JUDGE. And yet I can find no reason to postpone the case, as it is a clear one, and Alexandersson has no right to prove anything on his side.   Has anyone here anything to add or object?

ALEXANDER EKLUND.   I would just ask leave to make a general reflection.   A case like this, where one not only innocent, but offended against, has to take the punishment, while the thief has his so-called honour restored, may easily bring about that people grow less forbearing toward their fellow-men, and that taking cases to court grows more common.

JUDGE.   This is quite possible, but general reflections have no place in the proceedings, and the Court has to make a decision. Consequently my one question to the jury is: can Alexandersson be held guilty under Chapter Sixteen, Section Thirteen, of the Criminal Code?

ALL THE JURORS.   Yes.

JUDGE.   [*To the* SHERIFF.]   Call in the parties and the witnesses.

SCENE VIII

ALL *return.*

JUDGE.   In the case of Alma Jonsson against the farmer Alexandersson, Alexandersson is sentenced to pay a fine of one hundred crowns for slander.

ALEXANDERSSON.   But I saw her stealing with my own eyes! — That's what one gets for being kind!

LAWYER.   [*To* ALMA JONSSON.]   What did I tell you! If you only deny, everything is all right.   Alexandersson acted like a fool and denied nothing.   If I had been his counsel, and he had denied the charge, I should have challenged your witnesses, and there you would have been!—   Now we'll go out and settle up this business.   [*Goes out with* ALMA JONSSON *and the witnesses.*

ALEXANDERSSON.   [*To the* SHERIFF.]   And perhaps I have now got to give Alma her papers and write down that she has been honest and faithful?

SHERIFF.   That's none of my concern!

ALEXANDERSSON. [*To the* CONSTABLE.] And for a thing like this I am to lose house and land!   Who'd believe it, that justice means honour for the thief and a flogging for him that's robbed!

Damn it!— Come and have a cup of coffee with a stick in it afterward, Öman.

CONSTABLE. I'll come, but don't make a row.

ALEXANDERSSON. Yes, I'll be damned if I don't, even if it should cost me three months!

CONSTABLE. Now please don't make a row—don't make a row!

SCENE IX

The BARON *and the* BARONESS *enter after awhile.*

JUDGE. [*To the* SHERIFF.] Call the separation suit of Baron Sprengel and his wife, born Malmberg.

SHERIFF. Separation suit of Baron Sprengel and his wife, born Malmberg.

The BARON *and the* BARONESS *enter.*

JUDGE. In the proceedings entered against his wife, Baron Sprengel declares his intention of not continuing the marriage, and requests that, as the warnings of the Vestry Board have proved fruitless, order be issued for a year's separation in bed and board. What objection have you to make to this, Baroness?

BARONESS. To the separation I make no objection at all, if I can only have my child. That is my condition.

JUDGE. The law recognises no conditions in a case like this, and it is for the Court to dispose of the child.

BARONESS. Why, that's very peculiar!

JUDGE. For this reason it is of utmost importance that the Court learn who has caused the dissension leading to this suit. According to appended minutes of the Vestry Board, it appears that the wife has admitted having at times shown a quarrelsome and difficult disposition, while the husband has admitted no fault. Thus, Baroness, you appear to have admitted——

BARONESS. That's a lie!

JUDGE. I find it difficult to believe that the minutes of the Vestry Board, countersigned by the Pastor and eight other trust-worthy men, can be inaccurate.

BARONESS. The report is false!

JUDGE. Such remarks cannot be made with impunity before this Court.

BARON. May I call attention to the fact that I have voluntarily surrendered the child to the Baroness on certain conditions?

JUDGE. And I have to repeat once more what I said before, namely, that the case will be decided by the Court and not by the parties to it. Therefore: you deny having caused any dissension, Baroness?

BARONESS. Indeed, I do! And it is not the fault of one that two quarrel.

JUDGE. This is no quarrel, Baroness, but a criminal case; and furthermore, you seem now to be displaying a contentious temperament as well as inconsiderate behaviour.

BARONESS. Then you don't know my husband.

JUDGE. Will you please explain yourself, for I can base no decision on mere insinuations.

BARON. Then I must ask to have the case dismissed, so that I can obtain separation in other ways.

JUDGE. The case is already before the Court and will have to be carried to its conclusion— Baroness, you maintain then that your husband has caused the estrangement. Can this be proved?

BARONESS. Yes, it can be proved.

JUDGE. Please do so then, but bear in mind that it is a question of depriving the Baron of his parental rights and also of his rights to the property.

BARONESS. He has forfeited it many times over, and not the least when he denied me sleep and food.

BARON. I feel compelled to state that I have never refused to let the Baroness sleep. I have merely asked her not to sleep in the afternoon, because thereby the house was neglected and the child left without proper care. As to food, I have always left such matters to my wife, and I have only objected to some extravagant entertainments, as the neglected household could not bear such expenses.

BARONESS. And he has let me lie sick without calling in a physician.

BARON. The Baroness would always be taken sick when she

could not have her own way, but that kind of ailment did not last long as a rule. After I had brought a specialist from the city, and he had declared it to be nothing but tricks, I did not judge it necessary to call a physician the next time the Baroness was taken sick—because the new pier-glass cost fifty crowns less than originally intended.

JUDGE. All this is not of such nature that it can be considered when such a serious case has to be decided. There must be some deeper motives.

BARONESS. It ought to be counted a motive that the father will not permit the mother to bring up her own child.

BARON. First of all, the Baroness left the care of the child to a maid, and whenever she tried to assist, things went wrong. Secondly, she tried to bring up the boy as a woman, and not as a man. For instance, she dressed him as a girl until he was four years old; and to this very day, when he is eight years old, he carries his hair long as a girl, is forced to sew and crochet, and plays with dolls; all of which I regard as injurious to the child's normal development into a man. On the other hand, she has amused herself by dressing up the daughters of our tenants as boys, cutting their hair short, and putting them to work on things generally handled by boys. In a word, I took charge of my son's education because I noticed symptoms of mental derangement which before this have led to offences against the Eighteenth Chapter of the Criminal Code.

JUDGE. And yet you are now willing to leave the child in the hands of the mother?

BARON. Yes, for I have never been able to contemplate such a cruelty as to separate mother and child—and also because the mother has promised to mend her ways. And for that matter, I had only promised conditionally, and with the understanding that the law was not to be invoked in the matter. But since we have not been able to keep away from recriminations, I have changed my mind—especially as, from being the complainant, I have been turned into a defendant.

BARONESS. That's the way this man always keeps his promises.

BARON. My promises, like those of other people, have always

been conditional, and I have kept them as long as the conditions were observed.

BARONESS.   In the same way he had promised me personal freedom within the marriage.

BARON.   Naturally with the provision that the laws of decency were kept inviolate; but when all bounds were exceeded, and when ideas of license appeared under the name of freedom, then I regarded my promise as annulled.

BARONESS.   And for this reason he tormented me with the most absurd jealousy, and that is generally enough to make a common life unbearable.   He even made himself ridiculous to the extent of being jealous of the doctor.

BARON.   This alleged jealousy may be reduced to an advice on my part against the employment of a notorious and tattling masseur for an ailment commonly treated by women—unless the Baroness is having in mind the occasion when I showed our steward the door for smoking in my drawing-room and offering cigars to my wife.

BARONESS.   As we have not been able to keep away from scandal-mongering, it is just as well that the whole truth should get out: the Baron has been guilty of adultery.   Is not this enough to make him unworthy of bringing up my child alone?

JUDGE.   Can you prove this, Baroness?

BARONESS.   Yes, I can, and here are letters that show.

JUDGE.   [Receiving the letters.]   How long ago did this happen?

BARONESS.   A year ago.

JUDGE.   Of course, the time limit for prosecution has already expired, but the fact itself weighs heavily against the husband and may cause him to lose the child entirely as well as a part of the marriage portion.   Do you admit the truth of this charge, Baron?

BARON.   Yes, with remorse and mortification; but there were circumstances which ought to be held extenuating.   I was forced into humiliating celibacy by the calculated coldness of the Baroness, although I, and in all courtesy, asked as a favour, what the law allowed me to demand as a right.   I tired of buying her love, she having prostituted our marriage by selling her favours first for power and later for presents and money; and in the end

I found myself compelled, with the express consent of the Baroness, to take up an irregular relationship.

JUDGE. Had you given your consent, Baroness?

BARONESS. No, that is not true! I demand proofs!

BARON. It is true, but I cannot prove it, since the only witness, my wife, denies it.

JUDGE. What is unproved need not be untrue, but a compact of this kind, trespassing upon prevailing laws, must be held a *pactum turpe* and invalid in itself. Baron, so far everything is against you.

BARONESS. And as the Baron has confessed his guilt with remorse and shame, I, who have now become complainant instead of defendant, ask that the Court proceed to render a decision, as further details are not needed.

JUDGE. In my capacity as presiding officer of this Court, I wish to hear what the Baron has to say in justification, or at least in palliation.

BARON. I have just admitted the charge of adultery and have advanced as extenuating circumstances, partly that it was the result of pressing need when, after ten years of married life, I suddenly found myself unmarried, and partly that it was done with the consent of the Baroness herself. As I have now come to believe that all this was a trap set to make a case against me, it is my duty, for the sake of my son, to hold back no further——

BARONESS. [*Exclaims instinctively.*] Axel!

BARON. What caused me to break my marital vows was the faithlessness of the Baroness.

JUDGE. Baron, can you prove that the Baroness has been faithless to you?

BARON. No! For I was concerned about the honour of the family, and I destroyed all proofs that I obtained. But I still venture to believe that, in this matter, the Baroness will stand by the confession she once made to me.

JUDGE. Baroness, do you admit this offence as preceding and, therefore, probably causing the lapse of the Baron?

BARONESS. No!

JUDGE. Are you willing to repeat under oath that you are innocent of this charge?

BARONESS. Yes!

BARON. Good heavens! No, she must not do that! No perjury for my sake!

JUDGE. I ask once more is the Baroness willing to take the oath?

BARONESS. Yes.

BARON. Permit me to suggest that the Baroness just now appears as complainant, and a complaint is not made under oath.

JUDGE. As you have charged her with a criminal offence, she is defendant. What does the Jury hold?

EMMANUEL WICKBERG. As the Baroness is a party to this suit, it seems to me that she can hardly be allowed to testify in her own behalf.

SWEN OSCAR ERLIN. It seems to me that if the Baroness is to testify under oath, then the Baron should also be allowed to do so in the same matter, but as oath may not be put against oath, the whole matter remains in the dark.

AUGUST ALEXANDER VASS. I should say that it is not a question of testifying under oath here, but of taking an oath on one's own innocence.

ANDERS ERIC RUTH. Well, isn't that the question which has to be settled first of all?

AXEL WALLIN. But not in the presence of the parties, as the deliberations of the Court are not public.

CARL JOHAN SJÖBERG. The right of the Jury to express itself is not limited or conditioned by secrecy.

JUDGE. Out of so many meanings I can get no guidance. But as the guilt of the Baron can be proved, and that of the Baroness still remains unproved, I must demand that the Baroness take oath on her innocence.

BARONESS. I am ready!

JUDGE. No, wait a moment!— Baron, if you were granted time, would you be able to produce evidence or witnesses in support of your charge?

BARON. This I neither can nor will do, as I am not anxious to see my dishonour made public.

JUDGE. The proceedings of the Court will be adjourned while I consult with the chairman of the Vestry Board.

[*Steps down and goes out to the right.*

SCENE X

The JURORS *confer in low tones among themselves. The* BARON *and the* BARONESS *in the background. The* SPECTATORS *form groups and talk.*

BARON. [*To the* BARONESS.] You do not shrink from perjuring yourself?

BARONESS. I shrink from nothing when my child is concerned.

BARON. But if I have proofs?

BARONESS. Well, you have not.

BARON. The letters were burned, but certified copies of them are still in existence.

BARONESS. You lie to frighten me!

BARON. To show you how deeply I love my child, and to save the mother at least, as I seem to be lost, you—may have the proofs. But don't be ungrateful.

[*Hands her a bundle of letters.*

BARONESS. That you are a liar, I knew before, but that you were scoundrel enough to have the letters copied, that I could never have believed.

BARON. That is your thanks! But now both of us are lost.

BARONESS. Yes, let both go down—then there will be an end to the fight——

BARON. Is it better for the child to lose both its parents and be left alone in the world?

BARONESS. That will never occur!

BARON. Your absurd conceit, which makes you think yourself above all laws and above other human beings, has lured you into starting this fight, in which there can be only one loser: our son! What were you thinking of when you began this attack, which could not fail to provoke a defence? Not of the child, I am sure. But of revenge, I suppose? Revenge for what? For my discovery of your guilt?

BARONESS. The child? Were you thinking of the child when you dragged me in the mire before this rabble?

BARON. Helen!— Like wild beasts we have clawed each other bloody. We have laid our disgrace open to all these who take pleasure in our ruin, for in this room we have not a single friend. Our child will after this never be able to speak of his parents as respectable people; he will not be able to start life with a recommendation from father and mother; he will see the home shunned, the old parents isolated and despised, and so the time must come when he will flee us!

BARONESS. What do you want then?

BARON. Let us leave the country after selling the property.

BARONESS. And begin the same squabble all over again! I know what will happen: for a week you will be tame, and then you will abuse me.

BARON. Just think—now they are settling our fate in there. You cannot hope for a good word from the Pastor, whom you have just called a liar; and I, who am known to be no Christian, can expect no mercy either. Oh, I wish I were in the woods, so that I could crawl in under some big roots or put my head under a rock—this is more shame than I can bear!

BARONESS. It is true that the minister hates both of us, and it may happen as you say. Why don't you speak to him?

BARON. Of what? Making up?

BARONESS. Of anything you please, if it only be not too late! Oh, if it should be too late!— What can that man Alexandersson want that makes him prowl about us two all the time? I am afraid of that man!

BARON. Alexandersson is a nice fellow.

BARONESS. Yes, he is nice to you, but not to me—I have observed those glances before— Go and see the Pastor now; but take my hand first—I am scared!

BARON. Of what, dear, of what?

BARONESS. I don't know— Everything, everybody!

BARON. But not of me?

BARONESS. No, not now! It is as if our clothes had been caught in the mill wheels, and we had been dragged into the machinery. What have we been doing? What have we been

doing in our anger? How they will enjoy themselves, all these
who are now seeing the Baron and Baroness stripped naked and
flogging each other— Oh, I feel as if 1 were standing here
without a rag to cover me.   [*She buttons her coat.*

BARON. Calm yourself, my dear. It is not exactly the proper
place to tell you what I have said before: that there is only one
friend and one home—but we might start over again!— Well,
heaven knows! No, we cannot do it. You have gone too far.
It is all over. And this last—yes, let it be the last! And it had
to come after all the rest. No, we are enemies for life! And
if I let you go away with the child now, then you might marry
again— I see that now. And my child might have a step-
father; and I should have to watch another man going about
with my wife and child— Or I might myself be going about
with somebody else's wench hanging on my arm. No! Either
you or I! One of us must be struck down! You or I!

BARONESS. You! For if I let you take the child, you might
marry again, and I might have to see another woman taking my
place with my own child. The mere thought of it could make
me a murderess! A stepmother for *my* child!

BARON. You might have thought of it before! But when
you saw me champing at the chain of love that bound me to you,
then you believed me incapable of loving anybody but yourself.

BARONESS. Do you think I ever loved you?

BARON. Yes, once at least. When I had been faithless to
you. Then your love grew sublime. And your pretended scorn
made you irresistible. But my error caused you to respect me,
too. Whether it was the male or the criminal you admired most,
I don't know, but I believe it was both—it must have been both,
for you are the most typical woman I have ever met. And now
you are already jealous of a new wife whom I have never thought
of. What a pity that you became my mate! As my mistress,
your victory would have been unchallenged, and your infidelities
would only have seemed the bouquet of my new wine.

BARONESS. Yes, your love was always material.

BARON. Material as everything spiritual, and spiritual as all
that is material! My weakness for you, which gave strength to
my feeling, made you believe yourself the stronger, when you

were simply coarser, more ill-natured, and more unscrupulous than I.

BARONESS. You the stronger? You, who never want the same thing two minutes in a stretch! You, who as a rule never know what you want!

BARON. Yes, I know perfectly well what I want, but there is room in me for both love and hatred, and while I love you one minute, I hate you the next. And just now I hate you!

BARONESS. Are you now thinking of the child also?

BARON. Yes, now and always! And do you know why? Because he is our love that has taken flesh. He is the memory of our beautiful hours, the link that unites our souls, the common ground where we must ever meet without wishing to do so. And that is why we shall never be able to part, even if our separation be declared—Oh, if I could only hate you as I want to!

SCENE XI

The JUDGE *and the* PASTOR *enter in conversation and remain in the foreground.*

JUDGE. Thus I recognise the utter hopelessness of seeking justice or discovering truth. And it seems to me as if the laws were a couple of centuries behind our ideas of right. Did I not have to punish Alexandersson, who was innocent, and exonerate the girl, who was guilty of theft? And as for this separation suit, I know nothing at all about it at this minute, and I cannot take upon my conscience to render a decision.

PASTOR. But a decision has to be rendered.

JUDGE. Not by me! I shall give up my place and choose another profession.

PASTOR. Why, such a scandal would only bring you notoriety and close every career to you. Keep on judging a few years, and you will come to think it quite easy to crush human fates like egg shells. And for that matter, if you want to stand clear of this case, let yourself be outvoted by the jury. Then they must take the responsibility on themselves.

JUDGE. That is a way—and I suspect that they will be practically at one against me, for I have formed an opinion in this matter, which, however, is wholly intuitive and, therefore, not to be trusted— I thank you for your advice.

SHERIFF. [*Who has been talking with* ALEXANDERSSON, *steps up to the* JUDGE.] In my capacity of public prosecutor, I have to report the farmer Alexandersson as a witness against Baroness Sprengel.

JUDGE. In relation to the adultery charge?

SHERIFF. Yes.

JUDGE. [*To the* PASTOR.] Here is a new clue that may lead to a solution.

PASTOR. Oh, there are lots of clues, if you can only get hold of them.

JUDGE. But nevertheless it is horrible to see two persons who have loved trying to ruin each other. It is like being in a slaughter-house!

PASTOR. Well, that is love, Judge!

JUDGE. What then is hatred?

PASTOR. It is the lining of the coat.

[*The* JUDGE *goes over and speaks to the* JURORS.

BARONESS. [*Comes forward to the* PASTOR.] Help us, Pastor! Help us!

PASTOR. I cannot, and as a clergyman, I must not. And furthermore, did I not warn you not to play with such serious matters? You thought it so simple to part! Well, part then! The law will not prevent you, so don't put the blame on it.

SCENE XII

ALL *as before.*

JUDGE. The Court will now resume its proceedings. According to the report of the public prosecutor, Sheriff Wiberg, a new witness has appeared against the Baroness and is ready to affirm her guilt under the charge of adultery. Farmer Alexandersson!

ALEXANDERSSON. I am here.

JUDGE. How can you prove your assertion?

ALEXANDERSSON. I saw the offence committed.

BARONESS. He is lying!   Let him bring proof!

ALEXANDERSSON.   Proof?   I'm a witness now, ain't I?

BARONESS. Your assertion is no proof, although you happen to be called a witness for the moment.

ALEXANDERSSON.   Maybe the witness has to have two more witnesses, and those still others?

BARONESS. Yes, it might be needed when one cannot tell whether the whole lot are lying or not.

BARON.   The testimony of Alexandersson will not be required. I beg leave to offer the Court all the correspondence by which the marital infidelity of the Baroness stands completely proved— Here are the originals; copies of them will be found in the possession of defendant.

[*The* BARONESS *utters a cry but controls herself quickly.*

JUDGE.   And yet, Baroness, you were willing to take the oath a little while ago?

BARONESS.   But I didn't take it!   And now I think the Baron and I may cry quits.

JUDGE.   We do not let one crime cancel another.   The account of each one has to be settled separately.

BARONESS.   Then I want to file a claim at once against the Baron for my dowry which he has squandered.

JUDGE.   If you have squandered your wife's dowry, Baron, it might be well to settle that matter right here.

BARON.   The Baroness brought with her six thousand crowns in stock that was then unsaleable and soon became wholly worthless.   As at the time of our marriage she held a position as a telegrapher and declared herself unwilling to take support from her husband, we made a marriage contract and agreed that each one should be self-supporting.   But she lost her position after the marriage, and I have been supporting her ever since.   To this I had no objection whatever, but as she is now putting in bills, I shall ask leave to present one of my own to meet hers.   It totals up to thirty-five thousand crowns, this being one-third of the household expenses since the beginning of our marriage, and I being willing to take two-thirds upon myself.

JUDGE.   Have you this agreement in black and white, Baron?

BARON.   I have not.

JUDGE. Have you any documents to prove the disposition of your dowry, Baroness?

BARONESS. I didn't think at the time it would be necessary to get anything in writing, as I supposed myself to be dealing with honourable people.

JUDGE. Then this whole question cannot come under consideration here. The jury will please step into the small court-room for discussion of the case and formulation of a decision.

SCENE XIII

The JURY *and the* JUDGE *go out to the right.*

ALEXANDERSSON. [*To the* SHERIFF.] This here justice is more than I can get any sense out of.

SHERIFF. I think it would be wiser for you to go right home now, or you might have the same experience as the farmer from Mariestad. Did you ever hear of it?

ALEXANDERSSON. No.

SHERIFF. Well, he went to court as spectator, was dragged into the case as witness, became a party to it, and ended up with a flogging at the whipping-post.

ALEXANDERSSON. Oh, hell! But I believe it of 'em! I believe anything of 'em! [*Goes out.*

The BARON *joins the* BARONESS *in the foreground.*

BARONESS. You find it hard to keep away from me.

BARON. Now I have struck you down, and I am bleeding to death myself, for your blood is mine——

BARONESS. And how clever you are at making out bills!

BARON. Only when it comes to counter-claims! Your courage is that of despair, or that of a person sentenced to death. And when you leave here, you will collapse. Then you will no longer be able to load your sorrow and guilt on me, and you will be suffering from remorse. Do you know why I have not killed you?

BARONESS. Because you did not dare!

BARON. No! Not even the thought of hell could have held me back—for I don't believe in it. But this was the thought that did it: even if you get the child, you will be gone in five years. That is what the doctor tells me. And then the child might be left without either father or mother. Think of it—all alone in the world!

BARONESS. Five years!— It is a lie!

BARON. In five years! And then I am left behind with the child whether you want it or not.

BARONESS. Oh no! For then my family will bring suit to get the child away from you. I don't die when I die!

BARON. Evil never dies! That is so! But can you explain why you grudge me the child, and grudge the child me, whom it needs? Is it sheer malice—a craving for revenge that punishes the child? [*The* BARONESS *remains silent.*] Do you know, I remarked to the Pastor that I thought possibly you might have some doubts concerning the child's parentage, and that this might be a reason why you would not let me have the child, lest my happiness be built on a false foundation. And he replied: No, I don't think her capable of it—not of such a fine motive— I don't think you know yourself what makes you so fanatical about this one thing: it is the yearning for continued existence that goads you into maintaining your hold. Our son has your body, but my soul, and that soul you cannot rid him of. In him you will have me back when you least expect it; in him you will find my thoughts, my tastes, my passions, and for this reason you will hate him one day, as you hate me now. That is what I fear!

BARONESS. You still seem a little afraid that he may become mine?

BARON. In your quality of mother and woman, you have a certain advantage over me with our judges, and although justice may throw dice blindfolded, there is always a little lead on one side of each die.

BARONESS. You know how to pay compliments even in the moment of separation. Perhaps you don't hate me as much as you pretend?

BARON. Frankly speaking, I think that I hate not so much you as my dishonour, though you, too, come in for a share. And why this hatred? Perhaps I have overlooked that you are near the forties, and that a masculine element is making its appearance in you. Perhaps it is this element that I notice in your kisses, in your embraces—perhaps that is what I find so repulsive?

BARONESS. Perhaps. For the sorrow of my life has been, as you well know, that I was not born a man.

BARON. Perhaps that became the sorrow of my life! And now you try to avenge yourself on nature for having played with you, and so you want to bring up your son as a woman. Will you promise me one thing?

BARONESS. Will you promise me one thing?

BARON. What is the use of promising?

BARONESS. No, let us give no more promises.

BARON. Will you answer a question truthfully?

BARONESS. If I told the truth, you would think I lied.

BARON. Yes, so I should!

BARONESS. Can you see now that all is over, for ever?

BARON. For ever! It was for ever that we once swore to love each other.

BARONESS. It is too bad that such oaths must be taken!

BARON. Why so? It is always a bond, such as it is.

BARONESS. I never could bear with bonds!

BARON. Do you think it would have been better for us not to bind ourselves?

BARONESS. Better for me, yes.

BARON. I wonder. For then you could not have bound me.

BARONESS. Nor you me.

BARON. And so the result would have been the same—as when you reduce fractions. Consequently: not the law's fault; not our own; not anybody else's. And yet we have to assume the responsibility! [*The* SHERIFF *approaches.*] So! Now the verdict has been pronounced— Good-bye, Helen!

BARONESS. Good-bye—Axel!

BARON. It is hard to part! And impossible to live together. But the fight is over at least!

BARONESS. If it were! I fear it is just about to begin.

SHERIFF. The parties will retire while the Court takes action.

BARONESS. Axel, a word before it is too late! After all, they might take the child away from both of us. Drive home and take the boy to your mother, and then we will flee from here, far away!

BARON.   I think you are trying to fool me again.

BARONESS.   No, I am not.   I am no longer thinking of you, or of myself, or of my revenge.   Save the child only!   Listen, Axel—you must do it!

BARON.   I will.   But if you are deceiving me—   Never mind: I'll do it!

Goes out quickly.   The BARONESS *leaves through the door in the background.*

SCENE   XIV

The JURY *and the* JUDGE *enter and resume their seats.*

JUDGE.   As we now have the case complete before us, I shall ask each juror separately to state his opinion before decision is rendered.   Personally, I can only hold it reasonable that the child be given to the mother, as both parties are equally to blame for the estrangement, and as the mother must be held better adapted to the care of the child than the father.   [*Silence.*

ALEXANDER EKLUND.   According to prevailing law, it is the wife who takes her rank and condition from the husband, not the husband from the wife.

EMMANUEL WICKBERG.   And the husband is the proper guardian of his wife.

CARL JOHAN SJÖBERG.   The ritual, which gives binding force to the marriage, says that the wife should obey her husband, and so it is clear to me that the man takes precedence of the woman.

ERIC OTTO BOMAN.   And the children are to be brought up in the faith of the father.

ÄRENFRID SÖDERBERG.   From which may be concluded that children follow the father and not the mother.

OLOF ANDERSSON OF WIK.   But as in the case before us both man and wife are equally guilty, and, judging by what has come to light, equally unfit to rear a child, I hold that the child should be taken away from both.

CARL PETER ANDERSSON OF BERGA. In concurring with Olof Andersson, I may call to mind that in such cases the Court names two good men as guardians to take charge of children and property, so that out of the latter man and wife may have their support together with the child.

AXEL WALLIN. And for guardians I wish in this case to propose Alexander Eklund and Ärenfrid Söderberg, both of whom are well known to be of honest character and Christian disposition.

ANDERS ERIC RUTH. I concur with Olof Andersson of Wik as to the separation of the child from both father and mother, and with Axel Wallin as to the guardians, whose Christian disposition makes them particularly fitted to bring up the child.

SWEN OSCAR ERLIN. I concur in what has just been said.

AUGUST ALEXANDER VASS. I concur.

LUDWIG ÖSTMAN. I concur.

JUDGE. As the opinion expressed by a majority of the jurors is contrary to my own, I must ask the Jury to take a vote on the matter. And I think it proper first to put the motion made by Olof Andersson for the separation of the child from both father and mother, and for the appointment of guardians. Is it the unanimous will of the Jury that such action be taken?

ALL THE JURORS. Yes.

JUDGE. If anybody objects to the motion, he will hold up his hand. [*Silence.*] The opinion of the Jury has won out against my own, and I shall enter an exception on the minutes against what seems to me the needless cruelty of the decision— The couple will then be sentenced to a year's separation of bed and board, at the risk of imprisonment, if, during that period, they should seek each other. [*To the* SHERIFF.] Call in the parties.

SCENE XV

The BARONESS *and* SPECTATORS *enter.*

JUDGE. Is Baron Sprengel not present?

BARONESS. The Baron will be here in a moment.

JUDGE. Whoever does not observe the time, has only himself

to blame.   This is the decision of the County Court: that husband and wife be sentenced to a year's separation of bed and
board, and that the child be taken from the parents and placed in
charge of two guardians for education.   For this purpose the
Court has selected and appointed the jurors Alexander Eklund
and Ärenfrid Söderberg.

> *The* BARONESS *cries out and sinks to the floor.   The* SHERIFF
> *and the* CONSTABLE *raise her up and place her on a chair.*
> *Some of the* SPECTATORS *leave in the meantime.*

BARON.   [*Enters.*]   Your Honour!   I heard the sentence of
the Court from the outside, and I wish to enter a challenge, first
against the Jury as a whole, it being made up of my personal
enemies, and secondly against the guardians, Alexander Eklund
and Ärenfrid Söderberg, neither of whom possesses the financial
status demanded of guardians.   Furthermore, I shall enter proceedings against the Judge for incompetence displayed in the exercise of his office, in so far as he has failed to recognise that the
primary guilt of one led to the subsequent guilt of the other, so
that both cannot be held equally responsible.

JUDGE.   Whosoever be not satisfied with the decision rendered may appeal to the higher court within the term set by law.
Will the Jury please accompany me on house visitation to the
Rectory in connection with the suit pending against the communal
assessors?

> *The* JUDGE *and the* JURY *go out through the door in the*
> *background.*

SCENE XVI

> *The* BARON *and the* BARONESS.   *The* SPECTATORS *withdraw*
> *gradually.*

BARONESS.   Where is Emil?

BARON.   He was gone!

BARONESS.   That's a lie!

BARON.   [*After a pause.*]   Yes—   I did not bring him to
my mother, whom I cannot trust, but to the Rectory.

BARONESS.   To the minister!

BARON.   Your one reliable enemy!   Yes.   Who was there

else that I might trust? And I did it because a while ago I caught a glance in your eye which made me think that you possibly might kill yourself and the child.

BARONESS. You saw that!— Oh, why did I let myself be fooled into believing you.

BARON. Well, what do you say of all this?

BARONESS. I don't know. But I am so tired that I no longer feel the blows. It seems almost a relief to have received the final stab.

BARON. You give no thought to what is now going to happen: how your son is going to be brought up by two peasants, whose ignorance and rude habits will kill the child by slow torture; how he is going to be forced down into their narrow sphere; how his intelligence is going to be smothered by religious superstition; how he is going to be taught contempt for his father and mother——

BARONESS. Hush! Don't say another word, or I shall lose my reason. My Emil in the hands of peasant women, who don't know enough to wash themselves, who have their beds full of vermin, and who cannot even keep a comb clean! My Emil! No, it is impossible!

BARON. It is the actual reality, and you have nobody but yourself to blame for it.

BARONESS. Myself? But did I make myself? Did I put evil tendencies, hatred, and wild passions into myself? No! And who was it that denied me the power and will to combat all those things?— When I look at myself this moment, I feel that I am to be pitied. Am I not?

BARON. Yes, you are! Both of us are to be pitied. We tried to avoid the rocks that beset marriage by living unmarried as husband and wife; but nevertheless we quarrelled, and we were sacrificing one of life's greatest joys, the respect of our fellow-men—and so we were married. But we must needs steal a march on the social body and its laws. We wanted no religious ceremony, but instead we wriggled into a civil marriage. We did not want to depend on each other—we were to have no common pocket-book and to insist on no personal ownership of each other—and with that we fell right back into the old rut

again. Without wedding ceremony, but with a marriage contract! And then it went to pieces. I forgave your faithlessness, and for the child's sake we lived together in voluntary separation—and freedom! But I grew tired of introducing my
friend's mistress as my wife—and so we had to get a divorce.
Can you guess—do you know against whom we have been fighting? You call him God, but I call him nature. And that was
the master who egged us on to hate each other, just as he is egging
people on to love each other. And now we are condemned to
keep on tearing each other as long as a spark of life remains.
New proceedings in the higher court, reopening of the case,
report by the Vestry Board, opinion from the Diocesan Chapter,
decision by the Supreme Court. Then comes my complaint to
the Attorney-General, my application for a guardian, your objections and counter-suits: from pillory to post! Without hope
of a merciful executioner! Neglect of the property, financial
ruin, scamped education for the child! And why do we not put
an end to these two miserable lives? Because the child stays our
hands! You cry, but I cannot! Not even when my thought
runs ahead to the night that is waiting for me in a home laid
waste! And you, poor Helen, who must go back to your mother!
That mother whom you once left with such eagerness in order to
get a home of your own. To become her daughter once more—
and perhaps find it worse than being a wife! One year! Two
years! Many years! How many more do you think we can
bear to suffer?

BARONESS. I shall never go back to my mother. Never! I
shall go out on the high-roads and into the woods so that I may
find a hiding-place where I can scream—scream myself tired
against God, who has put this infernal love into the world as a
torment for us human creatures—and when night comes, I shall
seek shelter in the Pastor's barn, so that I may sleep near my child.

BARON. You hope to sleep to-night—you?

Curtain.

THE FATHER

A Tragedy

1887

CHARACTERS

A CAVALRY CAPTAIN
LAURA, *his wife*
BERTHA, *their daughter*
DR. ÖSTERMARK
THE PASTOR
THE NURSE
NÖJD
THE ORDERLY

THE FATHER

ACT I

A sitting-room at the Captain's. A door in the background to the right. In the middle of the room a large round table strewn with newspapers and magazines. To the right a leather-covered sofa and table. In the right-hand corner a private door. To the left a bureau with a clock on it, and a door to the inner rooms. Arms on the wall, also guns and gamebags. Clothes pegs by the door on which hang uniform coats. A lighted lamp on the large table.

SCENE I

The CAPTAIN *and the* PASTOR [*on the sofa*]. *The Captain in undress uniform and riding-boots with spurs. The Pastor in black with a white neckcloth, but without his clerical ruff; he is smoking a pipe.*

The CAPTAIN *rings.*

ORDERLY. Yes, sir.

CAPTAIN. Is Nöjd out there?

ORDERLY. Nöjd is waiting for orders in the kitchen.

CAPTAIN. Is he in the kitchen again! Fetch him in at once.

ORDERLY. Yes, sir. [*Goes.*

THE PASTOR. What is wrong now?

CAPTAIN. Oh, the rascal has got the girl into trouble again; he is a thoroughly bad lot.

PASTOR. Nöjd do you say? Why, he was to the fore in the spring, wasn't he?

CAPTAIN. Yes, don't you remember? But won't you be kind enough to say a few friendly words to him, and perhaps you may make some impression on him. I've sworn at him, and I've flogged him, too, but it hasn't the least effect.

PASTOR. And now you want me to lecture him. What impression do you suppose the Word of God will make on a trooper?

CAPTAIN. Well, it certainly has no effect on me, you know.

PASTOR. I know that well enough.

CAPTAIN. But on him! Try at all events.

SCENE II

The former. NÖJD.

CAPTAIN. What have you been doing now, Nöjd?

NÖJD. Begging your pardon, Captain, I can't possibly say while the Pastor is here.

PASTOR. Don't be bashful, my lad.

CAPTAIN. You had better confess, or you know how it will be.

NÖJD. Well, then, it was like this: we were at a dance at Gabriel's, and then—and then Ludwig said——

CAPTAIN. What has Ludwig to do with the story. Stick to the truth.

NÖJD. Yes, and then Emma said that we should go into the barn.

CAPTAIN. Ah, I suppose it was Emma who led you astray?

NÖJD. Well, that's about it. And I must say that unless the girl is willing nothing ever comes of it.

CAPTAIN. Once for all: are you the child's father or not?

NÖJD. How should I know?

CAPTAIN. What do you mean? Can't you tell that?

NÖJD. Why no, one can never be quite sure.

CAPTAIN. Were you not the only one then?

NÖJD. Yes, that time, but I can't be sure that I was the only one for all that.

CAPTAIN. Do you lay the blame on Ludwig then? Is that what you mean?

NÖJD. It isn't easy to know who to lay the blame on.

CAPTAIN. Yes, but you told Emma that you would marry her.

NÖJD. Oh, one always has to say that——

CAPTAIN. [*To* PASTOR.] This is really dreadful.

PASTOR. These are old stories! But listen, Nöjd, you are surely man enough to know whether you are the father or not.

NÖJD. Well, certainly, I and the girl . . . but you know yourself, Pastor, that it needn't come to anything for all that.

PASTOR. Look here, my lad, we are talking about you now. You will surely not leave the girl alone with the child. I suppose we can't compel you to marry her, but you shall provide for the child! that you *shall* do.

NÖJD. Well, then, Ludwig must too.

CAPTAIN. Then the case must go to the Courts. I can't disentangle all this, and after all it doesn't concern me. So now, be off.

PASTOR. Nöjd, one word! Don't you think it is dishonourable to leave a girl like that in absolute destitution with her child? Don't you think so? Heigh? Don't you see that such a mode of action . . . h'm . . . h'm.

NÖJD. Yes, if only I knew for certain that I was father to the child, but one can never be sure of that, Pastor, and to slave all one's life for another man's child is not pleasant. Surely you, Pastor, and the Captain, can understand that for yourselves.

CAPTAIN. Be off.

NÖJD. God keep you, Captain.   [*Goes.*

CAPTAIN. But don't go into the kitchen again, you rascal!

SCENE III

The CAPTAIN *and the* PASTOR.

CAPTAIN. Now why didn't you come down upon him?

PASTOR. What do you mean? Didn't I give it him?

CAPTAIN. Why, you only sat and muttered to yourself.

PASTOR. To tell the truth I really don't know what to say. It is a pity about the girl, certainly, but it is a pity about the lad, too. For just think if he were not the father. The girl can nurse the child for four months at the orphanage, and then it will be permanently provided for, but the lad can do no such thing. The girl will get a good place afterwards in some respectable house, but the lad's future may be ruined if he is dismissed from the regiment.

CAPTAIN. Upon my soul I should like to be in the Magistrate's shoes and judge this case. The lad is probably not quite innocent, one can't be sure, but the one thing one can be sure of is that the girl is guilty if there be any guilt in the matter.

PASTOR. Well, well, I judge no man! But what were we talking about when this tiresome story interrupted us? It was about Bertha and the confirmation, wasn't it?

CAPTAIN. Yes, but it was surely not about the confirmation particularly, but the whole of her education. This house is full of women who all want to educate my child. My mother-in-law wants to make a spiritualist of her; Laura insists on her being an artist; the governess wants to make her a Methodist, old Margret a Baptist, and the servant-girls a Salvationist. It won't do to try and make a soul in patches like that: especially when I, who have the chief right to form her character, have all *my* efforts opposed. I am determined to get her out of this house.

PASTOR. There are too many women here governing the house.

CAPTAIN. Yes, aren't there? It is like going into a cage full of tigers, and if I did not hold red-hot irons under their noses they might tear me to pieces at any moment! And you, you laugh, you villain. Was it not enough that I took your sister for my wife, without your palming off your old stepmother on me.

PASTOR. Well but, good Heavens, one cannot have stepmothers in one's house.

CAPTAIN. No, you think it better to have mothers-in-law instead—in other people's houses that is to say.

PASTOR. Ah well, everyone of us has his burden in this life.

CAPTAIN. Yes, but I have certainly too heavy a one. I have even my old nurse in addition, who treats me as if I ought to wear bibs still. She is a good old soul, Heaven knows, but she is not in the right place here.

PASTOR. You must keep order among the womenfolk, Adolf. You let them dictate to you far too much.

CAPTAIN. Now, look here, will you enlighten me as to how to keep order among the womenfolk?

PASTOR. Laura was treated with a firm hand, but then, although she is my own sister, I must admit she really *was* a little troublesome.

CAPTAIN. Laura has certainly her weak points, but with her they don't amount to much.

PASTOR. Pray speak quite plainly, I know her.

CAPTAIN. She has been brought up with romantic ideas and finds it a little difficult to accommodate herself to circumstances, but in any case she is my wife. . . .

PASTOR. And because she is your wife she is the best of them. No, my dear fellow, it is really she who oppresses you most.

CAPTAIN. In the meantime the whole house is turned upside down. Laura won't let Bertha leave her, and I can't let her remain in this bedlam.

PASTOR. Oh, Laura won't. Well, then, do you know, I'm afraid there will be difficulties. If she set her mind on anything when she was a child, she used to lie like a corpse till she got it, and then as likely as not she would give it back, explaining that she didn't care about the thing, whatever it was, but about getting her own way.

CAPTAIN. So she was like that even then? H'm—— She really sometimes gets into such passions that I am quite anxious about her and fear that she is ill.

PASTOR. But what do you wish to do with Bertha that is so unpardonable? Is no compromise possible?

CAPTAIN. You mustn't think that I wish to make a prodigy of her, or a copy of myself. I will not play the pander to my daughter and educate her exclusively for matrimony, for in that case she would have bitter days if she remained unmarried. But I will not, on the other hand, persuade her into a masculine career that requires a long course of training, which would be entirely thrown away in case she should wish to marry.

PASTOR. What do you intend then?

CAPTAIN. I intend her to be a teacher. If she remains unmarried she will be able to support herself and at any rate be in no worse position than the poor schoolmasters who have to share their

salaries with a family.   If she marries she can apply her knowledge to the education of her children.   Don't you think I'm
right?

PASTOR.   Perfectly right.   But hasn't she, on the other hand,
shown such talents for painting that it would outrage nature to
suppress them?

CAPTAIN.   No!   I have shown her performances to an
eminent painter, and he says that they are only the kind of thing
that can be learnt in schools.   But then a young fellow came
here in the summer who, of course, understood the matter much
better, and declared that she had a remarkable talent, and so it
was settled to Laura's satisfaction.

PASTOR.   Was he in love with the girl?

CAPTAIN.   I take that entirely for granted.

PASTOR.   Then God be with you, old fellow, for in that case
I see no help.   But all this is very tiresome, and, of course, Laura
has her supporters . . . in there.

CAPTAIN.   Yes, that you may depend on!   The whole house
is already up in arms, and, between ourselves, it is not exactly a
noble conflict that is waged from that quarter.

PASTOR.   [*Gets up.*]   Do you think I don't know that.

CAPTAIN.   You also?

PASTOR.   Also?

CAPTAIN.   But the worst of it is that it seems to me as if
Bertha's career was being determined by most objectionable
motives, in there.   They drop hints about man having to see that
woman can do this and can do that.   It is Man and Woman
against one another, incessantly all day long.   Must you go now?
Do stay for supper.   I have certainly nothing to offer you, but
still.   You know that I am expecting the new Doctor.   Have
you seen him?

PASTOR.   I caught a glimpse of him as I passed by.   He
looked pleasant and trustworthy.

CAPTAIN.   I'm glad of that.   Do you think it possible he
may side with me?

PASTOR.   Who knows?   It depends on how much he has been
accustomed to women.

CAPTAIN.   Oh! but won't you stay?

PASTOR. No thanks, my dear fellow; I promised to come home to supper, and the old lady gets so uneasy if I am late.

CAPTAIN. Uneasy? Angry you should say. Well, as you will. Let me help you with your overcoat.

PASTOR. It seems to be very cold this evening. Thanks. You must take care of your health, Adolf, you look so nervous.

CAPTAIN. Do I look nervous?

PASTOR. Yes, you are not really well.

CAPTAIN. Has Laura put that into your head? She has treated me these twenty years as if I were at the point of death.

PASTOR. Laura? No; but, but I'm really uneasy about you. Take care of yourself. That's my advice! Good-bye, dear old man; but didn't you want to talk about the confirmation?

CAPTAIN. Not at all! I assure you that matter will proceed in the ordinary course at the expense of the official conscience, for I have no intention of being either a confessor or a martyr. We have put all that behind us. Good-bye. Remember me at home.

PASTOR. Good-bye, Adolf. Love to Laura.

SCENE IV

The CAPTAIN, *afterwards* LAURA. *The* CAPTAIN *opens his desk, and seats himself at it with his accounts.*

CAPTAIN. Thirty-four . . . nine, forty-three . . . seven, eight, fifty-six.

LAURA. [*Enters from the inner rooms.*] Will you be so kind as to——

CAPTAIN. In a moment! Fifty-six . . ., seventy-one, eighty-four, eighty-nine, ninety-two, a hundred. What is it?

LAURA. Am I disturbing you?

CAPTAIN. Not at all. Housekeeping money, I suppose?

LAURA. Yes, housekeeping money.

CAPTAIN. Put the accounts down there and I will go through them.

LAURA. The accounts?

CAPTAIN. Yes.

LAURA. Am I to keep accounts now?

CAPTAIN. Of course you are to keep accounts now. Our affairs are in a precarious condition, and in case of a liquidation there must be accounts or one may be punished as a fraudulent debtor.

LAURA. It is not my fault that our affairs are in a precarious condition.

CAPTAIN. That is exactly what will be shown by the accounts.

LAURA. It is not my fault that the bailiff doesn't pay.

CAPTAIN. Who recommended the bailiff so warmly? You! Why did you recommend a—shall we say—a fool?

LAURA. And why did you take the fool, then?

CAPTAIN. Because I was not allowed to eat in peace, nor to sleep in peace, nor to work in peace, till you got the man here. You wanted him so that your brother might be rid of him, your mother wanted him because I didn't want him, the governess wanted him because he was a Scripture-reader, and old Margret because she had known his mother from her childhood. That's why I took him, and if I hadn't taken him I should be shut up in a mad-house now, or lying in the family grave. Meantime here is the housekeeping money and your allowance. You can give me the accounts presently.

LAURA. [Curtsies.] Thanks so much. Do you also keep accounts of what you spend besides the housekeeping money?

CAPTAIN. That does not concern you.

LAURA. No, that is true, just as little as my child's education concerns me. Have my lords made up their minds after the conference of this evening?

CAPTAIN. I had made up my mind beforehand, and it therefore only remained for me to announce my intention to the one friend I and the family have in common. Bertha is to board in town and starts in a fortnight.

LAURA. Where is she to board, if I may venture to ask?

CAPTAIN. At Auditor Säffberg's.

LAURA. That free thinker!

CAPTAIN. The law declares that children are to be brought up in their father's faith.

LAURA. And the mother is to have no voice in the matter?

CAPTAIN. None whatever. She has sold her birthright by a

legal transaction, and surrendered her rights in return for the man's undertaking to care for her and her children.

LAURA. Therefore she has no power over her child.

CAPTAIN. No, none whatever. When one has once sold one's goods, one cannot have them back and yet keep the money.

LAURA. But if both father and mother agree . . .

CAPTAIN. How could that happen? I wish her to live in town, you wish her to live at home. The arithmetical result would be that she remained at the railway station, midway between town and home. This is a knot that cannot be untied. Do you see?

LAURA. Then it must be broken! What was Nöjd doing here?

CAPTAIN. That is a professional secret.

LAURA. Which the whole kitchen knows.

CAPTAIN. Good, then you must know it.

LAURA. I do know it!

CAPTAIN. And have your judgment ready beforehand.

LAURA. My judgment is the law's judgment.

CAPTAIN. It is not written in "the judgment of the law" who the child's father is.

LAURA. No, but one can usually find that out.

CAPTAIN. Wise people say that one never can tell those things.

LAURA. That is remarkable. Can one never tell who is the father of a child?

CAPTAIN. No; so it is maintained.

LAURA. That is remarkable. How, then, can the father have such rights over the child!

CAPTAIN. He only has them when he has assumed the responsibility or has had the responsibility thrust on him. And in marriage there is, of course, no doubt about paternity.

LAURA. No doubt?

CAPTAIN. No, I should hope not.

LAURA. And in case the wife has been unfaithful?

CAPTAIN. This is no such case! Have you anything further to ask about?

LAURA. Nothing whatever.

CAPTAIN. Then I shall go up to my room, and perhaps you will be good enough to inform me when the Doctor comes.

[*Shuts the bureau and gets up.*

LAURA. Certainly.

[CAPTAIN *goes through the private door to right.*

CAPTAIN. As soon as he comes. For I don't wish to be rude to him. You understand. [*Goes.*

LAURA. I understand.

SCENE V

LAURA. *Alone, she gazes at the banknotes she holds in her hand.*

MOTHER-IN-LAW'S VOICE. [*Within.*] Laura!

LAURA. Yes.

MOTHER-IN-LAW'S VOICE. Is my tea ready?

LAURA. [*In the doorway to the inner rooms.*] You shall have it directly.

LAURA *goes towards the hall door in the background, as the orderly opens it and announces—*DOCTOR ÖSTERMARK.

DOCTOR. Madam!

LAURA. [*Goes towards him and gives him her hand.*] Good evening, Doctor? We are all very glad to see you here. The Captain is out, but he will be back directly.

DOCTOR. I beg your pardon for coming so late, but I have had to pay some professional visits already.

LAURA. Won't you sit down? Do.

DOCTOR. Thank you.

LAURA. Yes, there is a great deal of illness in the neighbourhood just now, but I hope that you will settle down comfortably all the same. It is so very important for lonely country people like us to find a doctor who is interested in his patients. And I hear so much good of you, Doctor, that I hope the happiest relations will prevail between us.

DOCTOR. You are much too kind, but I hope on the other hand that my visits to you may not too frequently be caused by necessity. Your family, I believe, is usually in good health. . . .

LAURA. We have fortunately not had any acute illness, but still things are not entirely as they ought to be.

DOCTOR. Indeed?

LAURA. They are, Heaven knows, not so satisfactory as we might wish.

DOCTOR. You really alarm me.

LAURA. There are circumstances in a family, which one is bound in honour and conscience to conceal from the whole world. . . .

DOCTOR. Excepting from the doctor.

LAURA. Exactly. It is, therefore, my painful duty to tell you the whole truth immediately.

DOCTOR. Can we not postpone this conference until I have had the honour of being introduced to the Captain?

LAURA. No! You must hear me before seeing him.

DOCTOR. It relates to him, then?

LAURA. Yes—to him, my poor, dear husband.

DOCTOR. You make me uneasy, Madam, and believe me, I sympathise with your misfortune.

LAURA. [*Taking out her handkerchief.*] My husband's mind is affected. Now you know all, and must judge for yourself when you see him.

DOCTOR. Is it possible! I have read the Captain's excellent treatises on mineralogy with great admiration, and have always found them display a clear and powerful intellect.

LAURA. Really? I should be delighted if his whole family should prove to be mistaken.

DOCTOR. But, of course, it is possible that his mind is disturbed in other directions. Let me hear.

LAURA. That is what we also fear. You see, he has sometimes the most extraordinary ideas, which, of course, one would expect in a learned man if they did not exercise a disastrous influence on the welfare of his whole family. For instance, he has a fancy for buying all manner of things.

DOCTOR. That is serious; but what does he buy?

LAURA. Whole boxes of books that he never reads.

DOCTOR. Oh, it is nothing out of the way for a scholar to buy books.

LAURA. You don't believe what I say?

DOCTOR. Yes, Madam, I am convinced that you believe what you say.

LAURA. Then is it reasonable to think that one can see, by looking in a microscope, what is going on in another planet?

DOCTOR. Does he say he can do that?

LAURA. Yes, he says so.

DOCTOR. In a microscope?

LAURA. In a microscope, yes.

DOCTOR. This is serious, if it is so.

LAURA. If it is so. Then you have no belief in me, Doctor, and I am sitting here and confiding the family secret in you. . . .

DOCTOR. Indeed, Madam, your confidence honours me, but as a physician I must investigate and observe before I can judge. Has the Captain ever shown any symptoms of uncertainty of temper, or instability of will?

LAURA. Has he ever? We have been married for twenty years and he has never yet made a decision without abandoning it afterwards.

DOCTOR. Is he obstinate?

LAURA. He always insists on having his own way, but when he has got it he drops the whole thing and asks me to decide.

DOCTOR. This is serious and requires close observation. The will, you see, is the mainspring of the mind, and if it is injured the whole mind collapses.

LAURA. And God knows that I have had to teach myself to meet his wishes half-way all through these long years of trial. Ah, if you only knew what a life I have endured with him—if you only knew?

DOCTOR. Your misfortune touches me deeply, and I promise you to see what can be done. I pity you with my whole heart, and I beg you to trust me absolutely. But after what I have heard I must impress one thing on you. Avoid suggesting any ideas that make a strong impression on the sufferer, for in a weak brain they are rapidly developed and readily turn to monomania or " Idées fixes." Do you understand?

LAURA. You mean, avoid rousing his suspicions?

Doctor. Exactly so. One can make the insane believe anything just because they are receptive to everything.

Laura. Indeed. Then I understand. Yes—yes. [*Ringing heard within.*] Excuse me, my mother has something to say to me. One moment . . . ah, there is Adolf.

SCENE VI

The Doctor *and the* Captain.

Captain. [*Enters by the private door.*] Ah, you are here already, Doctor. You are very welcome.

Doctor. Captain! It is a very great pleasure to me to make the acquaintance of so celebrated a man of science.

Captain. You are very good. My professional duties don't allow me to make any profound investigations, but I believe myself to be really on the track of a discovery.

Doctor. Really.

Captain. You see I have submitted meteoric stones to spectrum analysis, with the result that I have found coal, that is to say, a clear trace of organic life. What do you think of that?

Doctor. Can you see that in the microscope?

Captain. No, deuce take it, in the spectroscope.

Doctor. The spectroscope! Pardon. Well, then, you will soon be able to tell us what is happening in Jupiter.

Captain. Not what is happening, but what has happened. If only the confounded booksellers in Paris would send me the books; but I believe that all the booksellers in the universe have conspired against me. Just imagine that for the last two months not a single one has even answered my communications, either letters or abusive telegrams. I shall go frantic over it, and I can't imagine what it all means.

Doctor. Oh, they are generally unbusinesslike fellows, you mustn't take it so much to heart.

Captain. No, but the deuce is that I shall not get my treatise done in time, and I know that they are working on the same lines in Berlin. But that's not what we ought to be talking about . . . What about you? If you care to live here we have a small apartment at your disposal in the wing, or perhaps you would rather live in the old doctor's quarters.

DOCTOR.   Just as you like.

CAPTAIN.   No, as you like.   Which is it to be?

DOCTOR.   You must decide that, Captain.

CAPTAIN.   No, I shall decide nothing.   You must say what you wish.   I wish nothing, nothing whatever.

DOCTOR.   Oh, but I really cannot decide. . . .

CAPTAIN.   For God's sake, do say, Doctor, what you would like.   I have no will in this matter, no opinion, no wishes.   Are you so utterly feeble that you don't know what you wish?   Answer me or I shall get angry.

DOCTOR.   As it rests with me, I choose to live here.

CAPTAIN.   Good!   Thank you. . . .   Ah, forgive me, Doctor, but nothing annoys me so much as to hear people profess indifference about anything.   [*Rings.*]

Enter NURSE.

CAPTAIN.   Oh, there you are Margret.   Do you happen to know if the wing is in order for the Doctor?

NURSE.   Yes, sir, it is.

CAPTAIN.   All right.   Then I won't detain you, Doctor; you must be tired.   Good-bye and welcome again; we shall meet to-morrow, I hope.

DOCTOR.   Good evening, Captain.

CAPTAIN.   I presume that my wife explained our circumstances to you a little, so that you have some idea how the land lies.

DOCTOR.   Your excellent wife has given me a few hints about one thing and another such as were necessary to a stranger. Good evening, Captain.

SCENE VII

CAPTAIN *and* NURSE.

CAPTAIN.   What do you want, you old dear?   Is anything the matter?

NURSE.   Now, my dear Mr. Adolf, you must just listen.

CAPTAIN. Yes, old Margret. Talk away, you are the only one I can listen to without getting into a rage.

NURSE. Now just listen, Mr. Adolf. Don't you think you should go half-way and come to an agreement with Mistress about this fuss over the child. Just think of a mother. . . .

CAPTAIN. Think of a father, Margret.

NURSE. There, there, there! A father has something besides his child, but a mother has nothing but her child.

CAPTAIN. Just so, old lady. She has only one burden, but I have three, and I bear her burden, too. Don't you think that I should have had a better position in the world than a poor soldier's if I had not had her and her child.

NURSE. Yes, but it wasn't that I wanted to say.

CAPTAIN. No, I believe that, for you wanted to make me confess I was in the wrong.

NURSE. Don't you believe, Mr. Adolf, that I wish you well?

CAPTAIN. Yes, dear friend, I do believe it, but you don't know what is for my good. You see it isn't enough for me to have given the child life, I want to give her my soul too.

NURSE. I don't know anything about that. But I do think that you ought to be able to agree.

CAPTAIN. You are not my friend, Margret!

NURSE. I? Ah God! How can you say that, Mr. Adolf. Do you think I can forget that you were my child when you were little.

CAPTAIN. No, you dear, have I forgotten it? You have been like a mother to me, and have supported me hitherto when I had everybody against me, but now, when I really need you, you desert me and go over to the enemy.

NURSE. The enemy!

CAPTAIN. Yes, the enemy! You know well enough how things are in this house, you have seen everything from beginning to end.

NURSE. I have seen well enough! but, my God, why should two people torment the life out of one another; two people who are otherwise so good and wish all others well. Mistress is never like that to me or to anyone else. . . .

CAPTAIN. Only to me, I know it. But let me tell you,

Margret, that if you desert me now, you will do wrong. For they have begun to plot against me, and that doctor is not my friend.

NURSE. Ah, Mr. Adolf, you believe evil about everybody, but, you see, it's because you haven't the true faith, that's just what it is.

CAPTAIN. But you and the Baptists have found the only true faith. You are indeed happy!

NURSE. At any rate, I am not so unhappy as you, Mr. Adolf. Humble your proud heart and you will see that God will make you happy in love to your neighbour.

CAPTAIN. It is a strange thing that you no sooner speak of God and love than your voice becomes hard and your eyes evil. No, Margret, you have certainly not the true faith.

NURSE. Yes, you're proud and hard enough in your learning, but it doesn't amount to much when it comes to the pinch.

CAPTAIN. How arrogantly you talk, humble heart. I know well enough learning is of no use with such creatures as you.

NURSE. You should be ashamed of yourself! But in spite of everything, old Margret loves her great big boy best, and he will come back again, you'll see, like a good child, in the day of trouble.

CAPTAIN. Margret! Forgive me, but believe me there is no one here who wishes me well but you. Help me, for I am sure that something is going to happen. What it is I don't know, but some evil thing is on its way. [*Scream from within.*] What is it? Who is screaming?

SCENE VIII

The FORMER. BERTHA *enters from inner rooms.*

BERTHA. Father! Father! help me, save me!

CAPTAIN. What is it my darling child? Speak!

BERTHA. Help me. She is going to hurt me!

CAPTAIN. Who is going to hurt you. Speak! Speak!

BERTHA. Grandmother! But it's my fault for I deceived her!

CAPTAIN. Go on.

BERTHA. Yes, but you mustn't say anything about it! Do you hear! Promise!

CAPTAIN. Well, but tell me what it is.   [NURSE *goes.*

BERTHA. In the evening she generally turns down the lamp, and then she makes me sit at a table holding a pen over a piece of paper. And then she says that the spirits are to write.

CAPTAIN. What do you say? And you have never told me this?

BERTHA. Forgive me, but I dared not. For grandmother says that the spirits take revenge if one speaks about them. And then the pen writes, but I don't know if it is I. And sometimes it goes beautifully, but sometimes it can't do anything at all. And when I am tired nothing comes, but she wants it to come all the same. And this evening I thought I was writing beautifully, but then grandmother said it was all out of Stagnelius,[1] and that I was deceiving her, and then she got so fearfully angry.

CAPTAIN. Do you believe that there are spirits?

BERTHA. I don't know.

CAPTAIN. But I know that there are none.

BERTHA. But grandmother says that you don't understand, papa, and that you have much worse things that can see to other planets.

CAPTAIN. Does she say that! Does she say that! What else does she say?

BERTHA. She says that you can't work wonders.

CAPTAIN. I never said I could. You know what meteoric stones are—stones that fall down from other heavenly bodies. I can examine them and say whether they contain the same elements as our world. That is all that I can see.

BERTHA. But grandmother says there are things that she can see, but that you cannot see.

CAPTAIN. Then she lies!

BERTHA. Grandmother doesn't tell lies.

CAPTAIN. Why not?

BERTHA. Then mother tells lies too.

CAPTAIN. H'm.

[1] Erik Johan Stagnelius, poet and dramatist, 1793–1823.

BERTHA. If you say that mother tells lies, I will never believe you again.

CAPTAIN. I have not said so, and therefore you must believe me when I tell you, that your future welfare requires that you should leave your home. Will you? Will you go to town and learn something useful?

BERTHA. Ah, yes, I should love to go to town, away from here, anywhere! Only let me see you sometimes, often. Oh, it is always so gloomy and sad in there, as if it were a winter's night, but when you come, father, it is like some spring morning when they take out the inner window.

CAPTAIN. My beloved child. My dear child.

BERTHA. But, father, you must be good to mother, do you hear. She cries so often.

CAPTAIN. H'm. Then you will go to town?

BERTHA. Yes, yes.

CAPTAIN. But suppose mother will not let you go?

BERTHA. But she must let me.

CAPTAIN. But what if she won't?

BERTHA. Well, then, I don't know what will happen. But she must! She must!

CAPTAIN. Will you ask her?

BERTHA. You must ask her very nicely, for she doesn't care about me.

CAPTAIN. H'm! Now if you wish it, and I wish it, and she doesn't wish it, what shall we do then?

BERTHA. Ah, then, it will be all in a muddle again! Why can't you ask . . .   [*Enter* LAURA.

SCENE IX

The FORMER *and* LAURA.

LAURA. Ah, so Bertha is here! Then perhaps we may hear her own opinion, as the question of her future has to be decided.

CAPTAIN. The child can hardly have any well-founded opinion as to how a young girl's life is likely to shape itself, while we, on the contrary, can easily make an approximate calculation, for we have seen a great number of young girls' lives unfold themselves.

LAURA. But as we are of different opinions, Bertha's must be the determining one.

CAPTAIN. No, I let no one usurp my right, neither women nor children. Bertha, leave us.   [BERTHA *goes out.*

LAURA. You were afraid of hearing her opinion, because you thought it would be to my advantage.

CAPTAIN. I know that she wishes to go away from home, but I know also that you possess the power of changing her mind according to your pleasure.

LAURA. Am I really so powerful?

CAPTAIN. Yes, you have a fiendish power of getting your own way, but people who are not ashamed of interfering always have. How did you get Doctor Nordling away, for instance, and how did you get the new man here?

LAURA. Yes, how did I manage that?

CAPTAIN. You insulted the first, until he went, and made your brother scrape votes together for the other.

LAURA. Well, that was quite simple and perfectly legitimate. Is Bertha to leave home?

CAPTAIN. Yes, she is to start in a fortnight.

LAURA. Is that your determination?

CAPTAIN. Yes.

LAURA. Have you spoken to Bertha about it?

CAPTAIN. Yes.

LAURA. Then I must try to prevent it.

CAPTAIN. You cannot.

LAURA. Can't I? Do you really think I would trust my daughter to these wicked people to be told that everything her mother has taught her is mere foolishness? Why, she would despise me for the rest of her life!

CAPTAIN. Do you think that a father will allow ignorant and conceited women to teach his daughter that her father is a charlatan?

LAURA. It ought to mean less to the father.

CAPTAIN. Why so?

LAURA. Because the mother is nearer to the child, since it

has been discovered that no one can tell for certain who is the father of a child.

CAPTAIN.   What is the application in this case?

LAURA.   That you do not know whether you are Bertha's father.

CAPTAIN.   Do I not know?

LAURA.   No; what no one can know, you surely cannot know.

CAPTAIN.   Are you joking?

LAURA.   No; I am only making use of your own teaching. Besides, how can you tell that I have not been unfaithful to you?

CAPTAIN.   I believe a great deal of you, but not that, nor that you would talk about it if it were true.

LAURA.   Assume that I was prepared to bear anything, even scorn and rejection, for the sake of being allowed to keep and dispose of my child, and that I was truthful just now when I declared that Bertha is my child, but not yours.   Assume . . .

CAPTAIN.   Stop!

LAURA.   Only assume this: in that case your power would be at an end.

CAPTAIN.   Yes, when you had proved that I was not the father.

LAURA.   That would not be so difficult! Should you like me to do that?

CAPTAIN.   Stop!

LAURA.   I should, of course, only need to declare the name of the real father, give all details of place and time, for in- stance— when was Bertha born?   In the third year of our marriage.

CAPTAIN.   Stop, or . . .

LAURA.   Or what?   I am to stop now.   Just think for a moment of all you do and decide, and whatever you do, don't make yourself ridiculous.

CAPTAIN.   I consider all this most lamentable.

LAURA.   Which is more ridiculous than ever.

CAPTAIN.   And what of you?

LAURA.   Oh, I have managed too cleverly.

CAPTAIN.   That is why one cannot contend with you.

LAURA. Then why do you provoke contests with a superior enemy?

CAPTAIN. Superior?

LAURA. Yes, it is singular, but I have never looked at a man without knowing myself his superior.

CAPTAIN. Well, you shall be made to see your superior for once, so that you never shall forget it.

LAURA. That will be interesting.

NURSE. [*Enters.*] Supper is ready. Will you come in, Ma'am?

LAURA. Yes, directly.

[CAPTAIN *lingers; sits down in an arm-chair by the table.*]

LAURA. Won't you come in to supper?

CAPTAIN. No thanks, I don't want anything.

LAURA. What! Are you annoyed?

CAPTAIN. No, but I am not hungry.

LAURA. Come, or they will question me in a way that is—unnecessary. . . . Be good now. . . . You won't; then stay there. [*Goes.*

NURSE. Mr. Adolf! What is all this about?

CAPTAIN. I don't know what it is. Can you explain to me how it is that a grown man can be treated as if he were a child?

NURSE. I don't understand it, but it must be because you are all women's children, every man of you, great and small. . . .

CAPTAIN. But no women are born of men. Yes, but I am Bertha's father. Tell me, Margret, don't you believe it? Don't you?

NURSE. Lord, how childish you are. Of course you are your own child's father. Come and eat now, and don't sit there and brood. There, there, come now.

CAPTAIN. Get out, woman. To hell with the witches. [*Goes to the private door.*] Svärd, Svärd! [*Enter* ORDERLY.

ORDERLY. Yes, Captain.

CAPTAIN. Let them put the horses in the covered sleigh at once.

NURSE. Captain, just listen!

CAPTAIN. Out woman! At once!

NURSE.   Lord preserve us, what will come of all this.

[CAPTAIN *puts on his cap and prepares to go out.*

CAPTAIN.   Don't expect me home before midnight.

NURSE.   Jesus help us, what will be the end of this!

ACT II

The same scene as in the previous Act.   A lighted lamp on the table; it is night.

SCENE I

THE DOCTOR *and* LAURA.

DOCTOR.   From what I could find out in the course of our conversation, the case is not yet clearly proved to me.   To begin with, you had made one mistake in saying that he had arrived at these astonishing results about other celestial bodies by means of a microscope.   Now that I hear it was a spectroscope, he is not only entirely cleared of any suspicion of insanity, but is shown to have done a great service to science.

LAURA.   Yes, but I never said that.

DOCTOR.   Madam, I made careful notes of our conversation, and I remember that I asked about this very point because I thought that I could not have heard aright.   One must be scrupulous in making such assertions when a certificate of insanity is in question.

LAURA.   A certificate of insanity?

DOCTOR.   Yes, you must surely know that an insane person loses his civil and family rights.

LAURA.   No, I did not know that.

DOCTOR.   There was a further point that seems to me suspicious.   He spoke of his communications to his booksellers having remained unanswered.   Permit me to ask if you intercepted them from motives of mistaken kindness.

LAURA.   Yes, I did.   It was my duty to watch over the interests of the household and I could not let him ruin us all without intervention.

DOCTOR.   Pardon me, but I think that you cannot have considered the consequences of such an act. If he discovers your secret interference with his affairs, his suspicions will be aroused and will grow with the rapidity of an avalanche. But besides this, you have raised obstacles to his will and subsequently still further provoked his irritability. You must know how maddening it is to have your most ardent desires thwarted and your will restrained.

LAURA. As if I didn't know that!

DOCTOR. Then consider what he must have gone through.

LAURA. [*Getting up.*] It is midnight and he hasn't come home. We may fear the worst now.

DOCTOR. But tell me what actually happened this evening after I left. I must know everything.

LAURA. He talked in the wildest way about the most extraordinary things. Such fancies, for instance, as that he is not the father of his child.

DOCTOR. That is strange. How did such an idea come into his head?

LAURA. I really can't imagine, unless that he had to examine one of the men in a child maintenance case, and when I took the girl's part, he got excited and said that no one could tell who was father to a child. God knows that I did everything to calm him, but I fear that nothing can help him now. [*Cries.*]

DOCTOR. This really cannot be allowed to go on. Something must be done, without, of course, rousing his suspicions. Tell me, has the captain ever had such delusions before?

LAURA. Six years ago we had the same state of things and then he actually confessed, in his own letter to the doctor, that he feared for his reason.

DOCTOR. Ah, yes, this is of course a story that has deep roots, and the sanctity of family life—and so on—prevents . . . I cannot ask about everything, but must keep to the surface. What is done can't be undone, alas, and yet the remedy should have some application to the past. ——Where do you think he is now?

LAURA. I have no idea. He has such wild fancies now.

DOCTOR. Should you like me to stay till he returns? I could say, to avoid suspicion, that I had come to see your mother, who is unwell.

LAURA. Yes, that will do admirably. And do not leave us, Doctor; I can't tell you how anxious I am! But wouldn't it be better to tell him right out what you think of his condition?

DOCTOR. We never do that unless the patient speaks of the subject himself, and very rarely even then. It depends entirely on the direction the case takes. But we mustn't stay here; perhaps I had better go into the next room, it will look more natural.

LAURA. Yes, it will be better, and then Margret can sit here. She is accustomed to sit up when he is out, and she is the only one, too, who has any power over him. [*Goes to the door on the left.*] Margret, Margret!

NURSE. Yes, Ma'am. Is the master at home?

LAURA. No, but you are to sit here and wait for him, and when he comes you are to say that my mother is ill and that the Doctor is here because of that.

NURSE. Yes, Ma'am. I'll see that it is all right.

LAURA. [*Opens door to inner rooms.*] Will you come in here, Doctor?

DOCTOR. Thanks.

SCENE II

The NURSE *sits at the table and takes up a hymn-book and spectacles.*

NURSE. Ah yes, ah yes! [*Reads half aloud.*]

> Ah, woe is me, how sad a thing
> Is life within this vale of tears,
> Death's angel triumphs like a king
> And calls aloud to all the spheres—
> 'Tis vanity, all vanity.   Yes, yes! yes, yes!

> All that on earth hath life and breath
> Falls stricken down before his spear,
> And sorrow, saved alone from death,
> Inscribes above the mighty bier—
> 'Tis vanity, all vanity.   Yes, yes.

BERTHA. [*Enters with a coffee-pot and some needlework; she speaks low.*]

BERTHA. Margret, may I sit with you? It is so lonely up there.

NURSE. Oh! Good gracious, are you still up, Bertha.

BERTHA. I must work at papa's Christmas present, you see. And I've got something good for you here.

NURSE. Yes, but, dear heart, it won't do. You have to get up in the morning and it is past twelve o'clock.

BERTHA. Well, what does that matter? I dare not sit up there alone, I believe it's haunted.

NURSE. There now, didn't I say so! Yes, mark my words, this house is no good place. What did you hear?

BERTHA. Oh, just fancy, I heard someone singing up in the garret.

NURSE. In the garret? At this time of night!

BERTHA. And it was a very, very sad song, such as I never heard. And it seemed as if it came from the lumber-room, where the cradle stands, you know, on the left. . . .

NURSE. Oh dear, oh dear! And it's such fearful weather to-night! I believe the chimneys will blow down.

> Ah, what is then this earthly life
> But grief, affliction, trouble, strife?
> E'en when fairest it has seemed
> Vanity it must be deemed.

Yes, dear child, God send us a happy Christmas!

BERTHA. Margret, is it true that papa is ill?

NURSE. Yes; he is indeed.

BERTHA. Then we shan't be able to keep Christmas Eve. But how can he be up if he is ill?

NURSE. You see, my child, the kind of illness that he has doesn't prevent him from being up. Hush, there's someone out in the hall. Go to bed now and take the coffee-pot away, or the master will be angry.

BERTHA. [*Going out with the tray.*] Good night, Margret!

NURSE. Good night, my child. God bless you!

SCENE III

NURSE.   CAPTAIN [*takes off his overcoat.*]

CAPTAIN.   Are you still up!   Go to bed!

NURSE.   I was only waiting till . . .

CAPTAIN. *lights a candle, opens his desk, sits down at it, and takes letters and newspapers out of his pocket.*

NURSE.   Mr. Adolf.

CAPTAIN.   What do you want?

NURSE.   Old mistress is ill, and the doctor is here.

CAPTAIN.   Is it anything dangerous?

NURSE.   No, I don't think so.   It is only a cold.

CAPTAIN.   [*Gets up.*]   Who was the father of your child, Margret?

NURSE.   Oh, I have told you that many and many a time: it was that scamp Johansson.

CAPTAIN.   Are you sure that it was he?

NURSE.   How childish you are; of course I am sure of it, since he was the only one.

CAPTAIN.   Yes; but was he sure that he was the only one? No; he could not be, but you could be sure of it.   You see, that's the difference.

NURSE.   I can't see any difference.

CAPTAIN.   No; you cannot see it, but the difference is there all the same.   [*Turns over the pages of a photograph album that is on the table.*]   Do you think Bertha is like me?

[*Looks at a portrait in the album.*

NURSE.   Why, yes; you are as like as two peas.

CAPTAIN.   Did Johansson confess that he was the father?

NURSE.   He had no choice.

CAPTAIN.   How dreadful!   There is the doctor.

SCENE IV

CAPTAIN, NURSE, *and* DOCTOR.

CAPTAIN.   Good evening, Doctor.   How is my mother-in-law?

DOCTOR. Oh, it is not at all serious; it is merely a slight sprain of the left foot.

CAPTAIN. I thought Margret said that it was a cold. There seem to be different interpretations of the same case. Go to bed, Margret. [NURSE goes.

[A Pause.]

CAPTAIN. Do sit down, Doctor Östermark.

DOCTOR. [Sits down.] Thanks.

CAPTAIN. Is it true that you obtain striped foals if you cross a zebra and a mare?

DOCTOR. [Astonished.] Perfectly true.

CAPTAIN. Is it true that the foals continue to be striped if the breed is carried on with a stallion?

DOCTOR. Yes, that is also true.

CAPTAIN. Therefore, under certain conditions, a stallion can be sire to striped foals?

DOCTOR. Yes, so it appears.

CAPTAIN. That is to say, the offspring's likeness to the father proves nothing.

DOCTOR. Well . . .

CAPTAIN. That is to say, paternity cannot be proved.

DOCTOR. H'm . . . Well!

CAPTAIN. You are a widower and have had children?

DOCTOR. Ye-es.

CAPTAIN. Did you never see how ridiculous you were as a father? I know nothing so comical as to see a father leading his child about the streets, or to hear a father talk of his children. "My wife's children," he ought to say. Did you never realise how false your position was? Were you never troubled by doubts, I won't say suspicions, for I assume, as a gentleman, that your wife was above suspicion?

DOCTOR. No, really, I never was; and, indeed, Captain, a man must take his children on trust as Goethe, I think, says.

CAPTAIN. On trust when there is a woman in the case? That is risky.

DOCTOR. Oh! there are so many kinds of women.

CAPTAIN. Modern investigation has pronounced that there is only one kind! . . . When I was young I was strong and—if

I may boast—handsome. I can only remember two momentary impressions that in recalling them have caused me to doubt this. I was once on board a steamer sitting with a few friends in the fore-saloon. The young stewardess came and flung herself down by me, burst into tears, and told us that her sweetheart was drowned. We pitied her, and I ordered some champagne. After the second glass, I touched her foot, after the fourth her knee, and before morning I had consoled her.

DOCTOR. One swallow does not make a summer.

CAPTAIN. Now comes the second, and that was really a summer swallow. I was at Lysekil. A young woman was staying there. She had her children with her, but her husband was in town. She was religious, had extremely severe principles, preached morality to me, and was, I believe, entirely virtuous. I lent her some books, and when she was leaving she unexpectedly enough returned them. Three months later I found a visiting card in those very books with a fairly plain declaration. It was innocent, as innocent, that is to say, as a declaration of love from a married woman to a strange man who never made any advances can be. Now comes the moral. Whatever you do, don't believe too much.

DOCTOR. But don't believe too little either.

CAPTAIN. No. Not that either. But don't you see, Doctor Östermark, the woman was so unconsciously dishonest that she spoke of her infatuation for me to her husband. This very unconsciousness of their instinctive duplicity is what is so dangerous. It is, I grant you, an extenuating circumstance, but it cannot make me reverse my judgment, only soften it.

DOCTOR. Captain, your thoughts are taking a morbid direction, and you ought to control them.

CAPTAIN. You must not use the word morbid. All steam boilers, as you know, explode when the pressure gauge registers 100, but the scale is not the same for all boilers; do you understand? In the meantime you are here to watch me. If I only were not a man I should have the right of making accusations, or complaints as they are so cleverly called, and, perhaps, I should be able to give you the whole diagnosis, and, what is more, the history of my disease; but I am unfortunately a man, and there is nothing for me but to fold my arms across my breast like the Roman, and hold my breath till I die. Good night.

DOCTOR. Captain, if you are ill, it will not offend your dignity as a man to tell me all. Indeed, I am bound to hear the other side.

CAPTAIN. It is enough that you have heard the one, I imagine.

DOCTOR. No, Captain. And do you know when I heard Mrs. Alving eulogise her dead husband, I thought to myself it was a confounded pity the fellow was dead.

CAPTAIN. Do you suppose that he would have spoken if he had been alive! And do you suppose that any dead husbands would be believed if they were to come to life? Good night, Doctor. You hear that I am calm, and you can safely go to bed.

DOCTOR. Good night, then, Captain. I can take no further part in this affair.

CAPTAIN. Are we enemies?

DOCTOR. Far from it! Only it is pity that we cannot be friends. Good night. [*Goes.*

[*The* CAPTAIN *follows the* DOCTOR *to the door in the background, and then goes to the door at the left and opens it slightly.*

CAPTAIN. Come in, I want to talk to you! I heard you standing out there listening.

SCENE V

LAURA. [*Embarrassed.*] CAPTAIN. [*Sits down at the bureau.*]

CAPTAIN. It is late, but we must talk things out. Sit down. [*A pause.*] I have been at the post office this evening to fetch the letters. From these it appears that you have kept back my letters, both on their departure and arrival. The direct consequence of this is that the delay has entirely frustrated the results I hoped for from my work.

LAURA. It was an act of kindness on my part, since you neglected your professional duties for this other work.

CAPTAIN. It surely cannot have been kindness, for you knew quite well that I should one day win more renown from that than from the Service; but you were particularly anxious that I should not distinguish myself, lest your own insignificance should be eclipsed. In consequence of this I have intercepted letters addressed to you.

LAURA. That is very noble of you.

CAPTAIN. I see you have a high opinion of me. It appears from these letters that for some time past you have been arraying my former friends against me by spreading reports about my mental condition. And you have succeeded in your efforts, for now there is not more than one person, from the colonel down to the cook, who believes me to be sane. Now the facts about my illness are these: my reason is unaffected, as you know, so that I can discharge both my duties to the Service and my duties as a father; my nerves are still more or less under my control, and will continue so as long as my will remains fairly intact. You have, however, so thoroughly undermined it that it will soon be ready to fly off the cog-wheel, and then the whole mechanism will go to smash. I will not appeal to your feelings, for you have none, that is your strength; but I will appeal to your interests.

LAURA. Let me hear.

CAPTAIN. You have succeeded by this conduct in arousing my suspicions to such an extent that my judgment is nearly destroyed, and my thoughts begin to wander. This is that approaching insanity you are waiting for, and that may come now at any time. The question then arises for you: is it more to your interest that I should be sane or insane. Consider! If I succumb I shall have to leave the Service, and you will be in a very awkward position. If I die my life insurance will fall to you. But if I take my own life you will get nothing. It is therefore to your interest that I should live out my life.

LAURA. Is this a trap?

CAPTAIN. Of course! But it rests with you to avoid it or to run your head into it.

LAURA. You say that you will kill yourself? You shall not do it!

CAPTAIN. Don't be sure. Do you think a man can live when he has nothing and nobody to live for?

LAURA. You surrender then?

CAPTAIN. No, I offer you peace.

LAURA. The conditions?

CAPTAIN. That I may keep my reason. Deliver me from my suspicions and I throw up the struggle.

LAURA. What suspicions?

CAPTAIN. About Bertha's origin.

LAURA. Is there any doubt about that?

CAPTAIN. Yes, I have doubts, and you have awakened them.

LAURA. I?

CAPTAIN. Yes, you have dropped them like henbane in my ears, and circumstances have given them growth. Deliver me from uncertainty, tell me outright that my suspicions are justified, and I will forgive you in advance.

LAURA. You really can't expect me to take upon myself a sin that I have not committed.

CAPTAIN. What can it matter when you are certain that I shall not betray you? Do you think that a man would be likely to blazon his own shame abroad.

LAURA. If I say it is not true, you won't be convinced; but if I say it is true, you will be convinced. You seem to hope it is true?

CAPTAIN. Yes, strangely enough; no doubt because the first supposition can't be proved, only the last.

LAURA. Have you any reasons for your suspicions?

CAPTAIN. Yes, and no.

LAURA. I believe that you want to prove me guilty, so that you can get rid of me and have absolute control over the child. But you won't lure me into any such snare.

CAPTAIN. You surely don't think that I would adopt another man's child, if I were convinced of your guilt?

LAURA. No, I'm sure you wouldn't, and that convinces me that you lied just now when you said that you forgave me in advance.

CAPTAIN. [Gets up.] Laura, save me and my reason. You don't seem to understand what I say. If the child is not mine, I have no control over it, and don't want to have any, and that is precisely what you want, isn't it? You will have the power over the child, and I shall be left to maintain you both.

LAURA. The power, yes. Has this whole life and death struggle been fought for anything but the power?

CAPTAIN. You know I do not believe in a future life. The child was my future life. She was my conception of immortality, and perhaps the only one that has any analogy in reality. If you deprive me of that, you cut short my existence.

LAURA. Why did we not separate in time?

CAPTAIN. Because the child bound us together; but the bond became a chain. And how did it happen; how? I have never thought of this, but now the memory of it rises up in accusation, perhaps in condemnation. We had been married two years and had no child, you best know why. I fell ill and lay at the point of death. In an interval of the fever I heard voices outside in the drawing-room. You and the solicitor were talking about the fortune that I then still possessed. He explained that you could not inherit anything, because we had no children, and asked you if you were enceinte. What you answered I did not hear. I recovered, and we had a child. Who is its father?

LAURA. You.

CAPTAIN. No, it is not I. There is a buried crime here which begins to give off poisonous exhalations, and what a hellish crime. You have been tender enough about freeing black slaves, but you have kept white ones yourself. I have worked and slaved for you, your child, your mother, your servants; I have sacrificed career and promotion; I have endured torture, flagellation, sleeplessness, unrest for your sake, until my hair has grown grey; and all in order that you might enjoy a life without care, and when you grew old, enjoy it over again in your child. I have borne it all without complaint, because I thought myself the father of the child. This is the crudest form of theft, the most brutal slavery. I have had seventeen years of penal servitude and have been innocent. What can you give me in return for this?

LAURA. Now you are quite mad!

CAPTAIN. [Sits.]. That is your hope! ... And I have seen how you have laboured to conceal your sin. I have had sympathy with you because I did not understand your grief; I have often lulled your evil conscience to rest, because I thought I was chasing away a morbid thought; I have heard you cry out in your sleep without allowing myself to listen. Now I remember the night before last—Bertha's birthday—I was sitting up reading, between two and three in the morning. You screamed as if someone were strangling you " don't, don't! " I knocked on the wall because I wished to hear no more. I have long had my suspicions, but I did not dare to hear them confirmed. I have suffered this for you, what will you do for me?

LAURA. What can I do? I can swear by God and all that I hold sacred that you are Bertha's father.

CAPTAIN. Of what use is that, as you have said before that a mother can and ought to commit any crime for her child. I implore you by the memory of the past, I implore you as a wounded man begs for a death-blow, to tell me all. Don't you see that I am as helpless as a child, don't you hear that I am complaining as to a mother, won't you forget that I am a man, that I am a soldier who with a word can tame men and beasts; I simply implore pity like a sick man, I lay down the tokens of my power and pray for mercy on my life.

LAURA. [Approaches him and lays her hand on his brow.] What! You are crying, man!

CAPTAIN. Yes, I am crying, although I am a man. But has not a man eyes? Has not a man hands, limbs, senses, opinions, passions? Is he not fed with the same food, hurt by the same weapons, warmed and cooled by the same summer and winter as a woman is? If you prick us do we not bleed? If you tickle us do we not laugh? If you poison us do we not die? Why should not a man complain, a soldier cry? Because it is unmanly? Why is it unmanly?

LAURA. Cry then, my child, and you will have your mother with you again. Do you remember that it was as your second mother I first entered your life? Your great strong body was without nerve. You were a giant child that had either come too early into the world, or perhaps was not wanted.

CAPTAIN. Yes, that's just how it was. My father and mother did not want me and consequently I was born without a will.   I naturally enough thought that I was completing myself when you and I became one, and therefore you got the upper hand, and I, the commander in barracks and before the troops, became obedient to you, grew by you, looked up to you as a highly gifted being, listened to you as if I had been your ignorant child.

LAURA.   Yes, so it was, and therefore I loved you as my child.   But you know, you must have seen, when the nature of your feelings changed and you appeared as my lover, I blushed and the joy of your embraces turned to remorse as if my blood were ashamed.   The mother became the mistress.   Ugh!

CAPTAIN.   I saw but did not understand it.   And when I imagined that you despised me for my unmanliness, I wanted to win you as a woman by being a man.

LAURA.   Yes, but there was your mistake.   The mother was your friend, you see, but the woman was your enemy, and love between the sexes is strife.   Do not believe either that I gave myself; I did not give, but I took—what I wanted.   You had one advantage, however, that I realised and wanted you to realise.

CAPTAIN.   You always had the advantage.   You could hynotise me when I was wide awake, so that I neither saw nor heard, but merely obeyed; you could give me a raw potato and make me imagine it was a peach; you could force me to admire your foolish ideas as if they were strokes of genius; you could lead me into crime, yes, even into dishonourable actions.   For you were without understanding, and instead of carrying out my ideas you acted on your own initiative.   But when at last I awoke to reflection and realised that my honour was outraged, I wanted to blot out the memory by a great deed, an achievement, a discovery, or an honourable suicide.   I wanted to go to the wars, but was not permitted.   It was then that I threw myself into science.   And now, when I was about to stretch out my hand and gather in its fruits, you suddenly cut off my arm.   Now I am dishonoured and can live no longer, for a man cannot live without honour.

LAURA.   But a woman?

CAPTAIN.   Yes, for she has her children, which he has not. But we and the rest of mankind lived our lives, unconscious as children, full of imaginations, ideals, and illusions, and then we awoke; it was all over. But we awoke with our feet on the pillow, and he who waked us was himself a sleep-walker. When women grow old and cease to be women, they get beards on their chins; I wonder what men get who grow old and cease to be men. Those who crowed were no longer cocks but capons, and the pullets answered the call, so that when we thought the sun was about to rise we found ourselves in the bright moonlight amidst ruins, just as in the good old times. It had only been a little morning slumber with wild dreams, and there was no awakening.

LAURA. Do you know, you should have been a poet!

CAPTAIN. Very possibly.

LAURA. Now I am sleepy, so if you have any more fancies, keep them till to-morrow.

CAPTAIN. A word more first about realities. Do you hate me?

LAURA. Yes, sometimes, when you are a man.

CAPTAIN. This is race-hatred. If it is true that we are descended from monkeys, it must at least be from two separate species. We are not like one another, are we?

LAURA. What do you mean by all this?

CAPTAIN. I realise that one of us must go under in this struggle.

LAURA. Which?

CAPTAIN. The weaker, of course.

LAURA. And the stronger will be in the right.

CAPTAIN. Certainly, since he has the power.

LAURA. Then I am right.

CAPTAIN. Have you the power already, then?

LAURA. Yes, the power of the law, by means of which I shall put you under control to-morrow.

CAPTAIN. Under control!

LAURA. And then I shall educate my child myself without listening to your visions.

CAPTAIN. And who will pay for the education when I am not there?

LAURA. Your pension.

CAPTAIN. [*Goes menacingly towards her.*] How can you have me put under control?

LAURA. [*Takes out a letter.*] By means of this letter of

which an attested copy is lying before the Commissioners in Lunacy.

CAPTAIN. What letter?

LAURA. [*Moves backwards towards the door on the left.*] Yours! Your declaration to the doctor that you are insane.
[CAPTAIN *looks at her in silence.*

LAURA. Now you have fulfilled your function as an unfortunately necessary father and breadwinner. You are not needed any longer and you must go. You must go since you have realised that my intellect is as strong as my will, and since you will not stay and acknowledge it.

[*The* CAPTAIN *goes to the table, takes the lighted lamp, and throws it at* LAURA, *who escapes backwards through the door.*

ACT III

Same scene as in former acts. Another lamp—the private door is barricaded with a chair.

SCENE I

LAURA *and* NURSE.

LAURA. Did he give you the keys?

NURSE. Give them to me, no, heaven help us, but I took them from the things that Nöjd had out to brush.

LAURA. Then it is Nöjd who is on duty to-day.

NURSE. Yes, it is Nöjd.

LAURA. Give me the keys.

NURSE. Yes, but it seems like downright stealing. Do you hear his footsteps up there, Ma'am. Backwards and forwards, backwards and forwards.

LAURA. Is the door safely fastened?

NURSE. Oh yes, it's fastened safely enough.

LAURA. [*Opens the desk and sits down at it.*] Control your feelings, Margret. Nothing but calm can save us all. [*Knock.*] Who is it?

NURSE. [*Opens passage door.*] It is Nöjd.

LAURA. Let him come in.

NÖJD. [*Comes in.*]   A note from the colonel.

LAURA. Bring it here. [*Reads.*] Ah!——Nöjd, have you taken all the cartridges out of the guns and pouches?

NÖJD. I have done what you ordered, Ma'am.

LAURA. Then wait outside while I answer the colonel's letter.   [NÖJD *goes.*

LAURA [*writes*].

NURSE. Listen, Ma'am. Whatever is he doing up there now?

LAURA. Be silent while I write. [*The sound of sawing is heard.*]

NURSE. [*Half aloud to herself.*]   Oh, may God in His mercy help us all! Where will this end!

LAURA. There; give this to Nöjd. And my mother is to know nothing of all this. Do you hear? [*Nurse goes to door.*

[*Laura opens drawers in top of bureau and takes out papers.*]

SCENE II

LAURA *and* PASTOR. [*He takes a chair and sits by* LAURA *at the bureau.*]

PASTOR. Good evening, sister. I have been away all day as you heard, and have only just got back. Distressing things have happened here.

LAURA. Yes, brother, never before have I gone through such a night and such a day.

PASTOR. Ah, but at all events I see that you are none the worse.

LAURA. No, God be thanked; but think what might have happened!

PASTOR. Do tell me how it all began. I have heard so many different accounts.

LAURA. It began with his wild fancy that he was not Bertha's father, and ended with his throwing the lighted lamp in my face.

PASTOR. But that is dreadful! It is fully developed insanity. And what is to be done now?

LAURA. We must try to prevent further violence, and the

doctor has sent to the hospital for a strait-waistcoat. In the meantime I have written to the colonel, and am now trying to acquaint myself with the affairs of the household, which he has conducted in a most reprehensible manner.

PASTOR.   It is a sad story, but I have always expected something of the sort.   Fire and water must end in exploding!   What have you got there in the drawers?

LAURA.   [*Opens a drawer in the bureau.*]   Look, he seems to have kept everything here.

PASTOR.   [*Looking through the drawer.*]   Good heavens, he has your doll here; and there is your christening cap and Bertha's rattle; and your letters; and the locket. [*Dries his eyes.*] He must after all have loved you very dearly, Laura.   I never kept such things as these!

LAURA.   I believe that he used to love me, but time—time changes so many things.

PASTOR.   What is this great paper?   The receipt for a grave!   Yes, better the grave than the lunatic asylum!   Laura, tell me, are you blameless in all this?

LAURA.   I?   Why should I be to blame because a man goes out of his mind?

PASTOR.   Ah, well!   I shall say nothing!   Blood is thicker than water after all!

LAURA.   What do you dare to mean?

PASTOR.   [*Gazing at her.*]   Listen!

LAURA.   What?

PASTOR.   Listen!   You surely cannot deny that it is in conformity with your wishes that you will be able to educate your child yourself?

LAURA.   I don't understand.

PASTOR.   How I admire you!

LAURA.   Me?   H'm!

PASTOR.   And I shall become the guardian of that freethinker up there.   Do you know I have always considered him as a weed in our garden.

LAURA. [*Gives a short suppressed laugh, and then becomes suddenly grave.*]   And you dare to say that to me—his wife?

PASTOR.   You are strong, Laura, incredibly strong!   Like a trapped fox, you would rather bite off your own leg than let yourself be caught! Like a master thief—no accomplice, not even your own conscience! Look at yourself in the glass! You dare not!

LAURA. I never use a looking-glass!

PASTOR. No, you dare not! Let me look at your hand. Not a treacherous blood stain, not a trace of cunning poison? A little innocent murder that cannot be reached by the law; an unconscious sin; unconscious! That is a splendid invention! Do you hear how he is working up there? Beware! if the man gets out he will make short work of you.

LAURA. You talk as much as if you had a bad conscience. Accuse me if you can!

PASTOR. I cannot.

LAURA. You see! You cannot, and therefore I am innocent. You take care of your ward, and I will look after mine! There's the doctor.

SCENE III

The FORMER *and* DOCTOR.

LAURA. [*Getting up.*] Good evening, Doctor. You at least will help me, will you not? But, unfortunately, there is not much to be done. Do you hear how he is going on up there? Are you convinced now?

DOCTOR. I am convinced that an act of violence has been committed, but the question is whether that act of violence is to be considered as an outbreak of anger or of madness.

PASTOR. But apart from the actual outbreak you must acknowledge that his ideas are those of a monomaniac.

DOCTOR. I think that your ideas, Pastor, are much more those of a monomaniac.

PASTOR. My firmly-rooted convictions about the highest things——

DOCTOR. We will put convictions on one side. Madam, it rests with you to decide whether your husband has made himself liable to imprisonment and fine or to detention in an asylum! What do you think of the behaviour?

LAURA.   I will not answer for it now.

DOCTOR.   Then you have no firmly-rooted convictions as to what is most advantageous in the interests of the family?   What do you say, Pastor?

PASTOR.   Well, there will be scandal in either case.   It is not easy to say.

LAURA.   But if he is only sentenced to a fine for violence, he will be able to repeat the violence.

DOCTOR.   And if he is sent to prison he will soon be out again.   Therefore we consider it most advantageous for all parties that he should immediately be treated as insane.   Where is the nurse?

LAURA.   Why?

DOCTOR.   She must put the strait-waistcoat on the patient when I have talked to him and given the order!   But not before. I have—the—the garment out here.   [*Goes out into the hall and comes in with a large parcel.*]   Please ask the nurse to come in.   [LAURA *rings.*

PASTOR.   Shocking! Shocking!   [*Enter* NURSE.

DOCTOR.   [*Takes out the strait-waistcoat.*]   Please pay attention. I wish you to slip this strait-waistcoat on the Captain from behind when I consider that circumstances require it to prevent outbreaks of violence.   As you see, it has excessively long sleeves with the object of hindering his movements.   They are to be tied at the back.   There are two straps here that go through buckles, which are afterwards made fast to the arm of the chair, or the sofa or whatever is convenient.   Will you do this?

NURSE.   No, sir, I can't do that; I can't indeed!

LAURA.   Why don't you do it yourself, Doctor?

DOCTOR.   Because the patient distrusts me.   You, Madam, would appear the most obvious person, but I fear that he distrusts even you.

           [LAURA *makes an involuntary movement.*]

DOCTOR.   Perhaps you, Pastor.

PASTOR.   No, I must decline.

SCENE IV

The FORMER *and* NÖJD.

LAURA. Have you delivered the note already?

NÖJD. Yes, ma'am.

DOCTOR. Is that you, Nöjd? You know the circumstances here; you know that the Captain is out of his mind, and you must help us to look after him.

NÖJD. If there is anything I can do for the Captain, you may be sure I will do it.

DOCTOR. You are to put this jacket on him . . .

NURSE. No, he shan't touch him. Nöjd shall not hurt him. I would rather do it myself, very, very gently. But Nöjd can stand outside and help me if necessary. He may do that. [*Loud knocking at the private door.*]

DOCTOR. Here he is! Put the jacket under your shawl on that chair, and if you will all go out for the present, the Pastor and I will receive him, for that door will not hold out many minutes. Now go.

NURSE. [*Out to left.*] Lord Jesus help us!

[LAURA *locks bureau, and goes out to left.* NÖJD *goes out at back.*]

SCENE V

The private door is forced open, so that the chair is thrown forward on the floor and the lock is broken.

The CAPTAIN, DOCTOR, PASTOR.

[*The* CAPTAIN *comes in with a pile of books under his arm. Puts them on the table.*]

CAPTAIN. The whole thing is to be read here, and in every book. So I was not out of my mind! Here it is in the Odyssey, canto one, verse 215, page 6 of the Upsala translation. It is Telemakos who speaks to Athene. " My Mother indeed maintains that he, Odysseus, is my Father, but I myself know it not, for no man yet hath known his own origin." And this suspicion is harboured by Telemakos of Penelope, the most virtuous of

women. It is beautiful! Is it not? And here we have the
prophet Ezekiel: "The Fool saith; see here is my father, but
who can tell whose loins have engendered him."

It is quite clear. What have I got here? Merslákow's History of Russian Literature. "Alexander Puschkin, Russia's
greatest poet, was tortured to death by the reports that were cir-
culated about his wife's unfaithfulness rather than by the ball he
received in his breast in the duel. On his deathbed he swore that
she was innocent." Ass, Ass! How could he answer for it? In
the meantime you hear that I read my books—Ah, Jonas, are you
there? And the Doctor, of course? Have you heard how I
answered an English lady, when she complained of an Irishman
who used to throw lighted lamps in his wife's face. "God, what
women," I cried.—"Women," she lisped.—"Yes, of course,"
I answered. "When things go to such a length that a man, a
man who loved and worshipped a woman, takes a lighted lamp
and throws it in her face, then one can tell."

PASTOR. What can one tell?

CAPTAIN. Nothing. One never knows anything. Only
one believes. Is not that true, Jonas? One believes, and then
one is saved! Yes; so one would be. No, I know that one may
be lost by one's faith. I know that.

DOCTOR. Captain!

CAPTAIN. Hush! I will not speak to you; I will not hear
you repeating the chatter in there like a telephone! In there!
You know!—Listen, Jonas; do you believe that you are the
father of your children? I remember that you had a tutor in
the house who was good-looking, and who was a great deal
gossiped about.

PASTOR. Adolf, beware!

CAPTAIN. Grope about under your wig, and feel if there are
not two knobs there. By my soul, I believe he turns pale! Yes,
yes; they only talk; but, good Lord, there is so much talk. Still
we are nothing but ridiculous dupes for all that, we married men.
Don't you think so, Doctor? How was it with your marriage
bed? Had you not a lieutenant in the house, too? Wait, and I
will guess? His name is [*whispers in Doctor's ear*]. You see
he turns pale, too! Don't be unhappy now. She is dead and

buried, and what is done can't be undone? I knew him well, by the by, and he is now . . . look at me, Doctor . . . No, right into my eyes . . . a major of dragoons! By God, if I don't believe he has horns, too.

DOCTOR. [*Annoyed.*] Captain, won't you talk of something else?

CAPTAIN. Do you see. He immediately wants to talk of something else when I mention horns.

PASTOR. Do you know, Adolf, that you are insane?

CAPTAIN. Yes; I know that well enough. But if I only had the management of your crowned brains awhile, I should soon have you shut up, too! I am mad, but how did I become so? That does not matter to you, and it does not matter to any one! Will *you* talk of something else now? [*Takes photograph album from the table.*] Lord Jesus, is that my child! Mine! We cannot tell that. Do you know what would have to be done to make sure? First, one would have to marry to get a position in society, then immediately be divorced and become lovers, and finally adopt the children. Then one would at least be sure that they were one's adopted children. That is right enough. But how does all this help me now? What can help me now that you have taken my conception of immortality from me, what do science and philosophy avail me when I have nothing to live for, what can I do with life when I have no honour? I grafted my right arm, half my brain, half my marrow on to another stem, for I thought they would grow up together and knit themselves into a more perfect tree, and then someone came with a knife and cut them asunder below the graft, and now I am only half a tree. As for the other half, it goes on growing with my arm and my half brain, while I pine and die, for they were the best parts I gave away. Now I will die. Do what you like with me. I shall not be found any more.

[*The* DOCTOR *whispers to the* PASTOR, *and they go into the inner rooms on the left. Immediately afterwards* BERTHA *comes out.*

SCENE VI

The CAPTAIN *and* BERTHA.
[*The Captain sinks into a chair by the table.*]

BERTHA. [*Goes up to him.*]   Are you ill, father?

CAPTAIN. [*Looks up offended.*]   I?

BERTHA.   Do you know what you have done?   Do you know that you threw the lamp at mother?

CAPTAIN.   Did I?

BERTHA.   Yes, you did.   Just think if she had been hurt.

CAPTAIN.   What would that have mattered?

BERTHA.   You are not my father if you can talk like that.

CAPTAIN.   What do you say?   Am I not your father? How do you know that?   Who told you that?   And who is your father, then?   Who?

BERTHA.   Not you at any rate.

CAPTAIN.   Still not I!   Who, then?   Who?   You seem to be well informed!   Who told you?   That I should live to see my child come and tell me straight in the face that I am not her father!   But do you not know that you disgrace your mother when you say that?   Do you not know that it is her shame if it is so?

BERTHA.   Say nothing bad about mother; do you hear?

CAPTAIN.   No; you all hold together against me!   And so you have done all the time.

BERTHA.   Father!

CAPTAIN.   Do not say that word again!

BERTHA.   Father, father!

CAPTAIN. [*Drawing her to him.*]   Bertha, dearly beloved child, you are my child, are you not?   Yes, yes; it cannot be otherwise.   It is so.   The rest was only morbid thoughts which come on the wind like pestilence and fevers.   Look at me, and then I shall see my soul in your eyes!—But I see her soul, too! You have two souls, and you love me with one of them and hate me with the other.   But you must only love me!   You must only have one soul, or you will never have peace, nor I either.

You must only have one thought, which is the child of my thought; you must only have one will, which is mine.

BERTHA. But I will not. I want to be myself.

CAPTAIN. You must not. You see, I am a cannibal, and I will eat you. Your mother wanted to eat me, but she could not. I am Saturn who ate his children because it had been prophesied that they would eat him. To eat or be eaten! That is the question. If I do not eat you, you will eat me, and you have already showed me your teeth? But don't be frightened, my darling child; I won't do you any harm.

[*Goes to the trophy of weapons and takes down a revolver.*

BERTHA. [*Trying to escape.*] Help, mother, help, he's going to murder me!

NURSE. [*Coming in.*] Mr. Adolf, what is it?

CAPTAIN. [*Examines revolver.*] Have you taken the cartridges out?

NURSE. Yes, I just tidied them away, but sit down and be quiet, and I'll get them out again!

[*She takes the* CAPTAIN *by the arm and puts him in a chair, into which he sinks feebly. Then she takes out the strait-waistcoat and places herself behind the chair.*

[BERTHA *slips out on the left.*]

NURSE. Mr. Adolf, do you remember when you were my darling little child and I tucked you in of nights, and said " Gentle Jesus " to you, and do you remember how I got up in the night and gave you a drink; do you remember how I lighted the candle and talked about pretty things when you had bad dreams and couldn't sleep. Do you remember?

CAPTAIN. Go on talking, Margret, it soothes my head so. Go on talking again.

NURSE. Oh yes, but you must listen to me! Do you remember when you once took the great kitchen knife and wanted to cut out boats with it, and how I came in and had to get the knife away by tricking you. You were a little foolish child so I had to trick you, for you didn't believe that we meant well by you. " Give me that ugly snake," I said, " or it will bite you!" and then you gave up the knife. [*Takes the revolver out of the* CAPTAIN's *hand.*] And then when you had to dress yourself and didn't want to. Then I had to coax you and say that you should have a golden coat and be dressed like a prince. And then I took your little vest that was only made of green worsted, and held it up in front of you and said: " In with both arms," and then I said: " Sit nice and still while I button it down the back." [*She gets the jacket on.*] And then I said: " Get up now, and walk across the floor like a good boy so that I can see whether it's straight. [*She leads him to the sofa.*] And then I said: " Now you must go to bed."

CAPTAIN. What did you say? Was I to go to bed when I was dressed. . . . Damnation! What have you done with me. [*Tries to free himself.*] Ah! you infernally cunning woman! Who would have thought that you had so much wit. [*Lies down on the sofa.*] Trapped, shorn, outwitted, forbidden to die.

NURSE. Forgive me, Mr. Adolf, forgive me, but I wanted to hinder you from killing your child.

CAPTAIN. Why didn't you let me kill the child? For life is a hell and death a heaven, and children belong to heaven.

NURSE. How do you know what comes after death?

CAPTAIN. That is the only thing we do know, but of life we know nothing! Oh, if one had only known from the beginning.

NURSE. Mr. Adolf, humble your hard heart and cry to God for mercy, it is not yet too late. It was not too late for the thief on the cross when the Saviour said, " To-day·shalt thou be with Me in Paradise."

CAPTAIN. Are you croaking for a corpse already, old crow?
        [NURSE *takes a hymn-book out of her pocket.*]
CAPTAIN. [*Calls.*] Nöjd, is Nöjd there? [*Enter* NÖJD.
CAPTAIN. Fling that woman out! She is trying to strangle me with her hymn-book. Throw her out of the window, or up the chimney, or anywhere.

NÖJD. [*Looks at* NURSE.] Heaven help you, Captain, but I can't do that, I simply can't. If only it were six men, but a woman!

CAPTAIN. Have you never got the better of a woman, heigh?

NÖJD. Of course I have, but it is a very different thing to lay hands on a woman.

CAPTAIN. Why is it so different? Have they not laid hands on me?

NÖJD. Yes, but I can't, Captain. It is downright as if you were to ask me to strike the pastor. It's against nature! I can't.

SCENE VII

The FORMER. LAURA. [*She signs to* NÖJD *to go.*]

CAPTAIN. Omphale, Omphale! Now you play with the club while Hercules spins the wool.

[LAURA *comes forward to the sofa.*

LAURA. Adolf. Look at me. Do you think that I am your enemy?

CAPTAIN. Yes, I do think so. I believe that you are all my enemies! My mother, who did not want to bring me into the world because I was to be born with pain, was my enemy when she deprived my embryonic life of its nourishment and made a weakling of me. My sister was my enemy when she taught me that I was to be obedient to her. The first woman I embraced was my enemy, for she gave me ten years of illness in payment for the love I gave her. My daughter became my enemy when she had to choose between me and you. And you, my wife, you have been my arch-enemy, because you have never left me till I lay here lifeless.

LAURA. I don't know that I ever thought or intended what you think I did. It may be that an obscure desire to get rid of you as something troublesome may have existed within me, and if you see any plan in my conduct, it is possible that it was to be found there, although I was unconscious of it. I have never reflected about my actions, but they have proceeded on the lines that you yourself laid down, and before God and my conscience I consider myself innocent, even if I am not. Your existence has lain like a stone on my heart, which weighed so heavily that the heart sought to shake off the oppressive burden. These are the facts, and if I have wounded you to the death, I ask your forgiveness.

CAPTAIN. All that sounds plausible. But of what help is it

to me? And whose is the fault? Perhaps that of a spiritual marriage! Formerly, one married a wife, now one enters into partnership with a business woman, or goes to live with a friend. . . . And then one cheats the partner, and outrages the friend! What becomes of love, healthy physical love? It dies in the meantime. And what is the result of this love in shares, payable to the bearer without joint liability? Who is the bearer when the crash comes? Who is the fleshly father to the spiritual child?

LAURA. And with regard to your suspicions about the child, they are quite without foundation.

CAPTAIN. That is just what is so appalling! If at least there was any foundation for them, it would be something to take hold of, to cling to. Now there are only shadows that hide themselves in the bushes, and stick out their heads to grin; it is like fighting with the air, or firing blank cartridges at a sham-fight. A fatal reality would have called forth resistance, nerved life and soul to action; but now my thoughts dissolve into thin air, and my brain grinds a void until it is on fire. Put a pillow under my head and throw something over me, I am cold. I am so terribly cold.

[LAURA *takes her shawl and spreads it over him.* NURSE *goes to fetch a pillow.*

LAURA. Give me your hand, friend.

CAPTAIN. My hand! The hand that you have bound! Omphale! Omphale! . . . But I can feel your shawl against my mouth; it is as warm and soft as your arm, and it smells of vanilla, like your hair when you were young! Laura, when you were young, and we walked in the birchwoods, with the oxlips and the thrushes . . . glorious, glorious! Think how beautiful life was, and what it is now. You did not wish to have it so, and neither did I, and yet it happened. Who then rules over life?

LAURA. God alone rules . . .

CAPTAIN. The god of strife then! Or perhaps the goddess nowadays. Take away the cat that is lying on me. Take it away! [NURSE *brings in a pillow and takes away the shawl.*

CAPTAIN. Give me my uniform coat! Throw it over me! [NURSE *takes the coat from the clothes pegs and lays it over*

him.]   Ah, my rough lion skin that you wanted to take away
from me! Omphale! Omphale! Thou cunning woman
who wast the lover of peace and the deviser of disarmaments.
Wake, Hercules, before they take thy club from thee! You will
wile our armour off us, too, and make believe that it is tinsel.
No, it was iron, do you hear, before it became tinsel. In olden
days the smith made the cuirass, now it is the needlewoman.
Omphale! Omphale! rude strength has fallen before treacherous weakness.—Out on you, infernal woman, and damnation on
your sex! [*He raises himself to spit at her, but falls back on to
the sofa.*] What sort of a pillow have you given me, Margret?
It is so hard, and so cold, so cold! Come and sit here by me on
the chair. There now! May I lay my head on your lap? Ah,
that is warm! Bend over me so that I can feel your breast!
Oh, it is sweet to sleep on a woman's breast, a mother's or a mistress's, but the mother's is best.

LAURA.   Would you like to see your child, Adolf?

CAPTAIN.   My child?   A man has no children, it is only
women who have children, and therefore the future is theirs,
when we die childless. Oh, God! who lovest children!

NURSE.   Listen, he is praying to God.

CAPTAIN.   No, to you to put me to sleep, for I am tired,
so tired. Good night, Margret, and blessed be you among
women.

[*He raises himself but falls back on the nurse's lap with a cry*

SCENE VIII

LAURA *goes to the left and calls in the* DOCTOR *who enters
with the* PASTOR.

LAURA.   Help, Doctor, if it is not too late. Look, he has
ceased to breathe!

DOCTOR.   [*Feels the patient's pulse.*]   It is a fit.

PASTOR.   Is he dead?

DOCTOR.   No, he may still come back to life, but to what an
awakening we do not know.

PASTOR.   " First death, and then the judgment."

DOCTOR.   No judgment, and no accusations. You who believe that a God overrules the fortunes of men must ask of Him concerning this matter.

NURSE.   Ah, Pastor, he prayed to God in his last moments.

PASTOR.   [*To* LAURA.]   Is that true?

LAURA.   It is true.

DOCTOR.   In that case, of which I can judge just as little as of the origin of the illness, my science is at an end.   You try now, Pastor.

LAURA.   Is this all that you have to say by this death-bed, Doctor?

DOCTOR.   This is all!   I know no more.   Let him speak that knows more!

BERTHA.   [*Enters on the left and runs forward to her mother.*]   Mother!   Mother!

LAURA.   My child, my own child!

PASTOR.   Amen.

Curtain.

MISS JULIA

A Naturalistic Tragedy

1888

CHARACTERS

Miss Julia, *aged* 25
Jean, *a valet, aged* 30
Christine, *a cook, aged* 35

The action takes place on Midsummer Eve, in the kitchen of the count's country house.

AUTHOR'S PREFACE

LIKE almost all other art, that of the stage has long seemed to me a sort of *Biblia Pauperum*, or a Bible in pictures for those who cannot read what is written or printed. And in the same way the playwright has seemed to me a lay preacher spreading the thoughts of his time in a form so popular that the middle classes, from which theatrical audiences are mainly drawn, can know what is being talked about without troubling their brains too much. For this reason the theatre has always served as a grammar-school to young people, women, and those who have acquired a little knowledge, all of whom retain the capacity for deceiving themselves and being deceived—which means again that they are susceptible to illusions produced by the suggestions of the author. And for the same reason I have had a feeling that, in our time, when the rudimentary, incomplete thought processes operating through our fancy seem to be developing into reflection, research, and analysis, the theatre might stand on the verge of being abandoned as a decaying form, for the enjoyment of which we lack the requisite conditions. The prolonged theatrical crisis now prevailing throughout Europe speaks in favour of such a supposition, as well as the fact that, in the civilised countries producing the greatest thinkers of the age, namely, England and Germany, the drama is as dead as are most of the other fine arts.

In some other countries it has, however, been thought possible to create a new drama by filling the old forms with the contents of a new time. But, for one thing, there has not been time for the new thoughts to become so popularised that the public might grasp the questions raised; secondly, minds have been so inflamed by party conflicts that pure and disinterested enjoyment has been excluded from places where one's innermost feelings are violated and the tyranny of an applauding or hissing majority is exercised with the openness for which the theatre gives a chance; and, finally, there has been no new form devised for the new contents, and the new wine has burst the old bottles.

In the following drama I have not tried to do anything new—for that cannot be done—but I have tried to modernise the form in accordance with the demands which I thought the new men of a new time might be likely to make on this art. And with such a purpose in view, I have chosen, or surrendered myself to, a theme that might well be said to lie outside the partisan strife of the day: for the problem of social ascendancy or decline, of higher or lower, of better or worse, of men or women, is, has been and will be of lasting interest. In selecting this theme from real life, as it was related to me a number of years ago, when the incident impressed me very deeply, I found it suited to a tragedy, because it can only make us sad to see a fortunately placed individual perish, and this must be the case in still higher degree when we see an entire family die out. But perhaps a time will arrive when we have become so developed, so enlightened, that we can remain indifferent before the spectacle of life, which now seems so brutal, so cynical, so heartless; when we have closed up those lower, unreliable instruments of thought which we call feelings, and which have been rendered not only superfluous but harmful by the final growth of our reflective organs.

The fact that the heroine arouses our pity depends only on our weakness in not being able to resist the sense of fear that the same fate could befall ourselves. And yet it is possible that a very sensitive spectator might fail to find satisfaction in this kind of pity, while the man believing in the future might demand some positive suggestion for the abolition of evil, or, in other words, some kind of programme. But, first of all, there is no absolute evil. That one family perishes is the fortune of another family, which thereby gets a chance to rise. And the alternation of ascent and descent constitutes one of life's main charms, as fortune is solely determined by comparison. And to the man with a programme, who wants to remedy the sad circumstance that the hawk eats the dove, and the flea eats the hawk, I have this question to put: why should it be remedied? Life is not so mathematically idiotic that it lets only the big eat the small, but it happens just as often that the bee kills the lion, or drives it to madness at least.

That my tragedy makes a sad impression on many is their own fault. When we grow strong as were the men of the French revolution, then we shall receive an unconditionally good and joyful impression from seeing the national forests rid of rotting and superannuated trees that have stood too long in the way of others with equal right to a period of free growth—an impression good in the same way as that received from the death of one incurably diseased.

Not long ago they reproached my tragedy " The Father " with being too sad—just as if they wanted merry tragedies. Everybody is clamouring arrogantly for " the joy of life," and all theatrical managers are giving orders for farces, as if the joy of life consisted in being silly and picturing all human beings as so many sufferers from St. Vitus' dance or idiocy. I find the joy of life in its violent and cruel struggles, and my pleasure lies in knowing something and learning something. And for this reason I have selected an unusual but instructive case—an exception, in a word—but a great exception, proving the rule, which, of course, will provoke all lovers of the commonplace. And what also will offend simple brains is that my action cannot be traced back to a single motive, that the view-point is not always the same. An event in real life—and this discovery is quite recent—springs generally from a whole series of more or less deep-lying motives, but of these the spectator chooses as a rule the one his reason can master most easily, or else the one reflecting most favourably on his power of reasoning. A suicide is committed. Bad business, says the merchant. Unrequited love, say the ladies. Sickness, says the sick man. Crushed hopes, says the ship-wrecked. But now it may be that the motive lay in all or none of these directions. It is possible that the one who is dead may have hid the main motive by pushing forward another meant to place his memory in a better light.

In explanation of *Miss Julia's* sad fate I have suggested many factors: her mother's fundamental instincts; her father's mistaken upbringing of the girl; her own nature, and the suggestive influence of her fiancé on a weak and degenerate brain; furthermore, and more directly: the festive mood of the Midsummer Eve; the absence of her father; her physical condition; her preoccupation with the animals; the excitation of the dance; the dusk of the night; the strongly aphrodisiacal influence of the flowers; and lastly the chance forcing the two of them together in a secluded room, to which must be added the aggressiveness of the excited man.

Thus I have neither been one-sidedly physiological nor one-sidedly psychological in my procedure. Nor have I merely delivered a moral preachment. This multiplicity of motives I regard as praiseworthy because it is in keeping with the views of our own time. And if others have done the same thing before me, I may boast of not being the sole inventor of my paradoxes— as all discoveries are named.

In regard to the character-drawing I may say that I have tried to make my figures rather " characterless," and I have done so for reasons I shall now state.

In the course of the ages, the word character has assumed many meanings. Originally it signified probably the dominant ground-note in the complex mass of the self, and as such it was confused with temperament. Afterward it became the middle-class term for an automaton, so that an individual whose nature had come to a stand-still, or who had adapted himself to a certain part in life—who had ceased to grow, in a word—was named a character; while one remaining in a state of development—a skilful navigator on life's river, who did not sail with close-tied sheets, but knew when to fall off before the wind and when to luff again—was called lacking in character. And he was called so in a depreciatory sense, of course, because he was so hard to catch, to classify, and to keep track of. This middle-class notion about the immobility of the soul was transplanted to the stage, where the middle-class element has always held sway. There a character became synonymous with a gentleman fixed and finished once for all—one who invariably appeared drunk, jolly, sad. And for the purpose of characterisation nothing more was needed than some physical deformity like a club-foot, a wooden leg, a red nose; or the person concerned was made to repeat some phrase like " That's capital!" or " Barkis is willin'," or something of that kind. This manner of regarding human beings as homogeneous is preserved even by the great Molière. *Harpagon* is nothing but miserly, although *Harpagon* might as well have been at-once miserly and a financial genius, a fine father, and a public-spirited citizen. What is worse yet, his " defect " is of distinct advantage to his son-in-law and daughter, who are his heirs, and for that reason should not find fault with him, even if they have to wait a little for their wedding. I do not believe, therefore, in simple characters on the stage. And the summary judgments of the author upon men—this one stupid, and that one brutal, this one jealous, and that one stingy—should be challenged by the naturalists, who know the fertility of the soul-complex, and who realise that " vice " has a reverse very much resembling virtue.

Because they are modern characters, living in a period of transition more hysterically hurried than its immediate predecessor at least, I have made my figures vacillating, out of joint, torn between the old and the new. And I do not think it unlikely that, through newspaper reading and overheard conversations, modern ideas may have leaked down to the strata where domestic servants belong.

My souls (or characters) are conglomerates, made up of past and present stages of civilisation, scraps of humanity, torn-off pieces of Sunday clothing turned into rags—all patched together as is the human soul itself. And I have furthermore offered a touch of evolutionary history by letting the weaker repeat words stolen from the stronger, and by letting different souls accept " ideas "—or suggestions, as they are called—from each other.

Miss Julia is a modern character, not because the man-hating half-woman may not have existed in all ages, but because now, after her discovery, she has stepped to the front and begun to make a noise. The half-woman is a type coming more and more into prominence, selling herself nowadays for power, decorations, distinctions, diplomas, as formerly for money, and the type indicates degeneration. It is not a good type, for it does not last, but unfortunately it has the power of reproducing itself and its misery through one more generation. And degenerate men seem instinctively to make their selection from this kind of women, so that they multiply and produce indeterminate sexes to whom life is a torture. Fortunately, however, they perish in the end, either from discord with real life, or from the irresistible revolt of their suppressed instincts, or from foiled hopes of possessing the man. The type is tragical, offering us the spectacle of a desperate struggle against nature. It is also tragical as a Romantic inheritance dispersed by the prevailing Naturalism, which wants nothing but happiness: and for happiness strong and sound races are required.

But *Miss Julia* is also a remnant of the old military nobility which is now giving way to the new nobility of nerves and brain. She is a victim of the discord which a mother's " crime " produces in a family, and also a victim of the day's delusions, of the circumstances, of her defective constitution—all of which may be held equivalent to the old-fashioned fate or universal law. The naturalist has wiped out the idea of guilt, but he cannot wipe out the results of an action—punishment, prison, or fear—and for the simple reason that they remain without regard to his verdict. For fellow-beings that have been wronged are not so good-natured as those on the outside, who have not been wronged at all, can be without cost to themselves.

Even if, for reasons over which he could have no control, the father should forgo his vengeance, the daughter would take vengeance upon herself, just as she does in the play, and she would be moved to it by that innate or acquired sense of honour which the upper classes inherit—whence? From the days of barbarism, from the original home of the Aryans, from the chivalry of the Middle Ages? It is beautiful, but it has become disadvantageous to the preservation of the race. It is this, the nobleman's *hara-kiri*—or the law of the inner conscience compelling the Japanese to cut open his own abdomen at the insult of another—which survives, though somewhat modified, in the duel, also a privilege of the nobility. For this reason the valet, *Jean*, continues to live, but *Miss Julia* cannot live on without honour. In so far as he lacks this life-endangering superstition about honour, the serf takes precedence of the earl, and in all of us Aryans there is something of the nobleman, or of Don Quixote, which makes us sympathise with the man who takes his own life because he has committed a dishonourable deed and thus lost his honour. And we are noblemen to the extent of suffering from seeing the earth littered with the living corpse of one who was once great—yes, even if the one thus fallen should rise again and make restitution by honourable deeds.

Jean, the valet, is of the kind that builds new stock—one in whom the differentiation is clearly noticeable. He was a cotter's child, and he has trained himself up to the point where the future gentleman has become visible. He has found it easy to learn, having finely developed sense (smell, taste, vision) and an instinct for beauty besides. He has already risen in the world, and is strong enough not to be sensitive about using other people's services. He has already become a stranger to his equals, despising them as so many outlived stages, but also fearing and fleeing them because they know his secrets, pry into his plans, watch his rise with envy, and look forward to his fall with pleasure. From this relationship springs his dual, indeterminate character, oscillating between love of distinction and hatred of those who have already achieved it. He says himself that he is an aristocrat, and has learned the secrets of good company. He is polished on the outside and coarse within. He knows already how to wear the frock-coat with ease, but the cleanliness of his body cannot be guaranteed.

He feels respect for the young lady, but he is afraid of *Christine*, who has his dangerous secrets in her keeping. His emotional callousness is sufficient to prevent the night's happenings from exercising a disturbing influence on his plans for the future. Having at once the slave's brutality and the master's lack of squeamishness, he can see blood without fainting, and he can also bend his back under a mishap until able to throw it off. For this reason he will emerge unharmed from the battle, and will probably end his days as the owner of a hotel. And if he does not become a Roumanian count, his son will probably go to a university, and may even become a county attorney.

Otherwise, he furnishes us with rather significant information as to the way in which the lower classes look at life from beneath —that is, when he speaks the truth, which is not often, as he prefers what seems favourable to himself to what is true. When *Miss Julia* suggests that the lower classes must feel the pressure from above very heavily, *Jean* agrees with her, of course, because he wants to gain her sympathy. But he corrects himself at once, the moment he realises the advantage of standing apart from the herd.

And *Jean* stands above *Miss Julia* not only because his fate is in ascendancy, but because he is a man. Sexually he is the aristocrat because of his male strength, his more finely developed senses, and his capacity for taking the initiative. His inferiority depends mainly on the temporary social environment in which he has to live, and which he probably can shed together with the valet's livery.

The mind of the slave speaks through his reverence for the count (as shown in the incident with the boots) and through his religious superstition. But he reveres the count principally as a possessor of that higher position towards which he himself is striving. And this reverence remains even when he has won the daughter of the house, and seen that the beautiful shell covered nothing but emptiness.

I don't believe that any love relation in a " higher " sense can spring up between two souls of such different quality. And for this reason I let *Miss Julia* imagine her love to be protective or commiserative in its origin. And I let *Jean* suppose that, under different social conditions, he might feel something like real love for her. I believe love to be like the hyacinth, which has to strike roots in darkness *before* it can bring forth a vigorous flower. In this case it shoots up quickly, bringing forth blossom and seed at once, and for that reason the plant withers so soon.

Christine, finally, is a female slave, full of servility and sluggishness acquired in front of the kitchen fire, and stuffed full of morality and religion that are meant to serve her at once as cloak and scapegoat. Her church-going has for its purpose to bring her quick and easy riddance of all responsibility for her domestic thieveries and to equip her with a new stock of guiltlessness. Otherwise she is a subordinate figure, and therefore purposely sketched in the same manner as the minister and the doctor in " The Father," whom I designed as ordinary human beings, like the common run of country ministers and country doctors. And if these accessory characters have seemed mere abstractions to some people, it depends on the fact that ordinary men are to a

certain extent impersonal in the exercise of their callings.   This
means that they are without individuality, showing only one side
of themselves while at work.   And as long as the spectator does
not feel the need of seeing them from other sides, my abstract
presentation of them remains on the whole correct.

In regard to the dialogue, I want to point out that I have de-
parted somewhat from prevailing traditions by not turning my
figures into catechists who make stupid questions in order to call
forth witty answers.   I have avoided the symmetrical and mathe-
matical construction of the French dialogue, and have instead
permitted the minds to work irregularly as they do in reality,
where, during conversation, the cogs of one mind seem more or
less haphazardly to engage those of another one, and where no
topic is fully exhausted.   Naturally enough, therefore, the dialogue strays a good deal as, in the opening scenes, it acquires a
material that later on is worked over, picked up again, repeated,
expounded, and built up like the theme in a musical composition.

The plot is pregnant enough, and as, at bottom, it is concerned
only with two persons, I have concentrated my attention on these,
introducing only one subordinate figure, the cook, and keeping the
unfortunate spirit of the father hovering above and beyond the
action.   I have done this because I believe I have noticed that the
psychological processes are what interest the people of our own
day more than anything else.   Our souls, so eager for knowledge, cannot rest satisfied with seeing what happens, but must
also learn how it comes to happen!   What we want to see are
just the wires, the machinery.   We want to investigate the box
with the false bottom, touch the magic ring in order to find the
suture, and look into the cards to discover how they are marked.

In this I have taken for models the monographic novels of the
brothers de Goncourt, which have appealed more to me than any
other modern literature.

Turning to the technical side of the composition, I have tried
to abolish the division into acts.   And I have done so because I
have come to fear that our decreasing capacity for illusion might
be unfavourably affected by intermissions during which the spectator would have time to reflect and to get away from the suggestive influence of the author-hypnotist.   My play will probably

last an hour and a half, and as it is possible to listen that length of time, or longer, to a lecture, a sermon, or a debate, I have imagined that a theatrical performance could not become fatiguing in the same time. As early as 1872, in one of my first dramatic experiments, "The Outlaw," I tried the same concentrated form, but with scant success. The play was written in five acts and wholly completed when I became aware of the restless, scattered effect it produced. Then I burned it, and out of the ashes rose a single, well-built act, covering fifty printed pages, and taking an hour for its performance. Thus the form of the present play is not new, but it seems to be my own, and changing æsthetical conventions may possibly make it timely.

My hope is still for a public educated to the point where it can sit through a whole-evening performance in a single act. But that point cannot be reached without a great deal of experimentation. In the meantime I have resorted to three art forms that are to provide resting-places for the public and the actors, without letting the public escape from the illusion induced. All these forms are subsidiary to the drama. They are the monologue, the pantomime, and the dance, all of them belonging originally to the tragedy of classical antiquity. For the monologue has sprung from the monody, and the chorus has developed into the ballet.

Our realists have excommunicated the monologue as improbable, but if I can lay a proper basis for it, I can also make it seem probable, and then I can use it to good advantage. It is probable, for instance, that a speaker may walk back and forth in his room practising his speech aloud; it is probable that an actor may read through his part aloud, that a servant-girl may talk to her cat, that a mother may prattle to her child, that an old spinster may chatter to her parrot, that a person may talk in his sleep. And in order that the actor for once may have a chance to work independently, and to be free for a moment from the author's pointer, it is better that the monologues be not written out, but just indicated. As it matters comparatively little what is said to the parrot or the cat, or in one's sleep—because it cannot influence the action—it is possible that a gifted actor, carried away by the situation and the mood of the occasion, may improvise such matters better than they could be written by the author, who cannot figure out in advance how much may be said, and how long the talk may last, without waking the public out of their illusions.

It is well known that, on certain stages, the Italian theatre has returned to improvisations and thereby produced creative actors—who, however, must follow the author's suggestions—and this may be counted a step forward, or even the beginning of a new art form that might well be called *productive.*

Where, on the other hand, the monologue would seem unreal, I have used the pantomime, and there I have left still greater scope for the actor's imagination—and for his desire to gain independent honours. But in order that the public may not be tried beyond endurance, I have permitted the music—which is amply warranted by the Midsummer Eve's dance—to exercise its illusory power while the dumb show lasts. And I ask the musical director to make careful selection of the music used for this purpose, so that incompatible moods are not induced by reminiscences from the last musical comedy or topical song, or by folk-tunes of too markedly ethnographical distinction.

The mere introduction of a scene with a lot of " people " could not have taken the place of the dance, for such scenes are poorly acted and tempt a number of grinning idiots into displaying their own smartness, whereby the illusion is disturbed. As the common people do not improvise their gibes, but use ready-made phrases in which stick some double meaning, I have not composed their lampooning song, but have appropriated a little known folk-dance which I personally noted down in a district near Stockholm. The words don't quite hit the point, but hint vaguely at it, and this is intentional, for the cunning (*i.e.,* weakness) of the slave keeps him from any direct attack. There must, then, be no chattering clowns in a serious action, and no coarse flouting at a situation that puts the lid on the coffin of a whole family.

As far as the scenery is concerned, I have borrowed from impressionistic painting its asymmetry, its quality of abruptness, and have thereby, in my opinion, strengthened the illusion. Because the whole room and all its contents are not shown, there is a chance to guess at things—that is, our imagination is stirred into complementing our vision. I have made a further gain in getting rid of those tiresome exits by means of doors, especially as stage doors are made of canvas and swing back and forth at the lightest touch. They are not even capable of expressing the anger of an irate *pater familias* who, on leaving his home after a poor dinner, slams the door behind him " so that it shakes the whole house." (On the stage the house sways.) I have also contented myself with a single setting, and for the double purpose of making the figures become parts of their surroundings, and of breaking with the tendency towards luxurious scenery. But having only a single setting, one may demand to have it real. Yet nothing is more difficult than to get a room that looks something like a room, although the painter can easily enough produce waterfalls and flaming volcanoes. Let it go at canvas for the walls, but we might be done with the painting of shelves and kitchen utensils on the canvas. We have so much else on the stage that is conventional, and in which we are asked to believe, that we might at least be spared the too great effort of believing in painted pans and kettles.

I have placed the rear wall and the table diagonally across the stage in order to make the actors show full face and half profile to the audience when they sit opposite each other at the table. In the opera " Aïda " I noticed an oblique background, which led the eye out into unseen prospects. And it did not appear to be the result of any reaction against the fatiguing right angle.

Another novelty well needed would be the abolition of the foot-lights. The light from below is said to have for its purpose to make the faces of the actors look fatter. But I cannot help asking: why must all actors be fat in the face? Does not this light from below tend to wipe out the subtler lineaments in the lower part of the face, and especially around the jaws? Does it not give a false appearance to the nose and cast shadows upward over the eyes? If this be not so, another thing is certain: namely, that the eyes of the actors suffer from the light, so that the effective play of their glances is precluded. Coming from below, the light strikes the retina in places generally protected (except in sailors, who have to see the sun reflected in the water), and for this reason one observes hardly anything but a vulgar rolling of the eyes, either sideways or upwards, towards the galleries, so that nothing but the white of the eye shows. Perhaps the same cause may account for the tedious blinking of which especially the actresses are guilty. And when anybody on the stage wants to use his eyes to speak with, no other way is left him but the poor one of staring straight at the public, with whom he or she then gets into direct communication outside of the frame provided by the setting. This vicious habit has, rightly or wrongly, been named " to meet friends." Would it not be possible by means of strong side-lights (obtained by the employment of reflectors, for instance) to add to the resources already possessed by the actor? Could not his mimicry be still further strengthened by use of the greatest asset possessed by the face: the play of the eyes?

Of course, I have no illusions about getting the actors to play *for* the public and not *at* it, although such a change would be highly desirable. I dare not even dream of beholding the actor's back throughout an important scene, but I wish with all my heart that crucial scenes might not be played in the centre of the proscenium, like duets meant to bring forth applause. Instead, I should like to have them laid in the place indicated by the situation. Thus I ask for no revolutions, but only for a few minor modifications. To make a real room of the stage, with the fourth wall missing, and a part of the furniture placed back towards the audience, would probably produce a disturbing effect at present.

In wishing to speak of the facial make-up, I have no hope that the ladies will listen to me, as they would rather look beautiful than lifelike. But the actor might consider whether it be to his advantage to paint his face so that it shows some abstract type which covers it like a mask. Suppose that a man put a markedly choleric line between the eyes, and imagine further that some remark demands a smile of this face fixed in a state of continuous wrath. What a horrible grimace will be the result! And how can the wrathful old man produce a frown on his false forehead, which is smooth as a billiard ball?

In modern psychological dramas, where the subtlest movements of the soul are to be reflected on the face rather than by gestures and noise, it would probably be well to experiment with strong side-light on a small stage, and with unpainted faces, or at least with a minimum of make-up.

If, in addition, we might escape the visible orchestra, with its disturbing lamps and its faces turned towards the public; if we could have the seats on the main floor (the orchestra or the pit) raised so that the eyes of the spectators would be above the knees of the actors; if we could get rid of the boxes with their tittering parties of diners; if we could also have the auditorium completely darkened during the performance; and if, first and last, we could have a small stage and a small house: then a new dramatic art might rise, and the theatre might at least become an institution for the entertainment of people with culture. While waiting for this kind of theatre, I suppose we shall have to write for the " icebox," and thus prepare the repertory that is to come.

I have made an attempt. If it prove a failure, there is plenty of time to try over again.

MISS JULIA

SCENE

A large kitchen: the ceiling and the side walls are hidden by draperies and hangings. The rear wall runs diagonally across the stage, from the left side and away from the spectators. On this wall, to the left, there are two shelves full of utensils made of copper, iron, and tin. The shelves are trimmed with scalloped paper.

A little to the right may be seen three-fourths of the big arched doorway leading to the outside. It has double glass doors, through which are seen a fountain with a cupid, lilac shrubs in bloom, and the tops of some Lombardy poplars.

On the left side of the stage is seen the corner of a big cook-stove built of glazed bricks; also a part of the smoke-hood above it.

From the right protrudes one end of the servants' dining-table of white pine, with a few chairs about it.

The stove is dressed with bundled branches of birch. Twigs of juniper are scattered on the floor.

On the table end stands a big Japanese spice pot full of lilac blossoms.

An icebox, a kitchen-table, and a wash-stand.

Above the door hangs a big old-fashioned bell on a steel spring, and the mouthpiece of a speaking-tube appears at the left of the door.

CHRISTINE is standing by the stove, frying something in a pan. She has on a dress of light-coloured cotton, which she has covered up with a big kitchen apron.

JEAN enters, dressed in livery and carrying a pair of big, spurred riding-boots, which he places on the floor in such a manner that they remain visible to the spectators.

JEAN.   To-night Miss Julia is crazy again; absolutely crazy.
CHRISTINE.   So you're back again?

JEAN.   I took the count to the station, and when I came back by the barn, I went in and had a dance, and there I saw the young lady leading the dance with the gamekeeper.   But when she caught sight of me, she rushed right up to me and asked me to dance the ladies' waltz with her.   And ever since she's been waltzing like—well, I never saw the like of it.   She's crazy!

CHRISTINE.   And has always been, but never the way it's been this last fortnight, since her engagement was broken.

JEAN.   Well, what kind of a story was that, anyhow?   He's a fine fellow, isn't he, although he isn't rich?   Ugh, but they're so full of notions.   [*Sits down at the end of the table.*]   It's peculiar anyhow, that a young lady—h'm!—would rather stay at home with the servants—don't you think?—than go with her father to their relatives!

CHRISTINE.   Oh, I guess she feels sort of embarrassed by that rumpus with her fellow.

JEAN.   Quite likely.   But there was some backbone to that man just the same.   Do you know how it happened, Christine?   I saw it, although I didn't care to let on.

CHRISTINE.   No, did you?

JEAN. Sure, I did.   They were in the stable-yard one evening, and the young lady was training him, as she called it.   Do you know what that meant?   She made him leap over her horse-whip the way you teach a dog to jump.   Twice he jumped and got a cut each time.   The third time he took the whip out of her hand and broke it into a thousand bits.   And then he got out.

CHRISTINE.   So that's the way it happened!   You don't say!

JEAN.   Yes, that's how that thing happened.   Well, Christine, what have you got that's tasty?

CHRISTINE.   [*Serves from the pan and puts the plate before Jean.*]   Oh, just some kidney which I cut out of the veal roast.

JEAN.   [*Smelling the food.*]   Fine!   That's my great *délice.* [*Feeling the plate.*]   But you might have warmed the plate.

CHRISTINE.   Well, if you ain't harder to please than the count himself!   [*Pulls his hair playfully.*

JEAN.   [*Irritated.*]   Don't pull my hair!   You know how sensitive I am.

CHRISTINE. Well, well, it was nothing but a love pull, you know.

JEAN. [*Eats.*]

CHRISTINE *opens a bottle of beer.*

JEAN. Beer—on Midsummer Eve? No, thank you! Then I have something better myself. [*Opens a table-drawer and takes out a bottle of claret with yellow cap.*] Yellow seal, mind you! Give me a glass—and you use those with stems when you drink it *pure.*

CHRISTINE. [*Returns to the stove and puts a small pan on the fire.*] Heaven preserve her that gets you for a husband, Mr. Finicky!

JEAN. Oh, rot! You'd be glad enough to get a smart fellow like me. And I guess it hasn't hurt you that they call me your beau. [*Tasting the wine.*] Good! Pretty good! Just a tiny bit too cold. [*He warms the glass with his hands.*] We got this at Dijon. It cost us four francs per litre, not counting the bottle. And there was the duty besides. What is it you're cooking—with that infernal smell?

CHRISTINE. Oh, it's some devilry the young lady is going to give Diana.

JEAN. You should choose your words with more care, Christine. But why should you be cooking for a bitch on a holiday eve like this? Is she sick?

CHRISTINE. Ye-es, she is sick. She's been running around with the gate-keeper's pug—and now there's trouble—and the young lady just won't hear of it.

JEAN. The young lady is too stuck up in some ways and not proud enough in others—just as was the countess while she lived. She was most at home in the kitchen and among the cows, but she would never drive with only one horse. She wore her cuffs till they were dirty, but she had to have cuff buttons with a coronet on them. And speaking of the young lady, she doesn't take proper care of herself and her person. I might even say that she's lacking in refinement. Just now, when she was dancing in the barn, she pulled the gamekeeper away from Anna and asked him herself to come and dance with her. We wouldn't act in that way. But that's just how it is: when upper-class people want to demean themselves, then they grow—mean! But she's splendid! Magnificent! Oh, such shoulders! And—and so on!

CHRISTINE. Oh, well, don't brag too much! I've heard Clara talking, who tends to her dressing.

JEAN. Pooh, Clara! You're always jealous of each other. I, who have been out riding with her— And then the way she dances!

CHRISTINE. Say, Jean, won't you dance with me when I'm done?

JEAN. Of course I will.

CHRISTINE. Do you promise?

JEAN. Promise? When I say so, I'll do it. Well, here's thanks for the good food. It tasted fine!

[*Puts the cork back into the bottle.*

JULIA. [*Appears in the doorway, speaking to somebody on the outside.*] I'll be back in a minute. You go right on in the meantime.

JEAN *slips the bottle into the table-drawer and rises respectfully.*

JULIA. [*Enters and goes over to* CHRISTINE *by the washstand.*] Well, is it done yet?

CHRISTINE *signs to her that* JEAN *is present.*

JEAN. [*Gallantly.*] The ladies are having secrets, I believe.

JULIA. [*Strikes him in the face with her handkerchief.*] That's for you, Mr. Pry!

JEAN. Oh, what a delicious odour that violet has!

JULIA. [*With coquetry.*] Impudent! So you know something about perfumes also? And know pretty well how to dance—Now don't peep! Go away!

JEAN. [*With polite impudence.*] Is it some kind of witches' broth the ladies are cooking on Midsummer Eve—something to tell fortunes by and bring out the lucky star in which one's future love is seen?

JULIA. [*Sharply.*] If you can see that, you'll have good eyes, indeed! [*To* CHRISTINE.] Put it in a pint bottle and cork it well. Come and dance a *schottische* with me now, Jean.

JEAN. [*Hesitatingly.*] I don't want to be impolite, but I had promised to dance with Christine this time——

JULIA. Well, she can get somebody else—can't you, Christine? Won't you let me borrow Jean from you?

CHRISTINE. That isn't for me to say. When Miss Julia is so gracious, it isn't for him to say no. You just go along, and be thankful for the honour, too!

JEAN. Frankly speaking, but not wishing to offend in any way, I cannot help wondering if it's wise for Miss Julia to dance twice in succession with the same partner, especially as the people here are not slow in throwing out hints——

JULIA. [*Flaring up.*] What is that? What kind of hints? What do you mean?

JEAN. [*Submissively.*] As you don't want to understand, I have to speak more plainly. It don't look well to prefer one servant to all the rest who are expecting to be honoured in the same unusual way——

JULIA. Prefer! What ideas! I'm surprised! I, the mistress of the house, deign to honour this dance with my presence, and when it so happens that I actually want to dance, I want to dance with one who knows how to lead, so that I am not made ridiculous.

JEAN. As you command, Miss Julia! I am at your service!

JULIA. [*Softened.*] Don't take it as a command. To-night we should enjoy ourselves as a lot of happy people, and all rank should be forgotten. Now give me your arm. Don't be afraid, Christine! I'll return your beau to you!

JEAN *offers his arm to* MISS JULIA *and leads her out.*

PANTOMIME

Must be acted as if the actress were really alone in the place. When necessary she turns her back to the public. She should not look in the direction of the spectators, and she should not hurry as if fearful that they might become impatient.

CHRISTINE *is alone. A* schottische *tune played on a violin is heard faintly in the distance.*

While humming the tune, CHRISTINE *clears off the table after* JEAN, *washes the plate at the kitchen table, wipes it, and puts it away in a cupboard.*

Then she takes off her apron, pulls out a small mirror from one of the table-drawers and leans it against the flower jar on the table; lights a tallow candle and heats a hairpin, which she uses to curl her front hair.

Then she goes to the door and stands there listening. Returns to the table. Discovers the handkerchief which MISS JULIA has left behind, picks it up, and smells it, spreads it out absent-mindedly and begins to stretch it, smooth it, fold it up, and so forth.

———————

JEAN. [*Enters alone.*] Crazy, that's what she is! The way she dances! And the people stand behind the doors and grin at her. What do you think of it, Christine?

CHRISTINE. Oh, she has her time now, and then she is always a little queer like that. But are you going to dance with me now?

JEAN. You are not mad at me because I disappointed you?

CHRISTINE. No!—Not for a little thing like that, you know! And also, I know my place——

JEAN. [*Putting his arm around her waist.*] You are a sensible girl, Christine, and I think you'll make a good wife——

JULIA. [*Enters and is unpleasantly surprised; speaks with forced gaiety.*] Yes, you are a fine partner—running away from your lady.

JEAN. On the contrary, Miss Julia. I have, as you see, looked up the one I deserted.

JULIA. [*Changing tone.*] Do you know, there is nobody that dances like you!—But why do you wear your livery on an evening like this? Take it off at once!

JEAN. Then I must ask you to step outside for a moment, as my black coat is hanging right here.

[*Points towards the right and goes in that direction.*

JULIA. Are you bashful on my account? Just to change a coat? Why don't you go into your own room and come back again? Or, you can stay right here, and I'll turn my back on you.

JEAN. With your permission, Miss Julia.

[*Goes farther over to the right; one of his arms can be seen as he changes his coat.*

JULIA. [*To* CHRISTINE.] Are you and Jean engaged, that he's so familiar with you?

CHRISTINE. Engaged? Well, in a way. We call it that.

JULIA. Call it?

CHRISTINE. Well, Miss Julia, you have had a fellow of your own, and——

JULIA. We were really engaged——

CHRISTINE. But it didn't come to anything just the same——

JEAN *enters, dressed in black frock coat and black derby.*

JULIA. *Très gentil, Monsieur Jean! Très gentil!*

JEAN. *Vous voulez plaisanter, Madame!*

JULIA. *Et vous voulez parler français!* Where did you learn it?

JEAN. In Switzerland, while I worked as *sommelier* in one of the big hotels at Lucerne.

JULIA. But you look like a real gentleman in your frock coat! Charming!   [*Sits down at the table.*

JEAN. Oh, you flatter me.

JULIA. [*Offended.*] Flatter—you!

JEAN. My natural modesty does not allow me to believe that you could be paying genuine compliments to one like me, and so I dare to assume that you are exaggerating, or, as we call it, flattering.

JULIA. Where did you learn to use your words like that? You must have been to the theatre a great deal?

JEAN. That, too. I have been to a lot of places.

JULIA. But you were born in this neighbourhood?

JEAN. My father was a cotter on the county attorney's property right by here, and I can recall seeing you as a child, although you, of course, didn't notice me.

JULIA. No, really!

JEAN. Yes, and I remember one time in particular—but of that I can't speak.

JULIA. Oh, yes, do! Why—just for once.

JEAN. No, really, I cannot do it now. Another time, perhaps.

JULIA. Another time is no time.   Is it as bad as that?

JEAN. It isn't bad, but it comes a little hard.   Look at that one!

Points to CHRISTINE, *who has fallen asleep on a chair by the stove.*

JULIA. She'll make a pleasant wife.   And perhaps she snores, too.

JEAN. No, she doesn't, but she talks in her sleep.

JULIA. [*Cynically.*]   How do you know?

JEAN. [*Insolently.*]   I have heard it.

Pause during which they study each other.

JULIA. Why don't you sit down?

JEAN. It wouldn't be proper in your presence.

JULIA. But if I order you to do it?

JEAN. Then I obey.

JULIA. Sit down, then!—But wait a moment!   Can you give me something to drink first?

JEAN. I don't know what we have got in the icebox.   I fear it is nothing but beer.

JULIA. And you call that nothing?   My taste is so simple that I prefer it to wine.

JEAN. [*Takes a bottle of beer from the icebox and opens it; gets a glass and a plate from the cupboard, and serves the beer.*] Allow me!

JULIA. Thank you.   Don't you want some yourself?

JEAN. I don't care very much for beer, but if it is a command, of course——

JULIA. Command?—I should think a polite gentleman might keep his lady company.

JEAN. Yes, that's the way it should be.

[*Opens another bottle and takes out a glass.*

JULIA. Drink my health now!

JEAN *hesitates.*

JULIA. Are you bashful—a big, grown-up man?

JEAN. [*Kneels with mock solemnity and raises his glass.*] To the health of my liege lady!

JULIA. Bravo!—And now you must also kiss my shoe in order to get it just right.

JEAN *hesitates a moment; then he takes hold of her foot and touches it lightly with his lips.*

JULIA. Excellent! You should have been on the stage.

JEAN. [*Rising to his feet.*] This won't do any longer, Miss Julia. Somebody might see us.

JULIA. What would that matter?

JEAN. Oh, it would set the people talking—that's all! And if you only know how their tongues were wagging up there a while ago——

JULIA. What did they have to say? Tell me— Sit down now!

JEAN. [*Sits down.*] I don't want to hurt you, but they were using expressions—which cast reflections of a kind that—oh, you know it yourself! You are not a child, and when a lady is seen alone with a man, drinking—no matter if he's only a servant—and at night—then——

JULIA. Then what? And besides, we are not alone. Isn't Christine with us?

JEAN. Yes—asleep!

JULIA. Then I'll wake her. [*Rising.*] Christine, are you asleep?

CHRISTINE. [*In her sleep.*] Blub-blub-blub-blub!

JULIA. Christine!—Did you ever see such a sleeper.

CHRISTINE. [*In her sleep.*] The count's boots are polished—put on the coffee—yes, yes, yes—my-my—pooh!

JULIA. [*Pinches her nose.*] Can't you wake up?

JEAN. [*Sternly.*] You shouldn't bother those that sleep.

JULIA. [*Sharply.*] What's that?

JEAN. One who has stood by the stove all day has a right to be tired at night. And sleep should be respected.

JULIA. [*Changing tone.*] It is fine to think like that, and it does you honour—I thank you for it. [*Gives* JEAN *her hand.*] Come now and pick some lilacs for me.

During the following scene CHRISTINE *wakes up. She moves as if still asleep and goes out to the right in order to go to bed.*

JEAN. With you, Miss Julia?

JULIA. With me!

JEAN. But it won't do! Absolutely not!

JULIA. I can't understand what you are thinking of. You couldn't possibly imagine——

JEAN. No, not I, but the people.

JULIA. What? That I am fond of the valet?

JEAN. I am not at all conceited, but such things have happened—and to the people nothing is sacred.

JULIA. You are an aristocrat, I think.

JEAN. Yes, I am.

JULIA. And I am stepping down——

JEAN. Take my advice, Miss Julia, don't step down. Nobody will believe you did it on purpose. The people will always say that you fell down.

JULIA. I think better of the people than you do. Come and see if I am not right. Come along!   [*She ogles him.*

JEAN. You're mighty queer, do you know!

JULIA. Perhaps. But so are you. And for that matter, everything is queer. Life, men, everything—just a mush that floats on top of the water until it sinks, sinks down! I have a dream that comes back to me ever so often. And just now I am reminded of it. I have climbed to the top of a column and sit there without being able to tell how to get down again. I get dizzy when I look down, and I must get down, but I haven't the courage to jump off. I cannot hold on, and I am longing to fall, and yet I don't fall. But there will be no rest for me until I get down, no rest until I get down, down on the ground. And if I did reach the ground, I should want to get still farther down, into the ground itself— Have you ever felt like that?

JEAN. No, my dream is that I am lying under a tall tree in a dark wood. I want to get up, up to the top, so that I can look out over the smiling landscape, where the sun is shining, and so that I can rob the nest in which lie the golden eggs. And I climb and climb, but the trunk is so thick and smooth, and it is so far to the first branch. But I know that if I could only reach that first branch, then I should go right on to the top as on a ladder. I have not reached it yet, but I am going to, if it only be in my dreams.

JULIA. Here I am chattering to you about dreams! Come along! Only into the park!

She offers her arm to him, and they go towards the door.

JEAN. We must sleep on nine midsummer flowers to-night, Miss Julia—then our dreams will come true.

They turn around in the doorway, and JEAN *puts one hand up to his eyes.*

JULIA. Let me see what you have got in your eye.

JEAN. Oh, nothing—just some dirt—it will soon be gone.

JULIA. It was my sleeve that rubbed against it. Sit down and let me help you. [*Takes him by the arm and makes him sit down; takes hold of his head and bends it backwards; tries to get out the dirt with a corner of her handkerchief.*] Sit still now, absolutely still! [*Slaps him on the hand.*] Well, can't you do as I say? I think you are shaking—a big strong fellow like you! [*Feels his biceps.*] And with such arms!

JEAN. [*Ominously.*] Miss Julia!

JULIA. Yes, Monsieur Jean.

JEAN. *Attention! Je ne suis qu'un homme.*

JULIA. Can't you sit still!— There now! Now it's gone. Kiss my hand now, and thank me.

JEAN. [*Rising.*] Miss Julia, listen to me. Christine has gone to bed now— Won't you listen to me?

JULIA. Kiss my hand first.

JEAN. Listen to me!

JULIA. Kiss my hand first!

JEAN. All right, but blame nobody but yourself!

JULIA. For what?

JEAN. For what! Are you still a mere child at twenty-five? Don't you know that it is dangerous to play with fire?

JULIA. Not for me. I am insured.

JEAN. [*Boldly.*] No, you are not. And even if you were, there are inflammable surroundings to be counted with.

JULIA. That's you, I suppose?

JEAN. Yes. Not because I am I, but because I am a young man——

JULIA. Of handsome appearance—what an incredible conceit! A Don Juan, perhaps. Or a Joseph? On my soul, I think you are a Joseph!

JEAN. Do you?

JULIA. I fear it almost.

JEAN *goes boldly up to her and takes her around the waist in order to kiss her.*

JULIA. [*Gives him a cuff on the ear.*] Shame!

JEAN. Was that in play or in earnest?

JULIA. In earnest.

JEAN. Then you were in earnest a moment ago also. Your playing is too serious, and that's the dangerous thing about it. Now I am tired of playing, and I ask to be excused in order to resume my work. The count wants his boots to be ready for him, and it is after midnight already.

JULIA. Put away the boots.

JEAN. No, it's my work, which I am bound to do. But I have not undertaken to be your playmate. It's something I can never become— I hold myself too good for it.

JULIA. You're proud!

JEAN. In some ways, and not in others.

JULIA. Have you ever been in love?

JEAN. We don't use that word. But I have been fond of a lot of girls, and once I was taken sick because I couldn't have the one I wanted: sick, you know, like those princes in the Arabian Nights who cannot eat or drink for sheer love.

JULIA. Who was it?

JEAN *remains silent.*

JULIA. Who was it?

JEAN. You cannot make me tell you.

JULIA. If I ask you as an equal, ask you as—a friend: who was it?

JEAN. It was you.

JULIA. [*Sits down.*] How funny!

JEAN. Yes, as you say—it was ludicrous. That was the story, you see, which I didn't want to tell you a while ago. But now I am going to tell it. Do you know how the world looks from below—no, you don't. No more than do hawks and falcons, of whom we never see the back because they are always floating about high up in the sky. I lived in the cotter's hovel, together with seven other children, and a pig—out there on the grey plain, where there isn't a single tree. But from our windows I could see the wall around the count's park, and apple-trees above it. That was the Garden of Eden, and many fierce angels were guarding it with flaming swords. Nevertheless I and some other boys found our way to the Tree of Life—now you despise me?

JULIA. Oh, stealing apples is something all boys do.

JEAN. You may say so now, but you despise me nevertheless. However—once I got into the Garden of Eden with my mother to weed the onion beds. Near by stood a Turkish pavilion, shaded by trees and covered with honeysuckle. I didn't know what it was used for, but I had never seen a more beautiful building. People went in and came out again, and one day the door was left wide open. I stole up and saw the walls covered with pictures of kings and emperors, and the windows were hung with red, fringed curtains—now you know what I mean. I— [*breaks off a lilac sprig and holds it under* Miss JULIA's *nose*]— I had never been inside the manor, and I had never seen anything but the church—and this was much finer. No matter where my thoughts ran, they returned always—to that place. And gradually a longing arose within me to taste the full pleasure of —*enfin!* I sneaked in, looked, and admired. Then I heard somebody coming. There was only one way out for fine people, but for me there was another, and I could do nothing else but choose it.

JULIA, *who has taken the lilac sprig, lets it drop on the table.*

JEAN. Then I started to run, plunged through a hedge of raspberry bushes, chased right across a strawberry plantation, and came out on the terrace where the roses grow. There I caught sight of a pink dress and pair of white stockings—that was you! I crawled under a pile of weeds—right into it, you know—into stinging thistles and wet, ill-smelling dirt. And I saw you walking among the roses, and I thought: if it be possible for a robber to get into heaven and dwell with the angels, then it is strange that a cotter's child, here on God's own earth, cannot get into the park and play with the count's daughter.

JULIA. [*Sentimentally.*] Do you think all poor children have the same thoughts as you had in this case?

JEAN. [*Hesitatingly at first; then with conviction.*] If all poor—yes—of course. Of course!

JULIA. It must be a dreadful misfortune to be poor.

JEAN. [*In a tone of deep distress and with rather exaggerated emphasis.*] Oh, Miss Julia! Oh!— A dog may lie on her ladyship's sofa; a horse may have his nose patted by the young lady's hand, but a servant—[*changing his tone*]—oh well, here and there you meet one made of different stuff, and he makes a way for himself in the world, but how often does it happen?— However, do you know what I did? I jumped into the mill brook with my clothes on, and was pulled out, and got a licking. But the next Sunday, when my father and the rest of the people were going over to my grandmother's, I fixed it so that I could stay at home. And then I washed myself with soap and hot water, and put on my best clothes, and went to church, where I could see you. I did see you, and went home determined to die. But I wanted to die beautifully and pleasantly, without any pain. And then I recalled that it was dangerous to sleep under an elder bush. We had a big one that was in full bloom. I robbed it of all its flowers, and then I put them in the big box where the oats were kept and lay down in them. Did you ever notice the smoothness of oats? Soft to the touch as the skin of the human body! However, I pulled down the lid and closed my eyes— fell asleep and was woken up a very sick boy. But I didn't die, as you can see. What I wanted—that's more than I can tell. Of course, there was not the least hope of winning you—but you symbolised the hopelessness of trying to get out of the class into which I was born.

JULIA. You narrate splendidly, do you know? Did you ever go to school?

JEAN. A little. But I have read a lot of novels and gone to the theatre a good deal. And besides, I have listened to the talk of better-class people, and from that I have learned most of all.

JULIA. Do you stand around and listen to what we are saying?

JEAN. Of course! And I have heard a lot, too, when I was on the box of the carriage, or rowing the boat. Once I heard you, Miss Julia, and one of your girl friends——

JULIA. Oh!— What was it you heard then?

JEAN. Well, it wouldn't be easy to repeat. But I was rather surprised, and I couldn't understand where you had learned all those words. Perhaps, at bottom, there isn't quite so much difference as they think between one kind of people and another.

JULIA. You ought to be ashamed of yourself! We don't live as you do when we are engaged.

JEAN. [*Looking hard at her.*] Is it so certain?— Well, Miss Julia, it won't pay to make yourself out so very innocent to me——

JULIA. The man on whom I bestowed my love was a scoundrel.

JEAN. That's what you always say—afterwards.

JULIA. Always?

JEAN. Always, I believe, for I have heard the same words used several times before, on similar occasions.

JULIA. What occasions?

JEAN. Like the one of which we were speaking. The last time——

JULIA. [*Rising.*] Stop! I don't want to hear any more!

JEAN. Nor did *she*—curiously enough! Well, then I ask permission to go to bed.

JULIA. [*Gently.*] Go to bed on Midsummer Eve?

JEAN. Yes, for dancing with that mob out there has really no attraction for me.

JULIA. Get the key to the boat and take me out on the lake— I want to watch the sunrise.

JEAN. Would that be wise?

JULIA. It sounds as if you were afraid of your reputation.

JEAN. Why not? I don't care to be made ridiculous, and I don't care to be discharged without a recommendation, for I am trying to get on in the world. And then I feel myself under a certain obligation to Christine.

JULIA. So it's Christine now——

JEAN. Yes, but it's you also— Take my advice and go to bed!

JULIA. Am I to obey you?

JEAN. For once—and for your own sake! The night is far gone. Sleepiness makes us drunk, and the head grows hot. Go to bed! And besides—if I am not mistaken—I can hear the crowd coming this way to look for me. And if we are found together here, you are lost!

CHORUS. [*Is heard approaching*]:
> Through the fields come two ladies a-walking,
> Treederee-derallah, treederee-derah.
> And one has her shoes full of water,
> Treederee-derallah-lah.
>
> They're talking of hundreds of dollars,
> Treederee-derallah, treederee-derah.
> But have not between them a dollar
> Treederee-derallah-lah.
>
> This wreath I give you gladly,
> Treederee-derallah, treederee-derah.
> But love another madly,
> Treederee-derallah-lah.

JULIA. I know the people, and I love them, just as they love me. Let them come, and you'll see.

JEAN. No, Miss Julia, they don't love you. They take your food and spit at your back. Believe me. Listen to me—can't you hear what they are singing?— No, don't pay any attention to it!

JULIA. [*Listening.*] What is it they are singing?

JEAN. Oh, something scurrilous. About you and me.

JULIA. How infamous! They ought to be ashamed! And the treachery of it!

JEAN. The mob is always cowardly. And in such a fight as this there is nothing to do but run away.

JULIA. Run away? Where to? We cannot get out. And we cannot go into Christine's room.

JEAN. Oh, we cannot? Well, into my room, then! Necessity knows no law. And you can trust me, for I am your true and frank and respectful friend.

JULIA. But think only——think if they should look for you in there!

JEAN. I shall bolt the door. And if they try to break it open, I'll shoot!— Come! [*Kneeling before her.*] Come!

JULIA. [*Meaningly.*] And you promise me——?

JEAN. I swear!

MISS JULIA *goes quickly out to the right.* JEAN *follows her eagerly.*

BALLET

The peasants enter. They are decked out in their best and carry flowers in their hats. A fiddler leads them. On the table they place a barrel of small-beer and a keg of " brännvin," or white Swedish whiskey, both of them decorated with wreaths woven out of leaves. First they drink. Then they form a ring and sing and dance to the melody heard before:

" Through the fields come two ladies a-walking."

The dance finished, they leave singing.

JULIA. [*Enters alone. On seeing the disorder in the kitchen, she claps her hands together. Then she takes out a powder-puff and begins to powder her face.*

JEAN. [*Enters in a state of exaltation.*] There you see! And you heard, didn't you? Do you think it possible to stay here?

JULIA. No, I don't think so. But what are we to do?

JEAN. Run away, travel, far away from here.

JULIA. Travel? Yes—but where?

JEAN. To Switzerland, the Italian lakes—you have never been there?

JULIA. No. Is the country beautiful?

JEAN. Oh! Eternal summer! Orange trees! Laurels! Oh!

JULIA. But then—what are we to do down there?

JEAN.   I'll start a hotel, everything first class, including the customers.

JULIA.   Hotel?

JEAN.   That's the life, I tell you!   Constantly new faces and new languages.   Never a minute free for nerves or brooding.   No trouble about what to do—for the work is calling to be done: night and day, bells that ring, trains that whistle, buses that come and go; and gold pieces raining on the counter all the time.   That's the life for you!

JULIA.   Yes, that is life.   And I?

JEAN.   The mistress of everything, the chief ornament of the house.   With your looks—and your manners—oh, success will be assured!   Enormous!   You'll sit like a queen in the office and keep the slaves going by the touch of an electric button.   The guests will pass in review before your throne and timidly deposit their treasures on your table.   You cannot imagine how people tremble when a bill is presented to them—I'll salt the items, and you'll sugar them with your sweetest smiles.   Oh, let us get away from here—[*pulling a time-table from his pocket*]—at once, with the next train!   We'll be in Malmö at 6.30; in Hamburg at 8.40 to-morrow morning; in Frankfort and Basel a day later.   And to reach Como by way of the St. Gotthard it will take us—let me see—three days.   Three days!

JULIA.   All that is all right.   But you must give me some courage—Jean.   Tell me that you love me.   Come and take me in your arms.

JEAN.   [*Reluctantly.*]   I should like to—but I don't dare.   Not in this house again.   I love you—beyond doubt—or, can you doubt it, Miss Julia?

JULIA.   [*With modesty and true womanly feeling.*]   Miss? —Call me Julia.   Between us there can be no barriers hereafter.   Call me Julia!

JEAN.   [*Disturbed:*]   I cannot!   There will be barriers between us as long as we stay in this house—there is the past, and there is the count—and I have never met another person for whom I felt such respect.   If I only catch sight of his gloves on a chair I feel small.   If I only hear that bell up there, I jump like a shy horse.   And even now, when I see his boots standing there so stiff and perky, it is as if something made my back bend. [*Kicking at the boots.*] It's nothing but superstition and tradition hammered into us from childhood—but it can be as easily forgotten again. Let us only get to another country, where they have a republic, and you'll see them bend their backs double before my liveried porter. You see, backs have to be bent, but not mine. I wasn't born to that kind of thing. There's better stuff in me—character—and if I only get hold of the first branch, you'll see me do some climbing. To-day I am a valet, but next year I'll be a hotel owner. In ten years I can live on the money I have made, and then I'll go to Roumania and get myself an order. And I may—note well that I say *may* —end my days as a count.

JULIA. Splendid, splendid!

JEAN. Yes, in Roumania the title of count can be had for cash, and so you'll be a countess after all. My countess!

JULIA. What do I care about all I now cast behind me! Tell me that you love me me: otherwise—yes, what am I otherwise?

JEAN. I will tell you so a thousand times—later. But not here. And above all, no sentimentality, or everything will be lost. We must look at the matter in cold blood, like sensible people. [*Takes out a cigar, cuts off the point, and lights it.*] Sit down there now, and I'll sit here, and then we'll talk as if nothing had happened.

JULIA. [*In despair.*] Good Lord! Have you then no feelings at all?

JEAN. I? No one is more full of feeling than I am. But I know how to control myself.

JULIA. A while ago you kissed my shoe—and now!

JEAN. [*Severely.*] Yes, that was then. Now we have other things to think of.

JULIA. Don't speak harshly to me!

JEAN. No, but sensibly. One folly has been committed— don't let us commit any more! The count may be here at any moment, and before he comes our fate must be settled. What do you think of my plans for the future? Do you approve of them?

JULIA. They seem acceptable, on the whole. But there is one question: a big undertaking of that kind will require a big capital—have you got it?

JEAN. [*Chewing his cigar.*] I? Of course! I have my expert knowledge, my vast experience, my familiarity with several languages. That's the very best kind of capital, I should say.

JULIA. But it won't buy you a railroad ticket even.

JEAN. That's true enough. And that is just why I am looking for a backer to advance the needful cash.

JULIA. Where could you get one all of a sudden?

JEAN. It's for you to find him if you want to become my partner.

JULIA. I cannot do it, and I have nothing myself. [*Pause.*

JEAN. Well, then that's off——

JULIA. And——

JEAN. Everything remains as before.

JULIA. Do you think I am going to stay under this roof as your concubine? Do you think I'll let the people point their fingers at me? Do you think I can look my father in the face after this? No, take me away from here, from all this humiliation and disgrace!— Oh, what have I done? My God, my God! [*Breaks into tears.*

JEAN. So we have got around to that tune now!— What you have done? Nothing but what many others have done before you.

JULIA. [*Crying hysterically.*] And now you're despising me!—I'm falling, I'm falling!

JEAN. Fall down to me, and I'll lift you up again afterwards.

JULIA. What horrible power drew me to you? Was it the attraction which the strong exercises on the weak—the one who is rising on one who is falling? Or was it love? This—love! Do you know what love is?

JEAN. I? Well, I should say so! Don't you think I have been there before?

JULIA. Oh, the language you use, and the thoughts you think!

JEAN. Well, that's the way I was brought up, and that's the way I am. Don't get nerves now and play the exquisite, for now one of us is just as good as the other. Look here, my girl, let me treat you to a glass of something superfine.

He opens the table-drawer, takes out the wine bottle, and fills up two glasses that have already been used.

JULIA. Where did you get that wine?

JEAN. In the cellar.

JULIA. My father's Burgundy!

JEAN. Well, isn't it good enough for the son-in-law?

JULIA. And I am drinking beer—I!

JEAN. It shows merely that I have better taste than you.

JULIA. Thief!

JEAN. Do you mean to tell on me?

JULIA. Oh, oh! The accomplice of a house thief! Have I been drunk, or have I been dreaming all this night? Midsummer Eve! The feast of innocent games——

JEAN. Innocent—hm!

JULIA. [*Walking back and forth.*] Can there be another human being on earth so unhappy as I am at this moment?

JEAN. But why should you be? After such a conquest? Think of Christine in there. Don't you think she has feelings also?

JULIA. I thought so a while ago, but I don't think so any longer. No, a menial is a menial——

JEAN. And a whore a whore!

JULIA. [*On her knees, with folded hands.*] O God in heaven, make an end of this wretched life! Take me out of the filth into which I am sinking! Save me! Save me!

JEAN. I cannot deny that I feel sorry for you. When I was lying among the onions and saw you up there among the roses— I'll tell you now—I had the same nasty thoughts that all boys have.

JULIA. And you who wanted to die for my sake!

JEAN. Among the oats. That was nothing but talk.

JULIA. Lies, in other words!

JEAN. [*Beginning to feel sleepy.*] Just about. I think I read the story in a paper, and it was about a chimney-sweep who

crawled into a wood-box full of lilacs because a girl had brought
suit against him for not supporting her kid——

JULIA. So that's the sort you are——

JEAN. Well, I had to think of something—for it's the high-
faluting stuff that the women bite on.

JULIA. Scoundrel!

JEAN. Rot!

JULIA. And now you have seen the back of the hawk——

JEAN. Well, I don't know——

JULIA. And I was to be the first branch——

JEAN. But the branch was rotten——

JULIA. I was to be the sign in front of the hotel——

JEAN. And I the hotel——

JULIA. Sit at your counter, and lure your customers, and
doctor your bills——

JEAN. No, that I should have done myself——

JULIA. That a human soul can be so steeped in dirt!

JEAN. Well, wash it off!

JULIA. You lackey, you menial, stand up when I talk to
you!

JEAN. You lackey-love, you mistress of a menial—shut up
and get out of here! You're the right one to come and tell me
that I am vulgar. People of my kind would never in their lives
act as vulgarly as you have acted to-night. Do you think any
servant girl would go for a man as you did? Did you ever see
a girl in my class throw herself at anybody in that way? I have
never seen the like of it except among beasts and prostitutes.

JULIA. [*Crushed.*] That's right: strike me, step on me—I
haven't deserved any better! I am a wretched creature. But
help me! Help me out of this, if there be any way to do so!

JEAN. [*In a milder tone.*] I don't want to lower myself
by a denial of my share in the honour of seducing. But do you
think a person in my place would have dared to raise his eyes to
you, if the invitation to do so had not come from yourself? I
am still sitting here in a state of utter surprise——

JULIA. And pride——

JEAN. Yes, why not? Although I must confess that the
victory was too easy to bring with it any real intoxication.

JULIA. Strike me some more!

JEAN. [*Rising.*] No! Forgive me instead what I have been saying. I don't want to strike one who is disarmed, and least of all a lady. On one hand I cannot deny that it has given me pleasure to discover that what has dazzled us below is nothing but cat-gold; that the hawk is simply grey on the back also; that there is powder on the tender cheek; that there may be black borders on the polished nails; and that the handkerchief may be dirty, although it smells of perfume. But on the other hand it hurts me to have discovered that what I was striving to reach is neither better nor more genuine. It hurts me to see you sinking so low that you are far beneath your own cook—it hurts me as it hurts to see the fall flowers beaten by the rain and turned into mud.

JULIA. You speak as if you were already above me?

JEAN. Well, so I am. Don't you see: I could have made a countess of you, but you could never make me a count.

JULIA. But I am born of a count, and that's more than you can ever achieve.

JEAN. That's true. But I might be the father of counts—if——

JULIA. But you are a thief—and I am not.

JEAN. Thief is not the worst. There are other kinds still farther down. And thēn, when I serve in a house, I regard myself in a sense as a member of the family, as a child of the house, and you don't call it theft when children pick a few of the berries that load down the vines. [*His passion is aroused once more.*] Miss Julia, you are a magnificent woman, and far too good for one like me. You were swept along by a spell of intoxication, and now you want to cover up your mistake by making yourself believe that you are in love with me. Well, you are not, unless possibly my looks might tempt you—in which case your love is no better than mine. I could never rest satisfied with having you care for nothing in me but the mere animal, and your love I can never win.

JULIA. Are you so sure of that?

JEAN. You mean to say that might be possible? That I might love you: yes, without doubt—for you are beautiful, refined, [*goes up to her and takes hold of her hand*] educated, charming when you want to be so, and it is not likely that the flame will ever burn out in a man who has once been set on fire by you. [*Puts his arm around her waist.*]   You are like burnt wine with strong spices in it, and one of your kisses——

He tries to lead her away, but she frees herself gently from his hold.

JULIA.   Leave me alone!   In that way you cannot win me.

JEAN.   How then?—   Not in that way!   Not by caresses and sweet words!   Not by thought for the future, by escape from disgrace!   How then?

JULIA.   How?   How?   I don't know—   Not at all!   I hate you as I hate rats, but I cannot escape from you!

JEAN.   Escape *with* me!

JULIA.   [*Straightening up.*]   Escape?   Yes, we   must escape!——   But I am so tired.   Give me a glass of wine.

JEAN *pours out wine.*

JULIA.   [*Looks at her watch.*]   But we must talk first. We have still some time left.

[*Empties her glass and holds it out for more.*

JEAN.   Don't drink so much.   It will go to your head.

JULIA.   What difference would that make?

JEAN.   What difference would it make?   It's vulgar to get drunk——   What was it you wanted to tell me?

JULIA.   We must get away.   But first we must have a talk— that is, I must talk, for so far you have done all the talking. You have told me about your life.   Now I must tell you about mine, so that we know each other right to the bottom before we begin the journey together.

JEAN.   One moment, pardon me!   Think first, so that you don't regret it afterwards, when you have already given up the secrets of your life.

JULIA.   Are you not my friend?

JEAN.   Yes, at times—but don't rely on me.

JULIA.   You only talk like that—and besides, my secrets are known to everybody.   You see, my mother was not of noble birth, but came of quite plain people.   She was brought up in the ideas of her time about equality, and woman's independence, and

that kind of thing.   And she had a decided aversion to marriage.
Therefore, when my father proposed to her, she said she wouldn't
marry him—and then she did it just the same.   I came into the
world—against my mother's wish, I have come to think.   Then
my mother wanted to bring me up in a perfectly natural state,
and at the same time I was to learn everything that a boy is
taught, so that I might prove that a woman is just as good as a
man.   I was dressed as a boy, and was taught how to handle a
horse, but could have nothing to do with the cows.   I had to
groom and harness and go hunting on horseback.   I was even
forced to learn something about agriculture.   And all over the
estate men were set to do women's work, and women to do men's
—with the result that everything went to pieces and we became
the laughing-stock of the whole neighbourhood.   At last my
father must have recovered from the spell cast over him, for he
rebelled, and everything was changed to suit his own ideas.   My
mother was taken sick—what kind of sickness it was I don't
know, but she fell often into convulsions, and she used to hide
herself in the garret or in the garden, and sometimes she stayed
out all night.   Then came the big fire, of which you have heard.
The house, the stable, and the barn were burned down, and this
under circumstances which made it look as if the fire had been
set on purpose.   For the disaster occurred the day after our insurance expired, and the money sent for renewal of the policy
had been delayed by the messenger's carelessness, so that it came
too late.   [*She fills her glass again and drinks.*

JEAN.   Don't drink any more.

JULIA.   Oh, what does it matter!— We were without a
roof over our heads and had to sleep in the carriages.   My father
didn't know where to get the money for the rebuilding of the
house.   Then my mother suggested that he try to borrow from a
childhood friend of hers, a brick manufacturer living not far
from here.   My father got the loan, but was not permitted to
pay any interest, which astonished him.   And so the house was
built up again.   [*Drinks again.*]   Do you know who set fire to
the house?

JEAN.   Her ladyship, your mother!

JULIA.   Do you know who the brick manufacturer was?

JEAN.   Your mother's lover.

JULIA.   Do you know to whom the money belonged?

JEAN.   Wait a minute—no, that I don't know.

JULIA.   To my mother.

JEAN.   In other words, to the count, if there was no settlement.

JULIA.   There was no settlement.   My mother possessed a small fortune of her own which she did not want to leave in my father's control, so she invested it with—her friend.

JEAN.   Who copped it.

JULIA.   Exactly!   He kept it.   All this came to my father's knowledge.   He couldn't bring suit; he couldn't pay his wife's lover; he couldn't prove that it was his wife's money.   That was my mother's revenge because he had made himself master in his own house.   At that time he came near shooting himself—it was even rumoured that he had tried and failed.   But he took a new lease of life, and my mother had to pay for what she had done.   I can tell you that those were five years I'll never forget! My sympathies were with my father, but I took my mother's side because I was not aware of the true circumstances.   From her I learned to suspect and hate men—for she hated the whole sex, as you have probably heard—and I promised her on my oath that I would never become a man's slave.

JEAN.   And so you became engaged to the County Attorney.

JULIA.   Yes, in order that he should be my slave.

JEAN.   And he didn't want to?

JULIA.   Oh, he wanted, but I wouldn't let him.   I got tired of him.

JEAN.   Yes, I saw it—in the stable-yard.

JULIA.   What did you see?

JEAN.   Just that—how he broke the engagement.

JULIA.   That's a lie!   It was I who broke it.   Did he say he did it, the scoundrel?

JEAN.   Oh, he was no scoundrel, I guess.   So you hate men, Miss Julia?

JULIA.   Yes!   Most of the time.   But now and then— when the weakness comes over me—oh, what shame!

JEAN.   And you hate me too?

JULIA. Beyond measure! I should like to kill you like a wild beast——

JEAN. As you make haste to shoot a mad dog. Is that right?

JULIA. That's right!

JEAN. But now there is nothing to shoot with—and there is no dog. What are we to do then?

JULIA. Go abroad.

JEAN. In order to plague each other to death?

JULIA. No—in order to enjoy ourselves: a couple of days, a week, as long as enjoyment is possible. And then—die!

JEAN. Die? How silly! Then I think it's much better to start a hotel.

JULIA. [*Without listening to* JEAN.] At Lake Como, where the sun is always shining, and the laurels stand green at Christmas, and the oranges are glowing.

JEAN. Lake Como is a rainy hole, and I could see no oranges except in the groceries. But it is a good place for tourists, as it has a lot of villas that can be rented to loving couples, and that's a profitable business—do you know why? Because they take a lease for six months—and then they leave after three weeks.

JULIA. [*Naïvely.*] Why after three weeks?

JEAN. Because they quarrel, of course. But the rent has to be paid just the same. And then you cán rent the house again. And that way it goes on all the time, for there is plenty of love—even if it doesn't last long.

JULIA. You don't want to die with me?

JEAN. I don't want to die at all. Both because I am fond of living, and because I regard suicide as a crime against the Providence which has bestowed life on us.

JULIA. Do you mean to say that *you* believe in God?

JEAN. Of course, I do. And I go to church every other Sunday. Frankly speaking, now I am tired of all this, and now I am going to bed.

JULIA. So! And you think that will be enough for me? Do you know what you owe a woman that you have spoiled?

JEAN. [*Takes out his purse and throws a silver coin on the table.*] You're welcome! I don't want to be in anybody's debt.

JULIA. [*Pretending not to notice the insult.*] Do you know what the law provides——

JEAN. Unfortunately the law provides no punishment for a woman who seduces a man.

JULIA. [*As before.*] Can you think of any escape except by our going abroad and getting married, and then getting a divorce?

JEAN. Suppose I refuse to enter into this *mésalliance*?

JULIA. *Mésalliance*——

JEAN. Yes, for me. You see, I have better ancestry than you, for nobody in my family was ever guilty of arson.

JULIA. How do you know?

JEAN. Well, nothing is known to the contrary, for we keep no pedigrees——except in the police bureau. But I have read about your pedigree in a book that was lying on the drawing-room table. Do you know who was your first ancestor? A miller who let his wife sleep with the king one night during the war with Denmark. I have no such ancestry. I have none at all, but I can become an ancestor myself.

JULIA. That's what I get for unburdening my heart to one not worthy of it; for sacrificing my family's honour——

JEAN. Dishonour! Well, what was it I told you? You shouldn't drink, for then you talk. And you *must* not talk!

JULIA. Oh, how I regret what I have done! How I regret it! If at least you loved me!

JEAN. For the last time: what do you mean? Am I to jump over your whip? Am I to kiss you, and lure you down to Lake Como for three weeks, and so on? What am I to do? What do you expect? This is getting to be rather painful! But that's what comes from getting mixed up with women. Miss Julia! I see that you are unhappy; I know that you are suffering; but I cannot understand you. We never carry on like that. There is never any hatred between us. Love is to us a play, and we play at it when our work leaves us time to do so. But we have not the time to do so all day and all night, as you have. I believe you are sick——I am sure you are sick.

JULIA. You should be good to me——and now you speak like a human being.

JEAN. All right, but be human yourself. You spit on me, and then you won't let me wipe myself—on you!

JULIA. Help me, help me! Tell me only what I am to do— where I am to turn.

JEAN. O Lord, if I only knew that myself!

JULIA. I have been exasperated, I have been mad, but there ought to be some way of saving myself.

JEAN. Stay right here and keep quiet. Nobody knows anything.

JULIA. Impossible! The people know, and Christine knows.

JEAN. They don't know, and they would never believe it possible.

JULIA. [Hesitating.] But—it might happen again.

JEAN. That's true.

JULIA. And the results?

JEAN. [Frightened.] The results! Where was my head when I didn't think of that! Well, then there is only one thing to do—you must leave. At once! I can't go with you, for then everything would be lost, so you must go alone—abroad—anywhere!

JULIA. Alone? Where?—I can't do it.

JEAN. You must! And before the count gets back. If you stay, then you know what will happen. Once on the wrong path, one wants to keep on, as the harm is done anyhow. Then one grows more and more reckless—and at last it all comes out. So you must get away! Then you can write to the count and tell him everything, except that it was me. And he would never guess it. Nor do I think he would be very anxious to find out.

JULIA. I'll go if you come with me.

JEAN. Are you stark mad, woman? Miss Julia to run away with her valet! It would be in the papers in another day, and the count could never survive it.

JULIA. I can't leave! I can't stay! Help me! I am so tired, so fearfully tired. Give me orders! Set me going, for I can no longer think, no longer act——

JEAN. Do you see now what good-for-nothings you are! Why do you strut and turn up your noses as if you were the lords of creation? Well, I am going to give you orders. Go up and dress. Get some travelling money, and then come back again.

JULIA. [*In an undertone.*] Come up with me!

JEAN. To your room? Now you're crazy again! [*Hesitates a moment.*] No, you must go at once!

[*Takes her by the hand leads her out.*

JULIA. [*On her way out.*] Can't you speak kindly to me, Jean?

JEAN. An order must always sound unkind. Now you can find out how it feels!

JULIA *goes out.*

JEAN, *alone, draws a sigh of relief; sits down at the table; takes out a note-book and a pencil; figures aloud from time to time; dumb play until* CHRISTINE *enters dressed for church; she has a false shirt front and a white tie in one of her hands.*

CHRISTINE. Goodness gracious, how the place looks! What have you been up to, anyhow?

JEAN. Oh, it was Miss Julia who dragged in the people. Have you been sleeping so hard that you didn't hear anything at all?

CHRISTINE. I have been sleeping like a log.

JEAN. And dressed for church already?

CHRISTINE. Yes, didn't you promise to come with me to communion to-day?

JEAN. Oh, yes, I remember now. And there you've got the finery. Well, come on with it. [*Sits down;* CHRISTINE *helps him to put on the shirt front and the white tie.* [*Pause.*

JEAN. [*Sleepily.*] What's the text to-day?

CHRISTINE. Oh, about John the Baptist beheaded, I guess.

JEAN. That's going to be a long story, I'm sure. My, but you choke me! Oh, I'm so sleepy, so sleepy!

CHRISTINE. Well, what has been keeping you up all night? Why, man, you're just green in the face!

JEAN. I have been sitting here talking with Miss Julia.

CHRISTINE. She hasn't an idea of what's proper, that creature!

[*Pause.*

JEAN. Say, Christine.

CHRISTINE. Well?

JEAN. Isn't it funny anyhow, when you come to think of it? Her!

CHRISTINE. What is it that's funny?

JEAN. Everything! [*Pause.*

CHRISTINE. [*Seeing the glasses on the table that are only half emptied.*] So you've been drinking together also?

JEAN. Yes.

CHRISTINE. Shame on you! Look me in the eye!

JEAN. Yes.

CHRISTINE. Is it possible? Is it possible?

JEAN. [*After a moment's thought.*] Yes, it is!

CHRISTINE. Ugh! That's worse than I could ever have believed. It's awful!

JEAN. You are not jealous of her, are you?

CHRISTINE. No, not of her. Had it been Clara or Sophie, then I'd have scratched your eyes out. Yes, that's the way I feel about it, and I can't tell why. Oh my, but that was nasty!

JEAN. Are you mad at her then?

CHRISTINE. No, but at you! It was wrong of you, very wrong! Poor girl! No, I tell you, I don't want to stay in this house any longer, with people for whom it is impossible to have any respect.

JEAN. Why should you have any respect for them?

CHRISTINE. And you who are such a smarty can't tell that! You wouldn't serve people who don't act decently, would you? It's to lower oneself, I think.

JEAN. Yes, but it ought to be a consolation to us that they are not a bit better than we.

CHRISTINE. No, I don't think so. For if they're no better then it's no use trying to get up to them. And just think of the count! Think of him who has had so much sorrow in his day! No, I don't want to stay any longer in this house— And with a fellow like you, too. If it had been the County Attorney—if it had only been someone of her own sort——

JEAN. Now look here!

CHRISTINE. Yes, yes! You're all right in your way, but there's after all some difference between one kind of people and another— No, but this is something I'll never get over!—

And the young lady who was so proud, and so tart to the men, that you couldn't believe she would ever let one come near her—and such a one at that!   And she who wanted to have poor Diana shot because she had been running around with the gate-keeper's pug!— Well, I declare!— But I won't stay here any longer, and next October I get out of here.

JEAN.   And then?

CHRISTINE.   Well, as we've come to talk of that now, perhaps it would be just as well if you looked for something, seeing that we're going to get married after all.

JEAN.   Well, what could I look for?   As a married man I couldn't get a place like this.

CHRISTINE.   No, I understand that.   But you could get a job as a janitor, or maybe as a messenger in some government bureau. Of course, the public loaf is always short in weight, but it comes steady, and then there is a pension for the widow and the children——

JEAN.   [*Making a face.*]   That's good and well, but it isn't my style to think of dying all at once for the sake of wife and children.   I must say that my plans have been looking towards something better than that kind of thing.

CHRISTINE.   Your plans, yes—but you've got obligations also, and those you had better keep in mind!

JEAN.   Now don't you get my dander up by talking of obligations!   I know what I've got to do, anyhow.   [*Listening for some sound on the outside.*]   However, we've plenty of time to think of all this.   Go in now and get ready, and then we'll go to church.

CHRISTINE.   Who is walking around up there?

JEAN.   I don't know, unless it be Clara.

CHRISTINE.   [*Going out.*]   It can't be the count, do you think, who's come home without anybody hearing him?

JEAN.   [*Scared.*]   The count?   No, that isn't possible, for then he would have rung for me.

CHRISTINE.   [*As she goes out.*]   Well, God help us all! Never have I seen the like of it!

The sun has risen and is shining on the tree tops in the park.
The light changes gradually until it comes slantingly in

through the windows. JEAN *goes to the door and gives a signal.*

JULIA. [*Enters in travelling dress and carrying a small bird-cage covered up with a towel; this she places on a chair.*] Now I am ready.

JEAN. Hush! Christine is awake.

JULIA. [*Showing extreme nervousness during the following scene.*] Did she suspect anything?

JEAN. She knows nothing at all. But, my heavens, how you look!

JULIA. How do I look?

JEAN. You're as pale as a corpse, and—pardon me, but your face is dirty.

JULIA. Let me wash it then— Now! [*She goes over to the washstand and washes her face and hands.*] Give me a towel— Oh!— That's the sun rising!

JEAN. And then the ogre bursts. *And that breaks the spell.*

JULIA. Yes, ogres and trolls were abroad last night!— But listen, Jean. Come with me, for now I have the money.

JEAN. [*Doubtfully.*] Enough?

JULIA. Enough to start with. Come with me, for I cannot travel alone to-day. Think of it—Midsummer Day, on a stuffy train, jammed with people who stare at you—and standing still at stations when you want to fly. No, I cannot! I cannot! And then the memories will come: childhood memories of Midsummer Days, when the inside of the church was turned into a green forest—birches and lilacs; the dinner at the festive table with relatives and friends; the afternoon in the park, with dancing and music, flowers and games! Oh, you may run and run, but your memories are in the baggage-car, and with them remorse and repentance! *guilt.*

JEAN. I'll go with you—but at once, before it's too late. This very moment!

JULIA. Well, get dressed then. [*Picks up the cage.*

JEAN. But no baggage! That would only give us away.

JULIA. No, nothing at all! Only what we can take with us in the car.

JEAN. [*Has taken down his hat.*] What have you got there? What is it?

JULIA. It's only my finch. I can't leave it behind.

JEAN. Did you ever! Dragging a bird-cage along with us! You must be raving mad! Drop the cage!

JULIA. The only thing I take with me from my home! The only living creature that loves me since Diana deserted me! Don't be cruel! Let me take it along!

JEAN. Drop the cage, I tell you! And don't talk so loud——Christine can hear us.

JULIA. No, I won't let it fall into strange hands. I'd rather have you kill it!

JEAN. Well, give it to me, and I'll wring its neck.

JULIA. Yes, but don't hurt it. Don't—no, I cannot!

JEAN. Let me—I can!

JULIA. [*Takes the bird out of the cage and kisses it.*] Oh, my little birdie, must it die and go away from its mistress?

JEAN. Don't make a scene, please. Don't you know it's a question of your life, of your future? Come, quick!

Snatches the bird away from her, carries it to the chopping-block and picks up an axe. MISS JULIA *turns away.*

JEAN. You should have learned how to kill chickens instead of shooting with a revolver—[*brings down the axe*]—then you wouldn't have fainted for a drop of blood.

JULIA. [*Screaming.*] Kill me too! Kill me. You who can take the life of an innocent creature without turning a hair! Oh, I hate and despise you! There is blood between us! Cursed be the hour when I first met you! Cursed be the hour when I came to life in my mother's womb!

JEAN. Well, what's the use of all that cursing? Come on!

JULIA. [*Approaching the chopping-block as if drawn to it against her will.*] No, I don't want to go yet. I cannot—I must see—Hush! There's a carriage coming up the road. [*Listening without taking her eyes off the block and the axe.*] You think I cannot stand the sight of blood. You think I am as weak as that—oh, I should like to see your blood, your brains, on that block there. I should like to see your whole sex swimming in blood like that thing there. I think I could drink out of your skull, and bathe my feet in your open breast, and eat your heart from the spit!— You think I am weak; you think I love you because the fruit of my womb was yearning for your seed; you think I want to carry your offspring under my heart and nourish it with my blood—bear your children and take your name! Tell me, you, what are you called, anyhow? I have never heard your family name—and maybe you haven't any. I should become Mrs. "Hovel," or Mrs. "Backyard"—you dog there, that's wearing my collar; you lackey with my coat of arms on your buttons—and I should share with my cook, and be the rival of my own servant. Oh! Oh! Oh!— You think I am a coward and want to run away. No, now I'll stay—and let the lightning strike! My father will come home—will find his chiffonier opened—the money gone! Then he'll ring—twice for the valet—and then he'll send for the sheriff—and then I shall tell everything! Everything! Oh, but it will be good to get an end to it—if it only be the end! And then his heart will break, and he dies!— So there will be an end to all of us—and all will be quiet—peace—eternal rest!— And then the coat of arms will be shattered on the coffin—and the count's line will be wiped out—but the lackey's line goes on in the orphan asylum—wins laurels in the gutter, and ends in jail.

JEAN. There spoke the royal blood! Bravo, Miss Julia! Now you put the miller back in his sack!

CHRISTINE *enters dressed for church and carrying a hymn-book in her hand.*

JULIA. [*Hurries up to her and throws herself into her arms as if seeking protection.*] Help me, Christine! Help me against this man!

CHRISTINE. [*Unmoved and cold.*] What kind of performance is this on the Sabbath morning? [*Catches sight of the chopping-block.*] My, what a mess you have made!— What's the meaning of all this? And the way you shout and carry on!

JULIA. You are a woman, Christine, and you are my friend. Beware of that scoundrel!

JEAN. [*A little shy and embarrassed.*] While the ladies are discussing I'll get myself a shave. [*Slinks out to the right.*

JULIA. You must understand me, and you must listen to me.

CHRISTINE. No, really, I don't understand this kind of trolloping. Where are you going in your travelling dress—and he with his hat on—what?— What?

JULIA. Listen, Christine, listen, and I'll tell you everything——

CHRISTINE. I don't want to know anything——

JULIA. You must listen to me——

CHRISTINE. What is it about? Is it about this nonsense with Jean? Well, I don't care about it at all, for it's none of my business. But if you're planning to get him away with you, we'll put a stop to that!

JULIA. [*Extremely nervous.*] Please try to be quiet, Christine, and listen to me. I cannot stay here, and Jean cannot stay here—and so we must leave——

CHRISTINE. H'm, h'm!

JULIA. [*Brightening up.*] But now I have got an idea, you know. Suppose all three of us should leave—go abroad—go to Switzerland and start a hotel together—I have money, you know—and Jean and I could run the whole thing—and you, I thought, could take charge of the kitchen— Wouldn't that be fine! Say yes, now! And come along with us! Then everything is fixed!— Oh, say yes!

[*She puts her arms around* CHRISTINE *and pats her.*

CHRISTINE. [*Coldly and thoughtfully.*] H'm, h'm!

JULIA. [*Presto tempo.*] You have never travelled, Christine—you must get out and have a look at the world. You cannot imagine what fun it is to travel on a train—constantly new people—new countries—and then we get to Hamburg and take in the Zoological Gardens in passing—that's what you like—and then we go to the theatres and to the opera—and when we get to Munich, there, you know, we have a lot of museums, where they keep Rubens and Raphael and all those big painters, you know— Haven't you heard of Munich, where King Louis used to live—the king, you know, that went mad— And then we'll have a look at his castle—he has still some castles that are furnished just as in a fairy tale—and from there it isn't very far to Switzerland—and the Alps, you know—just think of the Alps, with snow on top of them in the middle of the summer—and there you have orange trees and laurels that are green all the year round——

> JEAN *is seen in the right wing, sharpening his razor on a strop which he holds between his teeth and his left hand; he listens to the talk with a pleased mien and nods approval now and then.*

JULIA. [*Tempo prestissimo.*] And then we get a hotel— and I sit in the office, while Jean is outside receiving tourists— and goes out marketing—and writes letters— That's a life for you— Then the train whistles, and the bus drives up, and it rings upstairs, and it rings in the restaurant—and then I make out the bills—and I am going to salt them, too— You can never imagine how timid tourists are when they come to pay their bills! And you—you will sit like a queen in the kitchen. Of course, you are not going to stand at the stove yourself. And you'll have to dress neatly and nicely in order to show yourself to people—and with your looks—yes, I am not flattering you— you'll catch a husband some fine day—some rich Englishman, you know—for those fellows are so easy [*slowing down*] to catch— and then we grow rich—and we build us a villa at Lake Como— of course, it is raining a little in that place now and then—but [*limply*] the sun must be shining sometimes—although it looks dark—and—then—or else we can go home again—and come back—here—or some other place.

CHRISTINE. Tell me, Miss Julia, do you believe in all that yourself?

JULIA. [*Crushed.*] Do I believe in it myself?

CHRISTINE. Yes.

JULIA. [*Exhausted.*] I don't know: I believe no longer in anything. [*She sinks down on the bench and drops her head between her arms on the table.*] Nothing! Nothing at all!

CHRISTINE. [*Turns to the right, where JEAN is standing.*] So you were going to run away!

JEAN. [*Abashed, puts the razor on the table.*] Run away? Well, that's putting it rather strong. You have heard what the young lady proposes, and though she is tired out now by being up all night, it's a proposition that can be put through all right.

CHRISTINE. Now you tell me: did you mean to act as cook for that one there——?

JEAN. [*Sharply.*] Will you please use decent language in speaking to your mistress! Do you understand?

CHRISTINE. Mistress!

JEAN. Yes!

CHRISTINE. Well, well! Listen to him!

JEAN. Yes, it would be better for you to listen a little more and talk a little less. Miss Julia is your mistress, and what makes you disrespectful to her now should make you feel the same way about yourself.

CHRISTINE. Oh, I have always had enough respect for myself——

JEAN. To have none for others!

CHRISTINE. —not to go below my own station. You can't say that the count's cook has had anything to do with the groom or the swineherd. You can't say anything of the kind!

JEAN. Yes, it's your luck that you have had to do with a gentleman.

CHRISTINE. Yes, a gentleman who sells the oats out of the count's stable!

JEAN. What's that to you who get a commission on the groceries and bribes from the butcher?

CHRISTINE. What's that?

JEAN. And so you can't respect your master and mistress any longer! You—you!

CHRISTINE. Are you coming with me to church? I think you need a good sermon on top of such a deed.

JEAN. No, I am not going to church to-day. You can go by yourself and confess your own deeds.

CHRISTINE. Yes, I'll do that, and I'll bring back enough forgiveness to cover you also. The Saviour suffered and died on the cross for all our sins, and if we go to him with a believing heart and a repentant mind, he'll take all our guilt on himself.

JULIA. Do you believe that, Christine?

CHRISTINE. It is my living belief, as sure as I stand here, and the faith of my childhood which I have kept since I was young, Miss Julia. And where sin abounds, grace abounds, too.

JULIA. Oh, if I had your faith! Oh, if——

CHRISTINE. Yes, but you don't get it without special grace of God, and that is not bestowed on everybody——

JULIA. On whom is it bestowed then?

CHRISTINE. That's just the great secret of the work of grace, Miss Julia, and the Lord has no regard for persons, but there those that are last shall be foremost——

JULIA. Yes, but that means he has regard for those that are last.

CHRISTINE. [*Going right on.*] —and it is easier for a camel to go through a needle's eye than for a rich man to get into heaven. That's the way it is, Miss Julia. Now I am going, however—alone—and as I pass by, I'll tell the stableman not to let out the horses if anybody should like to get away before the count comes home. Good-bye! [*Goes out.*

JEAN. Well, ain't she a devil!— And all this for the sake of a finch!

JULIA. [*Apathetically.*] Never mind the finch!— Can you see any way out of this, any way to end it?

JEAN. [*Ponders.*] No!

JULIA. What would you do in my place?

JEAN. In your place? Let me see. As one of gentle birth, as a woman, as one who has—fallen. I don't know—yes, I do know!

JULIA. [*Picking up the razor with a significant gesture.*] Like this?

JEAN. Yes!— But please observe that I myself wouldn't do it, for there is a difference between us,

JULIA. Because you are a man and I a woman? What is the difference?

JEAN. It is the same—as—that between man and woman.

JULIA. [*With the razor in her hand.*] I want to, but I cannot!— My father couldn't either, that time he should have done it.

JEAN. No, he should not have done it, for he had to get his revenge first.

JULIA. And now it is my mother's turn to revenge herself again, through me.

JEAN.   Have you not loved your father, Miss Julia?

JULIA.   Yes, immensely, but I must have hated him, too.   I think I must have been doing so without being aware of it.   But he was the one who reared me in contempt for my own sex—half woman and half man!   Whose fault is it, this that has happened?   My father's—my mother's—my own?   My own? Why, I have nothing that is my own.   I haven't a thought that didn't come from my father; not a passion that didn't come from my mother; and now this last—this about all human creatures being equal—I got that from him, my fiancé—whom I call a scoundrel for that reason!   How can it be my own fault?   To put the blame on Jesus, as Christine does—no, I am too proud for that, and know too much—thanks to my father's teachings— And that about a rich person not getting into heaven, it's just a lie, and Christine, who has money in the savings-bank, wouldn't get in anyhow.   Whose is the fault?—   What does it matter whose it is?   For just the same I am the one who must bear the guilt and the results——

JEAN.   Yes, but——

Two sharp strokes are rung on the bell.   MISS JULIA *leaps to her feet.*   JEAN *changes his coat.*

JEAN.   The count is back.   Think if Christine——

              [*Goes to the speaking-tube, knocks on it, and listens.*

JULIA.   Now he has been to the chiffonier!

JEAN.   It is Jean, your lordship!   [*Listening again, the spectators being unable to hear what the count says.*]   Yes, your lordship!   [*Listening.*]   Yes, your lordship!   At once! [*Listening.*]   In a minute, your lordship!   [*Listening.*]   Yes, yes!   In half an hour!

JULIA.   [*With intense concern.*]   What did he say?   Lord Jesus, what did he say?

JEAN.   He called for his boots and wanted his coffee in half an hour.

JULIA.   In half an hour then!   Oh, I am so tired.   I can't do anything; can't repent, can't run away, can't stay, can't live—can't die!   Help me now!   Command me, and I'll obey you like a dog!   Do me this last favour—save my honour, and save his name!   You know what my will ought to do, and what it cannot do—now give me your will, and make me do it!

JEAN. I don't know why—but now I can't either—I don't understand— It is just as if this coat here made a—I cannot command you—and now, since I've heard the count's voice— now—I can't quite explain it—but— Oh, that damned menial is back in my spine again. I believe if the count should come down here, and if he should tell me to cut my own throat—I'd do it on the spot!

JULIA. Make believe that you are he, and that I am you!— You did some fine acting when you were on your knees before me—then you were the nobleman—or—have you ever been to a show and seen one who could hypnotise people?

JEAN makes a sign of assent.

JULIA. He says to his subject: get the broom. And the man gets it. He says: sweep. And the man sweeps.

JEAN. But then the other person must be asleep.

JULIA. [*Ecstatically.*] I am asleep already—there is nothing in the whole room but a lot of smoke—and you look like a stove—that looks like a man in black clothes and a high hat—and your eyes glow like coals when the fire is going out—and your face is a lump of white ashes. [*The sunlight has reached the floor and is now falling on JEAN.*] How warm and nice it is! [*She rubs her hands as if warming them before a fire.*] And so light—and so peaceful!

JEAN. [*Takes the razor and puts it in her hand.*] There's the broom! Go now, while it is light—to the barn—and——
[*Whispers something in her ear.*

JULIA. [*Awake.*] Thank you! Now I shall have rest! But tell me first—that the foremost also receive the gift of grace. Say it, even if you don't believe it.

JEAN. The foremost? No, I can't do that!— But wait— Miss Julia—I know! You are no longer among the foremost— now when you are among the—last!

JULIA. That's right. I am among the last of all: I am the very last. Oh!— But now I cannot go— Tell me once more that I must go!

JEAN. No, now I can't do it either. I cannot!

JULIA. And those that are foremost shall be the last.

JEAN.   Don't think, don't think!   Why, you are taking away my strength, too, so that I become a coward— What?   I thought I saw the bell moving!—To be that scared of a bell! Yes, but it isn't only the bell—there is somebody behind it—a hand that makes it move—and something else that makes the hand move—but if you cover up your ears—just cover up your ears!   Then it rings worse than ever!   Rings and rings, until you answer it—and then it's too late—then comes the sheriff— and then—

Two quick rings from the bell.

JEAN.   [*Shrinks together; then he straightens himself up.*] It's horrid!   But there's no other end to it!— Go!

JULIA *goes firmly out through the door.*

Curtain.

THE STRONGER
A Scene
1890

CHARACTERS

MRS. X., *an actress, married.*
MISS Y., *an actress, unmarried.*

THE STRONGER

SCENE

A corner of a ladies' restaurant; two small tables of cast-iron, a sofa covered with red plush, and a few chairs.

MRS. X. *enters dressed in hat and winter coat, and carrying a pretty Japanese basket on her arm.*

MISS Y. *has in front of her a partly emptied bottle of beer; she is reading an illustrated weekly, and every now and then she exchanges it for a new one.*

MRS. X. Well, how do, Millie! Here you are sitting on Christmas Eve as lonely as a poor bachelor.

MISS Y. *looks up from the paper for a moment, nods, and resumes her reading.*

MRS. X. Really, I feel sorry to find you like this—alone—alone in a restaurant, and on Christmas Eve of all times. It makes me as sad as when I saw a wedding party at Paris once in a restaurant—the bride was reading a comic paper and the groom was playing billiards with the witnesses. Ugh, when it begins that way, I thought, how will it end? Think of it, playing billiards on his wedding day! Yes, and you're going to say that she was reading a comic paper—that's a different case, my dear.

A WAITRESS *brings a cup of chocolate, places it before* MRS. X., *and disappears again.*

MRS. X. [*Sips a few spoonfuls; opens the basket and displays a number of Christmas presents.*] See what I've bought for my tots. [*Picks up a doll.*] What do you think of this? Lisa is to have it. She can roll her eyes and twist her head, do you see? Fine, is it not? And here's a cork pistol for Carl.

[*Loads the pistol and pops it at* MISS Y.
MISS Y. *starts as if frightened.*

MRS. X. Did I scare you? Why, you didn't fear I was going to shoot you, did you? Really, I didn't think you could believe that of me. If you were to shoot *me*—well, that wouldn't surprise me the least. I've got in your way once, and I know you'll never forget it—but I couldn't help it. You still think I intrigued you away from the Royal Theatre, and I didn't do anything of the kind—although you think so. But it doesn't matter what I say, of course—you believe it was I just the same. [*Pulls out a pair of embroidered slippers.*] Well, these are for my hubby—tulips—I've embroidered them myself. Hm, I hate tulips—and he must have them on everything.

MISS Y. *looks up from the paper with an expression of mingled sarcasm and curiosity.*

MRS. X. [*Puts a hand in each slipper.*] Just see what small feet Bob has. See? And you should see him walk—elegant! Of course, you've never seen him in slippers.

MISS Y. *laughs aloud.*

MRS. X. Look here—here he comes.

[*Makes the slippers walk across the table.*
MISS Y. *laughs again.*

MRS. X. Then he gets angry, and he stamps his foot just like this: "Blame that cook who can't learn how to make coffee." Or: "The idiot—now that girl has forgotten to fix my study lamp again." Then there is a draught through the floor and his feet get cold: "Gee, but it's freezing, and those blanked idiots don't even know enough to keep the house warm."

[*She rubs the sole of one slipper against the instep of the other.*
MISS Y. *breaks into prolonged laughter.*

MRS. X. And then he comes home and has to hunt for his slippers—Mary has pushed them under the bureau. Well, perhaps it is not right to be making fun of one's own husband. He's pretty good for all that—a real dear little hubby, that's what he is. You should have such a husband—what are you laughing at? Can't you tell? Then, you see, I know he is faithful. Yes, I know, for he has told me himself—what in the world makes you giggle like that? That nasty Betty tried to get him away from me while I was on the road—can you think of anything more infamous? [*Pause.*] But I'd have scratched the eyes out of her face, that's what I'd have done if I had been at home when she tried it. [*Pause.*] I'm glad Bob told me all about it, so I didn't have to hear it first from somebody else. [*Pause.*]   And just think of it, Betty was not the only one!   I don't know why it is, but all women seem to be crazy after my husband.   It must be because they imagine his government position gives him something to say about the engagements.   Perhaps you've tried it yourself—you may have set your traps for him, too?   Yes, I don't trust you very far—but I know he never cared for you— and then I have been thinking you rather had a grudge against him.

Pause.   They look at each other in an embarrassed manner.

MRS. X.   Amèlia, spend the evening with us, won't you? Just to show that you are not angry—not with me, at least.   I cannot tell exactly why, but it seems so awfully unpleasant to have you—you—for an enemy.   Perhaps because I got in your way that time [*rallentando*] or—I don't know—really, I don't know at all——

Pause.   MISS Y. gazes searchingly at MRS. X.

MRS. X.   [*Thoughtfully.*]   It was so peculiar, the way our acquaintance—why, I was afraid of you when I first met you; so afraid that I did not dare to let you out of sight.   It didn't matter where I tried to go—I always found myself near you.   I didn't have the courage to be your enemy—and so I became your friend.   But there was always something discordant in the air when you called at our home, for I saw that my husband didn't like you—and it annoyed me—just as it does when a dress won't fit.   I tried my very best to make him appear friendly to you at least, but I couldn't move him—not until you were engaged. Then you two became such fast friends that it almost looked as if you had not dared to show your real feelings before, when it was not safe—and later—let me see, now!   I didn't get jealous —strange, was it not?   And I remember the baptism—you were acting as godmother, and I made him kiss you—and he did, but both of you looked terribly embarrassed—that is, I didn't think of it then—or afterwards, even—I never thought of it—till— *now!*   [*Rises impulsively.*]   Why don't you say something? You have not uttered a single word all this time.   You've just let me go on talking.   You've been sitting there staring at me only, and your eyes have drawn out of me all these thoughts which were lying in me like silk in a cocoon—thoughts—bad thoughts maybe—let me think. Why did you break your engagement? Why have you never called on us afterward? Why don't you want to be with us to-night?

Miss Y. *makes a motion as if intending to speak.*

Mrs. X. No, you don't need to say anything at all. All is clear to me now. So, that's the reason of it all. Yes, yes! Everything fits together now. Shame on you! I don't want to sit at the same table with you. [*Moves her things to another table.*] That's why I must put those hateful tulips on his slippers—because you love them. [*Throws the slippers on the floor.*] That's why we have to spend the summer in the mountains—because you can't bear the salt smell of the ocean; that's why my boy had to be called Eskil—because that was your father's name; that's why I had to wear your colour, and read your books, and eat your favourite dishes, and drink your drinks—this chocolate, for instance; that's why—great heavens!—it's terrible to think of it—it's terrible! Everything was forced on me by you—even your passions. Your soul bored itself into mine as a worm into an apple, and it ate and ate, and burrowed and burrowed, till nothing was left but the outside shell and a little black dust. I wanted to run away from you, but I couldn't. You were always on hand like a snake with your black eyes to charm me—I felt how my wings beat the air only to drag me down—I was in the water, with my feet tied together, and the harder I worked with my arms, the farther down I went—down, down, till I sank to the bottom, where you lay in wait like a monster crab to catch me with your claws—and now I'm there! Shame on you! How I hate you, hate you, hate you! But you, you just sit there, silent and calm and indifferent, whether the moon is new or full; whether it's Christmas or mid-summer; whether other people are happy or unhappy. You are incapable of hatred, and you don't know how to love. As a cat in front of a mouse-hole, you are sitting there!—you can't drag your prey out, and you can't pursue it, but you can outwait it. Here you sit in this corner—do you know they've nicknamed it "the mouse-trap" on your account? Here you read the papers to see if anybody is in trouble or if anybody is about to be discharged from the theatre. Here you watch your victims and calculate your chances and take your tributes. Poor Amèlia! Do you know, I pity you all the same, for I know you are unhappy—unhappy as one who has been wounded, and malicious because you are wounded. I ought to be angry with you, but really I can't—you are so small after all—and as to Bob, why that does not bother me in the least. What does it matter to me, anyhow? If you or somebody else taught me to drink chocolate—what of that? [*Takes a spoonful of chocolate; then sententiously.*] They say chocolate is very wholesome. And if I have learned from you how to dress—*tant mieux!*—it has only given me a stronger hold on my husband—and you have lost where I have gained. Yes, judging by several signs, I think you have lost him already. Of course, you meant me to break with him—as you did, and as you are now regretting—but, you see, *I* never would do that. It won't do to be narrow-minded, you know. And why should I take only what nobody else wants? Perhaps, after all, I am the stronger now. You never got anything from me; you merely gave—and thus happened to me what happened to the thief—I had what you missed when you woke up. How explain in any other way that, in your hand, everything proved worthless and useless? You were never able to keep a man's love in spite of your tulips and your passions—and I could; you could never learn the art of living from the books—as I learned it; you bore no little Eskil, although that was your father's name. And why do you keep silent always and everywhere—silent, ever silent? I used to think it was because you were so strong; and maybe the simple truth was you never had anything to say—because you were unable to think! [*Rises and picks up the slippers.*] I'm going home now—I'll take the tulips with me—your tulips. You couldn't learn anything from others; you couldn't bend—and so you broke like a dry stem—and I didn't. Thank you, Amèlia, for all your instructions. I thank you that you have taught me how to love my husband. Now I'm going home—to him! [*Exit.*]

Curtain.

THERE ARE CRIMES AND CRIMES

A Comedy

1899

CHARACTERS

MAURICE, *a playwright*
JEANNE, *his mistress*
MARION, *their daughter, five years old*
ADOLPHE, *a painter*
HENRIETTE, *his mistress*
EMILE, *a workman, brother of Jeanne*
MADAME CATHERINE
THE ABBÉ
A WATCHMAN
A HEAD WAITER
A COMMISSAIRE
TWO DETECTIVES
A WAITER
A GUARD
A SERVANT GIRL

All the scenes are laid in Paris.

THERE ARE CRIMES AND CRIMES

ACT I

SCENE I

The upper avenue of cypresses in the Montparnasse Cemetery at Paris. The background shows mortuary chapels, stone crosses on which are inscribed "O Crux! Ave Spes Unica!" and the ruins of a windmill covered with ivy.

A well-dressed woman in widow's weeds is kneeling and muttering prayers in front of a grave decorated with flowers.

JEANNE *is walking back and forth as if expecting somebody.*

MARION *is playing with some withered flowers picked from a rubbish heap on the ground.*

The ABBÉ *is reading his breviary while walking along the farther end of the avenue.*

WATCHMAN. [*Enters and goes up to* JEANNE.] Look here, this is no playground.

JEANNE. [*Submissively.*] I am only waiting for somebody who'll soon be here——

WATCHMAN. All right, but you're not allowed to pick any flowers.

JEANNE. [*To* MARION.] Drop the flowers, dear.

ABBÉ. [*Comes forward and is saluted by the* WATCHMAN.] Can't the child play with the flowers that have been thrown away?

WATCHMAN. The regulations don't permit anybody to touch even the flowers that have been thrown away, because it's believed they may spread infection—which I don't know if it's true.

ABBÉ. [*To* MARION.] In that case we have to obey, of course. What's your name, my little girl?

MARION. My name is Marion.

ABBÉ And who is your father?

169

MARION *begins to bite one of her fingers and does not answer.*

ABBÉ.   Pardon my question, madame.   I had no intention —I was just talking to keep the little one quiet.

The WATCHMAN *has gone out.*

JEANNE.   I understood it, Reverend Father, and I wish you would say something to quiet me also.   I feel very much disturbed after having waited here two hours.

ABBÉ.   Two hours—for him!   How these human beings torture each other!   O Crux!   Ave spes unica!

JEANNE.   What do they mean, these words you read all around here?

ABBÉ.   They mean: O cross, our only hope!

JEANNE.   Is it the only one?

ABBÉ.   The only certain one.

JEANNE.   I shall soon believe that you are right, Father.

ABBÉ.   May I ask why?

JEANNE.   You have already guessed it.   When he lets the woman and the child wait two hours in a cemetery, then the end is not far off.

ABBÉ.   And when he has left you, what then?

JEANNE.   Then we have to go into the river.

ABBÉ.   Oh, no, no!

JEANNE.   Yes, yes!

MARION.   Mamma, I want to go home, for I am hungry.

JEANNE.   Just a little longer, dear, and we'll go home.

ABBÉ.   Woe unto those who call evil good and good evil.

JEANNE.   What is that woman doing at the grave over there?

ABBÉ.   She seems to be talking to the dead.

JEANNE.   But you cannot do that?

ABBÉ.   She seems to know how.

JEANNE.   This would mean that the end of life is not the end of our misery?

ABBÉ.   And you don't know it?

JEANNE.   Where can I find out?

ABBÉ.   Hm!   The next time you feel as if you wanted to learn about this well-known matter, you can look me up in Our

Lady's Chapel at the Church of St. Germain— Here comes the one you are waiting for, I guess.

JEANNE. [*Embarrassed.*] No, he is not the one, but I know him.

ABBÉ. [*To* MARION.] Good-bye, little Marion! May God take care of you! [*Kisses the child and goes out.*] At St. Germain des Prés.

EMILE. [*Enters.*] Good morning, sister. What are you doing here?

JEANNE. I am waiting for Maurice.

EMILE. Then I guess you'll have a lot of waiting to do, for I saw him on the boulevard an hour ago, taking breakfast with some friends. [*Kissing the child.*] Good morning, Marion.

JEANNE. Ladies also?

EMILE. Of course. But that doesn't mean anything. He writes plays, and his latest one has its first performance to-night. I suppose he had with him some of the actresses.

JEANNE. Did he recognise you?

EMILE. No, he doesn't know who I am, and it is just as well. I know my place as a workman, and I don't care for any condescension from those that are above me.

JEANNE. But if he leaves us without anything to live on?

EMILE. Well, you see, when it gets that far, then I suppose I shall have to introduce myself. But you don't expect anything of the kind, do you—seeing that he is fond of you and very much attached to the child?

JEANNE. I don't know, but I have a feeling that something dreadful is in store for me.

EMILE. Has he promised to marry you?

JEANNE. No, not promised exactly, but he has held out hopes.

EMILE. Hopes, yes! Do you remember my words at the start: don't hope for anything, for those above us don't marry downward.

JEANNE. But such things have happened.

EMILE. Yes, they have happened. But would you feel at home in his world? I can't believe it, for you wouldn't even understand what they were talking of. Now and then I take my meals where he is eating—out in the kitchen is my place, of course—and I don't make out a word of what they say.

JEANNE. So you take your meals at that place?

EMILE. Yes, in the kitchen.

JEANNE. And think of it, he has never asked me to come with him.

EMILE. Well, that's rather to his credit, and it shows he has some respect for the mother of his child. The women over there are a queer lot.

JEANNE. Is that so?

EMILE. But Maurice never pays any attention to the women. There is something *square* about that fellow.

JEANNE. That's what I feel about him, too, but as soon as there is a woman in it, a man isn't himself any longer.

EMILE. [*Smiling.*] You don't tell me! But listen: are you hard up for money?

JEANNE. No, nothing of that kind.

EMILE. Well, then, the worst hasn't come yet— Look! Over there! There he comes. And I'll leave you. Good-bye, little girl.

JEANNE. Is he coming? Yes, that's him.

EMILE. Don't make him mad now—with your jealousy, Jeanne!   [*Goes out.*

JEANNE. No, I won't.

MAURICE *enters.*

MARION. [*Runs up to him and is lifted up into his arms.*] Papa, papa!

MAURICE. My little girl! [*Greets* JEANNE.] Can you forgive me, Jeanne, that I have kept you waiting so long?

JEANNE. Of course I can.

MAURICE. But say it in such a way that I can hear that you are forgiving me.

JEANNE. Come here and let me whisper it to you.

MAURICE *goes up close to her.* JEANNE *kisses him on the cheek.*

MAURICE. I didn't hear.

JEANNE *kisses him on the mouth.*

MAURICE. Now I heard! Well—you know, I suppose that

this is the day that will settle my fate? My play is on for to-night, and there is every chance that it will succeed—or fail.

JEANNE. I'll make sure of success by praying for you.

MAURICE. Thank you. If it doesn't help, it can at least do no harm— Look over there, down there in the valley, where the haze is thickest: there lies Paris. To-day Paris doesn't know who Maurice is, but it is going to know within twenty-four hours. The haze, which has kept me obscured for thirty years, will vanish before my breath, and I shall become visible, I shall assume definite shape and begin to be somebody. My enemies—which means all who would like to do what I have done—will be writhing in pains that shall be my pleasures, for they will be suffering all that I have suffered.

JEANNE. Don't talk that way, don't!

MAURICE. But that's the way it is.

JEANNE. Yes, but don't speak of it— And then?

MAURICE. Then we are on firm ground, and then you and Marion will bear the name I have made famous.

JEANNE. You love me then?

MAURICE. I love both of you, equally much, or perhaps Marion a little more.

JEANNE. I am glad of it, for you can grow tired of me, but not of her.

MAURICE. Have you no confidence in my feelings towards you?

JEANNE. I don't know, but I am afraid of something, afraid of something terrible——

MAURICE. You are tired out and depressed by your long wait, which once more I ask you to forgive. What have you to be afraid of?

JEANNE. The unexpected: that which you may foresee without having any particular reason to do so.

MAURICE. But I foresee only success, and I have particular reasons for doing so: the keen instincts of the management and their knowledge of the public, not to speak of their personal acquaintance with the critics. So now you must be in good spirits——

JEANNE. I can't, I can't. Do you know, there was an Abbé

here a while ago, who talked so beautifully to us. My faith—
which you haven't destroyed, but just covered up, as when you
put chalk on a window to clean it—I couldn't lay hold on it for
that reason, but this old man just passed his hand over the chalk,
and the light came through, and it was possible again to see that
the people within were at home— To-night I will pray for you
at St. Germain.

MAURICE. Now I am getting scared.

JEANNE. Fear of God is the beginning of wisdom.

MAURICE. God? What is that? Who is he?

JEANNE. It was he who gave joy to your youth, and strength
to your manhood. And it is he who will carry us through the
terrors that lie ahead of us.

MAURICE. What is lying ahead of us? What do you know?
Where have you learned of this? This thing that I don't know?

JEANNE. I can't tell. I have dreamt nothing, seen nothing,
heard nothing. But during these two dreadful hours I have
experienced such an infinity of pain that I am ready for the worst.

MARION. Now I want to go home, mamma, for I am
hungry.

MAURICE. Yes, you'll go home now, my little darling.

[*Takes her into his arms.*

MARION. [*Shrinking.*] Oh, you hurt me, papa!

JEANNE. Yes, we must get home for dinner. Good-bye
then, Maurice. And good luck to you!

MAURICE. [*To* MARION.] How did I hurt you? Doesn't
my little girl know that I always want to be nice to her?

MARION. If you are nice, you'll come home with us.

MAURICE. [*To* JEANNE.] When I hear the child talk like
that, you know, I feel as if I ought to do what she says. But
then reason and duty protest— Good-bye, my dear little girl!

[*He kisses the child, who puts her arms around his neck.*

JEANNE. When do we meet again?

MAURICE. We'll meet -to-morrow, dear. And then we'll
never part again.

JEANNE. [*Embraces him.*] Never, never to part again!
[*She makes the sign of the cross on his forhead.*] May God
protect you!

MAURICE. [*Moved against his own will.*] My dear, be-loved Jeanne!

JEANNE *and* MARION *go towards the right;* MAURICE *towards the left. Both turn around simultaneously and throw kisses at each other.*

MAURICE. [*Comes back.*] Jeanne, I am ashamed of my-self. I am always forgetting you, and you are the last one to remind me of it. Here are the tickets for to-night.

JEANNE. Thank you, dear, but—you have to take up your post of duty alone, and so I have to take up mine—with Marion.

MAURICE. Your wisdom is as great as the goodness of your heart. Yes, I am sure no other woman would have sacrificed a pleasure to serve her husband— I must have my hands free to-night, and there is no place for women and children on the battlefield—and this you understand!

JEANNE. Don't think too highly of a poor woman like my-self, and then you'll have no illusions to lose. And now you'll see that I can be as forgetful as you—I have bought you a tie and a pair of gloves which I thought you might wear for my sake on your day of honour.

MAURICE. [*Kissing her hand.*] Thank you, dear.

JEANNE. And then, Maurice, don't forget to have your hair fixed, as you do all the time. I want you to be good-looking, so that others will like you, too.

MAURICE. There is no jealousy in *you!*

JEANNE. Don't mention that word, for evil thoughts spring from it.

MAURICE. Just now I feel as if I could give up this evening's victory—for I am going to win——

JEANNE. Hush, hush!

MAURICE. And go home with you instead.

JEANNE. But you mustn't do that! Go now: your destiny is waiting for you.

MAURICE. Good-bye then! And may that happen which must happen! [*Goes out.*

JEANNE. [*Alone with* MARION.] O Crux! Ave spes unica!

Curtain.

SCENE II

*The Crêmerie.   On the right stands a buffet, on which are placed
an aquarium with goldfish and dishes containing vegetables,
fruit, preserves, etc.   In the background is a door leading to
the kitchen, where workmen are taking their meals.   At the
other end of the kitchen can be seen a door leading out to a
garden.   On the left, in the background, stands a counter on
a raised platform, and back of it are shelves containing all
sorts of bottles.   On the right, a long table with a marble top
is placed along the wall, and another table is placed parallel
to the first farther out on the floor.   Straw-bottomed chairs
stand around the tables.   The walls are covered with oil-
paintings.*

MME. CATHERINE *is sitting at the counter.*   MAURICE *stands
leaning against it.   He has his hat on and is smoking a
cigarette.*

MME. CATHERINE.   So it's to-night the great event comes
off, Monsieur Maurice?

MAURICE.   Yes, to-night.

MME. CATHERINE.   Do you feel upset?

MAURICE.   Cool as a cucumber.

MME. CATHERINE.   Well, I wish you luck anyhow, and you
have deserved it, Monsieur Maurice, after having had to fight
against such difficulties as yours.

MAURICE.   Thank you, Madame Catherine.   You have
been very kind to me, and without your help I should probably
have been down and out by this time.

MME. CATHERINE.   Don't let us talk of that now.   I help
along where I see hard work and the right kind of will, but I
don't want to be exploited— Can we trust you to come back
here after the play and let us drink a glass with you?

MAURICE.   Yes, you can—of course, you can, as I have
already promised you.

HENRIETTE *enters from the right.*   MAURICE *turns around,
raises his hat, and stares at* HENRIETTE, *who looks him over
carefully.*

HENRIETTE.   Monsieur Adolphe is not here yet?

MME. CATHERINE.   No, madame.   But he'll soon be here now.   Won't you sit down?

HENRIETTE.   No, thank you, I'd rather wait for him outside.
[*Goes out.*

MAURICE.   Who—was—that?

MME. CATHERINE.   Why, that's Monsieur Adolphe's friend.

MAURICE.   Was—that—her?

MME. CATHERINE.   Have you never seen her before?

MAURICE.   No, he has been hiding her from me, just as if he was afraid I might take her away from him.

MME. CATHERINE.   Ha-ha!—   Well, how did you think she looked?

MAURICE.   How she looked?   Let me see: I can't tell—I didn't see her, for it was as if she had rushed straight into my arms at once and come so close to me that I couldn't make out her features at all.   And she left her impression on the air behind her.   I can still see her standing there.   [*He goes towards the door and makes a gesture as if putting his arm around somebody.*] Whew!   [*He makes a gesture as if he had pricked his finger.*] There are pins in her waist.   She is of the kind that stings!

MME. CATHERINE.   Oh, you are crazy, you with your ladies!

MAURICE.   Yes, it's craziness, that's what it is.   But do you know, Madame Catherine, I am going before she comes back, or else, or else—   Oh, that woman is horrible!

MME. CATHERINE.   Are you afraid?

MAURICE.   Yes, I am afraid for myself, and also for some others.

MME. CATHERINE.   Well, go then.

MAURICE.   She seemed to suck herself out through the door, and in her wake rose a little whirlwind that dragged me along— Yes, you may laugh, but can't you see that the palm over there on the buffet is still shaking?   She's the very devil of a woman!

MME. CATHERINE.   Oh, get out of here, man, before you lose all your reason.

MAURICE.   I want to go, but I cannot—   Do you believe in fate, Madame Catherine?

MME. CATHERINE.   No, I believe in a good God, who protects us against evil powers if we ask him in the right way.

MAURICE.   So there are evil powers after all!   I think I can hear them in the hallway now.

MME. CATHERINE.   Yes, her clothes rustle as when the clerk tears off a piece of linen for you.   Get away now—through the kitchen.

> MAURICE *rushes towards the kitchen door, where he bumps into* EMILE.

EMILE.   I beg your pardon.   [*He retires the way he came.*

ADOLPHE.   [*Comes in first; after him* HENRIETTE.]. Why, there's Maurice.   How are you?   Let me introduce this lady here to my oldest and best friend.   Mademoiselle Henriette—Monsieur Maurice.

MAURICE.   [*Saluting stiffly.*]   Pleased to meet you.

HENRIETTE.   We have seen each other before.

ADOLPHE.   Is that so?   When, if I may ask?

MAURICE.   A moment ago.   Right here.

ADOLPHE.   O-oh!——   But now you must stay and have a chat with us.

MAURICE.   [*After a glance at* MME. CATHERINE.]   If I only had time.

ADOLPHE.   Take the time.   And we won't be sitting here very long.

HENRIETTE.   I won't interrupt, if you have to talk business.

MAURICE.   The only business we have is so bad that we don't want to talk of it.

HENRIETTE.   Then we'll talk of something else.   [*Takes the hat away from* MAURICE *and hangs it up.*]   Now be nice, and let me become acquainted with the great author.

> MME. CATHERINE *signals to* MAURICE, *who doesn't notice her.*

ADOLPHE.   That's right, Henriette, you take charge of him.
                    [*They seat themselves at one of the tables.*

HENRIETTE.   [*To* MAURICE.]   You certainly have a good friend in Adolphe, Monsieur Maurice.   He never talks of anything but you, and in such a way that I feel myself rather thrown in the background.

ADOLPHE.   You don't say so!   Well, Henriette on her side never leaves me in peace about you, Maurice. She has read your works, and she is always wanting to know where you got this and where that. She has been questioning me about your looks, your age, your tastes. I have, in a word, had you for breakfast, dinner, and supper. It has almost seemed as if the three of us were living together.

MAURICE. [*To* HENRIETTE.] Heavens, why didn't you come over here and have a look at this wonder of wonders? Then your curiosity could have been satisfied in a trice.

HENRIETTE. Adolphe didn't want it.

ADOLPHE *looks embarrassed.*

HENRIETTE. Not that he was jealous——

MAURICE. And why should he be, when he knows that my feelings are tied up elsewhere?

HENRIETTE. Perhaps he didn't trust the stability of your feelings.

MAURICE. I can't understand that, seeing that I am notorious for my constancy.

ADOLPHE. Well, it wasn't that——

HENRIETTE. [*Interrupting him.*] Perhaps that is because you have not faced the fiery ordeal——

ADOLPHE. Oh, you don't know——

HENRIETTE. [*Interrupting.*]——for the world has not yet beheld a faithful man.

MAURICE. Then it's going to behold one.

HENRIETTE. Where?

MAURICE. Here.

HENRIETTE *laughs.*

ADOLPHE. Well, that's going it——

HENRIETTE. [*Interrupting him and directing herself continuously to* MAURICE.] Do you think I ever trust my dear Adolphe more than a month at a time?

MAURICE. I have no right to question your lack of confidence, but I can guarantee that Adolphe is faithful.

HENRIETTE. You don't need to do so—my tongue is just running away with me, and I have to take back a lot—not only for fear of feeling less generous than you, but because it is the truth. It is a bad habit I have of only seeing the ugly side of things, and I keep it up although I know better.   But if I had a chance to be with you two for some time, then your company would make me good once more.   Pardon me, Adolphe!

[*She puts her hand against his cheek.*

ADOLPHE.   You are always wrong in your talk and right in your actions.   What you really think—that I don't know.

HENRIETTE.   Who does know that kind of thing?

MAURICE.   Well, if we had to answer for our thoughts, who could then clear himself?

HENRIETTE.   Do you also have evil thoughts?

MAURICE.   Certainly; just as I commit the worst kind of cruelties in my dreams.

HENRIETTE.   Oh, when you are dreaming, of course— Just think of it— No, I am ashamed of telling——

MAURICE.   Go on, go on!

HENRIETTE.   Last night I dreamt that I was coolly dissecting the muscles on Adolphe's breast—you see, I am a sculptor—and he, with his usual kindness, made no resistance, but helped me instead with the worst places, as he knows more anatomy than I.

MAURICE.   Was he dead?

HENRIETTE.   No, he was living.

MAURICE.   But that's horrible!   And didn't it make you suffer?

HENRIETTE.   Not at all, and that astonished me most, for I am rather sensitive to other people's sufferings.   Isn't that so, Adolphe?

ADOLPHE.   That's right.   Rather abnormally so, in fact, and not the least when animals are concerned.

MAURICE.   And I, on the other hand, am rather callous towards the sufferings both of myself and others.

ADOLPHE.   Now he is not telling the truth about himself. Or what do you say, Madame Catherine?

MME. CATHERINE.   I don't know of anybody with a softer heart than Monsieur Maurice.   He came near calling in the police because I didn't give the goldfish fresh water—those over there on the buffet.   Just look at them: it is as if they could hear what I am saying.

MAURICE.   Yes, here we are making ourselves out as white

as angels, and yet we are, taking it all in all, capable of any kind of polite atrocity the moment glory, gold, or women are concerned— So you are a sculptor, Mademoiselle Henriette?

HENRIETTE. A bit of one. Enough to do a bust. And to do one of you—which has long been my cherished dream—I hold myself quite capable.

MAURICE. Go ahead! That dream at least need not be long in coming true.

HENRIETTE. But I don't want to fix your features in my mind until this evening's success is over. Not until then will you have become what you should be.

MAURICE. How sure you are of victory!

HENRIETTE. Yes, it is written on your face that you are going to win this battle, and I think you must feel that yourself.

MAURICE. Why do you think so?

HENRIETTE. Because I can feel it. This morning I was ill, you know, and now I am well.

ADOLPHE *begins to look depressed.*

MAURICE. [*Embarrassed.*] Listen, I have a single ticket left—only one. I place it at your disposal, Adolphe.

ADOLPHE. Thank you, but I surrender it to Henriette.

HENRIETTE. But that wouldn't do?

ADOLPHE. Why not? And I never go to the theatre anyhow, as I cannot stand the heat.

HENRIETTE. But you will come and take us home at least after the show is over.

ADOLPHE. If you insist on it. Otherwise Maurice has to come back here, where we shall all be waiting for him.

MAURICE. You can just as well take the trouble of meeting us. In fact, I ask, I beg you to do so— And if you don't want to wait outside the theatre, you can meet us at the Auberge des Adrets— That's settled then, isn't it?

ADOLPHE. Wait a little. You have a way of settling things to suit yourself, before other people have a chance to consider them.

MAURICE. What is there to consider—whether you are to see your lady home or not?

ADOLPHE. You never know what may be involved in a simple act like that, but I have a sort of premonition.

HENRIETTE. Hush, hush, hush! Don't talk of spooks while the sun is shining. Let him come or not, as it pleases him. We can always find our way back here.

ADOLPHE. [*Rising.*] Well, now I have to leave you— model, you know. Good-bye, both of you. And good luck to you, Maurice. To-morrow you will be out on the right side. Good-bye, Henriette.

HENRIETTE. Do you really have to go?

ADOLPHE. I must.

MAURICE. Good-bye then. We'll meet later.

ADOLPHE *goes out, saluting* MME. CATHERINE *in passing.*

HENRIETTE. Think of it, that we should meet at last! ·

MAURICE. Do you find anything remarkable in that?

HENRIETTE. It looks as if it had to happen, for Adolphe has done his best to prevent it.

MAURICE. Has he?

HENRIETTE. Oh, you must have noticed it.

MAURICE. I have noticed it, but why should you mention it?

HENRIETTE. I had to.

MAURICE. No, and I don't have to tell you that I wanted to run away through the kitchen in order to avoid meeting you and was stopped by a guest who closed the door in front of me.

HENRIETTE. Why do you tell me about it now?

MAURICE. I don't know.

MME. CATHERINE *upsets a number of glasses and bottles.*

MAURICE. That's all right, Madame Catherine. There's nothing to be afraid of.

HENRIETTE. Was that meant as a signal or a warning?

MAURICE. Probably both.

HENRIETTE. Do they take me for a locomotive that has to have flagmen ahead of it?

MAURICE. And switchmen! The danger is always greatest at the switches.

HENRIETTE. How nasty you can be!

MME. CATHERINE. Monsieur Maurice isn't nasty at all.

So far nobody has been kinder than he to those that love him and trust in him.

MAURICE. Sh, sh, sh!

HENRIETTE. [*To* MAURICE.] The old lady is rather impertinent.

MAURICE. We can walk over to the boulevard, if you care to do so.

HENRIETTE. With pleasure. This is not the place for me. I can just feel their hatred clawing at me.   [*Goes out.*

MAURICE. [*Starts after her.*] Good-bye, Madame Catherine.

MME. CATHERINE. A moment! May I speak a word to you, Monsieur Maurice?

MAURICE. [*Stops unwillingly.*] What is it?

MME. CATHERINE. Don't do it! Don't do it!

MAURICE. What?

MME. CATHERINE. Don't do it!

MAURICE. Don't be scared. This lady is not my kind, but she interests me. Or hardly that even.

MME. CATHERINE. Don't trust yourself!

MAURICE. Yes, I do trust myself. Good-bye. [*Goes out.*

Curtain.

ACT II

SCENE I

The Auberge des Adrets: a café in sixteenth-century style, with a suggestion of stage effect. Tables and easy-chairs are scattered in corners and nooks. The walls are decorated with armour and weapons. Along the ledge of the wainscoting stand glasses and jugs.

MAURICE *and* HENRIETTE *are in evening dress and sit facing each other at a table on which stands a bottle of champagne and three filled glasses. The third glass is placed at that side of the table which is nearest the background, and there an easy-chair is kept ready for the still missing " third man."*

MAURICE. [*Puts his watch in front of himself on the table.*] If he doesn't get here within the next five minutes, he isn't coming at all.   And suppose in the meantime we drink with his ghost.
                    [*Touches the third glass with the rim of his own.*
HENRIETTE. [*Doing the same.*]   Here's to you, Adolphe!
MAURICE. He won't come.
HENRIETTE. He will come.
MAURICE. He won't.
HENRIETTE. He will.
MAURICE. What an evening!   What a wonderful day!   I can hardly grasp that a new life has begun.   Think only: the manager believes that I may count on no less than one hundred thousand francs.   I'll spend twenty thousand on a villa outside the city.   That leaves me eighty thousand.   I won't be able to take it all in until to-morrow, for I am tired, tired, tired. [*Sinks back into the chair.*]   Have you ever felt really happy?
HENRIETTE. Never.   How does it feel?
MAURICE. I don't quite know how to put it.   I cannot express it, but I seem chiefly to be thinking of the chagrin of my enemies.   It isn't nice, but that's the way it is.
HENRIETTE. Is it happiness to be thinking of one's enemies?
MAURICE. Why, the victor has to count his killed and wounded enemies in order to gauge the extent of his victory.
HENRIETTE. Are you as bloodthirsty as all that?
MAURICE. Perhaps not.   But when you have felt the pressure of other people's heels on your chest for years, it must be pleasant to shake off the enemy and draw a full breath at last.
HENRIETTE. Don't you find it strange that you are sitting here, alone with me, an insignificant girl practically unknown to you—and on an evening like this, when you ought to have a craving to show yourself like a triumphant hero to all the people, on the boulevards, in the big restaurants?
MAURICE. Of course, it's rather funny, but it feels good to be here, and your company is all I care for.
HENRIETTE. You don't look very hilarious.
MAURICE. No, I feel rather sad, and I should like to weep a little.
HENRIETTE. What is the meaning of that?

MAURICE. It is fortune conscious of its own nothingness and waiting for misfortune to appear.

HENRIETTE. Oh my, how sad! What is it you are missing anyhow?

MAURICE. I miss the only thing that gives value to life.

HENRIETTE. So you love her no longer then?

MAURICE. Not in the way I understand love. Do you think she has read my play, or that she wants to see it? Oh, she is so good, so self-sacrificing and considerate, but to go out with me for a night's fun she would regard as sinful. Once I treated her to champagne, you know, and instead of feeling happy over it, she picked up the wine list to see what it cost. And when she read the price, she wept—wept because Marion was in need of new stockings. It is beautiful, of course: it is touching, if you please. But I can get no pleasure out of it. And I do want a little pleasure before life runs out. So far I have had nothing but privation, but now, now—life is beginning for me. [*The clock strikes twelve.*] Now begins a new day, a new era!

HENRIETTE. Adolphe is not coming.

MAURICE. No, now he won't come. And now it is too late to go back to the Crêmerie.

HENRIETTE. But they are waiting for you.

MAURICE. Let them wait. They have made me promise to come, and I take back my promise. Are you longing to go there?

HENRIETTE. On the contrary!

MAURICE. Will you keep me company then?

HENRIETTE. With pleasure, if you care to have me.

MAURICE. Otherwise I shouldn't be asking you. It is strange, you know, that the victor's wreath seems worthless if you can't place it at the feet of some woman—that everything seems worthless when you have not a woman.

HENRIETTE. You don't need to be without a woman—you?

MAURICE. Well, that's the question.

HENRIETTE. Don't you know that a man is irresistible in his hour of success and fame?

MAURICE. No, I don't know, for I have had no experience of it.

HENRIETTE. You are a queer sort! At this moment, when

you are the most envied man in Paris, you sit here and brood. Perhaps your conscience is troubling you because you have neglected that invitation to drink chicory coffee with the old lady over at the milk shop?

MAURICE.   Yes, my conscience is troubling me on that score, and even here I am aware of their resentment, their hurt feelings, their well-grounded anger.   My comrades in distress had the right to demand my presence this evening.   The good Madame Catherine had a privileged claim on my success, from which a glimmer of hope was to spread over the poor fellows who have not yet succeeded.   And I have robbed them of their faith in me.   I can hear the vows they have been making: " Maurice will come, for he is a good fellow; he doesn't despise us, and he never fails to keep his word."   Now I have made them forswear themselves.

While he is still speaking, somebody in the next room has begun to play the finale of Beethoven's Sonata in D-minor (Op. 31, No.2).   The allegretto is first played piano, then more forte, and at last passionately, violently, with complete abandon.

MAURICE.   Who can be playing at this time of the night?

HENRIETTE.   Probably some nightbirds of the same kind as we.   But listen!   Your presentation of the case is not correct. Remember that Adolphe promised to meet us here.   We waited for him, and he failed to keep his promise.   So that you are not to blame——

MAURICE.   You think so?   While you are speaking, I believe you, but when you stop, my conscience begins again.   What have you in that package?

HENRIETTE.   Oh, it is only a laurel wreath that I meant to send up to the stage, but I had no chance to do so.   Let me give it to you now—it is said to have a cooling effect on burning foreheads.   [*She rises and crowns him with the wreath; then she kisses him on the forehead.*]   Hail to the victor!

MAURICE.   Don't.

HENRIETTE.   [*Kneeling.*]   Hail to the King!

MAURICE.   [*Rising.*]   No, now you scare me.

HENRIETTE.   You timid man!   You of little faith who are

afraid of fortune even! Who robbed you of your self-assurance and turned you into a dwarf?

MAURICE. A dwarf? Yes, you are right. I am not working up in the clouds, like a giant, with crashing and roaring, but I forge my weapons deep down in the silent heart of the mountain. You think that my modesty shrinks before the victor's wreath. On the contrary, I despise it: it is not enough for me. You think I am afraid of that ghost with its jealous green eyes which sits over there and keeps watch on my feelings—the strength of which you don't suspect. Away, ghost! [*He brushes the third, untouched glass off the table.*] Away with you, you superfluous third person—you absent one who has lost your rights, if you ever had any. You stayed away from the field of battle because you knew yourself already beaten. As I crush this glass under my foot, so I will crush the image of yourself which you have reared in a temple no longer yours.

HENRIETTE. Good! That's the way! Well spoken, my hero!

MAURICE. Now I have sacrificed my best friend, my most faithful helper, on your altar, Astarte! Are you satisfied?

HENRIETTE. Astarte is a pretty name, and I'll keep it—I think you love me, Maurice.

MAURICE. Of course I do— Woman of evil omen, you who stir up man's courage with your scent of blood, whence do you come and where do you lead me? I loved you before I saw you, for I trembled when I heard them speak of you. And when I saw you in the doorway, your soul poured itself into mine. And when you left, I could still feel your presence in my arms. I wanted to flee from you, but something held me back, and this evening we have been driven together as the prey is driven into the hunter's net. Whose is the fault? Your friend's, who pandered for us!

HENRIETTE. Fault or no fault: what does it matter, and what does it mean?— Adolphe has been at fault in not bringing us together before. He is guilty of having stolen from us two weeks of bliss, to which he had no right himself. I am jealous of him on your behalf. I hate him because he has cheated you out of your mistress. I should like to blot him from the host of the living, and his memory with him—wipe him out of the past even, make him unmade, unborn!

MAURICE. Well, we'll bury him beneath our own memories. We'll cover him with leaves and branches far out in the wild woods, and then we'll pile stone on top of the mound so that he will never look up again. [*Raising his glass.*] Our fate is sealed. Woe unto us! What will come next?

HENRIETTE. Next comes the new era— What have you in that package?

MAURICE. I cannot remember.

HENRIETTE. [*Opens the package and takes out a tie and a pair of gloves.*] That tie is a fright! It must have cost at least fifty centimes.

MAURICE. [*Snatching the things away from her.*] Don't you touch them!

HENRIETTE. They are from her?

MAURICE. Yes, they are.

HENRIETTE. Give them to me.

MAURICE. No, she's better than we, better than everybody else.

HENRIETTE. I don't believe it. She is simply stupider and stingier. One who weeps because you order champagne——

MAURICE. When the child was without stockings. Yes, she is a good woman.

HENRIETTE. Philistine! You'll never be an artist. But I am an artist, and I'll make a bust of you with a shopkeeper's cap instead of the laurel wreath!— Her name is Jeanne?

MAURICE. How did you know?

HENRIETTE. Why, that's the name of all housekeepers.

MAURICE. Henriette!

HENRIETTE *takes the tie and the gloves and throws them into the fireplace.*

MAURICE. [*Weakly.*] Astarte, now you demand the sacrifice of women. You shall have them, but if you ask for innocent children, too, then I'll send you packing.

HENRIETTE. Can you tell me what it is that binds you to me?

MAURICE. If I only knew, I should be able to tear myself

away. But I believe it must be those qualities which you have and I lack. I believe that the evil within you draws me with the irresistible lure of novelty.

HENRIETTE. Have you ever committed a crime?

MAURICE. No real one. Have you?

HENRIETTE. Yes.

MAURICE. Well, how did you find it?

HENRIETTE. It was greater than to perform a good deed, for by that we are placed on equality with others; it was greater than to perform some act of heroism, for by that we are raised above others and rewarded. That crime placed me outside and beyond life, society, and my fellow-beings. Since then I am living only a partial life, a sort of dream life, and that's why reality never gets a hold on me.

MAURICE. What was it you did?

HENRIETTE. I won't tell, for then you would get scared again.

MAURICE. Can you ever be found out?

HENRIETTE. Never. But that does not prevent me from seeing, frequently, the five stones at the Place de Roquette, where the scaffold used to stand; and for this reason I never dare to open a pack of cards, as I always turn up the five of diamonds.

MAURICE. Was it that kind of a crime?

HENRIETTE. Yes, it was that kind.

MAURICE. Of course, it's horrible, but it is interesting. Have you no conscience?

HENRIETTE. None, but I should be grateful if you would talk of something else.

MAURICE. Suppose we talk of—love?

HENRIETTE. Of that you don't talk until it is over.

MAURICE. Have you been in love with Adolphe?

HENRIETTE. I don't know. The goodness of his nature drew me like some beautiful, all but vanished memory of childhood. Yet there was much about his person that offended my eye, so that I had to spend a long time retouching, altering, adding, subtracting, before I could make a presentable figure of him. When he talked, I could notice that he had learned from you, and the lesson was often badly digested and awkwardly applied.

You can imagine then how miserable the copy must appear now, when I am permitted to study the original. That's why he was afraid of having us two meet; and when it did happen, he understood at once that his time was up.

MAURICE. Poor Adolphe!

HENRIETTE. I feel sorry for him, too, as I know he must be suffering beyond all bounds——

MAURICE. Sh! Somebody is coming.

HENRIETTE. I wonder if it could be he?

MAURICE. That would be unbearable.

HENRIETTE. No, it isn't he, but if it had been, how do you think the situation would have shaped itself?

MAURICE. At first he would have been a little sore at you because he had made a mistake in regard to the meeting-place—and tried to find us in several other cafés—but his soreness would have changed into pleasure at finding us—and seeing that we had not deceived him. And in the joy at having wronged us by his suspicions, he would love both of us. And so it would make him happy to notice that we had become such good friends. It had always been his dream—hm! he is making the speech now—his dream that the three of us should form a triumvirate that could set the world a great example of friendship asking for nothing— "Yes, I trust you, Maurice, partly because you are my friend, and partly because your feelings are tied up elsewhere."

HENRIETTE. Bravo! You must have been in a similar situation before, or you couldn't give such a lifelike picture of it. Do you know that Adolphe is just that kind of a third person who cannot enjoy his mistress without having his friend along?

MAURICE. That's why I had to be called in to entertain you— Hush! There is somebody outside— It must be he.

HENRIETTE. No, don't you know these are the hours when ghosts walk, and then you can see so many things, and hear them also. To keep awake at night, when you ought to be sleeping, has for me the same charm as a crime: it is to place oneself above and beyond the laws of nature.

MAURICE. But the punishment is fearful—I am shivering or quivering, with cold or with fear.

HENRIETTE. [*Wraps her opera cloak about him.*] Put this on. It will make you warm.

MAURICE. That's nice. It is as if I were inside of your skin, as if my body had been melted up by lack of sleep and were being remoulded in your shape. I can feel the moulding process going on. But I am also growing a new soul, new thoughts, and here, where your bosom has left an impression, I can feel my own beginning to bulge.

During this entire scene, the pianist in the next room has been practising the Sonata in D-minor, sometimes pianissimo, sometimes wildly fortissimo; now and then he has kept silent for a little while, and at other times nothing has been heard but a part of the finale: bars 96 to 107.

MAURICE. What a monster, to sit there all night practising on the piano. It gives me a sick feeling. Do you know what I propose? Let us drive out to the Bois de Boulogne and take breakfast in the Pavilion, and see the sun rise over the lakes.

HENRIETTE. Bully!

MAURICE. But first of all I must arrange to have my mail and the morning papers sent out by messenger to the Pavilion. Tell me Henriette: shall we invite Adolphe?

HENRIETTE. Oh, that's going too far! But why not? The ass can also be harnessed to the triumphal chariot. Let him come. [*They get up.*

MAURICE. [*Taking off the cloak.*] Then I'll ring.

HENRIETTE. Wait a moment!

[*Throws herself into his arms.*
Curtain.

SCENE II

A large, splendidly furnished restaurant room in the Bois de Boulogne. It is richly carpeted and full of mirrors, easy-chairs, and divans. There are glass doors in the background, and beside them windows overlooking the lakes. In the foreground a table is spread, with flowers in the centre, bowls full of fruit, wine in decanters, oysters on

*platters, many different kinds of wine glasses, and two
lighted candelabra. On the right there is a round table full
of newspapers and telegrams.*

MAURICE *and* HENRIETTE *are sitting opposite each other at
this small table.*

The sun is just rising outside.

MAURICE. There is no longer any doubt about it. The
newspapers tell me it is so, and these telegrams congratulate me
on my success. This is the beginning of a new life, and my fate
is wedded to yours by this night, when you were the only one to
share my hopes and my triumph. From your hand I received
the laurel, and it seems to me as if everything had come from
you.

HENRIETTE. What a wonderful night! Have we been
dreaming, or is this something we have really lived through?

MAURICE. [*Rising.*] And what a morning after such a
night! I feel as if it were the world's first day that is now being
illumined by the rising sun. Only this minute was the earth
created and stripped of those white films that are now floating off
into space. There lies the Garden of Eden in the rosy light of
dawn, and here is the first human couple— Do you know, I am
so happy I could cry at the thought that all mankind is not equally
happy— Do you hear that distant murmur as of ocean waves
beating against a rocky shore, as of winds sweeping through a
forest? Do you know what it is? It is Paris whispering my
name. Do you see the columns of smoke that rise skyward in
thousands and tens of thousands? They are the fires burning on
my altars, and if that be not so, then it must become so, for I will
it. At this moment all the telegraph instruments of Europe are
clicking out my name. The Oriental Express is carrying the
newspapers to the Far East, towards the rising sun; and the ocean
steamers are carrying them to the utmost West. The earth is
mine, and for that reason it it beautiful. Now I should like to
have wings for us two, so that we might rise from here and fly
far, far away, before anybody can soil my happiness, before envy
has chance to wake me out of my dream—for it is probably a
dream!

HENRIETTE. [*Holding out her hand to him.*] Here you can feel that you are not dreaming.

MAURICE. It is not a dream, but it has been one. As a poor young man, you know, when I was walking in the woods down there, and looked up to this Pavilion, it looked to me like a fairy castle, and always my thoughts carried me up to this room, with the balcony outside and the heavy curtains, as to a place of supreme bliss. To be sitting here in company with a beloved woman and see the sun rise while the candles were still burning in the candelabra: that was the most audacious dream of my youth. Now it has come true, and now I have no more to ask of life— Do you want to die now, together with me?

HENRIETTE. No, you fool! Now I want to begin living.

MAURICE. [*Rising.*] To live: that is to suffer! Now comes reality. I can hear his steps on the stairs. He is panting with alarm, and his heart is beating with dread of having lost what it holds most precious. Can you believe me if I tell you that Adolphe is under this roof? Within a minute he will be standing in the middle of this floor.

HENRIETTE. [*Alarmed.*] It was a stupid trick to ask him to come here, and I am already regretting it— Well, we shall see anyhow if your forecast of the situation proves correct.

MAURICE. Oh, it is easy to be mistaken about a person's feelings.

The HEAD WAITER *enters with a card.*

MAURICE. Ask the gentleman to step in. [*To* HEN-RIETTE.] I am afraid we'll regret this.

HENRIETTE. Too late to think of that now— Hush!

ADOLPHE *enters, pale and hollow-eyed.*

MAURICE. [*Trying to speak unconcernedly.*] There you are! What became of you last night?

ADOLPHE. I looked for you at the Hôtel des Arrêts and waited a whole hour.

MAURICE. So you went to the wrong place. We were waiting several hours for you at the Auberge des Adrets, and we are still waiting for you, as you see.

ADOLPHE. [*Relieved.*] Thank heaven!

HENRIETTE. Good morning, Adolphe. You are always ex-

pecting the worst and worrying yourself needlessly. I suppose
you imagined that we wanted to avoid your company. And
though you see that we sent for you, you are still thinking yourself superfluous.

ADOLPHE. Pardon me: I was wrong, but the night was
dreadful.

They sit down. Embarrassed silence follows.

HENRIÈTTE. [*To* ADOLPHE.] Well, are you not going to
congratulate Maurice on his great success?

ADOLPHE. Oh, yes! Your success is the real thing, and
envy itself cannot deny it. Everything is giving way before you,
and even I have a sense of my own smallness in your presence.

MAURICE. Nonsense!— Henriette, are you not going to
offer Adolphe a glass of wine?

ADOLPHE. Thank you, not for me—nothing at all!

HENRIETTE. [*To* ADOLPHE.] What's the matter with
you? Are you ill?

ADOLPHE. Not yet, but——

HENRIETTE. Your eyes——

ADOLPHE. What of them?

MAURICE. What happened at the Crêmerie last night? I
suppose they are angry with me?

ADOLPHE. Nobody is angry with you, but your absence
caused a depression which it hurt me to watch. But nobody was
angry with you, believe me. Your friends understood, and they
regarded your failure to come with sympathetic forbearance.
Madame Catherine herself defended you and proposed your
health. We all rejoiced in your success as if it had been our
own.

HENRIETTE. Well, those are nice people! What good
friends you have, Maurice.

MAURICE. Yes, better than I deserve.

ADOLPHE. Nobody has better friends than he deserves, and
you are a man greatly blessed in his friends— Can't you feel
how the air is softened to-day by all the kind thoughts and wishes
that stream toward you from a thousand breasts?

MAURICE *rises in order to hide his emotion.*

ADOLPHE. From a thousand breasts that you have rid of the

nightmare that had been crushing them during a life-time. Humanity had been slandered—and you have exonerated it: that's why men feel grateful towards you. To-day they are once more holding their heads high and saying: You see, we are a little better than our reputation after all. And that thought *makes* them better.

HENRIETTE *tries to hide her emotion.*

ADOLPHE. Am I in the way? Just let me warm myself a little in your sunshine, Maurice, and then I'll go.

MAURICE. Why should you go when you have only just arrived?

ADOLPHE. Why? Because I have seen what I need not have seen; because I know now that my hour is past. [*Pause.*] That you sent for me, I take as an expression of thoughtfulness, a notice of what has happened, a frankness that hurts less than deceit. You hear that I think well of my fellow-beings, and this I have learned from you, Maurice. [*Pause.*] But, my friend, a few moments ago I passed through the Church of St. Germain, and there I saw a woman and a child. I am not wishing that you had seen them, for what has happened cannot be altered, but if you gave a thought or a word to them before you set them adrift on the waters of the great city, then you could enjoy your happiness undisturbed. And now I bid you good-bye.

HENRIETTE. Why must you go?

ADOLPHE. And you ask that? Do you want me to tell you?

HENRIETTE. No, I don't.

ADOLPHE. Good-bye then.   [*Goes out.*

MAURICE. The Fall: and lo! "they knew that they were naked."

HENRIETTE. What a difference between this scene and the one we imagined! He is better than we.

MAURICE. It seems to me now as if all the rest were better than we.

HENRIETTE. Do you see that the sun has vanished behind cloud, and the woods have lost their rose colour?

MAURICE. Yes, I see, and the blue lake has turned to black. Let us flee to some place where the sky is always blue and the trees are always green.

HENRIETTE.   Yes, let us—but without any farewells.

MAURICE.   No, with farewells.

HENRIETTE.   We were to fly.   You spoke of wings—and your feet are of lead.   I am not jealous, but if you go to say farewell and get two pairs of arms around your neck—then you can't tear yourself away.

MAURICE.   Perhaps you are right, but only one pair of little arms is needed to hold me fast.

HENRIETTE.   It is the child that holds you then, and not the woman?

MAURICE.   It is the child.

HENRIETTE.   The child!   Another woman's child!   And for the sake of it I am to suffer.   Why must that child block the way where I want to pass, and must pass?

MAURICE.   Yes, why?   It would be better if it had never existed.

HENRIETTE.   [*Walks excitedly back and forth.*]   Indeed! But now it does exist.   Like a rock on the road, a rock set firmly in the ground, immovable, so that it upsets the carriage.

MAURICE.   The triumphal chariot!—   The ass is driven to death, but the rock remains.   Curse it!   [*Pause.*

HENRIETTE.   There is nothing to do.

MAURICE.   Yes, we must get married, and then *our* child will make us forget the other one.

HENRIETTE.   This will kill this!

MAURICE.   Kill!   What kind of word is that?

HENRIETTE. [*Changing tone.*]   Your child will kill our love.

MAURICE.   No, girl, our love will kill whatever stands in its way, but it will not be killed.

HENRIETTE.   [*Opens a deck of cards lying on the mantelpiece.*]   Look at it!   The five of diamonds—the scaffold! Can it be possible that our fates are determined in advance?   That our thoughts are guided as if through pipes to the spot for which they are bound, without chance for us to stop them?   But I don't want it, I don't want it!—   Do you realise that I must go to the scaffold if my crime should be discovered?

MAURICE.   Tell me about your crime.   Now is the time for it.

HENRIETTE. No, I should regret it afterwards, and you would despise me—no, no, no!— Have you ever heard that a person could be hated to death? Well, my father incurred the hatred of my mother and my sisters, and he melted away like wax before a fire. Ugh! Let us talk of something else. And, above all, let us get away. The air is poisoned here. To-morrow your laurels will be withered, the triumph will be forgotten, and in a week another triumphant hero will hold the public attention. Away from here, to work for new victories! But first of all, Maurice, you must embrace your child and provide for its immediate future. You don't have to see the mother at all.

MAURICE. Thank you! Your good heart does you honour, and I love you doubly when you show the kindness you generally hide.

HENRIETTE. And then you go to the Crêmerie and say good-bye to the old lady and your friends. Leave no unsettled business behind to make your mind heavy on our trip.

MAURICE. I'll clear up everything, and to-night we meet at the railroad station.

HENRIETTE. Agreed! And then: away from here—away towards the sea and the sun!

Curtain.

ACT III

SCENE I

In the Crêmerie. The gas is lit. MME. CATHERINE *is seated at the counter,* ADOLPHE *at a table.*

MME. CATHERINE. Such is life, Monsieur Adolphe. But you young ones are always demanding too much, and then you come here and blubber over it afterwards.

ADOLPHE. No, it isn't that. I reproach nobody, and I am as fond as ever of both of them. But there is one thing that makes me sick at heart. You see, I thought more of Maurice than of anybody else; so much that I wouldn't have grudged him anything that could give him pleasure—but now I have lost him, and it hurts me worse than the loss of her. I have lost both of them, and so my loneliness is made doubly painful. And then there is still something else which I have not yet been able to clear up.

MME. CATHERINE. Don't brood so much. Work and divert yourself. Now, for instance, do you ever go to church?

ADOLPHE. What should I do there?

MME. CATHERINE. Oh, there's so much to look at, and then there is the music. There is nothing commonplace about it, at least.

ADOLPHE. Perhaps not. But I don't belong to that fold, I guess, for it never stirs me to any devotion. And then, Madame Catherine, faith is a gift, they tell me, and I haven't got it yet.

MME. CATHERINE. Well, wait till you get it— But what is this I heard a while ago? Is it true that you have sold a picture in London for a high price, and that you have got a medal?

ADOLPHE. Yes, it's true.

MME. CATHERINE. Merciful heavens!—and not a word do you say about it?

ADOLPHE. I am afraid of fortune, and besides it seems almost worthless to me at this moment. I am afraid of it as of a spectre: it brings disaster to speak of having seen it.

MME. CATHERINE. You're a queer fellow, and that's what you have always been.

ADOLPHE. Not queer at all, but I have seen so much misfortune come in the wake of fortune, and I have seen how adversity brings out true friends, while none but false ones appear in the hour of success— You asked me if I ever went to church, and I answered evasively. This morning I stepped into the Church of St. Germain without really knowing why I did so. It seemed as if I were looking for somebody in there—somebody to whom I could silently offer my gratitude. But I found nobody. Then I dropped a gold coin in the poor-box. It was all I could get out of my church-going, and that was rather commonplace, I should say.

MME. CATHERINE. It was always something; and then it was fine to think of the poor after having heard good news.

ADOLPHE.   It was neither fine nor anything else: it was something I did because I couldn't help myself.   But something more occurred while I was in the church.   I saw Maurice's girl friend, Jeanne, and her child.   Struck down, crushed by his triumphal chariot, they seemed aware of the full extent of their misfortune.

MME. CATHERINE.   Well, children, I don't know in what kind of shape you keep your consciences.   But how a decent fellow, a careful and considerate man like Monsieur Maurice, can all of a sudden desert a woman and her child, that is something I cannot explain.

ADOLPHE.   Nor can I explain it, and he doesn't seem to understand it himself.   I met them this morning, and everything appeared quite natural to them, quite proper, as if they couldn't imagine anything else.   It was as if they had been enjoying the satisfaction of a good deed or the fulfilment of a sacred duty.   There are things, Madame Catherine, that we cannot explain, and for this reason it is not for us to judge.   And besides, you saw how it happened.   Maurice felt the danger in the air.   I foresaw it and tried to prevent their meeting.   Maurice wanted to run away from it, but nothing helped.   Why, it was as if a plot had been laid by some invisible power, and as if they had been driven by guile into each other's arms.   Of course, I am disqualified in this case, but I wouldn't hesitate to pronounce a verdict of " not guilty."

MME. CATHERINE.   Well, now, to be able to forgive as you do, that's what I call religion.

ADOLPHE.   Heavens, could it be that I am religious without knowing it.

MME. CATHERINE.   But then, to *let* oneself be driven or tempted into evil, as Monsieur Maurice has done, means weakness or bad character.   And if you feel your strength failing you, then you ask for help, and then you get it.   But he was too conceited to do that—   Who is this coming?   The Abbé, I think.

ADOLPHE.   What does he want here?

ABBÉ.   [*Enters.*]   Good evening, madame.   Good evening, monsieur.

MME. CATHERINE.   Can I be of any service?

ABBÉ.   Has Monsieur Maurice, the author, been here to-day?

MME. CATHERINE.   Not to-day.   His play has just been put on, and that is probably keeping him busy.

ABBÉ.   I have—sad news to bring him.   Sad in several respects.

MME. CATHERINE.   May I ask of what kind?

ABBÉ.   Yes, it's no secret.   The daughter he had with that girl, Jeanne, is dead.

MME. CATHERINE.   Dead!

ADOLPHE.   Marion dead!

ABBÉ.   Yes, she died suddenly this morning without any previous illness.

MME. CATHERINE.   O Lord, who can tell Thy ways!

ABBÉ.   The mother's grief makes it necessary that Monsieur Maurice look after her, so we must try to find him.   But first a question in confidence: do you know whether Monsieur Maurice was fond of the child, or was indifferent to it?

MME. CATHERINE.   If he was fond of Marion?   Why, all of us know how he loved her.

ADOLPHE.   There's no doubt about that.

ABBÉ.   I am glad to hear it, and it settles the matter so far as I am concerned.

MME. CATHERINE.   Has there been any doubt about it?

ABBÉ.   Yes, unfortunately.   It has even been rumoured in the neighbourhood that he had abandoned the child and its mother in order to go away with a strange woman.   In a few hours this rumour has grown into definite accusations, and at the same time the feeling against him has risen to such a point that his life is threatened and he is being called a murderer.

MME. CATHERINE.   Good God, what is *this*?   What does it mean?

ABBÉ.   Now I'll tell you my opinion—   I am convinced that the man is innocent on this score, and the mother feels as certain about it as I do.   But appearances are against Monsieur Maurice, and I think he will find it rather hard to clear himself when the police come to question him.

ADOLPHE.   Have the police got hold of the matter?

ABBÉ.   Yes, the police have had to step in to protect him

against all those ugly rumours and the rage of the people. Probably the Commissaire will be here soon.

MME. CATHERINE. [*To* ADOLPHE.] There, you see what happens when a man cannot tell the difference between good and evil, and when he trifles with vice. God will punish!

ADOLPHE. Then he is more merciless than man.

ABBÉ. What do you know about that?

ADOLPHE. Not very much, but I keep an eye on what happens——

ABBÉ. And you understand it also?

ADOLPHE. Not yet perhaps.

ABBÉ. Let us look more closely at the matter—— Oh, here comes the Commissaire.

COMMISSAIRE. [*Enters.*] Gentlemen--Madame Catherine —I have to trouble you for a moment with a few questions concerning Monsieur Maurice. As you have probably heard, he has become the object of a hideous rumour, which, by the by, I don't believe in.

MME. CATHERINE. None of us believes in it either.

COMMISSAIRE. That strengthens my own opinion, but for his own sake I must give him a chance to defend himself.

ABBÉ. That's right, and I guess he will find justice, although it may come hard.

COMMISSAIRE. Appearances are very much against him, but I have seen guiltless people reach the scaffold before their innocence was discovered. Let me tell you what there is against him. The little girl, Marion, being left alone by her mother, was secretly visited by the father, who seems to have made sure of the time when the child was to be found alone. Fifteen minutes after his visit the mother returned home and found the child dead. All this makes the position of the accused man very unpleasant—— The post-mortem examination brought out no signs of violence or of poison, but the physicians admit the existence of new poisons that leave no traces behind them. To me all this is mere coincidence of the kind I frequently come across. But here's something that looks worse. Last night Monsieur Maurice was seen at the Auberge des Adrets in company with a strange lady. According to the waiter, they were talking about

crimes.   The Place de Roquette and the scaffold were both mentioned.   A queer topic of conversation for a pair of lovers of
good breeding and good social position!   But even this may be
passed over, as we know by experience that people who have been
drinking and losing a lot of sleep seem inclined to dig up all the
worst that lies at the bottom of their souls.   Far more serious is
the evidence given by the head waiter as to their champagne
breakfast in the Bois de Boulogne this morning.   He says that he
heard them wish the life out of a child.   The man is said to
have remarked that, " It would be better if it had never existed."
To which the woman replied: " Indeed!   But now it does
exist."   And as they went on talking, these words occurred:
" This will kill this! "   And the answer was: " Kill!   What
kind of word is that? "   And also: " The five of diamonds—
the scaffold, the Place de Roquette."   All this, you see, will be
hard to get out of, and so will the foreign journey planned for
this evening.   These are serious matters.

ADOLPHE.   He is lost!

MME. CATHERINE.   That's a dreadful story.   One doesn't
know what to believe.

ABBÉ.   This is not the work of man.   God have mercy on
him!

ADOLPHE.   He is in the net, and he will never get out of it.

MME. CATHERINE.   He had no business to get in.

ADOLPHE.   Do you begin to suspect him also, Madame
Catherine?

MME. CATHERINE.   Yes and no.   I have got beyond having
an opinion in this matter.   Have you not seen angels turn into
devils just as you turn your hand, and then become angels again?

COMMISSAIRE.   It certainly does look queer.   However, we'll
have to wait and hear what explanations he can give.   No one
will be judged unheard.   Good evening, gentlemen.   Good
evening, Madame Catherine.   [Goes out.

ABBÉ.   This is not the work of man.

ADOLPHE.   No, it looks as if demons had been at work for the
undoing of man.

ABBÉ.   It is either a punishment for secret misdeeds, or it is
a terrible test.

JEANNE.   [*Enters, dressed in mourning.*]   Good evening.
Pardon me for asking, but have you seen Monsieur Maurice?

MME. CATHERINE.   No, madame, but I think he may be here
any minute.   You haven't met him then since——

JEANNE.   Not since this morning.

MME. CATHERINE.   Let me tell you that I share in your
great sorrow.

JEANNE.   Thank you, madame.   [*To the* ABBÉ.]   So you
are here, Father.

ABBÉ.   Yes, my child.   I thought I might be of some use to
you.   And it was fortunate, as it gave me a chance to speak to
the Commissaire.

JEANNE.   The Commissaire!   He doesn't suspect Maurice
also, does he?

ABBÉ.   No, he doesn't, and none of us here do.   But appearances are against him in a most appalling manner.

JEANNE.   You mean on account of the talk the waiters overheard—it means nothing to me, who has heard such things before
when Maurice had had a few drinks.   Then it is his custom to
speculate on crimes and their punishment.   Besides it seems to
have been the woman in his company who dropped the most
dangerous remarks.   I should like to have a look into that
woman's eyes.

ADOLPHE.   My dear Jeanne, no matter how much harm that
woman may have done you, she did nothing with evil intention—
in fact, she had no intention whatever, but just followed the
promptings of her nature.   I know her to be a good soul and one
who can very well bear being looked straight in the eye.

JEANNE.   Your judgment in this matter, Adolphe, has great
value to me, and I believe what you say.   It means that I cannot
hold anybody but myself responsible for what has happened.   It
is my carelessness that is now being punished.   [*She begins to cry.*

ABBÉ.   Don't accuse yourself unjustly!   I know you, and
the serious spirit in which you have regarded your motherhood.
That your assumption of this responsibility had not been sanc-
tioned by religion and the civil law was not your fault.   No, we
are here facing something quite different.

ADOLPHE.   What then?

ABBÉ. Who can tell?

HENRIETTE *enters, dressed in travelling suit.*

ADOLPHE. [*Rises with an air of determination and goes to meet* HENRIETTE.] You here?

HENRIETTE. Yes, where is Maurice?

ADOLPHE. Do you know—or don't you?

HENRIETTE. I know everything. Excuse me, Madame Catherine, but I was ready to start and absolutely had to step in here a moment. [*To* ADOLPHE.] Who is that woman?—Oh!

HENRIETTE *and* JEANNE *stare at each other.* EMILE *appears in the kitchen door.*

HENRIETTE. [*To* JEANNE.] I ought to say something, but it matters very little, for anything I can say must sound like an insult or a mockery. But if I ask you simply to believe that I share your deep sorrow as much as anybody standing closer to you, then you must not turn away from me. You mustn't, for I deserve your pity if not your forbearance. [*Holds out her hand.*

JEANNE. [*Looks hard at her.*] I believe you now—and in the next moment I don't. [*Takes* HENRIETTE's *hand.*

HENRIETTE. [*Kisses* JEANNE's *hand.*] Thank you!

JEANNE. [*Drawing back her hand.*] Oh, don't! I don't deserve it! I don't deserve it!

ABBÉ. Pardon me, but while we are gathered here and peace seems to prevail temporarily at least, won't you, Mademoiselle Henriette, shed some light into all the uncertainty and darkness surrounding the main point of accusation? I ask you, as a friend among friends, to tell us what you meant with all that talk about killing, and crime, and the Place de Roquette. That your words had no connection with the death of the child, we have reason to believe, but it would give us added assurance to hear what you were really talking about. Won't you tell us?

HENRIETTE. [*After a pause.*] That I cannot tell! No, I cannot!

ADOLPHE. Henriette, do tell! Give us the word that will relieve us all.

HENRIETTE. I cannot! Don't ask me!

ABBÉ. This is not the work of man!

HENRIETTE. Oh, that this moment had to come! And in

this manner!   [*To* JEANNE.]   Madame, I swear that I am not guilty of your child's death.   Is that enough?

JEANNE.   Enough for us, but not for Justice.

HENRIETTE.   Justice!   If you knew how true your words are!

ABBÉ.   [*To* HENRIETTE.]   And if you knew what you were saying just now!

HENRIETTE.   Do you know that better than I?

ABBÉ.   Yes, I do.

HENRIETTE looks fixedly at the ABBÉ.

ABBÉ.   Have no fear, for even if I guess your secret, it will not be exposed.   Besides, I have nothing to do with human justice, but a great deal with divine mercy.

MAURICE.   [*Enters hastily, dressed for travelling.   He doesn't look at the others, who are standing in the background, but goes straight up to the counter, where* MME. CATHERINE *is sitting.*]   You are not angry at me, Madame Catherine, because I didn't show up?   I have come now to apologise to you before I start for the South at eight o'clock this evening.

MME. CATHERINE *is too startled to say a word.*

MAURICE.   Then you are angry at me?   [*Looks around.*] What does all this mean?   Is it a dream, or what is it?   Of course, I can see that it is all real, but it looks like a wax cabinet— There is Jeanne, looking like a statue and dressed in black— And Henriette looking like a corpse—   What does it mean?

All remain silent.

MAURICE.   Nobody answers.   It must mean something dreadful.   [*Silence.*]   But speak, please!   Adolphe, you are my friend, what is it?   [*Pointing to* EMILE.]   And there is a detective!

ADOLPHE.   [*Comes forward.*]   You don't know then?

MAURICE.   Nothing at all.   But I must know!

ADOLPHE.   Well, then—Marion is dead.

MAURICE.   Marion—dead?

ADOLPHE.   Yes, she died this morning.

MAURICE.   [*To* JEANNE.]   So that's why you are in mourning.   Jeanne, Jeanne, who has done this to us?

JEANNE.   He who holds life and death in his hand.

MAURICE.   But I saw her looking well and happy this morning.   How did it happen?   Who did it?   Somebody must have done it?   [*His eyes seek* HENRIETTE.

ADOLPHE.   Don't look for the guilty one here, for there is none to be found.   Unfortunately, the police have turned their suspicion in a direction where none ought to exist.

MAURICE.   What direction is that?

ADOLPHE.   Well—you may as well know that your reckless talk last night and this morning has placed you in a light that is anything but favourable.

MAURICE.   So they were listening to us.   Let me see, what were we saying—I remember!—   Then I am lost!

ADOLPHE.   But if you explain your thoughtless words we will believe you.

MAURICE.   I cannot!   And I will not!   I shall be sent to prison, but it doesn't matter.   Marion is dead!   Dead!   And I have killed her!

General consternation.

ADOLPHE.   Think of what you are saying!   Weigh your words!   Do you realise what you said just now?

MAURICE.   What did I say?

ADOLPHE.   You said that you had killed Marion.

MAURICE.   Is there a human being here who could believe me a murderer, and who could hold me capable of taking my own child's life?   You who know me, Madame Catherine, tell me; do you believe, can you believe——

MME. CATHERINE.   I don't know any longer what to believe.   What the heart thinketh the tongue speaketh.   And your tongue has spoken evil words.

MAURICE.   She doesn't believe me!

ADOLPHE.   But explain your words, man!   Explain what you meant by saying that " your love would kill everything that stood in its way ".

MAURICE.   So they know that too—   Are you willing to explain it, Henriette?

HENRIETTE.   No, I cannot do that.

ABBÉ.   There is something wrong behind all this and you have lost our sympathy, my friend.   A while ago I could have sworn that you were innocent, and I wouldn't do that now.

MAURICE. [*To* JEANNE.] What you have to say means more to me than anything else.

JEANNE. [*Coldly.*] Answer a question first: who was it you cursed during that orgy out there?

MAURICE. Have I done that, too? Maybe. Yes, I am guilty, and yet I am guiltless. Let me go away from here, for I am ashamed of myself, and I have done more wrong than I can forgive myself.

HENRIETTE. [*To* ADOLPHE.] Go with him and see that he doesn't do himself any harm.

ADOLPHE. Shall I——?

HENRIETTE. Who else?

ADOLPHE. [*Without bitterness.*] You are nearest to it—Sh! A carriage is stopping outside.

MME. CATHERINE. It's the Commissaire. Well, much as I have seen of life, I could never have believed that success and fame were such short-lived things.

MAURICE. [*To* HENRIETTE.] From the triumphal chariot to the patrol wagon!

JEANNE. [*Simply.*] And the ass—who was that?

ADOLPHE. Oh, that must have been me.

COMMISSAIRE. [*Enters with a paper in his hand.*] A summons to Police Headquarters—to-night, at once—for Monsieur Maurice Gérard—and for Mademoiselle Henriette Mauclerc—both here?

MAURICE *and* HENRIETTE. Yes.

MAURICE. Is this an arrest?

COMMISSAIRE. Not yet. Only a summons.

MAURICE. And then?

COMMISSAIRE. We don't know yet.

MAURICE *and* HENRIETTE *go towards the door.*

MAURICE. Good-bye to all!

Everybody shows emotion. The COMMISSAIRE, MAURICE, *and* HENRIETTE *go out.*

EMILE. [*Enters and goes up to* JEANNE.] Now I'll take you home, sister.

JEANNE. And what do you think of all this?

EMILE. The man is innocent.

ABBÉ. But as I see it, it is, and must always be, something despicable to break one's promise, and it becomes unpardonable when a woman and her child are involved.

EMILE. Well, I should rather feel that way, too, now when it concerns my own sister, but, unfortunately, I am prevented from throwing the first stone because I have done the same thing myself.

ABBÉ. Although I am free from blame in that respect, I am not throwing any stones either, but the act condemns itself and is punished by its consequences.

JEANNE. Pray for him! For both of them!

ABBÉ. No, I'll do nothing of the kind, for it is an impertinence to want to change the counsels of the Lord. And what has happened here is, indeed, not the work of man.

Curtain.

SCENE II

The Auberge des Adrets. ADOLPHE *and* HENRIETTE *are seated at the same table where* MAURICE *and* HENRIETTE *were sitting in the second act. A cup of coffee stands in front of* ADOLPHE. HENRIETTE *has ordered nothing.*

ADOLPHE. You believe then that he will come here?

HENRIETTE. I am sure. He was released this noon for lack of evidence, but he didn't want to show himself in the streets before it was dark.

ADOLPHE. Poor fellow! Oh, I tell you, life seems horrible to me since yesterday.

HENRIETTE. And what about me? I am afraid to live, dare hardly breathe, dare hardly think even, since I know that somebody is spying not only on my words but on my thoughts.

ADOLPHE. So it was here you sat that night when I couldn't find you?

HENRIETTE. Yes, but don't talk of it. I could die from shame when I think of it. Adolphe, you are made of a different, a better, stuff than he or I——

ADOLPHE. Sh, sh, sh!

HENRIETTE. Yes, indeed! And what was it that made me stay here? I was lazy; I was tired; his success intoxicated me and bewitched me—I cannot explain it. But if you had come it would never have happened. And to-day you are great, and he is small—less than the least of all. Yesterday he had one hundred thousand francs. To-day he has nothing, because his play has been withdrawn. And public opinion will never excuse him, for his lack of faith will be judged as harshly as if he were the murderer, and those that see farthest hold that the child died from sorrow, so that he was responsible for it anyhow.

ADOLPHE. You know what my thoughts are in this matter, Henriette, but I should like to know that both of you are spotless. Won't you tell me what those dreadful words of yours meant? It cannot be a chance that your talk in a festive moment like that dealt so largely with killing and the scaffold.

HENRIETTE. It was no chance. It was something that had to be said, something I cannot tell you—probably because I have no right to appear spotless in your eyes, seeing that I am not spotless.

ADOLPHE. All this is beyond me.

HENRIETTE. Let us talk of something else— Do you believe there are many unpunished criminals at large among us, some of whom may even be our intimate friends?

ADOLPHE. [Nervously.] Why? What do you mean?

HENRIETTE. Don't you believe that every human being at some time or another has been guilty of some kind of act which would fall under the law if it were discovered?

ADOLPHE. Yes, I believe that is true, but no evil act escapes being punished by one's own conscience at least. [Rises and unbuttons his coat.] And—nobody is really good who has not erred. [Breathing heavily.] For in order to know how to forgive, one must have been in need of forgiveness—I had a friend whom we used to regard as a model man. He never spoke a hard word to anybody; he forgave everything and everybody; and he suffered insults with a strange satisfaction that we couldn't explain. At last, late in life, he gave me his secret in a single word: I am a penitent! [He sits down again.

HENRIETTE *remains silent, looking at him with surprise.*

ADOLPHE. [*As if speaking to himself.*] There are crimes not mentioned in the Criminal Code, and these are the worse ones, for they have to be punished by ourselves, and no judge could be more severe than we are against our own selves.

HENRIETTE. [*After a pause.*] Well, that friend of yours, did he find peace?

ADOLPHE. After endless self-torture he reached a certain degree of composure, but life had never any real pleasures to offer him. He never dared to accept any kind of distinction; he never dared to feel himself entitled to a kind word or even well-earned praise: in a word, he could never quite forgive himself.

HENRIETTE. Never? What had he done then?

ADOLPHE. He had wished the life out of his father. And when his father suddenly died, the son imagined himself to have killed him. Those imaginations were regarded as signs of some mental disease, and he was sent to an asylum. From this he was discharged after a time as wholly recovered—as they put it. But the sense of guilt remained with him, and so he continued to punish himself for his evil thoughts.

HENRIETTE. Are you sure the evil will cannot kill?

ADOLPHE. You mean in some mystic way?

HENRIETTE. As you please. Let it go at mystic. In my own family—I am sure that my mother and my sisters killed my father with their hatred. You see, he had the awful idea that he must oppose all our tastes and inclinations. Wherever he discovered a natural gift, he tried to root it out. In that way he aroused a resistance that accumulated until it became like an electrical battery charged with hatred. At last it grew so powerful that he languished away, became depolarised, lost his willpower, and, in the end, came to wish himself dead.

ADOLPHE. And your conscience never troubled you?

HENRIETTE. No, and furthermore, I don't know what conscience is.

ADOLPHE. You don't? Well, then you'll soon learn. [*Pause.*] How do you believe Maurice will look when he gets here? What do you think he will say?

HENRIETTE. Yesterday morning, you know, he and I tried to make the same kind of guess about you while we were waiting for you.

ADOLPHE. Well?

HENRIETTE. We guessed entirely wrong.

ADOLPHE. Can you tell me why you sent for me?

HENRIETTE. Malice, arrogance, outright cruelty!

ADOLPHE. How strange it is that you can admit your faults and yet not repent of them.

HENRIETTE. It must be because I don't feel quite responsible for them. They are like the dirt left behind by things handled during the day and washed off at night. But tell me one thing: do you really think so highly of humanity as you profess to do?

ADOLPHE. Yes, we are a little better than our reputation— and a little worse.

HENRIETTE. That is not a straightforward answer.

ADOLPHE. No, it isn't. But are you willing to answer me frankly when I ask you: do you still love Maurice?

HENRIETTE. I cannot tell until I see him. But at this moment I feel no longing for him, and it seems as if I could very well live without him.

ADOLPHE. It's likely you could, but I fear you have become chained to his fate—Sh! Here he comes.

HENRIETTE. How everything repeats itself. The situation is the same, the very words are the same, as when we were expecting you yesterday.

MAURICE. [*Enters, pale as death, hollow-eyed, unshaven.*] Here I am, my dear friends, if this be me. For that last night in a cell changed me into a new sort of being.

[*Notices* HENRIETTE *and* ADOLPHE.

ADOLPHE. Sit down and pull yourself together, and then we can talk things over.

MAURICE. [*To* HENRIETTE.] Perhaps I am in the way?

ADOLPHE. Now don't get bitter.

MAURICE. I have grown bad in these twenty-four hours, and suspicious also, so I guess I'll soon be left to myself. And who wants to keep company with a murderer?

HENRIETTE. But you have been cleared of the charge.

MAURICE. [*Picks up a newspaper.*] By the police, yes, but not by public opinion. Here you see the murderer Maurice Gérard, once a playwright, and his mistress, Henriette Mauclerc——

HENRIETTE. O my mother and my sisters—my mother! Jesus, have mercy!

MAURICE. And can you see that I actually look like a murderer? And then it is suggested that my play was stolen. So there isn't a vestige left of the victorious hero from yesterday. In place of my own, the name of Octave, my enemy, appears on the bill-boards, and he is going to collect my one hundred thousand francs. O Solon, Solon! Such is fortune, and such is fame! You are fortunate, Adolphe, because you have not yet succeeded.

HENRIETTE. So you don't know that Adolphe has made a great success in London and carried off the first prize?

MAURICE. [*Darkly.*] No, I didn't know that. Is it true, Adolphe?

ADOLPHE. It is true, but I have returned the prize.

HENRIETTE. [*With emphasis.*] That I didn't know! So you are also prevented from accepting any distinction—like your friend?

ADOLPHE. My friend? [*Embarrassed.*] Oh, yes, yes!

MAURICE. Your success gives me pleasure, but it puts us still farther apart.

ADOLPHE. That's what I expected, and I suppose I'll be as lonely with my success as you with your adversity. Think of it —that people feel hurt by your fortune! Oh, it's ghastly to be alive!

MAURICE. You say that! What am I then to say? It is as if my eyes had been covered with a black veil, and as if the colour and shape of all life had been changed by it. This room looks like the room I saw yesterday, and yet it is quite different. I recognise both of you, of course, but your faces are new to me. I sit here and search for words because I don't know what to say to you. I ought to defend myself, but I cannot. And I almost miss the cell, for it protected me, at least, against the curious glances that pass right through me. The murderer Maurice and his mistress! You don't love me any longer, Henriette, and no more do I care for you. To-day you are ugly, clumsy, insipid, repulsive.

Two men in civilian clothes have quietly seated themselves at a table in the background.

ADOLPHE. Wait a little and get your thoughts together. That you have been discharged and cleared of all suspicion must appear in some of the evening papers. And that puts an end to the whole matter. Your play will be put on again, and if it comes to the worst, you can write a new one. Leave Paris for a year and let everything become forgotten. You who have exonerated mankind will be exonerated yourself.

MAURICE. Ha-ha! Mankind! Ha-ha!

ADOLPHE. You have ceased to believe in goodness?

MAURICE. Yes, if I ever did believe in it. Perhaps it was only a mood, a manner of looking at things, a way of being polite to the wild beasts. When I, who was held among the best, can be so rotten to the core, what must then be the wretchedness of the rest?

ADOLPHE. Now I'll go out and get all the evening papers, and then we'll undoubtedly have reason to look at things in a different way.

MAURICE. [*Turning towards the background.*] Two detectives!—It means that I am released under surveillance, so that I can give myself away by careless talking.

ADOLPHE. Those are not detectives. That's only your imagination. I recognise both of them.

[*Goes towards the door.*

MAURICE. Don't leave us alone, Adolphe. I fear that Henriette and I may come to open explanations.

ADOLPHE. Oh, be sensible, Maurice, and think of your future. Try to keep him quiet, Henriette. I'll be back in a moment. [*Goes out.*

HENRIETTE. Well, Maurice, what do you think now of our guilt or guiltlessness?

MAURICE. I have killed nobody. All I did was to talk a lot of nonsense while I was drunk. But it is your crime that comes back, and that crime you have grafted on to me.

HENRIETTE.   Oh, that's the tone you talk now!—Was it not you who cursed your own child, and wished the life out of it, and wanted to go away without saying good-bye to anybody? And was it not I who made you visit Marion and show yourself to Madame Catherine?

MAURICE.   Yes, you are right.   Forgive me!   You proved yourself more human than I, and the guilt is wholly my own. Forgive me!   But all the same I am without guilt.   Who has tied this net from which I can never free myself?   Guilty and guiltless: guiltless and yet guilty!   Oh, it is driving me mad— Look, now they sit over there and listen to us—   And no waiter comes to take our order.   I'll go out and order a cup of tea.   Do you want anything?

HENRIETTE.   Nothing.

MAURICE *goes out.*

FIRST DETECTIVE.   [*Goes up to* HENRIETTE.]   Let me look at your papers.

HENRIETTE.   How dare you speak to me?

DETECTIVE.   Dare?   I'll show you!

HENRIETTE.   What do you mean?

DETECTIVE.   It's my job to keep an eye on street-walkers. Yesterday you came here with one man, and to-day with another. That's as good as walking the streets.   And unescorted ladies don't get anything here.   So you'd better get out and come along with me.

HENRIETTE.   My escort will be back in a moment.

DETECTIVE.   Yes, and a pretty kind of escort you've got— the kind that doesn't help a girl a bit!

HENRIETTE.   O God!   My mother, my sisters!—   I am of good family, I tell you.

DETECTIVE.   Yes, first-rate family, I am sure.   But you are too well known through the papers.   Come along!

HENRIETTE.   Where?   What do you mean?

DETECTIVE.   Oh, to the Bureau, of course.   There you'll get a nice little card and a license that brings you free medical care.

HENRIETTE.   O Lord Jesus, you don't mean it!

DETECTIVE.   [*Grabbing* HENRIETTE *by the arm.*]   Don't I mean it?

HENRIETTE. [*Falling on her knees.*] Save me, Maurice! Help!

DETECTIVE. Shut up, you fool!

MAURICE *enters, followed by* WAITER.

WAITER. Gentlemen of that kind are not served here. You just pay and get out! And take the girl along!

MAURICE. [*Crushed, searches his pocket-book for money.*] Henriette, pay for me, and let us get away from this place. I haven't a sou left.

WAITER. So the lady has to put up for her Alphonse! Alphonse! Do you know what that is?

HENRIETTE. [*Looking through her pocket-book.*] Oh, merciful heavens! I have no money either!—Why doesn't Adolphe come back?

DETECTIVE. Well, did you ever see such rotters! Get out of here, and put up something as security. That kind of ladies generally have their fingers full of rings.

MAURICE. Can it be possible that we have sunk so low?

HENRIETTE. [*Takes off a ring and hands it to the* WAITER.] The Abbé was right: this is not the work of man.

MAURICE. No, it's the devil's!— But if we leave before Adolphe returns, he will think that we have deceived him and run away.

HENRIETTE. That would be in keeping with the rest—But we'll go into the river now, won't we?

MAURICE. [*Takes* HENRIETTE *by the hand as they walk out together.*] Into the river—yes!

Curtain.

ACT IV

SCENE I

In the Luxembourg Gardens, at the group of Adam and Eve. The wind is shaking the trees and stirring up dead leaves, straws, and pieces of paper from the ground.

MAURICE *and* HENRIETTE *are seated on a bench.*

HENRIETTE. So you don't want to die?

MAURICE. No, I am afraid. I imagine that I am going to be very cold down there in the grave, with only a sheet to cover me and a few shavings to lie on. And besides that, it seems to me as if there were still some task waiting for me, but I cannot make out what it is.

HENRIETTE. But I can guess what it is.

MAURICE. Tell me.

HENRIETTE. It is revenge. You, like me, must have suspected Jeanne and Emile of sending the detectives after me yesterday. Such a revenge on a rival none but a woman could devise.

MAURICE. Exactly what I was thinking. But let me tell you that my suspicions go even further. It seems as if my sufferings during these last few days had sharpened my wits. Can you explain, for instance, why the waiter from the Auberge des Adrets and the head waiter from the Pavilion were not called to testify at the hearing?

HENRIETTE. I never thought of it before. But now I know why. They had nothing to tell, because they had not been listening.

MAURICE. But how could the Commissaire then know what we had been saying?

HENRIETTE. He didn't know, but he figured it out. He was guessing, and he guessed right. Perhaps he had had to deal with some similar case before.

MAURICE. Or else he concluded from our looks what we had been saying. There are those who can read other people's thoughts— Adolphe being the dupe, it seemed quite natural that we should have called him an ass. It's the rule, I understand, although it's varied at times by the use of " idiot " instead. But ass was nearer at hand in this case, as we had been talking of carriages and triumphal chariots. It is quite simple to figure out a fourth fact, when you have three known ones to start from.

HENRIETTE. Just think that we have let ourselves be taken in so completely.

MAURICE. That's the result of thinking too well of one's fellow beings. This is all you get out of it. But do you know,

I suspect somebody else behind the Commissaire, who, by the by, must be a full-fledged scoundrel.

HENRIETTE. You mean the Abbé, who was taking the part of a private detective.

MAURICE. That's what I mean. That man has to receive all kinds of confessions. And note you: Adolphe himself told us he had been at the Church of St. Germain that morning. What was he doing there? He was blabbing, of course, and bewailing his fate. And then the priest put the questions together for the Commissaire.

HENRIETTE. Tell me something: do you trust Adolphe?

MAURICE. I trust no human being any longer.

HENRIETTE. Not even Adolphe?

MAURICE. Him least of all. How could I trust an enemy—a man from whom I have taken away his mistress?

HENRIETTE. Well, as you were the first one to speak of this, I'll give you some data about our friend. You heard he had returned that medal from London. Do you know his reason for doing so?

MAURICE. No.

HENRIETTE. He thinks himself unworthy of it, and he has taken a penitential vow never to receive any kind of distinction.

MAURICE. Can that be possible? But what has he done?

HENRIETTE. He has committed a crime of the kind that is not punishable under the law. That's what he gave me to understand indirectly.

MAURICE. He, too! He, the best one of all, the model man, who never speaks a hard word of anybody and who forgives everything.

HENRIETTE. Well, there you can see that we are no worse than others. And yet we are being hounded day and night as if devils were after us.

MAURICE. He, also! Then mankind has not been slandered— But if he has been capable of *one* crime, then you may expect anything of him. Perhaps it was he who sent the police after you yesterday. Coming to think of it now, it was he who sneaked away from us when he saw that we were in the papers, and he lied when he insisted that those fellows were not detectives. But, of course, you may expect anything from a deceived lover.

HENRIETTE. Could he be as mean as that? No, it is impossible, impossible!

MAURICE. Why so? If he is a scoundrel?— What were you two talking of yesterday, before I came?

HENRIETTE. He had nothing but good to say of you.

MAURICE. That's a lie!

HENRIETTE. [*Controlling herself and changing her tone.*] Listen. There is one person on whom you have cast no suspicion whatever—for what reason, I don't know. Have you thought of Madame Catherine's wavering attitude in this matter? Didn't she say finally that she believed you capable of anything?

MAURICE. Yes, she did, and that shows what kind of person she is. To think evil of other people without reason, you must be a villain yourself.

HENRIETTE *looks hard at him. Pause.*

HENRIETTE. To think evil of others, you must be a villain yourself.

MAURICE. What do you mean?

HENRIETTE. What I said.

MAURICE. Do you mean that I——?

HENRIETTE. Yes, that's what I mean now! Look here! Did you meet anybody but Marion when you called there yesterday morning?

MAURICE. Why do you ask?

HENRIETTE. Guess!

MAURICE. Well, as you seem to know—I met Jeanne, too.

HENRIETTE. Why did you lie to me?

MAURICE. I wanted to spare you.

HENRIETTE. And now you want me to believe in one who has been lying to me? No, my boy, now I believe you guilty of that murder.

MAURICE. Wait a moment! We have now reached the place for which my thoughts have been heading all the time, though I resisted as long as possible. It's queer that what lies next to one is seen last of all, and what one doesn't *want* to believe cannot be believed— Tell me something: where did you go yesterday, after we parted in the Bois?

HENRIETTE. [*Alarmed.*] Why?

MAURICE. You went either to Adolphe—which you couldn't do, as he was attending a lesson—or you went to—Marion!

HENRIETTE. Now J am convinced that you are the murderer.

MAURICE. And I, that you are the murderess! You alone had an interest in getting the child out of the way—to get rid of the rock on the road, as you so aptly put it.

HENRIETTE. It was you who said that.

MAURICE. And the one who had an interest in it must have committed the crime.

HENRIETTE. Now, Maurice, we have been running around and around in this tread-mill, scourging each other. Let us quit before we get to the point of sheer madness.

MAURICE. You have reached that point already.

HENRIETTE. Don't you think it's time for us to part, before we drive each other insane?

MAURICE. Yes, I think so.

HENRIETTE. [*Rising.*] Good-bye then!

Two men in civilian clothes become visible in the background.

HENRIETTE. [*Turns and comes back to* MAURICE.] There they are again!

MAURICE. The dark angels that want to drive us out of the garden.

HENRIETTE. And force us back upon each other as if we were chained together.

MAURICE. Or as if we were condemned to lifelong marriage. Are we really to marry? To settle down in the same place? To be able to close the door behind us and perhaps get peace at last?

HENRIETTE. And shut ourselves up in order to torture each other to death; get behind locks and bolts, with a ghost for marriage portion; you torturing me with the memory of Adolphe, and I getting back at you with Jeanne—and Marion.

MAURICE. Never mention the name of Marion again!

Don't you know that she was to be buried to-day—at this very moment perhaps?

HENRIETTE. And you are not there? What does that mean?

MAURICE. It means that both Jeanne and the police have warned me against the rage of the people.

HENRIETTE. A coward, too?

MAURICE. All the vices! How could you ever have cared for me?

HENRIETTE. Because two days ago you were another person, well worthy of being loved——

MAURICE. And now sunk to such a depth!

HENRIETTE. It isn't that. But you are beginning to flaunt bad qualities which are not your own.

MAURICE. But yours?

HENRIETTE. Perhaps, for when you appear a little worse I feel at once a little better.

MAURICE. It's like passing on a disease to save one's self-respect.

HENRIETTE. And how vulgar you have become, too!

MAURICE. Yes, I notice it myself, and I hardly recognise myself since that night in the cell. They put in one person and let out another through that gate which separates us from the rest of society. And now I feel myself the enemy of all mankind: I should like to set fire to the earth and dry up the oceans, for nothing less than a universal conflagration can wipe out my dishonour.

HENRIETTE. I had a letter from my mother to-day. She is the widow of a major in the army, well educated, with old-fashioned ideas of honour and that kind of thing. Do you want to read the letter? No, you don't!— Do you know that I am an outcast? My respectable acquaintances will have nothing to do with me, and if I show myself on the streets alone the police will take me. Do you realise now that we have to get married?

MAURICE. We despise each other, and yet we have to marry: that is hell pure and simple! But, Henriette, before we unite our destinies you must tell me your secret, so that we may be on more equal terms.

HENRIETTE. All right, I'll tell you. I had a friend who got into trouble—you understand. I wanted to help her, as her whole future was at stake—and she died!

MAURICE. That was reckless, but one might almost call it noble, too.

HENRIETTE. You say so now, but the next time you lose your temper you will accuse me of it.

MAURICE. No, I won't. But I cannot deny that it has shaken my faith in you and that it makes me afraid of you. Tell me, is her lover still alive, and does he know to what extent you were responsible?

HENRIETTE. He was as guilty as I.

MAURICE. And if his conscience should begin to trouble him —such things do happen—and if he should feel inclined to confess: then you would be lost.

HENRIETTE. I know it, and it is this constant dread which has made me rush from one dissipation to another—so that I should never have time to wake up to full consciousness.

MAURICE. And now you want me to take my marriage portion out of your dread. That's asking a little too much.

HENRIETTE. But when I shared the shame of Maurice the murderer——

MAURICE. Oh, let's come to an end with it!

HENRIETTE. No, the end is not yet, and I'll not let go my hold until I have put you where you belong. For you can't go around thinking yourself better than I am.

MAURICE. So you want to fight me then? All right, as you please!

HENRIETTE. A fight on life and death!

The rolling of drums is heard in the distance.

MAURICE. The garden is to be closed. " Cursed is the ground for thy sake; thorns and thistles shall it bring forth to thee."

HENRIETTE. " And the Lord God said unto the woman——"

A GUARD. [*In uniform, speaking very politely.*] Sorry, but the garden has to be closed.

Curtain.

SCENE II

The Crêmerie. MME. CATHERINE *is sitting at the counter making entries into an account book.* ADOLPHE *and* HENRIETTE *are seated at a table.*

ADOLPHE. [*Calmly and kindly.*] But if I give you my final assurance that I didn't run away, but that, on the contrary, I thought you had played me false, this ought to convince you.

HENRIETTE. But why did you fool us by saying that those fellows were not policemen?

ADOLPHE. I didn't think myself that they were, and then I wanted to reassure you.

HENRIETTE. When you say it, I believe you. But then you must also believe me, if I reveal my innermost thoughts to you.

ADOLPHE. Go on.

HENRIETTE. But you mustn't come back with your usual talk of fancies and delusions.

ADOLPHE. You seem to have reason to fear that I may.

HENRIETTE. I fear nothing, but I know you and your scepticism— Well, and then you mustn't tell this to anybody —promise me!

ADOLPHE. I promise.

HENRIETTE. Now think of it, although I must say it's something terrible: I have partial evidence that Maurice is guilty, or at least, I have reasonable suspicions——

ADOLPHE. You don't mean it!

HENRIETTE. Listen, and judge for yourself. When Maurice left me in the Bois, he said he was going to see Marion alone, as the mother was out. And now I have discovered afterwards that he did meet the mother. So that he has been lying to me.

ADOLPHE. That's possible, and his motive for doing so may have been the best, but how can anybody conclude from it that he is guilty of a murder?

HENRIETTE. Can't you see that?— Don't you understand?

ADOLPHE. Not at all.

HENRIETTE. Because you don't want to!— Then there is

nothing left for me but to report him, and we'll see whether he can prove an alibi.

ADOLPHE.   Henriette, let me tell you the grim truth. You, like he, have reached the border-line of—insanity. The demons of distrust have got hold of you, and each of you is using his own sense of partial guilt to wound the other with. Let me see if I can make a straight guess: he has also come to suspect you of killing his child?

HENRIETTE.   Yes, he's mad enough to do so.

ADOLPHE.   You call his suspicions mad, but not your own.

HENRIETTE.   You have first to prove the contrary, or that I suspect him unjustly.

ADOLPHE.   Yes, that's easy. A new autopsy has proved that Marion died of a well-known disease, the queer name of which I cannot recall just now.

HENRIETTE.   Is it true?

ADOLPHE.   The official report is printed in to-day's paper.

HENRIETTE.   I don't take any stock of it. They can make up that kind of thing.

ADOLPHE.   Beware, Henriette—or you may, without knowing it, pass across that border line. Beware especially of throwing out accusations that may put you into prison. Beware! [*He places his hand on her head.*]   You hate Maurice?

HENRIETTE.   Beyond all bounds!

ADOLPHE.   When love turns into hatred, it means that it was tainted from the start.

HENRIETTE.   [*In a quieter mood.*]   What am I to do? Tell me, you who are the only one that understands me.

ADOLPHE.   But you don't want any sermons.

HENRIETTE.   Have you nothing else to offer me?

ADOLPHE.   Nothing else. But they have helped me.

HENRIETTE.   Preach away then!

ADOLPHE.   Try to turn your hatred against yourself. Put the knife to the evil spot in yourself, for it is there that *your* trouble roots.

HENRIETTE.   Explain yourself.

ADOLPHE.   Part from Maurice first of all, so that you cannot nurse your qualms of conscience together. Break off your career as an artist, for the only thing that led you into it was a craving for freedom and fun—as they call it. And you have seen how much fun there is in it. Then go home to your mother.

HENRIETTE. Never!

ADOLPHE. Some other place then.

HENRIETTE. I suppose you know, Adolphe, that I have guessed your secret and why you wouldn't accept the prize?

ADOLPHE. Oh, I assumed that you would understand a half-told story.

HENRIETTE. Well—what did you do to get peace?

ADOLPHE. What I have suggested: I became conscious of my guilt, repented, decided to turn over a new leaf, and arranged my life like that of a penitent.

HENRIETTE. How can you repent when, like me, you have no conscience? Is repentance an act of grace bestowed on you as faith is?

ADOLPHE. Everything is a grace, but it isn't granted unless you seek it— Seek!

HENRIETTE *remains silent.*

ADOLPHE. But don't wait beyond the allotted time, or you may harden yourself until you tumble down into the irretrievable.

HENRIETTE. [*After a pause.*] Is conscience fear of punishment?

ADOLPHE. No, it is the horror inspired in our better selves by the misdeeds of our lower selves.

HENRIETTE. Then I must have a conscience also?

ADOLPHE. Of course you have, but——

HENRIETTE. Tell me, Adolphe, are you what they call religious?

ADOLPHE. Not the least bit.

HENRIETTE. It's all so queer— What is religion?

ADOLPHE. Frankly speaking, I don't know! And I don't think anybody else can tell you. Sometimes it appears to me like a punishment, for nobody becomes religious without having a bad conscience.

HENRIETTE. Yes, it is a punishment. Now I know what to do. Good-bye, Adolphe!

ADOLPHE. You'll go away from here?

HENRIETTE. Yes, I am going—to where you said. Good-bye my friend! Good-bye, Madame Catherine!

MME. CATHERINE. Have you to go in such a hurry?

HENRIETTE. Yes.

ADOLPHE. Do you want me to go with you?

HENRIETTE. No, it wouldn't do. I am going alone, alone as I came here, one day in Spring, thinking that I belonged where I don't belong, and believing there was something called freedom, which does not exist. Good-bye! [*Goes out.*

MME. CATHERINE. I hope that lady never comes back, and I wish she had never come here at all!

ADOLPHE. Who knows but that she may have had some mission to fill here? And at any rate she deserves pity, endless pity.

MME. CATHERINE. I don't deny it, for all of us deserve that.

ADOLPHE. And she has even done less wrong than the rest of us.

MME. CATHERINE. That's possible, but not probable.

ADOLPHE. You are always so severe, Madame Catherine. Tell me: have you never done anything wrong?

MME. CATHERINE. [*Startled.*] Of course, as I am a sinful human creature. But if you have been on thin ice and fallen in, you have a right to tell others to keep away. And you may do so without being held severe or uncharitable. Didn't I say to Monsieur Maurice the moment that lady entered here: Look out! Keep away! And he didn't, and so he fell in. Just like a naughty, self-willed child. And when a man acts like that he has to have a spanking, like any disobedient youngster.

ADOLPHE. Well, hasn't he had his spanking?

MME. CATHERINE. Yes, but it does not seem to have been enough, as he is still going around complaining.

ADOLPHE. That's a very popular interpretation of the whole intricate question.

MME. CATHERINE. Oh, pish! You do nothing but philosophise about your vices, and while you are still at it the police come along and solve the riddle. Now please leave me alone with my accounts!

ADOLPHE. There's Maurice now.

MME. CATHERINE. Yes, God bless him!

MAURICE. [*Enters, his face very flushed, and takes a seat near* ADOLPHE.] Good evening.

MME. CATHERINE *nods and goes on figuring.*

ADOLPHE. Well, how's everything with you?

MAURICE. Oh, beginning to clear up.

ADOLPHE. [*Hands him a newspaper, which* MAURICE *does not take.*] So you have read the paper?

MAURICE. No, I don't read the papers any longer. There's nothing but infamies in them.

ADOLPHE. But you had better read it first——

MAURICE. No, I don't! It's nothing but lies— But listen: I have found a new clue. Can you guess who committed that murder?

ADOLPHE. Nobody, nobody!

MAURICE. Do you know where Henriette was during that quarter hour when the child was left alone?— She was *there*! And it is she who has done it!

ADOLPHE. You are crazy, man.

MAURICE. Not I, but Henriette, is crazy. She suspects me and has threatened to report me.

ADOLPHE. Henriette was here a while ago, and she used the self-same words as you. Both of you are crazy, for it has been proved by a second autopsy that the child died from a well-known disease, the name of which I have forgotten.

MAURICE. It isn't true!

ADOLPHE. That's what she said also. But the official report is printed in the paper.

MAURICE. A report? Then they have made it up!

ADOLPHE. And that's also what she said. The two of you are suffering from the same mental trouble. But with her I got far enough to make her realise her own condition.

MAURICE. Where did she go?

ADOLPHE. She went far away from here to begin a new life.

MAURICE. Hm, hm!— Did you go to the funeral?

ADOLPHE. I did.

MAURICE. Well?

ADOLPHE.   Well, Jeanne seemed resigned and didn't have a hard word to say about you.

MAURICE.   She is a good woman.

ADOLPHE.   Why did you desert her then?

MAURICE.   Because I *was* crazy—blown up with pride especially—and then we had been drinking champagne——

ADOLPHE.   Can you understand now why Jeanne wept when you drank champagne?

MAURICE.   Yes, I understand now—— And for that reason I have already written to her and asked her to forgive me—— Do you think she will forgive me?

ADOLPHE.   I think so, for it's not like her to hate anybody.

MAURICE.   Do you think she will forgive me completely, so that she will come back to me?

ADOLPHE.   Well, I don't know about *that*. You have shown yourself so poor in keeping faith that it is doubtful whether she will trust her fate to you any longer.

MAURICE.   But I can feel that her fondness for me has not ceased, and I know she will come back to me.

ADOLPHE.   How can you know that? How can you believe it? Didn't you even suspect her and that decent brother of hers of having sent the police after Henriette out of revenge?

MAURICE.   But I don't believe it any longer—that is to say, I guess that fellow Emile is a pretty slick customer.

MME. CATHERINE.   Now look here! What are you saying of Monsieur Emile? Of course, he is nothing but a workman, but if everybody kept as straight as he—— There is no flaw in him, but a lot of sense and tact.

EMILE [*Enters.*]   Monsieur Gérard?

MAURICE.   That's me.

EMILE.   Pardon me, but I have something to say to you in private.

MAURICE.   Go right on. We are all friends here.

The ABBÉ *enters and sits down.*

EMILE. [*With a glance at the* ABBÉ.]   Perhaps after——

MAURICE.   Never mind. The Abbé is also a friend, although he and I differ.

EMILE.   You know who I am, Monsieur Gérard?   **My**

sister has asked me to give you this package as an answer to your letter.

MAURICE *takes the package and opens it.*

EMILE.   And now I have only to add, seeing as I am in a way my sister's guardian, that, on her behalf as well as my own, I acknowledge you free of all obligations, now when the natural tie between you does not exist any longer.

MAURICE.   But you must have a grudge against me?

EMILE.   Must I?   I can't see why.   On the other hand, I should like to have a declaration from you, here in the presence of your friends, that you don't think either me or my sister capable of such a meanness as to send the police after Mademoiselle Henriette.

MAURICE.   I wish to take back what I said, and I offer you my apology, if you will accept it.

EMILE.   It is accepted.   And I wish all of you a good evening.   [*Goes out.*

EVERYBODY.   Good evening!

MAURICE.   The tie and the gloves which Jeanne gave me for the opening night of my play, and which I let Henriette throw into the fireplace.   Who can have picked them up?   Everything is dug up; everything comes back!—   And when she gave them to me in the cemetery, she said she wanted me to look fine and handsome, so that other people would like me also—   And she herself stayed at home—   This hurt her too deeply, and well it might.   I have no right to keep company with decent human beings.   Oh, have I done this?   Scoffed at a gift coming from a good heart; scorned a sacrifice offered to my own welfare.   This was what I threw away in order to get—a laurel that is lying on the rubbish heap, and a bust that would have belonged in the pillory—Abbé, now I come over to you.

ABBÉ.   Welcome!

MAURICE.   Give me the word that I need.

ABBÉ.   Do you expect me to contradict your self-accusations and inform you that you have done nothing wrong?

MAURICE.   Speak the right word!

ABBÉ.   With your leave, I'll say then that I have found your behaviour just as abominable as you have found it yourself.

MAURICE.   What can I do, what can I do, to get out of this?

ABBÉ.   You know as well as I do.

MAURICE.   No, I only know that I am lost, that my life is spoiled, my career cut off, my reputation in this world ruined for ever.

ABBÉ.   And so you are looking for a new existence in some better world, which you are now beginning to believe in?

MAURICE.   Yes, that's it.

ABBÉ.   You have been living in the flesh and you want now to live in the spirit.   Are you then so sure that this world has no more attractions for you?

MAURICE.   None whatever!   Honour is a phantom; gold, nothing but dry leaves; women, mere intoxicants.   Let me hide myself behind your consecrated walls and forget this horrible dream that has filled two days and lasted two eternities.

ABBÉ.   All right!   But this is not the place to go into the matter more closely.   Let us make an appointment for this evening at nine o'clock in the Church of St. Germain.   For I am going to preach to the inmates of St. Lazare, and that may be your first step along the hard road of penitence.

MAURICE.   Penitence?

ABBÉ.   Well, didn't you wish——

MAURICE.   Yes, yes!

ABBÉ.   Then we have vigils between midnight and two o'clock.

MAURICE.   That will be splendid!

ABBÉ.   Give me your hand that you will not look back.

MAURICE.   [*Rising, holds out his hand.*]   Here is my hand, and my will goes with it.

SERVANT GIRL.   [*Enters from the kitchen.*]   A telephone call for Monsieur Maurice.

MAURICE.   From whom?

SERVANT GIRL.   From the theatre.

MAURICE *tries to get away, but the* ABBÉ *holds on to his hand.*

ABBÉ.   [*To the* SERVANT GIRL.]   Find out what it is.

SERVANT GIRL.   They want to know if Monsieur Maurice is going to attend the performance to-night.

ABBÉ.   [*To* MAURICE, *who is trying to get away.*]   No, I won't let you go.

MAURICE.   What performance is that?

ADOLPHE.   Why don't you read the paper?

MME. CATHERINE *and the* ABBÉ.   He hasn't read the paper?

MAURICE.   It's all lies and slander.   [*To the* SERVANT GIRL.]   Tell them that I am engaged for this evening: I am going to church.

      The SERVANT GIRL *goes out into the kitchen.*

ADOLPHE.   As you don't want to read the paper, I shall have to tell you that your play has been put on again, now when you are exonerated.   And your literary friends have planned a demonstration for this evening in recognition of your indisputable talent.

MAURICE.   It isn't true.

EVERYBODY.   It is true.

MAURICE.   [*After a pause.*]   I have not deserved it!

ABBÉ.   Good!

ADOLPHE.   And, furthermore, Maurice——

MAURICE.   [*Hiding his face in his hands.*]   Furthermore!

MME. CATHERINE.   One hundred thousand francs!   Do you see now that they come back to you?   And the villa outside the city.   Everything is coming back except Mademoiselle Henriette.

ABBÉ.   [*Smiling.*]   You ought to take this matter a little more seriously, Madame Catherine.

MME. CATHERINE.   Oh, I cannot—I just can't keep serious any longer!

    [*She breaks into open laughter, which she vainly tries to smother with her handkerchief.*

ADOLPHE.   Say, Maurice, the play begins at eight.

ABBÉ.   But the church services are at nine.

ADOLPHE.   Maurice!

MME. CATHERINE.   Let us hear what the end is going to be, Monsieur Maurice.

      MAURICE *drops his head on the table, in his arms.*

ADOLPHE.   Loose him, Abbé.

ABBÉ.   No, it is not for me to loose or bind.   He must do that himself.

MAURICE. [*Rising.*] Well, I go with the Abbé.

ABBÉ. No, my young friend. I have nothing to give you but a scolding, which you can give yourself. And you owe a duty to yourself and to your good name. That you have got through with this as quickly as you have is to me a sign that you have suffered your punishment as intensely as if it had lasted an eternity. And when Providence absolves you there is nothing for me to add.

MAURICE. But why did the punishment have to be so hard when I was innocent?

ABBÉ. Hard? Only two days! And you were not innocent. For we have to stand responsible for our thoughts and words and desires also. And in your thought you became a murderer when your evil self wished the life out of your child.

MAURICE. You are right. But my decision is made. To-night I will meet you at the church in order to have a reckoning with myself—but to-morrow evening I go to the theatre.

MME. CATHERINE. A good solution, Monsieur Maurice.

ADOLPHE. Yes, that is the solution. Whew!

ABBÉ. Yes, so it is!

Curtain.

GUSTAVUS VASA
(GUSTAF VASA)
HISTORIC DRAMA IN FIVE ACTS
1899

CHARACTERS

GUSTAVUS I, *King of Sweden*

MARGARET LEIJONHUFVUD (*Lion-Head*), *his second Queen*

PRINCE ERIC, *the only son of the King's first marriage*

PRINCE JOHAN, *eldest son of the King's second marriage*

EBBA CARLSDAUGHTER, *a nun at the convent of Vreta and mother-in-law of the King*

MASTER OLAVUS PETRI, *commonly known as Master Olof*

CHRISTINE, *his wife*

REGINALD, *their son*

HERMAN ISRAEL, *a councillor of the free city of Luebeck*

JACOB ISRAEL, *his son*

MONS NILSSON OF ASPEBODA

ANDERS PERSSON OF RANKHYTTAN } *free miners*

INGHEL HANSSON } *of Dalecarlia*

NILS OF SÖDERBY

JORGHEN PERSSON, *secretary to* PRINCE ERIC

MASTER STIG, *pastor at Copperberg (Falun), Dalecarlia*

MONS NILSSON'S WIFE

BARBRO, *his daughter*

AGDA, *a barmaid*

KARIN MONSDAUGHTER, *a flower girl*

MARCUS } *Hanseatic clerks*

DAVID

ENGELBRECHT, *a free miner who was one of the Dalecarlian ski-runners that overtook* GUSTAVUS VASA *on his flight to Norway and brought him back to head the Dalecarlian revolt against King Christian II of Denmark*

CAPTAIN OF THE GUARD

A COURTIER

A MESSENGER

TWO BEGGARS

HISTORICAL NOTE

Gustavus Vasa, the maker of modern Sweden and founder of the Vasa dynasty, which ruled till 1818, was born in 1496. He belonged to the noble family of Ericson, the cognomen Vasa being a later addition. Sweden was at that time a somewhat restive partner in the union of the three Scandinavian countries under Christian II of Denmark, and in 1516 Gustavus was treacherously carried off to Denmark as a hostage. In 1519 he escaped to the Hansa town of Luebeck and in the following year, with help from Luebeck, made his way back to Sweden. For some time he lived among the peasants of Dalecarlia, trying to raise the country against the Danes, but was on the point of retiring to Norway in despair when news came of the massacre of some eighty Swedish nobles by the Danish king, known as the "blood-bath of Stockholm." The Dalecarlians now chose him as their leader, and after a struggle of about two years he succeeded, with help from Luebeck, in finally expelling the Danes in 1523, in which year he was elected King.

His long reign in some respects resembles those of the Tudors in England. His task, like theirs, was to bring order into a disorganised country and to build up, almost from scratch, an efficient central government on a sound financial basis. He accomplished this by an intensely laborious absolutism which found no detail too small for his personal attention and shrank from no means necessary to maintain his authority: he had, in fact, to put down numerous rebellions among his former friends the peasants, the last of them headed by Niels Dacke.

Both the nobles and the clergy had, on the whole, sided with the Danes in the struggle for independence, and Gustavus set himself to break the power of both. It was thus for political rather than religious reasons that he embraced the new doctrines which Olavus Petri (" Master Olof ") and some other ecclesiastics brought home with them from Germany. Protestantism

was formally established in 1527, and most of the rich estates of
the old Church fell to the Crown.   He also had to deal with the
pretensions of his old backer, Luebeck, which was determined to
keep its hold on the Baltic trade and whose demands as a
" creditor-nation " became intolerable—on one occasion the
largest bell in every church in Sweden was demanded in part
satisfaction of these claims—and finally led to a rupture, which
ended in a composition whereby the account was declared closed
and the commercial privileges of Luebeck greatly reduced
(1536).   In 1544 the Diet declared the crown hereditary in the
Vasa family; he died in 1560.

Gustavus was married three times.   His first wife, Catherine
of Saxe-Lauenberg, with whom he lived unhappily, was the
mother of his eldest son Eric.   His second, and far more successful, marriage was with a Swedish lady, Margaret Lejonhuvud,
who bore him four children, John, Magnus, Charles and Cecilia.
After her death he married her young niece, Catherine Stenbock.

He was succeeded by his eldest son Eric (Eric XIV).   The
new King was intelligent but unbalanced, and quarrelled with
his half-brothers, the nobles and Denmark, with which he became involved in a disastrous and unnecessary war.   (He also
attempted to marry Queen Elizabeth of England.)   By 1567
he had become manifestly insane, and in the next year he was
deposed in favour of his half-brother John.   His favourite,
Göran Persson, who was regarded as his evil genius, was executed.
He himself was thenceforth kept in close confinement and mur-
dered in 1577.

A. H.

GUSTAVUS VASA

SCENARIO

ACT I

ACT I

The main living-room in Mons Nilsson's *house at Copperberg (which is the old name of the present city of Falun in Dalecarlia).*

There is a door in the rear, with a window on either side, through which are visible small city houses with snow-covered roofs and the flames belching from many blast-furnaces. A large open fireplace with mantelpiece occupies the centre of the right wall. A fine log fire is going in the fireplace. On the same side, nearer the footlights, is a door

A long table fills the middle of the floor. At its farther end stands an armchair with cushions on the seat and bright textiles draped over the back and the arm supports. Wooden benches run along the two sides of the table.

Wooden seats are placed along the left wall.

237

Above the wainscoting of the walls appear large, simple frescoes
depicting the adventures of GUSTAVUS VASA *in Dalecarlia (at*
the beginning of the war of liberation). The one at the left
of the rear door shows him at the home of Master John at
Svärdsjö; the one at the right pictures him threshing in the
barn of ANDERS PERSSON OF RANKHYTTAN *(while Danish*
soldiers are searching the place for him).
The ringing of a church-bell is heard from the outside as the
curtain rises.

MONS NILSSON *is seated at the table, writing.   His* WIFE *is*
arranging tankards and beakers of silver on the mantelshelf.

MONS.   That's four o'clock, is it not?
WIFE.   Of course.
MONS.   Sounds like fire.
WIFE.   Is that any special sound?
MONS.   Yes, it sounds like " help-help, help-help! "
WIFE.   That's the way it has sounded ever since the King
carried off our bells, it seems to me.
MONS.   Be quiet!   And don't talk behind anybody's back.
The King will soon be here himself.
WIFE.   Has the King sent word of his visit, as you have put
everything in order to receive him?
MONS.   Not exactly, but when he sends word that he is coming
to Copperberg, it is not to be expected that he will pass by his
friend Mons Nilsson, who helped him in the days of trial, and
who has stood by him both against Master Knut and Peder the
Chancellor, not to speak of the False Sture.[1]   And he acted as
godfather for my girl besides.
WIFE.   That was a good while ago; but when the King's

[1] Peder Jacobsson Sunnanväder, bishop at Vesterås, and his archdeacon, Master
Knut, both members of the old Catholic clergy, tried to raise the Dalecarlians
against the King in 1524–5, when his hold on the new throne was still very precarious.   The False Sture was a young Dalecarlian named John Hansson, who
had acquired gentle manners as a servant in noble houses and who posed as the
natural son of Sten Sture the Younger, " National Director " of Sweden until
1520.   This pretender, who headed another Dalecarlian uprising in 1527, figures
also in Ibsen's early historical drama, " Lady Inger."   The taking of the church-
bells mentioned by Mons Nilsson's wife took place in 1531 and resulted in the
killing of several of the King's representatives by the Dalecarlians.

bailiff came here to get the bells two years ago, you helped to kill him.

MONS. That was two years ago, and I guess he was set on having our heads at that time. But just then King Christian broke into the country from Norway. Our own King turned meek as a lamb at once, and when he asked us for help, we Dalecarlians stood by him like one man, and gave him all the help he wanted. So I think we can call it even.

WIFE. So *you* think, but the King never calls it even except when it is to his own advantage.

MONS. Perhaps not. But as long as Christian still is free, he will not dare to break with us.

WIFE. Well, is Christian still free?

MONS. I have heard nothing to the contrary. Anyhow, the King owes us such a lot of money that, leaving old friendship aside . . .

WIFE. God bless you! And I hope He will protect you from the friend that is always breaking his word and safe-conduct!

MONS. Don't open the old wounds, but let bygones be bygones.

WIFE. If you do that, and he won't, you can hardly call it a reconciliation. Take care!

MONS. The sound of that bell is really dreadful!

WIFE. So it is to my ears, because it always reminds me of the big Mary, which the bailiff took away. Do you remember when the Mary was cast out of the best refined copper and the whole town brought milk and cream to give the clay of the form more firmness—and then, when the melt was ready, we threw in one-half of our table silver to improve the tone? It was baptised at Candlemas and rung for the first time at the burial of my father. . . . And then it went to Herman Israel at Luebeck, who made coin out of it.

MONS. All that is perfectly true, but now it *must* be forgotten—or we shall never have peace.

BARBRO, *their daughter, enters with a basket full of finely chopped spruce branches; she is dressed in black and white, and so are several younger children who follow her, also carrying baskets. All of them begin to spread the chopped spruce over the floor.*

WIFE. [*To* MONS.] Is there to be a funeral?

MONS. No, but not being the season, we couldn't get any leaves.

WIFE. I think the children might put off their mourning at least.

MONS. No, that's just what they should not do, because when the King asks whom they are mourning—well, what are they to answer, Barbro?

BARBRO. "We mourn our beloved teacher, Pastor John at Svärdsjö."

MONS. And what are you to say, if the King asks you why?

BABRO. "Because he was an early friend of King Gustavus and saved his precious life for our country."

MONS. What year was that?

BARBRO. "The very year when Christian the Tyrant cut the head off the Swedish nobility."[1]

MONS. That's right, children. And over there you see the picture of Master John when he is holding the towel for the outlaw who has been threshing in the barn. [*To his* WIFE.] On the other hand, it is not necessary to tell the children that the King took his friend's head two years ago.

WIFE. Have you really that much sense left?—Do you think the King likes any reminder of a deed that has brought him so little honour?

MONS. Let him like it or dislike it, he'll have to swallow it. It was an ugly deed, and Master John was a saint and a martyr, who died for his faith—the faith of his childhood, which he would not forswear.

BARBRO. [*Standing by the armchair at the end of the table.*] Is the King to sit here?

[1] In 1520 Christian II of Denmark made a temporarily successful effort to bring Sweden back into the union with the other two Scandinavian kingdoms. Having defeated the Swedish "National Director," Sten Sture the Younger, and been admitted to the city of Stockholm, he caused about eighty of the most influential members of the Swedish nobility to be beheaded in a single day. That was the "Bloodbath of Stockholm," by which King Gustavus lost his father and brother-in-law. On the same occasion his mother and sister were imprisoned, and both died before they could be set free.

MONS. Yes, child, that's where the marvellous man of God is to sit when he visits his friend Mons Nilsson of Aspeboda. His whole life is like a miracle story, children: how the Lord guided him out of a Danish prison up to Dalecarlia, and how, after many hardships, he finally freed his country from oppression. Those pictures on the walls tell you the whole story, down to the moment when the ski-runner overtook him at Sälen, close by the Norwegian border-line.

BABRO. [*Looking at the picture just indicated.*] Is it true, father, that the ski-runner was named Engelbrecht, like the great chieftain we had in the past century?

MONS. Yes, it's true, child, and we used to speak of it as " the finger of God," but now we call it mere superstition.

WIFE. Don't put that sort of thing into the children's heads!

MONS. Oh, keep quiet! I teach the children nothing but what is right and proper.—And bear in mind, little girls, that, no matter what you may hear, you must never believe or say anything bad of the King. Earth bears no heavier burden than a thankless man. And for that reason you must sing the ballad of King Gustav when he comes here. Do you still remember it?

BARBRO. Oh, yes!

MONS. Let me hear you read it then.

BARBRO. [*Reciting.*]
> " King Gustav, he rode his trusty steed
>   Across the battle-field;
> Have thanks, my brave Dalecarlians,
>   For your true loyalty."

CHILDREN. [*In chorus.*]
> " Have thanks, my brave Dalecarlians,
>   For your true loyalty."

BARBRO.
> " You have by my side been fighting
>   Like faithful Swedish men.
> If God will spare my life-blood,
>   I'll do you ·good in stead."

CHILDREN.
> " If God will spare my life-blood,
>   I'll do you good in stead!"

MONS. That's good, children. Go back to your own room now, and be ready when the time comes.

BARBRO *and the* CHILDREN. [*As they start to go out to the right.*] But won't the King frighten us?

MONS. Oh, he is not at all dangerous, and he is very fond of children. Besides, he is your godfather, Barbro.

BARBRO *and the* CHILDREN *leave the room.*

WIFE. Do you know what you are doing?

MONS. Hope so! Of course, I know what you mean.

WIFE. What do I mean?

MONS. That I should take your advice. So I have done in in the past, and it has ended badly every time.

WIFE. Try it once more!

MONS. No!

WIFE. Then—may the will of God be done!   [*Pause.*

MONS. That's the longest afternoon I have ever lived through!—And my friends don't seem to be coming.

WIFE. Yes, I think I hear them outside.

MONS. Well, you were right that time!

The stamping of feet is heard from the hallway outside. Then enter: ANDERS PERSSON OF RANKHYTTAN, NILS SÖDERBY, INGHEL HANSSON, *and* MASTER STIG [*in clerical costume*]. *Each one says as he comes into the room:* "Good evening, everybody!"

MONS. [*Shaking hands with them.*] God be with you, Anders Persson! God be with you, Nils Söderby! God be with you, Inghel Hansson! God be with you, Master Stig! Come forward and be seated.

All seat themselves at the long table.

ANDERS. You are getting ready, I see.

MONS. So we are.—And where's the King?

ANDERS. The other side of the hill, says the ski-runner that just returned.

MONS. As near as that?—And what errand is supposed to bring him here?

ANDERS. Ask Nils of Söderby.

NILS. They say he is headed for Norway to fight Christian.

INGHEL. There are others who think that he is coming to

thank us Dalecarlians for the good help rendered in his last fight.

STIG.   That would not be like him.

ANDERS.   To thank anybody—no, indeed!

MONS.   Do you think there is any cause for fear?

NILS.   Not while Christian is still free.

INGHEL.   It's queer that we should have to look to Christian for safety.

STIG.   We knew what we had, but not what we might get. Christian took the heads of the noble lords and left the people alone.   This one leaves the lords alone and rides roughshod over the people.   Who should be called a tyrant?

MONS.   Be quiet now!

ANDERS.   In other words, the last war of liberation was fought *against* our liberator.   Did we know at all what we were doing at that time?

INGHEL.   We were to clear the country of the Danes; and the first man to raise his hand for the King against the Danes in our parts was Rasmus Dane, who killed Nils Westgoth.   That was a strange beginning. . . .

NILS.   A strange beginning, indeed, but just like the ending. [*To* MONS'S WIFE.]   Look out for the silver, goodwife!

She turns and looks inquiringly at him.

NILS.   The King is coming.

MONS.   In the name of the Lord, be quiet!   That kind of talk will bring no peace.—All that you say is true, of course, but what has happened was the will of Providence——

STIG.   Which let the children have their will in order that they should see their own folly.

ANDERS.   Are you quite sure that the King will visit you, Mons Nilsson?

MONS.   What a question!

ANDERS.   Remember Master John!

MONS.   Let us forget!   Everything must be forgotten.

ANDERS.   No wonder if you and Nils want to forget that you burned the King's house at Hedemora and looted Räfvelstad two years ago!   But *he* will never forget it.

The roll of muffled drums is heard from the outside.

ALL.   [*Leaping to their feet.*]   What's that?

MONS. Don't you know the hornet that buzzes before it stings?

ANDERS. That's the kind of noise he made that Ash Wednesday at Tuna Flat.

INGHEL. Don't mention that blood-bath, or I can't control myself. [*Passionately.*] Don't talk of it!

NILS. Hear him spinning, spinning like a cat! No, don't trust him!

The roll of the drums comes nearer.

STIG. Might it not be wise for you, as personal friends of the King, to meet him and bid the stern master welcome?

MONS. I wonder. Then he might not come here afterwards. . . .

WIFE. Stay, Mons! Stay where you are!

MONS. Oh, the place smells of spruce, and the drums are flattened as for a funeral. [*Somebody raps three times at the door from the outside.*] Who's that?

[*He goes to the door and opens it.*

WIFE. [*To* MASTER STIG *as she leaves the room by the door at the right.*] Pray for us!

MASTER OLAVUS *and* HERMAN ISRAEL *enter.*

MONS. Who is doing me the honour?

OLAVUS. I am the acting secretary of his Highness, the King. And this is the venerable representative of the free city of Luebeck.

MONS. Come in, my good sirs, and—let us hear the news!

OLAVUS. The King is here and has pitched his camp on Falu Flat. Personally he has taken his abode at the Gildhall of Saint Jorghen.

MONS. What is the errand that has made the King cross Långhed Forest and Brunbeck Ford without permission and safe-conduct?[1]

---

[1] Långheden is a wooded upland plain on the southern border of Dalecarlia. Brunbeck Ferry or Ford was for centuries the main crossing point of the Dal River for all who entered the province of Dalecarlia from the south. Rendered arrogant by the part they had played in the wars of liberation between 1434 and 1524, the Dalecarlians had established a claim that not even the King himself had the right to pass those two border points at the head of an armed force without first having obtained their permission.

OLAVUS. He hasn't told.

MONS. Then I had better go and ask him.

OLAVUS. With your leave, this is the message our gracious lord, the King, sends you through us: " Greetings to the goodly miners of the Copperberg, and let every man stay in his own house." If he desires speech with any one, that one will be called.

MONS. What is the meaning of it?

OLAVUS. [*Seating himself.*] I don't know.   [*Pause.*

ANDERS. Has the Danish war come to an end, sir?

OLAVUS. I don't know.

ANDERS. Do you know with whom you are talking?

OLAVUS. No, I don't.

ANDERS. I am Anders Persson of Rankhyttan. Have you ever heard that name before?

OLAVUS. Yes—it's a good name.

HERMAN ISRAEL *has in the meantime been studying the wall paintings and the silver on the mantelpiece. He wears a pair of large, horn-rimmed eye-glasses. At last he seats himself in the armchair at the end of the table.*

MONS. [*Indicating* ISRAEL *to* OLAVUS.] Is that chap from Luebeck a royal person, too?

OLAVUS. [*In a low voice.*]. No, he is not, but he is in charge of the national debt, and we must never forget that our gracious King was able to free our country of the Danes *only* with the help of Luebeck.

MONS. With the help of Luebeck *only?* And how about the Dalecarlians?

OLAVUS. Oh, of course, they helped, too.

MONS. Does he speak Swedish?

OLAVUS. I don't think so, but I am not sure of it.

MONS. Is that so?

OLAVUS. We happened to arrive together, but I have not yet spoken to him.

MONS. Very strange! I suppose the King has sent him?

OLAVUS. Probably.

MONS. Perhaps he is the fellow who buys up the bells?

OLAVUS. Perhaps.

MONS. And the church silver!

OLAVUS. And the church silver, too!

MONS. What was his name again?

OLAVUS. Herman Israel.

MONS. Oh, Israel!

He whispers to ANDERS PERSSON, *who, in turn, whispers to the rest.*

A rap at the door is heard. MASTER OLAVUS *gets up quickly and opens the door.*

A MESSENGER *in full armour enters, whispers something to* MASTER OLAVUS, *and leaves again.*

OLAVUS. Our gracious lord, the King, requests Inghel Hansson to meet him at Saint Jorghen's Gild.

INGHEL. [*Rising.*] Well, well, am I to be the first?

NILS. The oldest first.

MONS. Stand up for yourself, Inghel, and tell the truth. The King is a gracious gentleman who won't mind a plain word in proper time.

INGHEL. Don't you worry. I have said my say to kings before now.   [*He goes out.*

OLAVUS. Well, Nils, how is the mining nowadays?

NILS. Not bad, thank you. The last fall flood left a little water in the mine, but otherwise we have nothing to complain of.

OLAVUS. Times are good, then?

NILS. Well, you might say so. . . . Hm! Good times will mean better taxes, I suppose?

OLAVUS I know nothing about the taxes. [*Pause; then to* ANDERS PERSSON.] And how about the crops? I hear you have plenty of tilled ground, too.

ANDERS. Oh, yes, and plenty of cattle in the pastures, too.

OLAVUS. Old Dalecarlia is a pretty good country, is it not?

MONS [*Giving* ANDERS *a poke with his elbow.*] Yes, everything is fat here—dripping with fat, so that one can eat the bark off the trees even.

OLAVUS. Yes, they have told me that you have to eat bark and chew resin now and then. Is that a common thing or does it happen only once in a while?

NILS. When the famine comes, you have to eat what you can get.

OLAVUS. [*To* MASTER STIG, *who has been keeping in the background.*] There is something you should know, Master Stig. How was it during the last famine, when the King sent grain to be distributed here: did it go to those who needed it?

STIG. Yes, it did, although there was not enough of it.

OLAVUS. [*To* ANDERS.] Was there not enough of it?

ANDERS. That depends on what you mean by "enough."

OLAVUS. [*To* MONS.] Do you know what is meant by "enough," Mons Nilsson?

MONS. Oh, well, everybody knows that.

OLAVUS. [*To* STIG.] As we now know what is meant by "enough," I ask you, Master Stig Larsson, if anybody perished from hunger during the last famine.

STIG. Man doth not live by bread only. . . .

OLAVUS. There you spoke a true word, Master Stig, but . . .

A rap on the door is heard. MASTER OLAVUS *opens. The same* MESSENGER *appears, whispers to him, and leaves again.*

OLAVUS. The King requests Nils Söderby to meet him at Saint Jorghen's Gildhall.

NILS. Won't Inghel Hansson come back first?

OLAVUS. I don't know.

NILS. Well, nobody is afraid here, and . . .

OLAVUS. What have you to be afraid of?

NILS. Nothing! [*To his friends.*] The big bell at Mora has not been taken out of Siljan valley yet, Anders Persson and Mons Nilsson. That's a devil of a bell, and when it begins to tinkle, they can hear it way over in Norway, and fourteen thousand men stand like one!

OLAVUS. I don't understand what you mean.

NILS. [*Shaking hands with* ANDERS *and* MONS.] But you two understand! God bless you and defend you!

MONS. What do you mean?

ANDERS. What are you thinking of, Nils?

NILS. Oh, my thoughts are running so fast that I can't keep up with them. But one thing I am sure of: that it's going hard with Inghel Hansson. [*He goes out.*

OLAVUS. Is this sulphur smoke always hanging over the place?

Mons. Mostly when the wind is in the east.

Mons *and* Anders *withdraw to the left corner of the room and sit down there.* Master Stig *shows plainly that he is much alarmed.*

Olavus. Is it the quartz or the pyrites that make the worst smoke?

Anders. Why do you ask?

Olavus. That's a poor answer!

Mons. May I ask you in return whether King Christian still is free?

Olavus. [*Looking hard at him.*] Do you put your trust in the enemy? [*Pause.*] What kind of a man is Nils of Söderby?

Mons. His friends think him better and his enemies worse than anybody else.

Olavus. What kind of a bell in the Siljan valley was that you spoke of?

Mons. It's the largest one in all Dalecarlia.

Olavus. Have you many bells of that kind?

Anders. Of the kind that calls the people to arms we have still a lot.

Mons *pokes him warningly.*

Olavus. I am glad to hear it, and I am sure it will please his Highness still more. Are the people attending church diligently, Master Stig?

Stig. I can't say that they are.

Olavus. Are the priests bad, or is the pure word of God not preached here?

Stig. There are no bad priests here, and nothing but the pure word of God is preached!

Olavus. That's the best thing I have heard yet! Nothing but the pure word of God, you say! [*Pause.*] Nils intimated a while ago that fourteen thousand men will take up arms when you ring the big bell at Mora. That was mere boasting, I suppose?

Mons. Oh, if you ring it the right way, I think sixteen thousand will come. What do you say, Anders Persson?

Anders. Sixteen, you say? I should say eighteen!

OLAVUS. Fine!   Then we shall ring it the right way when the Dane comes next time.   Only seven thousand answered the last call—to fight the *enemies* of our country.

MONS. [*To* ANDERS.]   That fellow is dangerous. We had better keep quiet after this.

STIG. [*To* OLAVUS.]   Why has Inghel Hansson not come back?

OLAVUS. I don't know.

STIG. Then I'll go and find out.

He goes to the door and opens it, but is stopped by the MES-SENGER, *who is now accompanied by several pikemen.*

MASTER OLAVUS *meets the* MESSENGER, *who whispers to him.*

OLAVUS. Master Stig Larsson is commanded before the King at once!

STIG. Commanded?   Who commands here?

OLAVUS. The King.

MONS. [*Leaping to his feet.*]   Treachery!

OLAVUS. Exactly: treachery and traitors!—If you don't go at once, Master Stig, you'll ride bareback!

STIG. To hell!

OLAVUS. Yes, *to* hell!—Away!

[MONS *and* ANDERS *rise and start for the door.*

MONS. Do you know who I am—that I am a free miner and a friend of the King?

OLAVUS. Be seated then, and keep your peace. If you are a friend of the King, there has been a mistake.   Sit down, Anders Persson and Mons Nilsson!   No harm will befall you or anybody else who is innocent.   Let Master Stig go, and don't get excited.   Where does the thought of violence come from, if not from your own bad conscience?

STIG. That's true.   We have done nothing wrong, and no one has threatened us.   Be quiet, friends.   I shall soon be back.

[*He goes out.*

MONS. That's right!

OLAVUS. Throw a stick at the pack, and the one that is hit will yelp.

ANDERS. `[*To* MONS.]   That was stupid of us!   Let us keep calm!   [*Aloud.*]   You see, doctor, one gets suspicious as one grows old, particularly after having seen so many broken words and promises. . . .

OLAVUS. I understand. In these days, when people change masters as the snake changes its skin, a certain instability of mind is easily produced. In young men it may be pardonable, but it is absolutely unpardonable in old and experienced persons.

MONS. As far as age is concerned, there is nothing to say about the King, who still is in his best years. . . .

OLAVUS. And for that reason pardonable. . . .

MONS. [*To* ANDERS.] I think he must be the devil himself!

ANDERS. [*To* OLAVUS.] How long are we to wait here? And what are we to wait for?

OLAVUS. The King's commands, as you ought to know.

MONS. Are we regarded as prisoners, then?

OLAVUS. By no means, but it is not wise to venture out for a while yet.

MONS *and* ANDERS *move from one chair to another and give other evidence of agitation.*

MONS. Some great evil is afoot. I can feel it within me.

ANDERS. It must be very hot in here. . . . I am sweating. Would you like a glass of beer, doctor?

OLAVUS. No, thank you.

ANDERS. Or a glass of wine?

OLAVUS. Not for me, thanks!

MONS. But it's real hock.

MASTER OLAVUS *shakes his head. At that moment drumbeats are heard outside.*

ANDERS. [*Beyond himself.*] In the name of Christ, will this never come to an end?

OLAVUS. [*Rising.*] Yes, this is the end!

[*He goes to the door and opens it.*

The MESSENGER *enters and throws on the table the bloodstained coats of* INGHEL HANSSON, NILS OF SÖDERBY, *and* MASTER STIG.

OLAVUS. Look!

MONS *and* ANDERS. Another blood-bath!

MONS. Without trial or hearing!

OLAVUS. The trial took place two years ago, and sentence was passed. But the King put mercy above justice and let the traitors remain at large to see whether their repentance was seriously meant. When he learned that they remained incorrigible and went on with their rebellious talk as before, he decided to execute the sentences. That's how the matter looks when presented truthfully.

MONS. And yet there was a lot of talk about everything being forgiven and forgotten. . . .

OLAVUS. So it was, provided the same offence was not repeated. But it was repeated, and what might have been forgotten was again remembered. All that is clear as logic. [*To* HERMAN ISRAEL.] These two trustworthy men. . . . [*To* MONS *and* ANDERS.] You are trustworthy, are you not?

MONS *and* ANDERS. Hope so!

OLAVUS. Answer yes or no! Are you trustworthy?

MONS *and* ANDERS. Yes!

OLAVUS. [*To* ISRAEL.] In the presence of you as my witness, syndic, these two trustworthy men have given a true report of conditions in Dalecarlia. They have unanimously assured us that the mines are being worked profitably; that agriculture and cattle-breeding prosper no less than the mining; that famines occur but rarely, and that, during the last one, our gracious King distributed grain in quantities not insufficient, which went to those that really were in need. These trustworthy and upright miners have also confirmed the following facts: that bells to summon the congregations still remain in all the churches; that no bad priests are spreading devices of men, and that nothing is preached here but the pure word of God. You have likewise heard them say, syndic, that the province of Dalecarlia can raise from sixteen to eighteen thousand men capable óf bearing arms—the figures vary as their courage falls or rises. Being in charge of the current debt, and for that reason entitled to know the actual *status* of the country, you have now heard the people declare with their own lips, that all the Dalecarlian grievances are unwarranted, and that those who have spread reports to the contrary are traitors and liars.

MONS. *Veto!*

ANDERS.   I deny it!

OLAVUS.   If you deny your own words, then you are liars twice over!

MONS.   He is drawing the noose tighter!   Better keep silent!

ANDERS.   No, I must speak.   [*To* OLAVUS.]   I want to know what our fate is to be.

OLAVUS.   So you shall.   Your fate is in your own hands. You are invited to Stockholm and given full safe-conduct.   You can travel freely by yourselves.   This is granted you as old friends of the King, to whom he acknowledges a great debt of gratitude.

MONS.   More guile!

OLAVUS.   No guile at all.   Here is the King's safe-conduct, signed by his own hand.

ANDERS.   We know all about his safe-conducts!

MONS.   [*To* ANDERS.]   We must consent and submit in order to gain time!   [*To* OLAVUS.]   Will you let us go into the next room and talk the matter over?

OLAVUS.   You can now go wherever you want—except to the King.

> MONS *and* ANDERS *go towards the left.*

MONS.   [*As he opens the door.*]   We'll bring you an answer shortly.

OLAVUS.   As you please, and when you please.

> [MONS *and* ANDERS *go out.*

OLAVUS.   [*To* ISRAEL.]   A stiff-necked people, true as gold, but full of distrust.

ISRAEL.   A very fine people.

OLAVUS.   Rather stupid, however.   Did you notice how I trapped them?

ISRAEL.   That was good work.   How did you learn to do it?

OLAVUS.   By long observation of innumerable human beings I have been led to conclude at last that vanity is the primal sin and mother of all the vices.   To get the truth out of criminals, I have merely to set them boasting.

ISRAEL.   What wisdom!   What wisdom!   And you are not yet an old man!   But there are modest people, too, and out of these you cannot get the truth, according to what you have just said.

OLAVUS. Modest people boast of their modesty, so that is all one.

ISRAEL. [*Looking attentively at him.*] If you'll pardon me—Master Olavus was your name, I think? You cannot be Olavus Petri?

OLAVUS. I am.

ISRAEL. [*Surprised.*] Who carried out the Reformation?

OLAVUS. I am that man.

ISRAEL. And who was subsequently tried for high treason on suspicion of having known about a plot against the King's life?

OLAVUS. Confidences given me under the seal of confession, so that I had no right to betray them.

ISRAEL. [*Gazing curiously at* OLAVUS.] Hm-hm! [*Pause.*] A mysterious story it was, nevertheless.

OLAVUS. No, I don't think so. Gorius Holst and Hans Bökman were found guilty. And it was so little of a secret, that the people of Hamburg heard of the King's murder as an accomplished fact long before the plot was exposed at Stockholm.

ISRAEL. That is just what I call mysterious, especially as we knew nothing about it at Luebeck.

OLAVUS. Yes, I call that mysterious, too, because the road to Hamburg goes through Luebeck as a rule. [ISRAEL *makes no reply.*] And it was rumoured at the time that Marcus Meyer and Juerghen Wollenweber were no strangers to the plot.

ISRAEL. I have never heard of it, and I don't believe it. [*Pause; then, pointing to the blood-stained coats.*] Must those things stay here?

OLAVUS. Yes, for the present.

ISRAEL. It seems to me that these royal visits are rather sanguinary affairs.

OLAVUS. I don't allow myself to pass judgment on the actions of my King, partly because I am not capable of doing so, and partly because I know there is a judge above him, too, who guides his destiny.

ISRAEL. That is beautifully said and thought. Have you always been equally wise?

OLAVUS. No, but what you have not been you frequently become.   [*Pause.*

ISRAEL. Won't those people in there try to get away?

OLAVUS. That, too, has been foreseen, just as their desire to discuss the matter had been reckoned with. Do you know what they are talking of?

ISRAEL. No, I have not the slightest idea.

OLAVUS. They still imagine that King Christian is free, and they are planning to seek help from him.

ISRAEL. What a senseless thought!

OLAVUS. Especially as Christian is a prisoner.

ISRAEL. It sounds like madness, but when you hear how devoted these good men of the mining districts are to their King, it cannot surprise you that they may have in mind the oath binding them to their only lawful sovereign. . . .

OLAVUS. Now, with your pardon, I *am* surprised. . . .

ISRAEL. Oh, mercy, I am merely putting myself in their place.

OLAVUS. It is always dangerous to put oneself in the place of traitors.   [*Pause.*

BARBRO. [*Entering from the right, followed by the smaller children.*] Is father here? [*She looks around and discovers* ISRAEL *seated in the armchair prepared for the King.*] Goodness, here is the King!

[*She kneels, the other children following her example.*

ISRAEL. No, no, dear children, I am not the King. I am only a poor merchant from Luebeck.

OLAVUS. A noble answer! [*To the children.*] This is Herman Israel, the far-famed and influential councillor, who, with Cord König and Nils Bröms, saved our King out of Danish captivity and enabled him to carry out the war of liberation. You will find him on the picture in Saint Jorghen's Gildhall which represents Gustavus Vasa appearing before the City Council of Luebeck. Honour to the man who has honour deserved. Give homage to the friend of your country and your King.

BARBRO *and the* CHILDREN *clap their hands.*

ISRAEL. [*Rises, evidently touched.*] My dear little friends. . . . All I can do is to thank you. . . . I have really not deserved this. . . . You see, a merchant does nothing except for payment, and I have been richly paid.

OLAVUS. Don't believe him! But bear in mind that there are services that can never be paid, and beautiful deeds that can never be wiped out by ingratitude or forgetfulness— Go back to your own room now. Your father will come in a moment.

[BARBRO *and the* CHILDREN *go out to the right.*

ISRAEL. I had never expected such a thing of you, doctor.

OLAVUS. I think I understand why. However, my dear syndic, don't compel us to become ungrateful. Ingratitude is such a heavy burden to carry.

ISRAEL. What is the use of talking of it? There is nothing of that kind to be feared.

MONS NILSSON *and* ANDERS PERSSON *enter from the left.*

MONS. After talking it over, we have decided to go to Stockholm with the King's good word and safe-conduct, so that we can quietly discuss the matter with him and the lords of the realm.

OLAVUS. Then my errand here is done, and both of us can leave. I wish you, Mons Nilsson, and you, Anders Persson, welcome to the capital.

MONS. Thank you, doctor.

[MASTER OLAVUS *and* HERMAN ISRAEL *go out.*

MONS. [*Picking up the blood-stained coats as soon as they are out of sight.*] These shall be our blood-stained banners! King Christian will furnish the staffs, and then—on to Stockholm!

ANDERS. And down with it!

OLAVUS [*Returning unexpectedly.*] There was one thing I forgot to tell you. Do you hear?

ANDERS. [*Angrily.*] Well!

OLAVUS. King Christian has been captured and made a prisoner at Sönderberg Castle, in the island of Als.

MONS *and* ANDERS *show how deeply the news hits them; neither one has a word to say.*

OLAVUS. You understand, don't you?—Sönderberg Castle, in the island of Als?

Curtain.

ACT II

SCENE I

The office of HERMAN ISRAEL. *A large room, the walls of which are covered by cupboards. Door in the rear; doors in both side walls; few windows, and these very small. A fireplace on the left-hand side. A large table in the middle of the floor; armchairs about it. Above the rear door and the fireplace appears the coat of arms of Luebeck, in black, red, and silver.*

At the right, a desk with writing material and a pair of scales. The room contains also several sets of shelves filled with goods in bundles.

One of the cupboard doors stands open, disclosing a number of altar vessels of gold and silver.

MARCUS *is weighing some of the vessels at the desk, while* DAVID *is noting down the weights given him.*

MARCUS. A crucifix of silver, gilded; weighs twelve ounces.

DAVID. [*Writing.*] Twelve ounces. . . .

MARCUS. Item: a monstrance of gold—a perfect thumper. Weighs . . . Let me see now. . . . Oh, it's hollow—and the base is filled with lead. . . . Put down a question-mark.

DAVID. Question-mark it is.

MARCUS. A paten of silver—well, I don't know. [*He tests the vessel with his teeth.*] It tastes like copper at least. Put it down as " white metallic substance."

DAVID. White metallic substance.—Do you think those rustics are cheating us?

MARCUS. Us? Nobody can cheat us!

DAVID. Don't be too certain. Niegels Bröms, the goldsmith, says that interlopers from Holland are going through the country selling church vessels full of coggery, probably meant to be exchanged for the genuine goods.

MARCUS. We'll have to get it back on the bells, which contain a lot of silver, according to old traditions.

DAVID. The bells—yes, they were to go to Luebeck, but instead they are going to the royal gun-foundry to be cast into culverins and bombards.

MARCUS. So it is said. If only the Dalecarlians knew of it, they would come galloping across the border forests, I suppose.

DAVID. I think their galloping came to an end with the recent fall slaughter.

MARCUS. No, there will be no end to it while the two blackest rogues are still at leisure. . . .

DAVID. You mean Mons Nilsson of Aspeboda and Anders Persson of Rankhyttan, who are still hanging about the town, hoping to get an audience with the King?

MARCUS. Those are the ones.

DAVID. Calling them rogues is rather an exaggeration, and our Principal seems to put great store on them.

MARCUS. Now, David, don't forget the first and last duty of a Hanseatic clerk—which is to keep his mouth closed. And bear in mind the number of talkative young fellows who have vanished for ever through water-gates and cellar holes. You had better remember!

DAVID. I'll try, although it seems about time for the Hansa itself to be thinking of the great silence. [*Pause.*

MARCUS. Do you know where the Principal is?

DAVID. With the King, I suppose, taking an inventory of Eskil's Chamber.[1]

JACOB ISRAEL. [*Enters; he is the son of* HERMAN ISRAEL; *a richly dressed young man, carrying a racket in his hand; his forehead is bandaged.*] Is my father here?

MARCUS. No, he is not. I think the Principal is with the King.

JACOB. Then I'll sit down here and wait. Go on with your writing. I won't disturb you. [*He seats himself at the big table.*

PRINCE ERIC. [*Enters; he is somewhat older than* JACOB.] Why did you leave me, Jacob?

JACOB. I was tired of playing.

---

[1] A subterranean vault in the Royal Palace at Stockholm used by the thrifty King Gustavus for the storing of gold and silver and other valuables. Compare the warning of Nils Söderby to Mons Nilsson's wife in the first act: " Look out for the silver—the King is coming."

ERIC.   I don't think that was the reason.   Someone offended you—someone who is not my friend.

JACOB.   No one has offended me, Prince, but I have such a strong feeling that I ought not to appear at court.

ERIC.   Oh, Jacob, my friend, why do you cease to call your old schoolmate by name?   And why do you look at me like a stranger?   Give me your hand. . . .   You won't?. . . .   And I, who have been lonely and deserted ever since my mother died; who am hated by my stepmother, by my father, and by my half-brother; I am begging for the friendship which you gave me once and which you are now taking back.

JACOB.   I am not taking back anything, Eric, but we are not allowed to be friends.   The fact that we two, as mere boys, formed ties of friendship that were nursed by common sufferings, has been ignored or tolerated by our fathers so far.   Now, when you are about to marry a foreign princess and take possession of a duchy, it has been deemed politic to separate us.

ERIC.   Your words are stilted, as if you meant to hide your own thoughts, but your feelings are not to be concealed. . . .

JACOB.   Pardon me, Eric, but this is not the place for a conversation like this. . . .

ERIC.   Because this is a place for trading, you mean—as if the parties to such a transaction were degraded by it?   I don't object to it, although I am rather inclined to think the seller more broad-minded than the buyer.

JACOB *indicates by a gesture the presence of the two clerks.*

ERIC.   Oh, let them hear.   Marcus and I are old friends, and we met at the Blue Dove last night.

JACOB.   Ugh!   Why do you visit a vulgar place like that, Prince?

ERIC.   Where can I go?   I have no one to talk with at home; and it seems to me, for that matter, that people are equally good or bad everywhere—although I prefer what is generally called bad company.—Do you know John Andersson?

JACOB.   [*Embarrassed.*]   I have never heard his name even. Who is he?   [MARCUS *and* DAVID *go quietly out to the left.*

ERIC.   A man from Småland who is full of sensible ideas.— Do you still need to have your forehead bandaged?

JACOB. Do you think I wear the bandage as an ornament, or as a souvenir of the city mob?

ERIC. You should not bear a grudge against the good folk because some scamp has misbehaved himself.

JACOB. I don't, my friend, and I know perfectly well what a stranger must expect in a hostile country. If you come to Luebeck, you will see how they stone Swedes.

ERIC. You talk just like Jorghen Persson. Do you know him?

JACOB. I don't.

ERIC. He looks at everything in the same way as you do.

JACOB. How do you mean?

ERIC. He thinks everyone is right, and that whatever happens is *juste*. There is something sensible and enlightened in his view of life. That's why my father hates him. . . .

JACOB. Don't talk badly of your father. It sounds dreadful —if you will pardon me!

ERIC. But if he acts badly, why shouldn't I say so? And I hate him, for that matter!

JACOB. Don't say that—don't! The greatness of your royal father is so boundless that you can't grasp it.

ERIC. It only looks that way—I know! Last night he came up to me and put his arm around my shoulders—for the first time in my life—and I, who have been living in the belief that I barely came up to his hip, found to my surprise that I am as tall as he. But as soon as I looked at him from a distance again, he grew taller and turned into a giant.

JACOB. That's what he is. And he resembles one of Buonarotti's prophets—Isaiah, I think. And, verily, the Lord on high is with him.

ERIC. Do you really believe in God?

JACOB. Are you not ashamed of yourself?

ERIC. Well, what are you to believe in times like these, when kings and priests persecute the faithful and profane everything that used to be held sacred. And yet they call themselves " defenders of the faith."

JACOB. Can't we talk of something else? Please, let us!

ERIC. That's what the King always says when I go after

him, and for that reason I hate him still more—as he hates me!
Do you know that it was your father who brought my mother to
him from Lauenburg? [1]

JACOB. No, I didn't know that.

ERIC. Yes, but the marriage turned out badly. They hated
each other beyond all bounds—and one day [*he rises in a state of
great agitation*] I saw him raise his stick against her—[*roaring
out the words*] against my mother—and he struck her!
That day I lost my youth [2]—and I can never forgive him—
never!

JACOB. [*Leaps to his feet and puts his arms about* ERIC.]
Look at me, Eric! Look at me! I have a stepmother, too—
who is always tormenting me when I am at home—but hush,
hush! If it can help you to hear that I am worse off than you—
very much worse—then—you know it now! Remember that it
won't last for ever, as we are growing up to freedom. . . .

ERIC. And you don't hate her?

JACOB. Such a feeling has no place beside the new one that is
now filling my soul.

ERIC. That means—you are in love.

JACOB. That's what we may call it. . . . And when your
own time comes, you, too, will see your hatred change form and
vanish.

ERIC. I wonder!—Perhaps you are right. . . . The love-
lessness in which I was born and brought up has turned into a
flame that is consuming my soul. My blood was poisoned at
my birth, and I doubt the existence of an antidote. . . . Why
do you leave me?

JACOB. Because . . . because we are not allowed to be
friends—because we cannot be friends.

ERIC. Do you think me so vile?

[1] The first wife of Gustavus was the Princess Catherine of Saxe-Lauenburg,
whom he married in 1531, and who died in 1535. She was of a very peculiar
temperament and caused much trouble between the King and his relatives by her
reckless talk. Prince Eric was born in 1533.

[2] This is an excellent illustration of the freedom taken by Strindberg in regard
to the actual chronology of the historical facts he is using. Eric was little more
than a year old when his mother died. Strindberg knew perfectly well what he
was doing, his reason being that the motive ascribed to Eric's hatred of his father
strengthens the dramatic quality of the play in a very high degree.

JACOB. No, no!—But I mustn't say anything more. Let us part. I shall always watch your fate with sympathy, for I think you were born to misfortune.

ERIC. What makes you utter what I have thought so many times? Do you know that I was also born to be in the way. I stand in the way of my father's desire to see Johan on the throne. I stand in the way of his wish to forget the hated German woman. My mind has not the true Swedish quality, and the fault lies in my German blood. Although I am a Vasa, I am Saxony, too, and Lauenburg, and Brunswick. I am so little of a Swede that it gives me pleasure when the free city of Luebeck imposes a penal tax on my country—and keeps it humiliated.

JACOB. [*Looking hard at him.*] Is that the truth, or do you merely talk like that out of politeness?

ERIC. [*Puts his hand to his sword, but regains self-control immediately.*] Do you notice how much I love .you, seeing that I pardon such a question?—Yes, my friend, the first words taught me by my mother were German, and in German I learned to say my evening prayers—that old and beautiful " Heil dir, Maria, Mutter Gottes ". . . . Oh, that time—that time. . . . [*He weeps.*] Oh, damn it! I am crying, I think!— Come to the Blue Dove to-night, Jacob. . . . There you'll find Rhine wine and merry maidens! Jorghen will be there, too. He's a man you should know.

JACOB. [*Coldly and shrewdly.*] I—shall—come.

ERIC. Thank you, friend! [*Rising.*] Really, the place has a look of pawn-shop.

JACOB. [*Sharply.*] That was just what I had in mind before.

ERIC. Well, then we agree to that extent at least. Until to-night, then! Do you know Agda?

JACOB. [*Brusquely.*] No!

ERIC. [*Haughtily, giving him two fingers to shake,* JACOB *pretending not to notice it.*] Farewell!—What became of those two little pawnbrokers?

JACOB *does not answer.*

ERIC. [*Arrogantly.*] Good-bye, then, Baruch!—Have you read the Book of Baruch?

*Going towards the background, he jingles the altar vessels as
he passes them.*

> " The ring of gold, and rattling dice,
> And wine brings light to tipsy eyes.
> But in the night, that light must lack,
> To wenches leads each crooked track."

That's a good one, isn't it?   I made it myself!

[*He goes out through the rear door.*

HERMAN ISRAEL. [*Enters from the right.*]   Are you
alone?

JACOB.   Yes, father.

ISRAEL.   I heard somebody speaking.

JACOB.   That was the Heir Apparent.

ISRAEL.   What did he want?

JACOB.   I don't think he has the slightest idea of what he
wants.

ISRAEL.   Is he your friend?

JACOB.   Yes, so he calls himself, but I am not his.   Because
he thinks that he is honouring me with his friendship, he flatters
himself with the belief that I return it.

ISRAEL.   You are frightfully wise for a young man of your
age.

JACOB.   Why, it's an axiom in the art of living, that you must
not be the friend of your enemy.

ISRAEL.   Can he be made useful?

JACOB.   Running errands, perhaps, provided you keep him
wholesomely ignorant of the matter at stake.   Otherwise I don't
think I ever saw an heir apparent more useless than this one.

ISRAEL.   Do you hate him?

JACOB.   No, I pity him too much for that.   He is more unfortunate than he deserves.   That he will end badly, seems
pretty certain.   It seems clear to himself, too, and to such an
extent that he appears anxious to hasten the catastrophe.

ISRAEL.   Listen, my son.   I have long noticed that I can
keep no secrets from you, and so I think it is better for me to tell
you everything.   Sit down and give me your attention while I

walk back and forth. . . .   I can think only when I am
walking. . . .

JACOB.   Talk away, father.   I am thinking all the time.

ISRAEL.   You have probably guessed that some great event is
preparing under the surface. . . . You have probably noticed that
our free city of Luebeck is fighting for its rights here in the North.
I speak of rights, because we have the right of the pioneer who
has broken new roads—roads of trade in this case—to demand
compensation and profit from the country on which he has spent
his energy.   We have taught these people to employ their natural
products and to exchange them with profit; and we have set
Sweden free.   Having used us, they wish now to cast us aside.
That's always the way: use—and cast aside!   But there are
greater and more powerful interests than those of trade that
should compel the North to join hands with the free cities.   The
Emperor and the Pope are one.   Our free cities made themselves independent first of the Emperor and then of the Pope.
Now, when this country has been helped by us and its great King
to do the same, we must, willy-nilly, remain allies against the
common enemy.   And until quite recently we did stick together.
Then an evil spirit seemed to take possession of this Vasa.
Whether misled by pride or fatigue, he wishes now to enter a
path that must lead us all to disaster.

JACOB. Wait a little.—All of us, you say? You had better say
" us of Luebeck," for the Swedes will gain by entering that path.

ISRAEL.   Are you on their side?

JACOB.   No, I am not.   But I can perfectly well see where
their advantage lies.   And I beg you, father, don't try to fight
against Vasa, for he is guided by the hand of the Lord!   Have
you not recognised that already?

ISRAEL.   I wonder how I could be such a fool as to give my
confidence to one still in his nonage!

JACOB.   It won't hurt you to have your plans discussed from
another point of view than your own while there is still time to
correct them.   And you know, of course, that you can rely on
me.   Go on, now!

ISRAEL.   No, I can't now.

JACOB.   The pen won't write when its point has been broken.

If you will not get angry, I can tell you a little more myself.

MARCUS. [*Enters.*] The one you have been waiting for is outside, sir.

JACOB. I suppose it is John Andersson.

ISRAEL. Let him wait. [*Motions* MARCUS *out of the room; then to* JACOB.] Do you know him, too?

JACOB. I have never seen him, but now I can figure out who he is.

ISRAEL. [*Astounded.*] You can figure it out, you say?

JACOB. I merèly add one thing to another. Now, when the Dalecarlians have been squelched, a new beginning will have to be made with the good folk of Småland.

ISRAEL. Of Småland, you say?

JACOB. Yes, I understand that this John Andersson is from Småland. I don't think his name is John Andersson, however, but—[*in a lower voice*] Nils Dacke! [1]

ISRAEL. Have you been spying?

JACOB. No, I merely listen, and look, and add together.

ISRAEL. Well, you have made a false calculation this time.

JACOB. Thus you tell me that there are two persons concerned in the matter, and that Nils Dacke is the silent partner who will not appear until the war has begun.

ISRAEL. I am afraid of you.

JACOB. You shouldn't be, father. I dare not do anything wrong, because then I am always made to suffer.

ISRAEL. Do you think I am doing anything wrong?

JACOB. You are more likely than I to do so, because, like Prince Eric, you believe in nothing.

ISRAEL. And such a thing I must hear from my own child!

---

[1] A peasant chieftain, who headed the most dangerous rebellion Gustavus had to contend with during his entire reign. The southern province of Småland had for years been the scene of peasant disturbances when, in 1541, Dacke took command of the scattered flocks and merged them into an army which defied the King's troops for nearly two years. Dacke was as able as he was ambitious. He was in communication with the German Emperor and other foreign enemies of Gustavus, and on one occasion the latter had actually to enter into negotiations with the rebel. In accordance with his invariable custom, Gustavus did not rely on hired soldiery, but turned to the people of the other provinces, explaining and appealing to them with such success that a sufficient army was raised and Dacke beaten and killed in 1543.

JACOB. It is better than to hear it from other people's children—later on.

MARCUS. [*Enters.*] Two Dalecarlians ask to see you.

ISRAEL. Tell them to wait. [MARCUS *goes out.*

JACOB. They'll pay for it with their heads.

ISRAEL. Who are they, then?

JACOB. Anders Persson of Rankhyttan and Mons Nilsson of Aspeboda, who have tried in vain to get an audience with the King, and who are now moved by their futile anger to turn to you for revenge.

ISRAEL. So you know that, too?

JACOB. Without wishing to show you any disrespect, father—how can a man of your age believe that secrets exist?

ISRAEL. Time has run away from me. I don't know any longer where I stand.

JACOB. Now you speak the truth! And I don't think that you estimate the results of your venture correctly.

ISRAEL. That will appear in due time. But now you must go, for even if you know of my venture, you must not become involved in it.

JACOB. I shall obey, but you must listen to me.

ISRAEL. No, you must listen to me! Tell Marcus that I shall expect my visitors in the hall of state. You stay here with David and pack all valuables into boxes ready to be sent southward.

JACOB. Father!

ISRAEL. Silence!

JACOB. One word: don't rely on me if you should do anything wrong!

ISRAEL. There is one thing *you* may rely on; that, having power of life and death in this house, I shall see that every traitor is tried and executed, whether he be my own son or no. First comes my country, then my family; but first and last—my duty! [*He puts his hand on his sword.*] And now—go!

Curtain.

SCENE II

*A large room in the Blue Dove Inn. Wainscoted walls,
with tankards and jugs ranged along the shelf above the
panels.   Benches fastened to the walls and covered with
cushions and draperies. In the background, a corner-stand
with potted flowers and bird-cages.   Sconces containing
wax candles are hung on the walls; candelabra stand on a
table that also contains bowls of fruit, beakers, goblets,
tumblers, dice, playing-cards, and a lute.*

It is night. PRINCE ERIC *and* JORGHEN PERSSON *are seated
at the table.   They are looking pale and tired, and have
ceased drinking.*

ERIC.   You want to go to sleep, Jorghen, and I prefer to
dream while still awake.   To go to bed is to me like dying: to be
swathed in linen sheets and stretched out in a long bed like a coffin.
And then the corpse has the trouble of washing itself and reading
its own burial service.

JORGHEN.   Are you afraid of death, Prince?

ERIC.   As the children are afraid of going to bed, and I am
sure I'll cry like a child when my turn comes.   If I only knew
what death is!

JORGHEN.   Some call it a sleep, and others an awakening, but
no one knows anything with certainty.

ERIC.   How could we possibly know anything of that other
life, when we know so little of this one?

JORGHEN.   Yes, what is life?

ERIC.   One large madhouse, it seems to me!   Think of my
sane and shrewd and sensible father—doesn't he act like a mad-
man?   He rids the country of foreigners and takes the heads of
those that helped him.   He rids the country of foreigners only to
drag in a lot of others, like Peutinger and Norman,[1] whom he

---

[1] In his effort to reorganise the country and its administration on a businesslike
basis, Gustavus turned first to Swedes like Olavus Petri and Laurentius Andreæ,
his first chancellor.   But these were as independent of mind as he was himself,
and there was not a sufficient number of them.   Then Gustavus turned to
Germany, whence a host of adventurers as well as able, honest men swarmed into
the country.   The two best known and most trusted of these foreigners were

puts above the lords of the realm and all other authorities. He
is mad, of course!—He rids the Church of human inventions
only to demand the acceptance of new inventions at the penalty
of death. This liberator is the greatest tyrant that ever lived,
and yet this tyrant is the greatest liberator that ever lived! This
evening, you know, he wanted to prohibit me from coming here;
and when I insisted on going all the same, he threw his Hun-
garian war-hammer after me, as if he had been the god Thor
chasing the trolls. He came within an inch of killing me, just
as it is said—which you may not have heard—that he killed my
mother.

JORGHEN. [*Becoming attentive.*] No, I never heard of
that.

ERIC. That's what they say. And I can understand it.
There is greatness in it. To feel raised above all human con-
siderations; to kill whatever stands in the way, and trample
everything else. . . . Sometimes, you know, when I see him
coming in his big, soft hat and his blue cloak, using his boar-
spear in place of a stick, I think he is Odin himself. When he
is angry, the people say that they can hear him from the top
storey down to the cellars, and that the sound of it is like thunder.
But I am not afraid of him, and that's why he hates me. At the
same time he has a great deal of respect for me. [JORGHEN
smiles sceptically.] Yes, you may smile! That's only because
you have no respect for anything; not even for yourself.

JORGHEN. That least of all.

ERIC. Are you really such a beast?

JORGHEN. That's what everyone thinks me, so I suppose I
must believe it.

ERIC. [*Returning to his previous idea.*] And . . . There
is a thought that pursues me. . . . He looks like old Odin, I
said: Odin who has returned to despoil the temples of the Chris-
tians just as they once robbed his temples. . . . You should
have seen them weighing and counting church treasures at Herman Israel's yesterday. It was ghastly! . . . And do you

Georg Norman, who rendered valuable services in organising the civil administration, and Conrad von Pyhy, said to be a plain charlatan named Peutinger, who
was made Chancellor of the Realm.

know, he is lucky in everything he undertakes. There is a favourable wind whenever he goes sailing; the fish bite whenever he goes fishing; he wins whenever he gambles. They say that he was born with a caul. . . .

JORGHEN. A most unusual man.

ERIC. Do you know young Jacob, the son of Herman Israel? He promised to come here to-night. Rather precocious, perhaps, but with sensible ideas on certain subjects—and I think I admire some of his qualities because I lack them myself.

JORGHEN. · Is that so?

ERIC. Otherwise he is probably a perfect rascal like his father.

JORGHEN. Then I shall be pleased to make his acquaintance.

ERIC. Because he is a rascal? Ha-ha!

JORGHEN. In spite of it!

AGDA. [*Enters from the left.*] Did you call me, Prince?

ERIC. No, but you are always welcome. Sit down here.

AGDA. The honour is too great for me.

ERIC. Of course, it is!

AGDA. And so I leave—to save my honour.

ERIC. Dare you sting, you gnat?

AGDA. That's your fancy only. I am too sensible and humble to hurt the feelings of a great lord like yourself, my Prince.

ERIC. Very good! Very good, indeed! Come here and talk to me a little more.

AGDA. If your lordship commands, I must talk, of course, but . . .

ERIC. Give me the love that I have begged for so long!

AGDA. What one does not have one cannot give away.

ERIC. Alas!

AGDA. Not loving your lordship, I cannot give you any love.

ERIC. *Diantre!*—Give me your favour, then!

AGDA. Favours are not given away, but sold.

ERIC. Listen to that! It is as if I heard my wise Jacob himself philosophising. [*To* JORGHEN.] Did you ever hear anything like it?

JORGHEN. All wenches learn that kind of patter from their lovers.

ERIC. Don't talk like that! This girl has won my heart.

JORGHEN. And someone else has won hers.

ERIC. How do you know?

JORGHEN. You can hear it at once, even though the proofs be not visible.

ERIC. Do you believe in love?

JORGHEN. In its existence, yes, but not in its duration.

ERIC. Do you know how a woman's love is to be won?

JORGHEN. All that's necessary is to be " the right one." If you are not, your case is hopeless.

ERIC. That's a riddle.

JORGHEN. One of the greatest.

ERIC. Who do you think can be my rival?

JORGHEN. Some clerk, or pikeman, or rich horsemonger.

ERIC. And I who am not afraid of tossing my handkerchief to the proud virgin-queen that rules Britannia!

JORGHEN. Yet it's true.

ERIC. Perhaps Agda is too modest—and does not dare to believe in the sincerity of my feelings?

JORGHEN. I don't believe anything of the kind.

A noise is heard outside the door in the rear.

PRINCE JOHAN. [*Enters.*] I hope my dear brother will pardon my intrusion at this late hour, but I have been sent by our father out of fond concern for my dear brother's . . .

ERIC. Be quick and brief, Jöns, or sit down and use a beaker as punctuation mark! The sum of it is: the old man wants me to come home and go to bed. Reply: the Heir Apparent decides for himself when he is to sleep.

JOHAN. I shall not convey such a reply, especially as my dear brother's disobedience may have serious results in this case.

ERIC. Won't you sit down and drink a goblet, Duke?

JOHAN. Thank you, Prince, but I don't wish to cause my father sorrow.

ERIC. How dreadfully serious that sounds!

JOHAN. It is serious. Our father has new and greater worries to face because disturbances have been reported from the southern provinces, especially from Småland. . . . And as it is possible that the King may have to leave his capital, he looks to the

Heir Apparent for assistance in the administration of the government.

ERIC.　Half of which is nothing but lies, of course—and then there are such a lot of people governing already.　Go in peace, my brother.　I shall come when I come.

JOHAN.　My duty is done, and all I regret is being unable to gain more of my brother's ear; of his heart I possess no part at all!　　　　　　　　　　　　　　　　　　　　　　　　　　[*He goes out.*

ERIC.　[*To* JORGHEN.]　Can you make anything out of that boy?

JORGHEN.　I can't.

ERIC.　I wonder if he believes in his own preachings?

JORGHEN.　That is just the worst of it.　Ordinary rascals like you and me, who don't believe in anything, can't get words of that kind over their lips; and for that reason we can never deceive anybody.

ERIC.　You *are* a beast, Jorghen.

JORGHEN.　Of course, I am.

ERIC.　Is there nothing good in you at all?

JORGHEN.　Not a trace!　And besides—what is good? [*Pause.*]　My mother was always saying that I should end on the gallows.　Do you think one's destiny is predetermined?

ERIC.　That's what Master Dionysius asserts—the Calvinist who uses Holy Writ to prove that the dispensation of grace is not at all dependent on man.

JORGHEN.　Come on with the gallows, then!　That's the grace dispensed to me.

ERIC.　That fellow Jacob says always that I was born to misfortune, and that's what father says, too, when he gets angry. What do you think my end will be?

JORGHEN.　Was it not Saint Augustine who said that he who has been coined into a groat can never become a ducat?

ERIC.　That's right.　But I don't think we have drunk enough to make us start any theological disputes.　Here we have been disputing for a lifetime now, and every prophet has been fighting all the rest.　Luther has refuted Augustine, Calvin has refuted Luther, Zwingli has refuted Calvin, and John of Leyden has refuted all of them.　So we know now just where we stand!

JORGHEN. Yes, it's nothing but humbug, and if it were not for that kind of humbug, I should never have been born.

ERIC. What do you mean?

JORGHEN. Oh, you know perfectly well that my father was a monk who went off and got married when they closed the monasteries. It means that I am a product of perjury and incest, as my father broke his oath and established an illicit relationship like any unclean sheep.

ERIC. You *are* a beast, Jorghen!

JORGHEN. Have I ever denied it?

ERIC. No, but there are limits. . . .

JORGHEN. Where?

ERIC. Here and there! A certain innate sense of propriety generally suggests the—approximate limits.

JORGHEN. Are you dreaming again, you dreamer?

ERIC. Take care! There are limits even to friendship. . . .

JORGHEN. No, mine is limitless!

JACOB *is shown into the room by* AGDA, *whose hand he presses.*

ERIC. [*Rising.*] There you are at last, Jacob! You have kept me waiting a long time, and just now I was longing for you.

JACOB. Pardon me, Prince, but my thoughts were so heavy that I did not wish to bring them into a merry gathering.

ERIC. Yes, we are devilishly merry, Jorghen and I! This is Jorghen Persson, you see—my secretary, and a very enlightened and clever man, but a perfect rascal otherwise, as you can judge from his horrible looks and treacherous eyes.

JORGHEN. At your service, my dear sir!

ERIC. Sit down and philosophise with us, Jacob. Of course, I promised you pretty maidens, but we have only one here, and she is engaged.

JACOB. [*Startled.*] What do you mean by—engaged?

ERIC. That she has bestowed her heart on somebody, so that you may save yourself the trouble of searching her bosom for it.

JACOB. Are you talking of Agda?

ERIC. Do you know Agda the Chaste, who has told us that she would sell her favours, but never give them away?

AGDA. My God, I never, never meant anything of the kind!

JACOB. No, she cannot possibly have meant it that way.

ERIC. She has said it.

JACOB. It must be a lie.

ERIC. [*His hand on his sword-hilt.*] The devil, you say!

JORGHEN. A tavern brawl of the finest water! The words have been given almost correctly, but they were not understood as they were meant.

ERIC. Do you dare to take sides against me, you rascal?

JORGHEN. Listen, friends. . . .

ERIC. *With* a hussy *against* your master. . . .

JACOB. She's no hussy!

AGDA. Thank you, Jacob! Please tell them everything. . . .

ERIC. Oh, there is something to tell, then? Well, well! [*To* JORGHEN.] And you must needs appear as the defender of innocence!

He makes a lunge at JORGHEN, *who barely manages to get out of the way.*

JORGHEN. Why the deuce must you always come poking after me when somebody else has made a fool of himself? Stop it, damn you!

ERIC. [*To* JACOB.] So this is my rival! Ha-ha-ha! A fellow like you! *Ventre-saint-gris!*

He loses all control of himself and finally sinks on a chair, seized with an epileptic fit.

JACOB. Once you honoured me with your friendship, Prince, for which I could only give you pity in return. As I did not wish to be false, I asked you to let me go. . . .

ERIC. [*Leaping to his feet.*] Go to the devil!

JACOB. Yes, I am going, but first you must hear what I and Agda have in common—something you can never understand, as you understand nothing but hatred, and for that reason never can win love. . . .

ERIC. *Diantre!* And I who can have the virgin-queen, the proud maiden of Britannia, at my feet any time I care. . . . Ha-ha, ha-ha!

JACOB. King David had five hundred proud maidens, but for happiness he turned to his humble servant's only wife. . . .

ERIC. Must I hear more of that sort of thing?

JACOB. A great deal more!

ERIC. [*Rushing at* JACOB.] Die, then!

The guard enters by the rear door.

CAPTAIN OF THE GUARD. [*An old, white-bearded man.*] Your sword, if you please, Prince Eric!

ERIC. What is this?

CAPTAIN. [*Handing* ERIC *a document.*] The King's order. You are under arrest. . . .

ERIC. Go to the devil, old Stenbock!

CAPTAIN. That's not a princely answer to a royal command!

ERIC. Yes, talk away!

CAPTAIN. [*Goes up to* ERIC *and wrests the sword out of his hand; then he turns him over to the guard.*] Away with him! And put him in the tower! That's order number one! [ERIC *is led towards the door.*] Then comes number two—Mr. Secretary! [*To the guard.*] Put on the handcuffs! And then— to the Green Vault with him! To-morrow at cockcrow—ten strokes of the rod!

JORGHEN. [*As he is seized by the guard.*] Must I be spanked because *he* won't go to bed?

ERIC. Do you dare to lay hands on the Heir Apparent? 'Sdeath!

CAPTAIN. God is still alive, and so is the King!—March on!——

ERIC *and* JORGHEN *are led out by the guard.*

CAPTAIN. [*To* AGDA.] And now you'll close your drink-shop. That's the final word. And as there is no question about it, you need not make any answer.

[*He goes out after the guard and the prisoners.*

JACOB. Always this titanic hand that is never seen and always felt! Now it has been thrust out of a cloud to alter our humble fates. The liberator of the country has descended during the darkness of night to set my little bird free.—Will you take flight with me?

AGDA. Yes, with you—and far away!

JACOB. But where?

AGDA. The world is wide!

JACOB. Come, then!

Curtain.

ACT III

*The King's study.   The background consists almost wholly of
large windows, some of which have panes of stained glass.
Several of the windows are open, and through these may be
seen trees in the first green of spring.   Mast tops with flying
flags, and church spires are visible above the tops of the
trees.*

*Beneath the windows are benches set in the walls.   Their seats
are covered by many-coloured cushions.*

*At the right, a huge open fireplace, richly decorated.   The
recently adopted national coat of arms appears on the mantelpiece.   A door on the same side leads to the waiting-room.*

*A chair of state with canopy occupies the centre of the left wall.
In front of it stands a long oak table covered with green cloth.
On the table are a folio Bible, an inkstand, candlesticks, a war-
hammer, and a number of other things.   A door on the same
side, nearer the background, leads to the royal apartments.*

The floor is covered with animal skins and rugs.

*The walls display paintings of Old Testament subjects.   The
most conspicuous of these represents " The Lord appearing
unto Abraham in the plains of Mamre."   The picture of
Abraham bears a strong resemblance to the King.*

*An Arabian water-bottle of clay and a silver cup stand on a small
cabinet.*

*Near the door at the right hang a long and wide blue cloak and a
big black felt hat.   A short boar-spear is leaned against the
wall.*

The KING, *lost in thought, stands by one of the open windows
where the full sunlight pours over him.   He has on a black
dress of Spanish cut, with yellow linings that show in the seams
and through a number of slits.   Over his shoulders is thrown
a short cloak trimmed with sable.   His hair is blond, and his
tremendous beard, reaching almost to his waist is still lighter
in colour.*

The QUEEN *enters from the left.   She wears a yellow dress with
black trimmings.*

KING. [*Kissing her brow.*]   Good morrow, my rose!

QUEEN.   A splendid morning!

KING.   The first spring day after a long winter.

QUEEN.   Is my King in a gracious mood to-day?

KING.   My graciousness is not dependent on weather or wind. —Go on now!   Is it a question of Eric?

QUEEN.   It is.

KING.   Well, he has my good grace once more after having slept himself sober in the tower.   And Jorghen comes next, I suppose?

QUEEN.   Yes.

KING.   He, on the other hand, will not have my good grace until he reforms.

QUEEN.   But . . .

KING.   He is bad through and through, and he is spoiling Eric.   Whatever may be the cause of his badness, I cannot dispose of it, but I can check the effects.   Have you any more protégés of the same kind?

QUEEN.   I won't say anything more now.

KING.   Then we can talk of something else.   How is my mother-in-law?

QUEEN.   Oh, you know.

KING.   And Johan?   Where is Johan?

QUEEN.   He is not far away.

KING.   I wish he were still nearer—nearer to me—so near that he could succeed me when the time comes.

QUEEN.   It is not right to think like that, and still less to talk like that, when a higher Providence has already decided in favour of Prince Eric.

KING.   Well, I can't tell whether it was vanity that fooled me into looking for a foreign princess or wisdom that kept me away from the homes of our Swedish nobility—one hardly ever knows what one is doing.

QUEEN.   That's true.

KING.   But the fact that I became the brother-in-law of the Danish king helped the country to get peace, and so nobody has any right to complain.

QUEEN.   The country first!

KING. The country first and last! That's why Eric must be married.

QUEEN. Do you really think he has any hopes with the English queen.

KING. I don't know, but we must find out—that is, without risking the honour of the country. It is not impossible. We have had a British princess on the throne before.

QUEEN. Who was that?

KING. Don't you know that Queen Philippa was a daughter of King Henry IV?[1]

QUEEN. No, I didn't know that.

KING. Then I suppose you don't know, either, that the Folkungs were among your ancestors, and that you are also descended from King Waldemar, the Conqueror of Denmark?[2]

QUEEN. No, no! I thought the bloody tale of the Folkungs was ended long ago.

KING. Let us hope it is! But your maternal ancestor was nevertheless a daughter of Eric Ploughpenny of Denmark and had a son with her brother-in-law, King Waldemar of Sweden, the son of Earl Birger. . . .

QUEEN. Why do you tell me all these dreadful stories?

KING. I thought it might amuse you to know that you have royal blood in your veins, while I have peasant blood. You are too modest, Margaret, and I wish to see you exalted—so high that that fool Eric will be forced to respect you.

QUEEN. To have sprung from a crime should make one more modest.

KING. Well, that's enough about that. Was there anything else?

The QUEEN *hesitates.*

[1] Philippa of England, who died in 1430, was the queen of Eric of Pomerania, who succeeded the great Queen Margaret on the united thrones of the three Scandinavian kingdoms. She was as sweet and fine as he was stupid and worthless, and to this day her memory survives among the people.

[2] The Folkungs were the descendants of the puissant Earl Birger of Håtuna, who, as an uncrowned king, ruled Sweden in very much the same spirit as King Gustavus himself. The Folkung dynasty reigned from 1250 to 1389—and spent much of that time in fighting among themselves. King Waldemar II gained the name of "Conqueror" by adding Esthonia and other Baltic districts to Denmark.

KING. You are thinking of Anders Persson and Mons Nilsson, but I won't let you talk of them.

The QUEEN *kneels before him.*

KING. Please, get up! [*As she remains on her knees.*] Then I must leave you. [*He goes out to the left.*

PRINCE ERIC *enters from the right; he is pale and unkempt, and his face retains evidence of the night's carouse.*

The QUEEN *rises, frightened.*

ERIC. Did I scare you?

QUEEN. Not exactly.

ERIC. I can take myself out of the way. I was only looking for a glass of water.

He goes to the water-bottle, fills a cup full of water, and gulps it down; then another, and still another.

QUEEN. Are you sick?

ERIC. [*Impertinently.*] Only a little leaky.

QUEEN. What do you mean?

ERIC. Well, dry, if you please. The more wine you drink, the dryer gets your throat. The wetter, the dryer—that's madness, like everything else.

QUEEN. Why do you hate me?

ERIC. [*Cynically.*] Because I am not allowed to love you. [*In the meantime he continues to pour down one glass of water after the other.*] You must not be in love with your stepmother, and yet you must love her: that's madness, too.

QUEEN. Why do you call me stepmother?

ERIC. Because that's the word, and that's what you are. Is that clear? If it is, then that isn't madness at least.

QUEEN. You have the tongue of a viper.

ERIC. And the reason, too.

QUEEN. But no heart!

ERIC. What could I do with it? Throw it at the feet of the women to be defiled by them?—My heart lies buried in my mother's coffin in the vault of Upsala cathedral. I was only four years old when it was put there, but there it lies with her, and they tell me there was a hole in her head as if she had been struck by the hammer of Thor—which I did not see, however. When I asked to see my mother for the last time at the burial, they had already screwed on the coffin lid. Well, there lies my heart—the only one I ever had. . . . What have you to do with my entrails, for that matter? Or with my feelings?—Look out for my reason; that's all! I grasp your thoughts before you have squeezed them out of yourself. I understand perfectly that you would like to see the crown placed on the red hair of that red devil whom you call son, and whom I must needs call brother. He insists that he has more ancestors than I, and that he is descended from Danish kings. If that's so, he has a lot of fine relatives. Eric Ploughpenny had his head cut off. Abel killed his brother and was killed in turn. Christofer was poisoned. Eric the Blinking was stuck like a pig.—I have no elegant relatives like those, but if heredity counts, I must keep an eye on my dear brother.

QUEEN. Nobody can talk of anything but blood and poison to-day. The sun must have risen on the wrong side this fine morning!

ERIC. The sun is a deceiver; don't trust it. Blood will be shed in this place before nightfall. Eric and Abel were the names of those elegant relatives; not Cain and Abel! And that time it was Abel who killed Cain—no, Eric, I mean! That's a fine omen to start with! Eric was killed! Poor Eric!

QUEEN. Alas, alas!

ERIC. But it is of no use to take any stock of superstition, as I entered this vale of misery with my fist full of blood.

QUEEN. Now you do scare me!

ERIC. [Laughing.] That's more than Jorghen would believe—that I could scare anybody.

QUEEN. What blood is to be shed here to-day?

ERIC. I am not sure, but it is said that those Dalecarlians will have their heads cut off.

QUEEN. Can it not be prevented?

ERIC. If it is to be, it cannot be prevented, but must come as thunder must come after lightning. And besides, what does it matter? Heads are dropping off here like ripe apples.

The KING enters reading a document. The QUEEN meets him with a supplicating look.

KING. [*Hotly.*] If you have any faith in me at all, Margaret, cease your efforts to judge in matters of state. I have been investigating for two years without being able to make up my mind. How can you, then, hope to grasp this matter?—Go in to the children now. I have a word to say to Eric!

> *The* QUEEN *goes out.*

KING. If you could see yourself as you are now, Eric, you would despise yourself!

ERIC. So I do anyhow!

KING. Nothing but talk! If you did despise yourself, you would change your ways.

ERIC. I cannot make myself over.

KING. Have you ever tried?

ERIC. I have.

KING. Then your bad company must counteract your good intentions.

ERIC. Jorghen is no worse than anybody else, but he has the merit of knowing himself no better than the rest.

KING. Do you bear in mind that you are to be king some time?

ERIC. Once I am king, the old slips will be forgotten.

KING. There you are mistaken again. I am still paying for old slips. However, if you are not willing to obey me as a son, you must obey me as a subordinate.

ERIC. The Heir Apparent is no subject!

KING. That's why I used the word "subordinate." And all are subordinate to the King.

ERIC. Must I obey blindly?

KING. As long as you are blind, you must obey blindly. When you get your sight, you will obey with open eyes. But obey you must!—Wait only till you have begun to command, and you will soon see how much more difficult that is, and how much more burdensome.

ERIC. [*Pertly.*] Pooh!

KING. [*Angrily.*] Idiot!—Go and wash the dirt off yourself, and see that your hair is combed. And rinse that filthy mouth of yours first of all, so that you don't stink up my rooms. Go now—or I'll give you a week in the tower to sober up. And if that should not be enough, I'll take off your ears, so that you can never wear a crown. Are those words plain enough?

ERIC. The law of succession. . . .

KING. I make laws of that kind to suit myself! Do you understand now?—That's all!—Away!

PRINCE ERIC *goes out.*

COURTIER. [*Enters from the right.*] Herman Israel, Councillor of Luebeck!

KING. Let him come.

The COURTIER *goes out.* HERMAN ISRAEL *enters shortly afterwards.*

KING. [*Meets him and shakes his hand; then he puts his arm about his neck and leads him across the floor in that manner.*] Good day, my dear old friend, and welcome! Sit down, sit down! [*He seats himself on the chair of state, and* ISRAEL *sits down across the table.*] So you have just come from Dalecarlia?

ISRAEL. That's where I was lately.

KING. I was there, too, as you know, to straighten out the mess left after the False Sture and the fight about the bells, but you stayed on when I left.—Did you keep an eye on Master Olavus Petri? What sort of a man has he turned out? Can I trust him?

ISRAEL. Absolutely! He is not only the most faithful, but the cleverest negotiator I have seen.

KING. Really, Herman? I am glad to hear that. Do you really think so, Herman? Well, you know the old affair between him and me, and how that was settled. But it *was* settled!—So much for that. Let us talk of our affairs now.

ISRAEL. As you say. But let us keep our words as well as actions under control.

KING. [*Playing with the war-hammer.*] All right! Control yours as much as you please.

ISRAEL. [*Pointing at the hammer.*] For the sake of old friendship and good faith, can't we put that away?

KING. Ha-ha! With pleasure, if you are afraid of it, Herman!—Go on now! But cut it short!

ISRAEL. Then I'll start at the end. The country's debt to Luebeck has been paid, and we are about to part.

KING. That sounds like writing! However, we shall part as friends.

ISRAEL. As allies rather. . . .

KING. So *that's* what you are aiming at, Israel?—No, I have had enough of dependence.

ISRAEL. Listen, your Highness, or Majesty, or whatever I am to call you. . . .

KING. Call me Gustav, as you used to do when I called you father.

ISRAEL. Well, my son, there are many things that drive us apart—many, indeed—but there is one thing that keeps us together: our common, legitimate opposition to the Emperor. . . .

KING. Right you are! And that's the reason why we can rely on each other without any written treaties.

ISRAEL. You forget one thing, my son: that I am a merchant. . . .

KING. And I the customer. Have you been paid?

ISRAEL. Paid? Yes. . . . But there are things that cannot be paid in money. . . .

KING. It is for me to speak of the gratitude I owe you and the free city of Luebeck ever since the day I first came to you— a young man who thought himself deserted by God, and who knew himself deserted by all humanity. Be satisfied to find my gratitude expressed in the friendly feelings I harbour and show towards you. A debt like that cannot be paid in money, and still less in treaties.—Why do you want any treaties? In order to tie me and the country for a future of uncertain duration?— Don't force me to become ungrateful, Herman! On my soul, I have enough as it is to burden me—far too much!

ISRAEL. What is weighing on you, my son?

KING. This . . . Oh, will you believe me, Herman, old friend, that I never form a decision or pass a judgment without having turned to the Eternal and Almighty Lord for advice? When, after fasting, prayer, and meditation, I have got the answer from above that I was asking for, then I strike gladly, even if it be my own heart-roots that must be cut off. But . . . you remember Master John. . . . John, the old friend of my youth, who assisted me in that first bout with Christian? He changed heart and incited the Dalecarlians to rise against me. His head had to fall, and it did fall! [*Rising.*] Since that day my peace is gone. My nearest and dearest don't look at me in the same way they used to do. My own wife, my beloved Margaret. . . . She turns away from me when I want to kiss her pure brow, and . . . can you imagine? . . . Yesterday, at the dinner-table, she kept looking at my hand as if she had seen blood on it!—I don't regret what I did. I have no right to regret it. I was right—by God, I was right! But nevertheless—my peace is gone!

ISRAEL. [*Pensively.*] Those feelings are an honour to your heart, my son, and I must admit that I didn't think you quite as sensitive. . . .

KING. Never mind! It was not meant as a boast. But now I find myself in the same situation again. Tell me, Herman, what you think of Ander Persson and Mons Nilsson.

ISRAEL. [*Disturbed.*] Will my opinion have any influence on their fate, or have you already made up your mind?

KING. I am still in doubts, as you ought to know.

ISRAEL. Then I must ask permission to remain silent.

KING. Are you my friend?

ISRAEL. Yes, up to a certain point. But you must not trust me too far, as I am not my own master and have no right to give away what is not mine.

KING. Fie on such astuteness!

ISRAEL. You should get some of it yourself!

KING. I'll try.—First of all you must give me a final receipt for the country's paid-up debt.

ISRAEL. I don't carry such documents with me, and the receipt has to be signed by the Council in regular session.

KING. [*Smiting the table with the hammer.*] Herman!

ISRAEL. Please put that thing away!

KING. I can see that you wish to lead me where I don't want to go. You have some purpose in mind that I can't make out. Speak out, old man, or you'll have me in a rage! You want to coax me into signing some kind of paper. What is it?

ISRAEL. Nothing but a treaty providing for mutual friendship and mutual trade. That's all!

KING. And that I will never sign! I know all about Luebeck's friendship as well as its trade. Talk of something else!

ISRAEL. I have nothing else to talk of. Why don't you believe me?

KING. Because you lie!

ISRAEL. Because you are unfortunate enough to think that I lie, you will never know the truth.

KING. Yes, unfortunate, indeed—as unfortunate as a man can be, for I have not a single friend.

ISRAEL. It hurts me to hear you talk like that, Gustav, and —and it makes me sad to see that your greatness and your exalted office have brought you so little true happiness. I shall say nothing more about gratitude, because the idea of it is too vague in human minds, but I have loved you like a son ever since that hour when the Lord of Hosts put your fate in my hands. I have followed your brilliant course as if it had been my own. I have joyed over your successes, and I have sorrowed over your sorrows. . . . Frequently my duties towards my own people have kept me from lending you a helping hand. Frequently, too, your own hardness has stood between us. But now, when I behold you so deeply crushed, and when you have treated me with a confidence that I may well call filial, I shall forget for a moment that I am your enemy—which I must be as a man of Luebeck, while as Herman Israel I am your friend. I shall forget that I am a merchant, and—[Pause] I hope that I may never regret it— [Pause] and—and . . . Do you know John Andersson?

KING. I don't.

ISRAEL. But I do, and I know Anders Persson and Mons Nilsson, too! They called on me yesterday, and—to-morrow the southern provinces will rise in rebellion!

KING. So *that's* what was coming? Oh! Who is John Andersson?

ISRAEL. Hard to tell. But behind his face appears another one that looks like the devil's own. Have you heard the name of Dacke?

KING. Yes, but only in a sort of dream. Dacke?—Dacke? —It sounds like the cawing of a jackdaw.—Who is he?

ISRAEL. Nobody knows. It is the name of one invisible,

whom all know and none have seen. But that name has been seen on a letter signed by—the Emperor.

KING. The Emperor?

ISRAEL. The Emperor of the Holy Roman and German Empire!

KING. Fairy-tales!

ISRAEL. You won't believe me? Investigate!

KING. I believe you and I thank you!—You say that Anders Persson and Mons Nilsson have been plotting with the rebels right here in my own city?

ISRAEL. As surely as I have ears to hear with.

KING. My God! My God!—Then I know what to do with them! Two years of struggle with myself and my conscience, and at last I know what to do with them! At last!

COURTIER. [*Bringing in* JACOB ISRAEL.] Jacob Israel of Luebeck!

KING. Who dares to disturb me?

JACOB. [*Throwing himself at the* KING's *feet without noticing his father.*] My noble King, an humble youth has ventured to disturb you because your life is at stake!

KING. Speak up! What more! Who are you?

JACOB. I am Jacob Israel, your Highness.

KING. [*To* ISRAEL.] It's your Jacob, is it not?

JACOB *is thunderstruck at the sight of his father.*

ISRAEL. It's my boy.

KING. What do you want? Speak quickly, or away with you!

JACOB *does not answer.*

KING. Who is after my life? If you mean John Andersson or Dacke, I know it already.—For the sake of your good intention and your youth, but particularly for the sake of your father, I shall forgive you.

ISRAEL. But I have no right to forgive so quickly.—You came here to accuse your father? Answer me yes or no.

JACOB. Yes!

ISRAEL. Go then, and take my curse with you!

JACOB. [*Kneeling before* ISRAEL.] Forgive, father!

ISRAEL. No more your father! You silly, impudent youth,

who think that you understand the art of statesmanship and the laws of honour better than he who brought you into the world! What you did not foresee was that I might change my mind.

KING. Oh, forgive him, Herman!

ISRAEL. I have forgiven him already, but our sacred laws will never do so. Take this ring, Jacob, and go to—you know whom!—But bid me good-bye first.

JACOB. [*Throwing himself into the arms of his father.*] Take away your curse, father!

ISRAEL *wets one of his fingers, makes a sign with it on his son's forehead, and mutters a few inaudible words. Then he kisses* JACOB *on both cheeks and leads him to the door at the right, through which the young man disappears.*

KING. What are you two doing?

ISRAEL. [*Deeply stirred.*] That is a family secret. Now we can go on.

KING. Or quit. You have given me proof of your unswerving friendship, Herman, and I thank you for the last time. Give me your hand!

ISRAEL. Not to promise anything that cannot be kept!

KING. No promises, then! Farewell, and peace be with you!

ISRAEL. [*Moved.*] I thank you!

KING. What is that? You are crying?

ISRAEL. Perhaps, for now I am your equal in misfortune. I have lost my son!

KING. He'll come back to you.

ISRAEL. [*As he is leaving.*] Never!—Good-bye!

KING. [*Escorting him to the door.*] Good-bye, Herman, old friend! [HERMAN ISRAEL *goes out.*

The KING's MOTHER-IN-LAW *enters from the left in the white dress of a Cistercian nun.*

KING. [*Greeting her kindly.*] Good morning, mother-in-law.

MOTHER-IN-LAW. Are you busy?

KING. Very much so.

MOTHER-IN-LAW. But not so much that you cannot hear the justified complaint of a subject.

KING. You are too modest. However, let me decide whether

your complaint be justified or no.   I must hear too many unjusti-
fied ones, God wot!

MOTHER-IN-LAW.   If I condescend to make a complaint,
you may be sure that I have reasons for it.

KING.   But they must be good.   Most reasons are no good at
all.—Is it a question of Anders Persson and Mons Nilsson?

MOTHER-IN-LAW.   No, of myself.

KING.   Then you should be well informed at least.

MOTHER-IN-LAW.   Is there law and justice in this country?

KING.   Both law and justice, but also a lot of wrong-
doing.

MOTHER-IN-LAW.   Do you know that the Queen's mother—
that is, I—has been insulted by the mob?

KING.   No, I didn't know, but I have long expected it, as I
have told you before this.

MOTHER-IN-LAW   You think it right, then? . . .

KING.   No, I think it wrong of you to wear that dress in
public, when it is forbidden.   And it is only out of respect for
yourself and your—hm!—sex, that I have not long ago ordered
you to be stripped of it.

MOTHER-IN-LAW.   Ha-ha!

KING.   And it has been wrong of me to leave the Convent of
Vreta standing for you to live in, when the law demands that it
be torn down.

MOTHER-IN-LAW.   Ha-ha!

KING.   Since you, by persuading me into letting the convent
remain, have placed me before the public in the awkward position of a perverter of justice, you should, at least, show me the
consideration of not appearing on the streets in that dress.   And
as I have given you permission to come here *at your own risk;*
you must bear that risk yourself.   To show you that justice exists,
however, I shall see that those who insulted you be found—they
had no right to insult you, even if you had been the humblest
woman of the people.   Now that matter is settled!   [*He goes
to the door at the right and summons the* COURTIER, *who appears
in the doorway.*]   Call four of the guards.   Put two at that
door [*indicating the door at the left*] and two at the other [*indicating the right-hand door*].

MOTHER-IN-LAW. Thus I am treated like a thief and a murderer by my own kinsman. . . .

KING. No you are not! But no one knows what may happen. . . . It depends on your own conduct.

MOTHER-IN-LAW. [*With a threat in her glance.*] Do you call that freedom?

KING. It is freedom for me—to be free from unreasonable people.

Two guards enter from the right.

KING. [*Pointing at the left-hand door.*] Outside that door. And no one can get in here; literally no one! [*As the guards hesitate.*] If anybody should come, whoever it be, mind you—and try to force his way in here, cut him down—cut him down! [*To his* MOTHER-IN-LAW.] I cannot show you the door, but I must warn you that two executions will take place in this room within a few minutes.

MOTHER-IN-LAW. Here?

KING. Yes, here! Do you wish to look on?

MOTHER-IN-LAW. [*Approaching the door at the left.*] I shall go in a moment, but first you must hear something for your own benefit. . . .

KING. If it is for *my* benefit, I can guess the nature of it. Well, spit it out now!

MOTHER-IN-LAW. This man Herman Israel, whom you regard as a friend, is speaking ill of you on your back.

KING. When I do what's ill, he has the right to speak ill of me—has he not?

MOTHER-IN-LAW. [*Going out in a huff.*] Oh, it's impossible to reason with you!

KING. Have you really discovered that at last?—At last! [*He goes to the door at the right.*] Let Master Olavus Petri come in.

MASTER OLAVUS *enters.*

KING. Good day, Olof. I have read your report on the conditions at Copperberg, and I am pleased with you.—Have Anders Persson and Mons Nilsson been arrested?

OLAVUS. They have been locked up since last night.

KING. [*Goes to the door at the right.*] Order Anders

Persson and Mons Nilsson to be brought up here at once. [*To* OLAVUS.] Have you any proof that the prisoners have been plotting with John Andersson?

OLAVUS.   Proof and witnesses.

KING.   Good!—Tell me something. . . .   What do you think of Herman Israel—as a man, and more particularly in his relationship to me?

OLAVUS.   He seems to me a good and faithful friend of your Highness.   As a private person he is honest in every respect, big-minded, and straight in all his actions.

KING.   I am glad to hear it just now, when I have all but lost my faith in friendship.   So you think I can rely on him?

OLAVUS.   Absolutely.

KING.   Have you heard of the restlessness in the southern provinces?

OLAVUS.   Yes, I am sorry to say.

KING.   They say that it is pretty serious.

OLAVUS.   So serious that nothing but quick and determined action can save the country.

KING.   Have you heard the Emperor's name mentioned in this connection?

OLAVUS.   I have.

KING.   I want a piece of advice, although I may not take it. What would you, in my place, do with Anders Persson and Mons Nilsson?

OLAVUS.   Have them executed before the sun has set.

KING.   You are a stern man, Olof!

OLAVUS.   Yes, why not?

KING.   Do you think you could sleep nights—having shown that kind of—sternness?

OLAVUS.   Only then should I be able to sleep in peace. . . .

KING.   Very well!   Have you anything to ask me about?

OLAVUS.   I have—but it's a delicate question.

KING.   Let's see!

OLAVUS.   It concerns the mother of the Queen. . . .

KING.   The people are muttering?

OLAVUS.   The people think that when the King has ordered

the introduction of a new faith, he should not for family reasons overlook the violation of the established law. . . .

KING. It's not the people, but you, who are saying that. . . .

OLAVUS. Suppose I took the liberty of telling my King the truth. . . .

KING. You're no court fool who needs to run about dropping truths wherever you go! [*Pause.*] Now, I am willing to admit that the indiscretion of my gracious mother-in-law puts me in a false position towards the adherents of the new faith. . . . But this is not the bedchamber, and we'll let that question stay where it belongs; behind the bed curtains. Is there anything else?

OLAVUS. Nothing else. But this question. . . .

KING. [*Hotly.*] I'll solve it myself!

OLAVUS. Can your Highness solve it?

KING. I think you ask too many questions!

OLAVUS. If it were a private matter, yes—but as it concerns the whole country. . . .

KING. Which I am looking after! I am looking after the whole country. And if you must know, I have just settled that very question, so that your advice is a little belated. The Convent of Vreta will be closed before you have time to write another sermon. Do you realise now that I have a right to be angry with your needless and unsolicited questions?

OLAVUS. I stand corrected!

KING. I have got you on account of my sins, and I suppose I must take your faults with your merits, which are great. Now we are done with *that*! Go back and roar in your pulpit now. Here I do the roaring!

[MASTER OLAVUS *goes out by the door at the right.*

KING. [*Standing in front of that door with folded hands and speaking in a barely audible voice.*] Eternal Lord, who rules the destinies of princes and of peoples, illumine my mind and strengthen my will, so that I may not judge unrighteously! [*He makes the sign of the cross and mutters a brief prayer; then he opens the door.*] Bring in the prisoners!

The door remains open while the KING *seats himself in the chair of state.*

ANDERS PERSSON *and* MONS NILSSON *are brought in. They look around the room uneasily at first; then they start towards the* KING.

KING. Stay where you are! [*Pause.*] Once I called you my friends, Anders Persson and Mons Nilsson. You know why. But that was long ago. I let you keep life and goods when you had forfeited both, and thus Providence rid me mercifully of the debt of gratitude I had come to owe you. Two years ago you withdrew your oath of loyalty and opened war on me for the sake of those bells. Being victorious, I had a right to your heads, but I let you go. That's how my debt was paid. Your ingratitude wiped up my gratitude, and so *that* bill was settled. Now the time has come for a new settlement, and this time the balance is against you. To find out just where you stood, I invited you to my capital, and you might have guessed that I would keep my eyes on you. My ears have been open, too, and I have learned that you have begun plotting all over again. Do you know John Andersson?

ANDERS *and* MONS. No!

KING. [*Rising and approaching them angrily.*] Do you know Dacke?

ANDERS *and* MONS. [*Falling on their knees.*] Mercy!

KING. Yes, mercy! But there will be no more mercy. You have had it once, and twice is too much.

ANDERS *and* MONS *make movements to speak.*

KING. Silence! I am doing the speaking now! You were going to talk about friendship, of course. I cannot be the friend of my enemies, and having cancelled your acquaintance, I don't even know you. Were I to let old devotion influence my judgment, I should not be acting as an unbiased judge. And he who has incurred the disfavour of the law cannot be helped by any favour of mine! That's enough words spent on this matter! [*Goes to the door at the right.*] Take away these culprits, guard!

ANDERS. What is the sentence?

KING. That you lose life, honour, and property.

MONS *makes a gesture as if wishing to shake hands with the* KING.

King. *My* hand? Oh, no! Shake hands with the heads-
man, and kiss the block—that's good enough for you!

Anders. One word!

King. Not one!

[Anders Persson *and* Mons Nilsson *are led out.*
The King *turns his back on them and goes to the chair of state,*
where he sinks down, burying his face in his hands.

Curtain.

ACT IV

SCENE I

A square at the foot of Brunkeberg. A fountain stands in the
centre. The Hansa House appears at the right. It is built
of red bricks, with windows in Gothic style. The windows
are barred outside and have shutters within. The gates are
fastened with heavy wooden beams. Above the gateway
appear the flag and coat of arms of Luebeck.

At the left is a tavern with a sign-board bearing the inscription:
" The Golden Apple." There are trees in front of it, and
under these tables and benches. Next the foreground is a
bower with a table and benches within it.

The hillside of Brunkeberg forms the background. It contains
a number of gallows, wheels, and similar paraphernalia.

There is a bench in front of the Hanseatic office.

Agda *and* Karin *are standing at the fountain when the cur-*
tain rises. Agda *carries a water-jar, while* Karin *has a*
basket full of flowers and wreaths.

Agda. You ask what that big red house is? It used to be
the Convent of St. Clara. Now it is the Hanseatic office.

Karin. Do they ever buy any flowers there?

Agda. Not now, I think. I used to bring flowers there
when an image of the Virgin Mary stood at the corner.—I wish
she were there still!

Karin. What do they do in that house? They tell so many
queer stories about it, and no one is ever admitted. . . .

AGDA. Have you heard that, too?   I suppose they buy and
sell, like all that come from Luebeck.

KARIN.   Of course, but they say that people have disappeared
in that house and that those who live there are heathens who
sacrifice. . . .

AGDA.   You have heard that, too?   But it can't be true!   Do
you think so?

KARIN.   How could I tell?   And why are you so disturbed
by those stories?   [AGDA *does not reply*.]   Gossip says that you
used to have a friend in there.   Is it true?

AGDA.   Well, as you have heard about it. . . .   But whether
he still be there. . . .   Oh, if I only knew!

KARIN.   I'll ring and ask.

AGDA. No, no!   You don't know what kind of people they are!

KARIN.   Do you think they'll eat me?   [*She goes up to the
gateway and pulls a string; a bell is heard ringing inside.*]
Listen!   That's the old vesper bell!   I know it!   Bing-bong!
Bing-bong!

AGDA.   Stop it!   Somebody might come.

KARIN.   Isn't that what we want?   But no one does come,
my dear.—It's a gruesome place.   And I shall leave it alone now.
—Do you know Prince Eric, Agda?

AGDA.   Yes, it was on his account they closed up the Blue
Dove.   Now I am working over there, at the Golden Apple.

KARIN.   They say that he used to be very polite to you.

AGDA.   No, he was most impolite, not to say nasty.

KARIN.   He had been drinking then.   Otherwise he is merely
miserable, they say.

AGDA.   Do you know him?

KARIN.   No, I have only seen him, but I cannot forget his
sad eyes and his long face.   He looks so much like a doll I had
once—I called it Blinkie Bloodless. . . .   I suppose they are not
kind to him at home, either.

AGDA.   Probably not, but a man has no right to act like a
brute because he is unhappy.

KARIN.   Why do you talk like that?   He drinks a lot of
wine, like most young men . . . and . . . Hush!   Somebody
is coming. . . .

AGDA.   Good-bye, Karin.   I have to run. . . .

> [*She hurries into the tavern at the left.*

KARIN.   [*As she goes to the right.*]   I'll be back.

PRINCE ERIC *and* JORGHEN PERSSON *enter from the rear.*

ERIC.   Here's my new well-spring of wine.   Come quick to the bower here.

JORGHEN.   And Agda is here, too!

ERIC.   Well, what of it?   [*Rapping on the table.*

> AGDA *appears.*

ERIC.   [*To* AGDA.]   Bring us some Rhine wine and then make yourself invisible.   [*To* JORGHEN.]   You know, Jorghen, I am facing a crucial moment and must be ready to act at once.   The King has lost his reason and is committing acts that cannot be defended.   Yesterday he cut off the heads of those Dalecarlians.   To-day comes the news that his troops have been beaten by the peasants of Småland, who are now crossing Holaved Forest.[1]   Now the Dalecarlians will rise, of course, and everything is lost.

JORGHEN.   What does that concern us?   Let the world perish, and I shall laugh at it.

ERIC.   But this is what beats everything else for madness. Finding his treasury empty, the King, in his incredible simplicity, tries to borrow money from these Luebeckians, who are his enemies.

JORGHEN.   Well, if you need money, your enemies are the best ones to take it from.

ERIC.   If I am not crazy already, you'll make me so!   Please be serious a moment!

JORGHEN.   [*Recites.*]

> " The ring of gold, and rattling dice,
> And wine brings light to tipsy eyes.
> But in the night, that light must lack,
> To wenches leads each crooked track."

At that moment AGDA *appears with the wine.*

---

[1] A rough and inaccessible forest region on the eastern shore of Lake Vettern, marking the border-line between the province of Småland in the south and Östergötland (East Gothia) in the north.

ERIC. [*Laughing idiotically at* JORGHEN's *recitation.*] Ha-
ha! That's a good one. But then, I made it myself.—Well,
Agda, or Magda, or what it is, where's your pawnbroker to-day?

AGDA *does not reply.*

ERIC. Do you know that those Hanseatic people are in the
habit of butchering little boys and selling them to the Turk?

AGDA. Is that true?

ERIC. There is some truth in it, I think.

JORGHEN. Let the maiden go before she begins to cry. I
can't bear tears.

ERIC. I suppose you have never cried, Jorghen?

JORGHEN. Twice: when I was born, and once after that—
out of rage.

ERIC. You are a beast, Jorghen.

AGDA *goes back into the tavern.*

JORGHEN. However—you wish to figure out what is to happen, and to form a decision on the basis of your false calculations.
Have you not noticed how all our plans are foiled? That's the
game of the gods. Sometimes we act wisely, and everything goes
to the devil, and then we act like fools, and everything turns out
right. It's nothing but humbug—all of it!

ERIC. I think so, too, and yet there must be some sort of
sense in it.

JORGHEN. Not as far as I can see. It's just like dicing.

ERIC. Let the dice rattle, then!

JORGHEN. Let them rattle! That's the right word for it.
Now it's a question of head or tail, however—whether the King
is to be the tail, and the man from Småland the head. . . .
Look, who comes here!

KARIN *enters from the right.*

ERIC. [*Staring at her.*] Who—is—that?

JORGHEN. A flower girl.

ERIC. No—this is—something else! Do you see?

JORGHEN. What?

ERIC. What I see—but, of course, you can't.

KARIN *comes forward, kneels before* ERIC *and offers him a
wreath.*

ERIC. [*Rises, takes the wreath, and places it on the head of*

KARIN; *then to* JORGHEN.] Look! Now the wreath has been added to the crown.[1]

JORGHEN. What crown?

ERIC. Didn't you see? [*To* KARIN.] Get up, child! You should not be kneeling to me, but I to you. I don't want to ask your name, for I know who you are, although I have never seen you or heard of you before.—What do you ask of me? Speak!

KARIN. [*Unaffectedly.*] That your Grace buy my flowers.

ERIC. Put your flowers there. [*He takes a ring from one of his fingers and gives it to her.*] There!

KARIN. No, I cannot wear that ring, your Grace—it's much too grand for me. And if I try to sell it, I shall be seized as a thief.

ERIC. You are as wise as you are beautiful.

[*He gives her money.*

KARIN. I thank your Grace, but it is too much.

ERIC. As you named no price, I can do so myself.

[KARIN *goes out. A long pause follows.*

ERIC. Did you see?

JORGHEN. Not a thing.

ERIC. Didn't you hear, either? Didn't you notice her voice?

JORGHEN. A voice like that of any jade—rather pert.

ERIC. Stop your tongue, Jorghen! I love her!

JORGHEN. She is not the first.

ERIC. Yes, the first, and the only one!

JORGHEN. Well, seduce her if you must.

ERIC. [*Drawing his sword.*] Take care, or by God! . . .

JORGHEN. Have we now got to the poking point again?

ERIC. I don't know what has happened, but this moment has made me despise you. The same city can't hold you and me. Your eyes defile me, and your whole being stinks. I shall leave you, and I don't want to see you face to face again.—It is as if an angel had come to take me away from the habitations of the

---

[1] As far back as we know the two principal ornaments of a Swedish bride have been the crown—sometimes woven out of myrtle and sometimes made of metal and semi-precious stones—and the wreath, always made of myrtle.

damned.   I despise my whole past, as I despise you and myself.

[*He goes out in the same direction as* KARIN *went before.*

JORGHEN.   Seems to be serious this time.   But I guess you'll come back.   [*He raps on the table.*

AGDA *appears.*

JORGHEN.   Do you know Karin, the flower girl?

AGDA.   Yes, I do.

JORGHEN.   What kind of a piece is she?

AGDA.   A nice and decent girl, of whom I have never heard anything bad.

JORGHEN.   Can you see anything beautiful about her?

AGDA.   No, but she is rather pretty, and there is like a halo of sweetness about her.

JORGHEN.   Oh, it was that he saw, then!

AGDA.   Tell me, secretary, are you really as hard as people say?

JORGHEN.   I am not hard to anybody, child, but the world has been hard to me ever since I was born.

AGDA.   Why don't you always speak like that?

JORGHEN.   . . . However, the Prince is enamoured, bewitched.

AGDA.   Poor fellow!— Tell me, secretary, is the Prince quite right?

JORGHEN.   You and your questions are very amusing.   Let me ask you one now.   Hm!   Do you think a woman could possibly—hm!—love me?

AGDA.   No, I don't.   [JORGHEN *looks offended.*]   Not unless you try to be good.

JORGHEN.   How the devil is that to be done?

AGDA.   Shame!   Shame!

JORGHEN.   If you never see anything good, how can you believe in it?

AGDA.   Tell me, secretary, did the Prince mean what he said about the Hanseatic people and what they are doing in that house?

JORGHEN.   No, child!   That was only a cruel jest.   But no Swedish authority can interfere with what they are doing in there. That much you should know, if you are worrying about your Jacob.

AGDA. Will you do me a favour? It won't cost you anything.

JORGHEN. With the greatest pleasure, my dear girl.

AGDA. Find Jacob for me! He had promised to meet me, and he never came. We have been ringing the bell at the door, but no one answers.

JORGHEN. I don't want to hurt you, Agda, but, unfortunately, I have reason to believe that all the Luebeck people have gone away on account of the new rebellion.

AGDA. And he won't come back, you think?

JORGHEN. I don't like to prophesy, because it generally turns out the other way, but I don't think he will be back soon.

AGDA. [*Sinking to the ground.*] Lord Jesus!

JORGHEN. [*Rises and helps her to her feet.*] What is it, girl?—Tell me! [*In a lower voice.*] A child?

AGDA. He had given me his promise.

JORGHEN. [*Genuinely moved.*] Poor woman!

AGDA *watches him closely.*

JORGHEN. Misery, always misery, wherever love gets in its work!

AGDA. And you don't despise me?

JORGHEN. I pity you, as I pity all of us.

AGDA. Can you see now that good exists?

JORGHEN. Where?

AGDA. Within yourself.

JORGHEN. Pooh!—Is there anything else I can do for you?

AGDA. Yes, secretary, if you would write to Luebeck and ask Jacob . . .

JORGHEN. I have not much use for love-affairs, but I'll write, nevertheless, provided we find that he really has gone away.

AGDA. [*Tries to kiss his hand, which he pulls away.*] Thank you!

JORGHEN. What are you doing, woman? I am no bishop! —But hush! Here comes illustrious company. So I think I'll sneak off!

The stage has grown darker in the meantime.

AGDA. Please, secretary, don't forget me now!

JORGHEN. So you don't trust me? Well, there is not much
to trust in!   [*He goes out to the left.*

The KING *enters, wearing his big blue cloak and his soft black
hat. He is using his boar-spear as a staff.*

PRINCE JOHAN *is with him, dressed very simply, as if to avoid
recognition.*

KING. [*Looking about.*] Do you think we have been recognised?

JOHAN. No, I don't think so, father.

KING. Ring, then.

JOHAN. [*Pulls the bell-rope outside the Hanseatic office.*]
The bell does not ring.

KING. Knock.

JOHAN. [*Rapping on the door.*] Nobody seems to answer.

KING. [*Seating himself on the bench outside.*] I must get
hold of Herman Israel this very evening—I must!

JOHAN. You are worried, father?

KING. I am certainly not at ease.   [*Pause.*

JOHAN. Money cares again?

KING. Oh, don't talk of it!—Knock again.

JOHAN. [*Rapping at the door.*] There is no one there.

*A crowd of beggars enter and kneel in front of the King with
hands held out in supplication.*

KING. Are you mocking me?

FIRST BEGGAR. We are perishing, my noble lord!

KING. I am perishing, too!—Why are you begging, anyhow?

SECOND BEGGAR. I'll tell you. Because the King has seized
the tithes that went to the poor before. And when he did so, he
said: " You can beg! "

KING. And what is he doing with the tithes of the poor?

FIRST BEGGAR. Paying Prince Eric's le-lecheries!

KING. No, paying the country's debt, you knaves!   [*To*
JOHAN.] Give them money, so we get rid of them.

JOHAN. [*Distributing coins.*] You'll have to share it between you, and then away—at once!

[*The* BEGGARS *leave.*

KING. I wonder who sent them? Somebody must have sent
them!—Knock again. [JOHAN *does so.*] *What unspeakable*

humiliation! You see, my son, that no matter how high up you get, now and then you have to climb down again. But of anything like this I never dreamt.

> [*He takes off his hat and wipes his forehead.*

JOHAN. May I speak?

KING. No, you may not, for I know what you mean to say.

MONS NILSSON's WIDOW *enters, led by* BARBRO. *Both are in mourning, and* BARBRO *carries a document in her hand.*

BARBRO. [*To her mother.*] That must be the Councillor himself.

WIDOW. Can that be Herman Israel who is sitting there? My eyes have grown blind with sorrow.

BARBRO. It must be him.

> *The two women approach the* KING.

BARBRO. [*To the* KING.] Are you the Councillor?

KING. What do you want of him?

BARBRO. Mr. Syndic, we are the bereaved dependents of Mons Nilsson, and we have come to pray that you put in a good word for us with the King.

KING. Why do you think the Councillor's word will be of any help?

BARBRO. We have been told that he is the King's only friend, and we thought he might help us to get back the property of which we have been unjustly deprived.

KING. Unjustly, you say? As a traitor, Mons Nilsson was judged forfeit of life *and* goods—which was only just!

BARBRO. But the dower of the innocent widow should not have been taken with the rest.

KING. What is your name?

BARBRO. I was baptised with the name of Barbro, and the King himself acted as my godfather when he was in Dalecarlia at that time.

KING. [*Rises, but sits down again immediately.*] Barbro? —Have you ever seen the King?

BARBRO. Not since I was too small to know him. But the last time he visited Copperberg, my father was expecting him, and we children were to greet him with a song.

KING. What song was that?

BARBRO.   I cannot sing since my father came to his death so miserably, but it was a song about King Gustavus and the Dalecarlians, and this is the way it ended:

> " You have by my side been fighting
> Like sturdy Swedish men.
> If God will spare my life-blood,
> I'll do you good in stead."

KING.   Say something really bad about the King!

BARBRO.   No, father told us we must never do that, no matter what we might hear other people say.

KING.   Did your father tell you that?

BARBRO.   Yes, he did.

KING.   Go in peace now.   I shall speak to the King, and you shall have your rights, for he wants to do right, and he tries to do it.

BARBRO.   [*Kneels and takes hold of the* KING's *hand, which she kisses.*]   If the King were as gracious as you are, Councillor, there would be no cause for worry.

KING.   [*Placing his hand on* BARBRO's *head.*]   He is, my child, and I know that he won't refuse his goddaughter anything. Go in peace now!   [*The two women leave.*

KING.   [*To* JOHAN.]   Who can have sent them?   Who? —Here I have to sit like a defendant—I, the highest judge of the land!

JOHAN.   May I say a word?

KING.   No, because I can tell myself what you want to say. I can tell that the hand of the Lord has been laid heavily upon me, although I cannot tell why.   If the Lord speaks through conscience and prayer, then it is he who has made me act as I have acted.   Why my obedience should be punished, I cannot grasp.   But I submit to a higher wisdom that lies beyond my reason.—That girl was my goddaughter, and her father was my friend, and I had to take his head. . . .   Oh, cruel life, that has to be lived nevertheless!   [*Pause.*]   Knock again.

MARCUS.   [*In travelling clothes, enters from the right.*] Your Highness!   [*He kneels.*

KING.   Still more?

MARCUS.   A message from Herman Israel.

KING. At last!—Speak!

MARCUS. Herman Israel has this afternoon set sail for Luebeck.

KING. [*Rising.*] Then I am lost!—God help me!

JOHAN. And all of us!

The KING *and* JOHAN *go out.* MARCUS *goes over to the tavern and raps on one of the tables.*

AGDA. [*Appearing.*] Is that you, Marcus?

MARCUS. Yes, Agda, it's me.

AGDA. Where is Jacob?

MARCUS. He has started on a journey—a very long one.

AGDA. Where?

MARCUS. I cannot tell. But he asked me to bring you his greeting and to give you this ring.

AGDA. As a keepsake only, or as a plight of his troth?

MARCUS. Read what it says.

AGDA. [*Studying the ring.*] Yes, I can spell a little. . . . "For ever," it says. What does it mean?

MARCUS. I fear it means—farewell for ever.

AGDA. [*With a cry.*] No, no, it means that he is dead!

MARCUS *does not answer.*

AGDA. Who killed him?

MARCUS. The law and his own crime. He rebelled against his father and betrayed his country.

AGDA. To save mine!—Oh, what is to become of me?

MARCUS. [*Shrugging his shoulders.*] That's the way of the world. Nothing but deceit and uncertainty.

AGDA. Alas, he was like all the rest!

MARCUS. Yes, all human beings are pretty much alike. He who is no worse than the rest is no better, either. Good-bye!

Curtain.

SCENE II

The study of MASTER OLAVUS PETRI. *There is a door on either side of the room.*

OLAVUS *is writing at a table.*

CHRISTINE *is standing beside the table with a letter in her hand.*

CHRISTINE.   Do I disturb you?

OLAVUS.   [*Quietly and coldly.*]   Naturally, as I am writing.

CHRISTINE.   Are you sure that you are writing?

OLAVUS.   Absolutely sure.

CHRISTINE.   But I have not seen your pen move for a long while.

OLAVUS.   That was because I was thinking.

CHRISTINE.   Once . . .

OLAVUS.   Yes, once upon a time!

CHRISTINE.   Can Reginald come in and say good-bye?

OLAVUS.   Are we that far already?

CHRISTINE.   The carriage is waiting and all his things have been packed.

OLAVUS.   Let him come, then.

CHRISTINE.   Are you certain that he is going to Wittenberg to study?

OLAVUS.   I have seen too much uncertainty, as you know, to be certain of anything.   If you have reason to doubt the feasibility of his plans, you had better say so.

CHRISTINE.   If I had any doubts, I would not disturb you with them.

OLAVUS.   Always equally amiable!   Will you please ask Reginald to come here?

CHRISTINE.   I'll do whatever you command.

OLAVUS.   And as I never command, but merely ask. . . .

CHRISTINE.   If you would command your precious son now and then, he might be a little more polite and obedient to his mother.

OLAVUS.   Reginald is hard, I admit, but you do wrong in trying to educate him to suit your own high pleasure.

CHRISTINE.   Do you side with the children against their parents?

OLAVUS.   If I am not mistaken, I have always done so when the natural rights of the children were concerned.

CHRISTINE.   Have the children any natural rights to anything?

OLAVUS.   Of course, they have!   You haven't forgotten how we . . .

CHRISTINE. Yes, I have forgotten every bit of that old tommy-rot! I have forgotten how you swore to love me. I have forgotten the noise made about the pope's beard, and the stealing of the church silver, and the humbug with the bells, and the *pure* faith, and roast ducks and cackling swans, and martyrs with a taste for fighting, and the following of Christ with wine and women, and the scratching of eyes and tearing of hair, until we now have twenty-five brand-new faiths in place of a holy Catholic Church. . . . I have forgotten every bit of it!

OLAVUS. Perhaps that was the best thing you could do. And will you please ask Reginald to come here now?

CHRISTINE. Certainly, I'll ask him to come here, and it will be a great pleasure to do so. [*She goes out to the left.*

OLAVUS. [*Alone, speaking to himself.*] Happy she, who has been able to forget! I remember everything!

CHRISTINE *returns with* REGINALD.

REGINALD. I want mother to go out, because I can't talk when she is here.

OLAVUS. There won't be so very much to talk about.

CHRISTINE. I won't say a word; only listen—and look at you. [*She seats herself.*

REGINALD. No, you mustn't look at us.

OLAVUS. Be quiet, boy, and be civil to your mother! When you go travelling, there is no telling whether you ever come back.

REGINALD. So much the better!

OLAVUS. [*Painfully impressed.*] What's that?

REGINALD. I am tired of everything, and I just wish I were dead!

OLAVUS. Yes, that's the way youth talks nowadays!

REGINALD. And why? Because we don't know what to believe!

OLAVUS. Oh, you don't? And how about the articles of confession? Don't you believe in them?

REGINALD. Believe, you say? Don't you know that belief comes as a grace of God?

OLAVUS. Are you a Calvinist?

REGINALD. I don't know what I am. When I talk with

Prince Johan, he says I am a papist, and when I meet Prince Eric, he tells me I am a follower of Zwingli.

OLAVUS.   And now you wish to go to Wittenberg to learn the true faith from Doctor Martin Luther?

REGINALD.   I know his teachings and don't believe in them.

OLAVUS.   Is that so?

REGINALD.   To him belief is everything, and deeds nothing. I have believed, but it didn't make my deeds any better at all, and so I felt like a perfect hypocrite in the end.

OLAVUS.   Is Prince Johan a Catholic?

REGINALD.   So he must be, as he sticks to deeds, which ought to be the main thing.

OLAVUS.   And Prince Eric belongs to the Reformed Church, you say?

REGINALD.   Yes, in so far as he believes in the dispensation of grace.   And Jorghen Persson must be a Satanist, I think. And young Sture is absolutely an Anabaptist. . . .

OLAVUS.   Well, this is news to me!   I thought the days of schism were past. . . .

REGINALD.   Schism, yes—that's the word Prince Johan is using always.   We had a Catholic Church, and then . . .

OLAVUS.   Oh, shut your mouth and go to Wittenberg!

REGINALD.   As it is your wish, father—but I won't study any more theology.

OLAVUS.   Why not?

REGINALD.   I think it is a device of the devil to make people hate each other.

CHRISTINE.   Good for you, Reginald!

OLAVUS.   And it had to come to this in my own house! *Pulchre, bene, recte!*—Who, Reginald, do you think has caused this dissension under which you young people are suffering now?

REGINALD.   That's easily answered.

OLAVUS.   Of course.   We old ones, you mean?   But we, too, were children of our time, and were stripped of our faith by our prophets.   Who is, then, to blame?

REGINALD.   No one.

OLAVUS.   And what do you mean to do with your future?

REGINALD.   My future?   It appears to me like a grey mist

without a ray of sunlight. And should a ray ever break through, it will at once be proved a will-o'-the-wisp leading us astray.

OLAVUS. That's just how I felt once! At your age I could see my whole future as in a vision. I foresaw the bitter cup and the pillory. And yet I had to go on. I had to enter the mist, and I myself had to carry the will-o'-the-wisp that *must* lead the wanderers astray. I foretold this very moment, even, when my son would stand before me saying: "Thus I am, because thus you have made me!" You noticed, perhaps, that I was not surprised —and this is the reason.

REGINALD. What am I to do? Advise me!

OLAVUS. You, no more than I, will follow the advices given you.

REGINALD. Inform me, then! Tell me: what is life?

OLAVUS. That's more than I know. But I think it must be a punishment or an ordeal. At your years I thought I knew everything and understood everything. Now I know nothing and understand nothing. For that reason I rest satisfied with doing my duty and bearing what comes my way.

REGINALD. But I want to know!

OLAVUS. You want to know what is not allowed to be known. Try to know and you will perish!—However, do you want to go or stay?

REGINALD. I am going to Wittenberg to pull Luther to pieces!

OLAVUS. [*Wholly without irony.*] That's the way to speak! O thou splendid youth with thy Alexandrian regret that there are no more things to pull to pieces!

REGINALD. Are you not a Lutheran?

OLAVUS. I am a Protestant.

CHRISTINE. If you have finished now, I shall ask permission to tell in a single word what Luther is—just one word!

OLAVUS. Oh, do, before you burst!

CHRISTINE. Luther is dead!

OLAVUS. Dead?

CHRISTINE. That's what my brother-in-law writes me in this letter from Magdeburg.

OLAVUS. [*Rising.*]   Dead!   [*To* REGINALD.]   My poor Alexander, what will you pull to pieces now?

REGINALD.   First the universe, and then myself.

OLAVUS.   [*Pushing him towards the door at the left.*]   Go ahead, then, but begin with yourself.   The universe will always remain.

CHRISTINE.   [*As she rises and is about to go out with* REGI-NALD.]   Will there be peace on earth now?

OLAVUS.   That will never be!—Let me have that letter.

[CHRISTINE *and* REGINALD *go out to the left.*
While OLAVUS *is reading the letter, a hard knock is heard at the right-hand door.*

OLAVUS.   Come!

The knock is repeated. OLAVUS *goes to the door and opens it.   The* KING *enters, wearing his big hat and his cloak, which he throws off.*

OLAVUS.   The King!

KING.   [*Very excited.*]   Yes, but for how long?   Do you know who Dacke is?—A farm labourer who has killed a bailiff; a common thief and incendiary, who is now writing to me with a demand of answer.   I am to take pen in hand and open corre-spondence with a scamp like him!   Do you know that he has crossed the Kolmord Forests and stands with one foot in West Gothia and the other in East Gothia?—Who is behind him? The Emperor, the Elector Frederick of the Palatinate, Magnus Haraldsson, the runaway Bishop of Skara, the Duke of Mecklen-burg.   The Emperor wishes to put the children of Christian the Tyrant back on the throne.[1]   But what troubles me more than anything else is to find the Luebeckians and Herman Israel on the same side—my old friend Herman!   I ask you how it can be possible.   And who has done this to me?   Who?—Have you not a word to say?

OLAVUS.   What can I say, and what—*may* I say?

KING.   Don't be hard on me, Olof, and don't be vengeful. I am nothing but an unfortunate human creature who has had to

---

[1] The Elector Frederick was a son-in-law of the deposed Christian II of Den-mark, and also one of the trusted liegemen of Emperor Charles V, who hoped to see him the head of a reunited Scandinavia dominated by German influences.

drink humiliation like water, and I come to you as my spiritual
guide. I am in despair because I fear that the Lord has deserted
me for ever.—What an infernal notion of mine that was to take
the head of the Dalecarlians just now, when I am in such need
of them! Do you think that deed was displeasing to the Lord?
But if I have sinned like David, you must be my Nathan.

OLAVUS. I have lost the power of prophecy, and I am not
the right man to inflict punishment.

KING. Console me, then, Olof.

OLAVUS. I cannot, because only those who repent can accept
consolation.

KING. You mean that I have transgressed—that I have gone
too far? Speak up! But do it like a servant of the Lord, and
not like a conceited schoolmaster. . . . Have I gone too
far?

OLAVUS. That is not the way to put the question. The
proper way is to ask whether the others have any right on their
side.

KING. Go ahead and ask!

OLAVUS Dacke is the mouthpiece of warranted dissatisfaction. Being the brother-in-law of Christian II, the Emperor is
the guardian of his children, and they have inherited a claim to
the Swedish throne, as the constitution cannot be cancelled by a
rebellion.[1] Bishop Magnus Haraldsson is the spokesman of all
the illegally exiled bishops.

KING. Illegally, you say?

OLAVUS. [Raising his voice.] Yes, because the law of
Sweden does not drive any man away on account of his faith.

KING. Take care!

OLAVUS. Too late now!—The dissatisfaction of the peasants
is warranted, because the Riksdag at Vesterås authorised the King
to seize only the property of bishops and convents. When he
took what belonged to parish churches and private persons, he
became guilty of a crime.

KING. You are a daring man!

OLAVUS. Nothing compared with what I used to be!—As far
as Herman Israel is concerned, he called recently on the King to

[1] Christian II was married to Isabelle, sister of Charles V.

offer a treaty of friendship, and it was stupid of the King to reject it.

KING. Stop!

OLAVUS. Not yet!—The gold and silver of the churches was meant to pay the debt to Luebeck, and much of it was used for that purpose, but a considerable part found its way to Eskil's Chamber under the Royal Palace, and has since been wasted on Prince Eric's silly courtships among other things. . . .

KING. The devil you say!

OLAVUS. Well, Queen Elizabeth is merely making fun of him.

KING. Do you know that?

OLAVUS. I do.—The bells were also to be used in payment of the debt to Luebeck, but a part of them went to the foundry and were turned into cannon, which was not right.

KING. Is that so?

OLAVUS. Add also that the Convent of Vreta was left un-molested in violation of the ordinance concerning the closing of all such places—and for no other reason than that the King's mother-in-law happened to be a Catholic. This is a cowardly and mischievous omission that has caused much bad blood.

KING. The convent is to be closed.

OLAVUS. It should be closed *now*, and it is not!—If I were to sum up what is reprehensible in my great King, I should call it a lack of piety.

KING. That's the worst yet! What do you mean?

OLAVUS. Piety is the respect shown by the stronger—even if he be a man of destiny—for the feelings of the weaker, when these spring from a childlike, and for that reason religious, mind.

KING. Oh, is that what it is?

OLAVUS. Now I have said my say.

KING. Yes, so you have—time and again.

OLAVUS. And if my King had been willing to listen now and then, he would have learned a great deal more. But it is a common fault of princes that they won't listen to anybody but themselves.

KING. Well, I never heard the like of it! I am astounded —most of all because I haven't killed you on the spot!

OLAVUS. Why don't you?

KING. [*Rises and goes towards* OLAVUS, *who remains standing unabashed, looking firmly at the approaching* KING; *the latter withdraws backward and sits down again; for a few moments the two men stare at each other in silence; then the* KING *says*] Who are you?

OLAVUS. A humble instrument of the Lord, shaped to serve what is really great—that marvellous man of God, to whom it was granted to unite all Swedish men and lands.

KING. That was granted Engelbrecht, too, and his reward was the axe that split his head.[1] Is that to be my reward, too?

OLAVUS. I don't think so, your Highness, but it depends on yourself.

KING. What am I to do?

OLAVUS. What you advised me to do when I was carried away by the zeal of my youth.

KING. And you think it necessary to return that advice to me now?

OLAVUS. Why not? I have learned from life, and you have forgotten.

KING. What am I to do?

OLAVUS. Answer Dacke's letter.

KING. Never! Am I to bow down to a vagabond?

OLAVUS. The Lord sometimes uses mere vagabonds for our humiliation. Picture it to yourself as an ordeal by fire.

KING. [*Rising and walking the floor.*] There is truth in what you say. I can feel it, but it does not fetch bottom in my mind. Say one word more.

---

[1] Engelbrecht Engelbrechtsson, a free miner of Dalecarlia, was the first one of a series of notable chieftains who led the Swedish people in their determination to rid the country of the Danish kings, after these had shown a growing inclination to treat Sweden as a Danish province, and not as an independent kingdom, united on equal terms with Denmark and Norway. At the head of the Dalecarlians, Engelbrecht began the work of liberation in 1434, and was remarkably successful in a short time. Unfortunately, he was treacherously and shamefully killed while crossing the Lake Maelaren only two years later. To the Swedes he has ever since been the symbol of their national independence and unity, and he, the simple country squire, remains to this day one of the most beloved and revered figures in Swedish history. It is to him Barbro refers in the opening scenes of the play, and his name is heard again in the closing scenes, with the appearance of his simpler namesake.

OLAVUS.   Dacke will be right as long as you are in the wrong, and God will be with him until you take your place on the side of right.

KING.   I can't bend!

OLAVUS.   Then you'll be broken by someone else.

KING.   [*Walking back and forth.*]   Are you thinking of the Dalecarlians?   Have you heard of a rising among them on account of the executions?

OLAVUS.   Such a thing has been rumoured.

KING.   I am lost.

OLAVUS.   Write to Dacke!

KING.   [*Without conviction.*]   I won't.

OLAVUS.   The Emperor does.

KING.   That's true!   If the Emperor can write to him, why shouldn't I?—But it is perfectly senseless.   Who is this mysterious man who never appears?

OLAVUS.   Perhaps another marvellous man of God—in his own way.

KING.   I must see him face to face.   I'll write and offer him safe-conduct, so that I can talk with him.   That's what I'll do. —Bring me pen and paper!   Or you write, and I'll dictate.

OLAVUS *seats himself at the table.*

KING.   How do we begin?   What am I to call him?

OLAVUS.   Let us merely put down " To Nils Dacke."

KING.   Oh, his name is Nils?   After St. Nicolaus, who comes with rods for children on the sixth of December? [1] [*Pause.*]   Write now. . . .   No, I'll go home and do the writing myself. . . .   Have you heard that Luther is dead?

OLAVUS.   I have, your Highness.

KING.   He was a splendid man!   May he rest in peace!— Yes, such as he was, he was a fine man, but we got rather too much of him.

OLAVUS.   Too many dogmas and not enough of religion.

KING.   He was an obstinate fellow and went too far.   What

[1] An old Swedish custom and superstition, prescribing that every child must be spanked on the date mentioned in order to ensure its obedience during the whole ensuing year.   That custom still survived when the translator was a child, although for many decades the spanking had been a mere formality serving as an excuse for some little gift or treat.

he needed was a taskmaster like you to call him to terms now and then.

OLAVUS. I hope the time of schism and dissension will come to an end now.

KING. A time of dissension you may well call it!—Goodbye, Olof. [*As* OLAVUS *makes a mien of saying something.*] Yes, yes, I *will* write!

Curtain.

ACT V

The terrace in front of the Royal Palace, with trimmed hedges, statuary, and a fountain. Chairs, benches, and tables are placed about. The near background shows a balustrade with Tuscan columns, on which are placed flowers in faïence pots. Beyond the balustrade appear tree tops, and over these tower the tops of masts, from which blue and yellow flags are flying. In the far background, a number of church spires.

The MOTHER-IN-LAW *of the* KING *is on the terrace in her Cistercian dress.*

QUEEN. [*Enters.*] For the last time I beg you, mother, don't wear that dress!

MOTHER-IN-LAW. It is my festive garb, and I am as proud of it as you of your ermine robe.

QUEEN. What is the use of being proud? The day of disaster is upon us all, and we must hold together.

MOTHER-IN-LAW. Let us do so then, and have peace.

QUEEN. Yes, so you say, but you won't even change dress for the sake of the country's peace.

MOTHER-IN-LAW. I don't change faith as you change clothes, and there is a solemn vow to God connected with this dress. The people are making threats against my life. Let them take it! I have my grave-clothes on.

QUEEN. Don't you know that we may have to flee this very day, if the news should prove as bad as yesterday?

MOTHER-IN-LAW. I will not flee.

QUEEN. Everything has already been packed by order of the King, and our sloop lies at the foot of the southern hills, ready to hoist sail.

MOTHER-IN-LAW. I have nothing to pack, because I own nothing. " Be thou faithful unto death, and I will give thee a crown of life." That's what I used to learn. But you have sold your birthright for a crown which soon will no longer be yours.

QUEEN. Go on and punish me; it feels like a relief.

PRINCE ERIC *appears on the terrace; his dress and appearance are orderly, and his mien subdued.*

MOTHER-IN-LAW. Can you tell me what has come over Eric these last days? He looks quite submissive, and something new has come into his face that used to be so hard.

QUEEN. I don't know, but they say that he has changed his ways and cannot bear the company of Jorghen. I have heard whispers about a serious affection. . . .

MOTHER-IN-LAW. No!

QUEEN. [*To* ERIC.] What news do you bring?

ERIC. [*Gently and respectfully.*] No news at all, mother.

QUEEN. [*To her mother.*] He called me mother! [*To* ERIC.] How fare you, Eric? Is life heavy?

ERIC. Heavier than it was the day before yesterday.

QUEEN. What happened yesterday?

ERIC. What happens to a human being only once in a life-time.—Are you much wiser now?

QUEEN. [*To her mother.*] How childlike he has grown! [*To* ERIC.] Have you heard anything of your friend Jacob?

ERIC. Yes, he was my real friend, and so they took his head.

QUEEN. Now you are unjust. There has been no attempt to take the head of Jorghen. . . .

ERIC. He is no longer my friend. [*Peevishly.*] But now I dont want to be questioned any longer, least of all about my secrets—that is, about the secrets of my heart.

QUEEN. [*To her mother.*] He is quite charming in his childishness. Apparently he would love to talk of his secret.

PRINCE JOHAN *enters.*

ERIC. [*Going to meet him.*] Soon we may have nothing

left to fight over, brother Johan, and so—it seems to me we may as well be friends.

JOHAN.   With a right good heart, brother!   Nothing could give me greater pleasure.

ERIC.   Give me your hand!   [*They shake hands.*]   I don't want to be the enemy of any human being after this.

[*He goes out, deeply moved.*]

MOTHER-IN-LAW.   [*To* JOHAN.]   What's the matter with Eric?

JOHAN.   He has found a sweetheart, they say.

QUEEN.   What did I say?

MOTHER-IN-LAW.   Are you coming with me to the mass in the chapel, Johan?   [*When Johan hesitates and does not answer, she says sharply*]   Johan!

QUEEN.   Mother!

MOTHER-IN-LAW.   Is he free to follow his conscience, or is he not?

QUEEN.   If you will leave his conscience alone, he will be free.

MOTHER-IN-LAW.   Well, I am going, and you know where, Johan.   [*She goes out.*

QUEEN.   Johan!

JOHAN.   What do you wish?

QUEEN.   That you do not desert your childhood faith.

JOHAN.   My childhood faith, which I got from my nurse, and not from you, was also the childhood faith of my father.   Why did you not give me yours?

QUEEN.   Yes, punish me.   You have a right to do so.   Everything comes home to us now.   I was young then.   Life was nothing but a game.   The King demanded my company at banquets and festivities, and so your cradle was left unattended and unguarded.   Those were the days when we were drunk with victory and happiness.   And now!—Go where you find it possible to worship, Johan, and pray for your mother!

JOHAN.   If it hurts my gracious mother, I won't go.

QUEEN.   Pray for us all!   [*In a lowered voice.*]   I do not know the new prayers and must not use the old ones!—Hush now!   The King is coming.

[PRINCE JOHAN *goes in the direction previously taken by the* KING'S MOTHER-IN-LAW. -

The KING *enters, holding a letter in his hand. He is accompanied by* MASTER OLAVUS PETRI.

KING. [*To the* QUEEN.] Have everything ready for the start. We are lost!

QUEEN. The will of God be done!

KING. That's what seems to be happening. Go and look after your house, child.   [*The* QUEEN *goes out.*

KING. [*To* OLAVUS.] This is the situation. Dacke answers that he does not care to see " that rebel, and perjurer, and breaker of safe-conducts, Ericsson." He calls me Ericsson, mind you. His people have reached as far north as Södermanland— which means that they are right at our gates! Furthermore, two thousand Dalecarlians are encamped at the North Gate. Their intentions are not known, but can easily be guessed. A fine prophet you are, Olof!

OLAVUS. We have not seen the end yet.

KING. Where do you get your confidence from?

OLAVUS. That's more than I can tell, but I know that everything will end well.

KING. You say that you know? How do you know? I have ceased to believe in anything—except in the wrath of God, which has been turned against me. I am now waiting for the axe. Good and well! I have done my service and am now to be discharged. That's why I wish to leave before I am kicked out.—Do you know what day it is to-day? Nobody has thought of it, and I didn't remember until just now. . . . It is Midsummer Day: *my* day, which no one celebrates. A generation ago I made my entry into the capital on this day. That was the greatest moment of my life. I thought the work of liberation was done, and I thanked God for it!—But it had not been done, and I am not done with it yet.—The Dalecarlians rose. I subdued them, and thought that I was done, which I was not. Twice more they rose, and each time I gave thanks to God, thinking I had done—which was not the case. The lords of West Gothia rose. I squelched them, and was happy, thinking that I surely must have done by that time—which I had not. And now,

Olof?—We are never done until done for—and that's where I am now!

OLAVUS. Oh, no, there is a whole lot left.

KING. Where do you get your fixed ideas from? Have you heard some bird sing, or have you been dreaming?

OLAVUS. Neither.

KING. [*Listening.*] Listen! That's the sound of birch-horns. Do they mean to give me a crown of birch, like the one I gave to Peder the Chancellor and Master Knut? Or is it the scaffold that . . . that? . . .

OLAVUS. Oh, don't!

KING. What was it you called that thing—piety? Much it would have availed me to have piety at Larv Heath or Tuna Plain! [1]—No, I have been right, right, right, so God help me, amen!

OLAVUS makes no answer.

KING. [*Listening.*] They have drums, too.—Oh, everything comes home!—Do you think I can get out of this, Olof?

OLAVUS. I do! And let me give you a final piece of advice: don't leave!

KING. I don't see how it can be avoided. Do you think I'll let them take my head?—Do you know, I can actually hear the tramp-tramp of their feet as they come marching through the North Gate. And that's the Dalecarlians—my own Dalecarlians! Oh, life is cruel! Can you hear it? Tramp—tramp—tramp! Do you think I can get out of this?

OLAVUS. I do.

KING. When the sun rises to-morrow I shall know my fate. I wish I were that far already!—Now I hear something else! [*The reading of a litany in Latin is faintly heard from the outside.*] What is that?

OLAVUS. [*Goes to the balustrade and looks over it.*] The Queen's mother is reading the Romish litany.

KING. But I hear a male voice, too.

[1] Larv Heath was the place where the dissatisfied lords of West Gothia summoned the peasants to meet them in 1529, when they tried to raise the province against the King. Tuna Plain, to which Mons Nilsson and his friends refer a number of times in the first act, was the place where Gustav settled his first score with the obstreperous Dalecarlians.

OLAVUS.   That's Prince Johan.

KING.   Johan?—So I must drink that cup, too!   I wonder if the cup is full yet?   Is everything that I have built to be torn down?

OLAVUS.   Everything you have torn down must be built up again.

KING.   Johan a papist, and Eric a Calvinist!—Do you remember the days when we were crying in the words of Von Hutten: " The souls are waking up, and it is a joy to live "?   A joy to live, indeed—ha-ha!   And the souls woke up to find their feet on the pillows!   Was it you who said that the gods are playing with us?—Hush!   I was mistaken a while ago!   It's the North Bridge they are crossing!   Can't you hear their heavy tread on the planking of the bridge?   Let us fly!   [*He puts a document on a table.*]   Here I place my resignation.

OLAVUS.   [*Seizing the document.*]   I'll take care of that. I'll keep it—as a memento!   And now we'll hoist a flag of truce.

He pulls a white cloth from one of the tables and ties it to the branch of a tree.

PRINCE ERIC.   [*Enters.*]   Father!

KING.   Croak away, raven!

ERIC.   Our last hope is gone!   The sloop has dragged its anchor and gone ashore.

KING.   [*In desperation.*]   And lightning has struck the nursery, and the grasshoppers have eaten the crops, and the waters are rising, and . . .

ERIC.   The Dalecarlians are negotiating with the palace guards, and they are awfully drunk.

KING.   [*Sitting down.*]   Come on, death!

ERIC.   [*Listening.*]   I can hear their wooden shoes on the garden stairs!   [*He goes to the balustrade.*

KING.   [*Counting on his fingers.*]   Anders Persson, Mons Nilsson, Master John.

ERIC.   [*Drawing his sword.*]   Now he is here!

He can be seen following somebody on the other side of the balustrade with his eyes.

KING.   [*As before.*]   Inghel Hansson, Master Stig, Nils of Söderby.   God is just!

ENGELBRECHT. [*Enters; he is in the happy stage of intoxication, but in full control of his movements for all that; he looks about with a broad grin on his face, a little embarrassed, and yet pleased; then he says to* ERIC.] Are you the King?

He puts his hat on the ground and takes off his wooden shoes.

KING. [*Rising and pushing* ERIC *aside.*] No, I am the King!

ENGELBRECHT. Yes, so I see now!

KING. Who are you?

ENGELBRECHT. [*Faltering.*] Don't you know me? . . .

KING. I don't.

ENGELBRECHT. [*Pulls a dagger with silver handle out of his long stocking and shows it to the* KING, *grinning more broadly than ever.*] Well, don't you know this one?

KING. I don't understand at all. What is your name?

ENGELBRECHT. Well—it happens to be Engelbrecht!

KING. Eng-el-brecht?

ENGELBRECHT. It sounds mighty big, but I am not of *that* family.—You see, it was like this—once upon a time the King—who was no king at all then—oh, mercy, but I am drunk! . . . Well, it was me who followed you on skis to the border of Norway, and that time you gave me this here dagger and said: "If you ever need me, come on!" Now I've come, and here I am! And I wish only that I was not so frightfully drunk!

KING. And what do you want?

ENGELBRECHT. What I want?—I want to fight that man Dacke, of course, and that's what the rest of them want, too.

KING. You want to *fight* Dacke?

ENGELBRECHT. Why do you think we have come, anyhow?

KING. [*Raising his arms towards heaven.*] Eternal God, now you have punished me!

ENGELBRECHT. Is it all right? You see, the rest are down there and they'd like to do something to celebrate the day.

KING. *Is it all right?*—Ask me for a favour?

ENGELBRECHT. [*After thinking hard.*] I'd like to shake hands!

The KING *holds out his hand.*

ENGELBRECHT. [*Looking at the* KING's *hand.*] My, what

a fist! Hard as nails, but clean! Yes, and a devil of a fellow you are, all in all!—I must say I was rather scared when I came here!

KING. Are all the rest of them as drunk as you are?

ENGELBRECHT. About the same! But they can toot the horns for all that. [*He goes to the balustrade, waves his hand, and utters the yell used by the Dalecarlians in calling their cows.*] Poo-ala! Poo-ala! Poo Oy-ala! Oy-ala! Oy!

The blowing of horns and beating of drums is heard from the outside. The KING *goes to the balustrade and waves his hand. The* MOTHER-IN-LAW *appears in court dress. The* QUEEN *enters and goes to the King, who folds her in his arms.* PRINCE JOHAN *enters and goes to the balustrade.*

KING. [*With raised arms.*] You have punished me, O Lord, and I thank thee.

Curtain.

THE DANCE OF DEATH
1901
PART I

CHARACTERS

EDGAR, *Captain in the Coast Artillery*
ALICE, *his wife, a former actress*
CURT, *Master of Quarantine*
JENNY
THE OLD WOMAN } *Subordinate characters*
THE SENTRY

THE DANCE OF DEATH

PART I

The scene is laid inside of a round fort built of granite.

In the background, a gateway, closed by huge, swinging double doors; in these, small square window panes, through which may be seen a seashore with batteries and the sea beyond.

On either side of the gateway, a window with flower pots and bird cages.

To the right of the gateway, an upright piano; farther down the stage, a sewing-table and two easy-chairs.

On the left, half-way down the stage, a writing-table with a telegraph instrument on it; farther down, a whatnot full of framed photographs. Beside it, a couch that can be used to sleep on. Against the wall, a buffet.

A lamp suspended from the ceiling. On the wall near the piano hang two large laurel wreaths with ribbons. Between them, the picture of a woman in stage dress.

Beside the door, a hat-stand on which hang accoutrements, sabres, and so forth. Near it, a chiffonier.

To the left of the gateway hangs a mercurial barometer.

It is a mild autumn evening. The doors stand open, and a sentry is seen pacing back and forth on the short battery. He wears a helmet with a forward-pointed brush for a crest. Now and then his drawn sabre catches the red glare of the setting sun. The sea lies dark and quiet.

The CAPTAIN *sits in the easy-chair to the left of the sewing-table, fumbling an extinguished cigar. He has on a much-worn undress uniform and riding-boots with spurs. Looks tired and bored.*

ALICE sits in the easy-chair on the right, doing nothing at all. Looks tired and expectant.

CAPTAIN. Won't you play something for me?

ALICE. [*Indifferently, but not snappishly.*] What am I to play?

CAPTAIN. Whatever suits you.

ALICE. You don't like my repertory.

CAPTAIN. Nor you mine.

ALICE. [*Evasively.*] Do you want the doors to stay open?

CAPTAIN. If you wish it.

ALICE. Let them be, then. [*Pause.*] Why don't you smoke?

CAPTAIN. Strong tobacco is beginning not to agree with me.

ALICE. [*In an almost friendly tone.*] Get weaker tobacco then. It is your only pleasure, as you call it.

CAPTAIN. Pleasure—what is that?

ALICE. Don't ask me. I know it as little as you—— Don't you want your whisky yet?

CAPTAIN. I'll wait a little. What have you for supper?

ALICE. How do I know? Ask Christine.

CAPTAIN. The mackerel ought to be in season soon—now the autumn is here.

ALICE. Yes, it is autumn!

CAPTAIN. Within and without. But leaving aside the cold that comes with the autumn, both within and without, a little broiled mackerel, with a slice of lemon and a glass of white Burgundy, wouldn't be so very bad.

ALICE. Now you grow eloquent.

CAPTAIN. Have we any Burgundy left in the wine-cellar?

ALICE. So far as I know, we have had no wine-cellar these last five years——

CAPTAIN. You never know anything. However, we *must* stock up for our silver wedding.

ALICE. Do you actually mean to celebrate it?

CAPTAIN. Of course!

ALICE. It would be more seemly to hide our misery—our twenty-five years of misery——

CAPTAIN. My dear Alice, it has been a misery, but we have also had some fun—now and then. One has to avail oneself of what little time there is, for afterwards it is all over.

ALICE. Is it over? Would that it were!

CAPTAIN. It is over! Nothing left but what can be put on a wheel-barrow and spread on the garden beds.

ALICE. And so much trouble for the sake of the garden beds!

CAPTAIN. Well, that's the way of it. And it is not of my making.

ALICE. So much trouble! [*Pause.*] Did the mail come?

CAPTAIN. Yes.

ALICE. Did the butcher send his bill?

CAPTAIN. Yes.

ALICE. How large is it?

CAPTAIN. [*Takes a paper from his pocket and puts on his spectacles, but takes them off again at once.*] Look at it yourself. I cannot see any longer.

ALICE. What is wrong with your eyes?

CAPTAIN. Don't know.

ALICE. Growing old?

CAPTAIN. Nonsense! I?

ALICE. Well, not I!

CAPTAIN. Hm!

ALICE. [*Looking at the bill.*] Can you pay it?

CAPTAIN. Yes, but not at this moment.

ALICE. Some other time, of course! In a year, when you have been retired with a small pension, and it is too late! And then, when your trouble returns——

CAPTAIN. Trouble? I never had any trouble—only a slight indisposition once. And I can live another twenty years.

ALICE. The doctor thought otherwise.

CAPTAIN. The doctor!

ALICE. Yes, who else could express any valid opinion about sickness?

CAPTAIN. I have no sickness, and never had. I am not going to have it either, for I shall die all of a sudden—like an old soldier.

ALICE. Speaking of the doctor—you know they are having a party to-night?

CAPTAIN. [*Agitated.*] Yes, what of it? We are not invited because we don't associate with those people, and we don't associate with them because we don't want to—because we despise both of them.   Rabble—that's what they are!

ALICE.   You say that of everybody.

CAPTAIN.   Because everybody is rabble.

ALICE.   Except yourself.

CAPTAIN.   Yes, because I have behaved decently under all conditions of life.   That's why I don't belong to the rabble.

[*Pause.*

ALICE.   Do you want to play cards?

CAPTAIN.   All right.

ALICE.   [*Takes a pack of cards from the drawer in the sewing-table and begins to shuffle them.*]   Just think, the doctor is permitted to use the band for a private entertainment!

CAPTAIN.   [*Angrily.*]   That's because he goes to the city and truckles to the Colonel.   Truckle, you know—if one could only do that!

ALICE.   [*Deals.*]   I used to be friendly with Gerda, but she played me false——

CAPTAIN.   They are all false!   What did you turn up for trumps?

ALICE.   Put on your spectacles.

CAPTAIN.   They are no help——   Well, well!

ALICE.   Spades are trumps.

CAPTAIN.   [*Disappointed.*]   Spades——?

ALICE.   [*Leads.*]   Well, be that as it may, our case is settled in advance with the wives of the new officers.

CAPTAIN.   [*Taking the trick.*]   What does it matter?   We never give any parties anyhow, so nobody is the wiser.   I can live by myself—as I have always done.

ALICE.   I, too.   But the children?   The children have to grow up without any companionship.

CAPTAIN.   Let them find it for themselves in the city——   I take that!   Got any trumps left?

ALICE.   One——   That's mine!

CAPTAIN.   Six and eight make fifteen——

ALICE.   Fourteen—fourteen!

CAPTAIN.   Six and eight make fourteen.   I think I am

also forgetting how to count. And two makes sixteen—
[*Yawns.*] It is your deal.

ALICE. You are tired?

CAPTAIN. [*Dealing.*] Not at all.

ALICE. [*Listening in direction of the open doors.*] One
can hear the music all this way. [*Pause.*] Do you think Curt
is invited also?

CAPTAIN. He arrived this morning, so I guess he has had
time to get out his evening clothes, though he has not had time
to call on us.

ALICE. Master of Quarantine—is there to be a quarantine
station here?

CAPTAIN. Yes.

ALICE. He is my own cousin after all, and once I bore the
same name as he——

CAPTAIN. In which there was no particular honour——

ALICE. See here! [*Sharply.*] You leave my family alone,
and I'll leave yours!

CAPTAIN. All right, all right—don't let us begin again!

ALICE. Must the Master of Quarantine be a physician?

CAPTAIN. Oh, no, he's merely a sort of superintendent or
book-keeper—and Curt never became anything in particular.

ALICE. He was not much good——

CAPTAIN. And he has cost us a lot of money. And when
he left wife and children, he became disgraced.

ALICE. Not quite so severe, Edgar!

CAPTAIN. That's what happened! What has he been doing
in America since then? Well, I cannot say that I am longing
for him—but he was a nice chap, and I liked to argue with him.

ALICE. Because he was so tractable——

CAPTAIN. [*Haughtily.*] Tractable or not, he was at least
a man one could talk to. Here, on this island, there is not *one*
person who understands what I say—it's a community of idiots!

ALICE. It is rather strange that Curt should arrive just in
time for our silver wedding—whether we celebrate it or not——

CAPTAIN. Why is that strange? Oh, I see! It was he
who brought us together, or got you married, as they put it.

ALICE. Well, didn't he?

CAPTAIN. Certainly! It was a kind of fixed idea with him—— I leave it for you to say what kind.

ALICE. A wanton fancy——

CAPTAIN. For which we have had to pay, and not he!

ALICE. Yes, think only if I had remained on the stage! All my friends are stars now.

CAPTAIN. [*Rising.*] Well, well, well! Now I am going to have a drink. [*Goes over to the buffet and mixes a drink, which he takes standing up.*] There should be a rail here to put the foot on, so that one might dream of being at Copenhagen, in the American Bar.

ALICE. Let us put a rail there, if it will only remind us of Copenhagen. For there we spent our best moments.

CAPTAIN. [*Drinks quickly.*] Yes, do you remember that *navarin aux pommes*?

ALICE. No, but I remember the concerts at the Tivoli.

CAPTAIN. Yes, your tastes are so—exalted!

ALICE. It ought to please you to have a wife whose taste is good.

CAPTAIN. So it does.

ALICE. Sometimes, when you need something to brag of——

CAPTAIN. [*Drinking.*] I guess they must be dancing at the doctor's—I catch the three-four time of the tuba: boom—boom-boom!

ALICE. I can hear the entire melody of the Alcazar Waltz. Well, it was not yesterday I danced a waltz——

CAPTAIN. You think you could still manage?

ALICE. Still?

CAPTAIN. Ye-es. I guess you are done with dancing, you like me!

ALICE. I am ten years younger than you.

CAPTAIN. Then we are of the same age, as the lady should be ten years younger.

ALICE. Be ashamed of yourself! You are an old man—and I am still in my best years.

CAPTAIN. Oh, I know, you can be quite charming—to others, when you make up your mind to it.

ALICE. Can we light the lamp now?

CAPTAIN. Certainly.

ALICE. Will you ring, please.

The CAPTAIN *goes languidly to the writing-table and rings a bell.* JENNY *enters from the right.*

CAPTAIN. Will you be kind enough to light the lamp, Jenny?

ALICE. [*Sharply.*] I want you to light the hanging lamp.

JENNY. Yes, ma'am.

Lights the lamp while the CAPTAIN *watches her.*

ALICE. [*Stiffly.*] Did you wipe the chimney?

JENNY. Sure.

ALICE. What kind of an answer is that?

CAPTAIN. Now—now——

ALICE. [*To* JENNY.] Leave us. I will light the lamp myself. That will be better.

JENNY. I think so, too. [*Starts for the door.*

ALICE. [*Rising.*] Go!

JENNY. [*Stops.*] I wonder, ma'am, what you'd say if I did go?

ALICE *remains silent.*

[JENNY *goes out.*

The CAPTAIN *comes forward and lights the lamp.*

ALICE. [*With concern.*] Do you think she will go?

CAPTAIN. Shouldn't wonder. And then we are in for it——

ALICE. It's your fault! You spoil them.

CAPTAIN. Not at all. Can't you see that they are always polite to me?

ALICE. Because you cringe to them. And you always cringe to inferiors, for that matter, because, like all despots, you have the nature of a slave.

CAPTAIN. There—there!

ALICE. Yes, you cringe before your men, and before your sergeants, but you cannot get on with your equals or your superiors.

CAPTAIN. Ugh!

ALICE. That's the way of all tyrants— Do you think she will go?

CAPTAIN. Yes, if you don't go out and say something nice to her.

ALICE. I?

CAPTAIN. Yes, for if I should do it, you would say that I was flirting with the maids.

ALICE. Mercy, if she should leave! Then I shall have to do the work, as I did the last time, and my hands will be spoiled.

CAPTAIN. That is not the worst of it. But if Jenny leaves, Christine will also leave, and then we shall never get a servant to the island again. The mate on the steamer scares away every one that comes to look for a place—and if he should miss his chance, then my corporals attend to it.

ALICE. Yes, your corporals, whom I have to feed in my kitchen, and whom you dare not show the door——

CAPTAIN. No, for then they would also go when their terms were up—and we might have to close up the whole gun shop!

ALICE. It will be our ruin.

CAPTAIN. That's why the officers have proposed to petition His Royal Majesty for special expense money.

ALICE. For whom?

CAPTAIN. For the corporals.

ALICE. [Laughing.] You are crazy!

CAPTAIN. Yes, laugh a little for me. I need it.

ALICE. I shall soon have forgotten how to laugh——

CAPTAIN. [Lighting his cigar.] That is something one should never forget—it is tedious enough anyhow!

ALICE. Well, it is not very amusing— Do you want to play any more?

CAPTAIN. No, it tires me. [Pause.

ALICE. Do you know, it irritates me nevertheless that my cousin, the new Master of Quarantine, makes his first visit to our enemies.

CAPTAIN. Well, what's the use of talking about it?

ALICE. But did you see in the paper that he was put down as rentier? He must have come into some money then.

CAPTAIN. Rentier! Well, well—a rich relative. That's really the first one in this family.

ALICE. In your family, yes. But among my people many have been rich.

CAPTAIN. If he has money, he's conceited, I suppose, but I'll hold him in check—and he won't get a chance to look at my cards.

The telegraph receiver begins to click.

ALICE. Who is it?

CAPTAIN. [*Standing still.*] Keep quiet, please.

ALICE. Well, are you not going to look——

CAPTAIN. I can hear—I can hear what they are saying—— It's the children.

Goes over to the instrument and sends an answer; the receiver continues to click for awhile, and then the CAPTAIN *answers again.*

ALICE. Well?

CAPTAIN. Wait a little—[*Gives a final click.*] The children are at the guard-house in the city. Judith is not well again and is staying away from school.

ALICE. Again! What more did they say?

CAPTAIN. Money, of course!

ALICE. Why is Judith in such a hurry? If she didn't pass her examinations until next year, it would be just as well.

CAPTAIN. Tell her, and see what it helps.

ALICE. You should tell her.

CAPTAIN. How many times have I not done so? But children have their own wills, you know.

ALICE. Yes, in this house at least. [*The* CAPTAIN *yawns.*] So, you yawn in your wife's presence!

CAPTAIN. Well, what can I do? Don't you notice how day by day we are saying the same things to each other? When, just now, you sprang that good old phrase of yours, " in this house at least," I should have come back with my own stand-by, " it is not my house only." But as I have already made that reply some five hundred times, I yawned instead. And my yawn could be taken to mean either that I was too lazy to answer, or " right you are, my angel," or " supposing we quit."

ALICE. You are very amiable to-night.

CAPTAIN. Is it not time for supper soon?

ALICE. Do you know that the doctor ordered supper from the city—from the Grand Hotel?

CAPTAIN. No! Then they are having ptarmigans—tschk! Ptarmigan, you know, is the finest bird there is, but it's clear barbarism to fry it in bacon grease——

ALICE. Ugh! Don't talk of food.

CAPTAIN. Well, how about wines? I wonder what those barbarians are drinking with the ptarmigans?

ALICE. Do you want me to play for you?

CAPTAIN. [*Sits down at the writing-table.*] The last resource! Well, if you could only leave your dirges and lamentations alone—it sounds too much like music with a moral. And I am always adding within myself " Can't you hear how unhappy I am! Meow, meow! Can't you hear what a horrible husband I have! Brum, brum, brum! If he would only die soon! Beating of the joyful drum, flourishes, the finale of the Alcazar Waltz, Champagne Galop! " Speaking of champagne, I guess there are a couple of bottles left. What would you say about bringing them up and pretending to have company?

ALICE. No, we won't, for they are mine—they were given to me personally.

CAPTAIN. You are so economical.

ALICE. And you are always stingy—to your wife at least!

CAPTAIN. Then I don't know what to suggest. Perhaps I might dance for you?

ALICE. No, thank you—I guess you are done with dancing.

CAPTAIN. You should bring some friend to stay with you.

ALICE. Thanks! You might bring a friend to stay with you.

CAPTAIN. Thanks! It has been tried, and with mutual dissatisfaction. But it was interesting in the way of an experiment, for as soon as a stranger entered the house, we became quite happy—to begin with——

ALICE. And then!

CAPTAIN. Oh, don't talk of it!

There is a knock at the door on the left.

ALICE. Who can be coming so late as this?

CAPTAIN. Jenny does not knock.

ALICE. Go and open the door, and don't yell " come "—it has a sound of the workshop.

CAPTAIN. [*Goes towards the door on the left.*] You don't like workshops.

ALICE. Please, open!

CAPTAIN. [*Opens the door and receives a visiting-card that is held out to him*]. It is Christine— Has Jenny left? [*As the public cannot hear the answer, to* ALICE.] Jenny has left.

ALICE. Then I become servant-girl again!

CAPTAIN. And I man-of-all-work.

ALICE. Would it not be possible to get one of your gunners to help along in the kitchen?

CAPTAIN. Not these days.

ALICE. But it couldn't be Jenny who sent in her card?

CAPTAIN. [*Looks at the card through his spectacles and then turns it over to* ALICE.] You see what it is—I cannot.

ALICE. [*Looks at the card.*] Curt—it is Curt! Hurry up and bring him in.

CAPTAIN. [*Goes out to the left.*] Curt! Well, that's a pleasure!

Alice arranges her hair and seems to come to life.

CAPTAIN. [*Enters from the left with* CURT.] Here he is, the traitor! Welcome, old man! Let me hug you!

ALICE. [*Goes to* CURT.] Welcome to my home, Curt!

CURT. Thank you—it is some time since we saw each other.

CAPTAIN. How long? Fifteen years! And we have grown old——

ALICE. Oh, Curt has not changed, it seems to me.

CAPTAIN. Sit down, sit down! And first of all—the programme. Have you any engagement for to-night?

CURT. I am invited to the doctor's, but I have not promised to go.

ALICE. Then you will stay with your relatives.

CURT. That would seem the natural thing, but the doctor is my superior, and I might have trouble afterwards.

CAPTAIN. What kind of talk is this? I have never been afraid of my superiors——

CURT. Fear or no fear, the trouble cannot be escaped.

CAPTAIN. On this island I am master. Keep behind my back, and nobody will dare to touch you.

ALICE. Oh, be quiet, Edgar! [*Takes* CURT *by the hand.*] Leaving both masters and superiors aside, you must stay with us. That will be found both natural and proper.

CURT. Well, then—especially as I feel welcome here.

CAPTAIN. Why should you not be welcome. There is nothing between us— [CURT *tries vainly to hide a sense of displeasure.*] What could there be? You were a little careless as a young man, but I have forgotten all about it. I don't let things rankle.

ALICE *looks annoyed. All three sit down at the sewing-table.*

ALICE. Well, you have strayed far and wide in the world?

CURT. Yes, and now I have a harbour with you——

CAPTAIN. Whom you married off twenty-five years ago.

CURT. It was not quite that way, but it doesn't matter. It is pleasing to see that you have stuck together for twenty-five years.

CAPTAIN. Well, we have borne with it. Now and then it has been so-so, but, as you say, we have stuck together. And Alice has had nothing to complain of. There has been plenty of everything—heaps of money. Perhaps you don't know that I am a celebrated author—an author of text-books——

CURT. Yes, I recall that, when we parted, you had just published a volume on rifle practice that was selling well. Is it still used in the military schools?

CAPTAIN. It is still in evidence, and it holds its place as number one, though they have tried to substitute a worse one—which is being used now, but which is totally worthless.

[*Painful silence.*

CURT. You have been travelling abroad, I have heard.

ALICE. We have been down to Copenhagen five times—think of it?

CAPTAIN. Well, you see, when I took Alice away from the stage——

ALICE. Oh, you took me?

CAPTAIN. Yes, I took you as a wife should be taken——

ALICE. How brave you have grown!

CAPTAIN. But as it was held up against me afterward that I had spoiled her brilliant career—hm!—I had to make up for it by promising to take my wife to Copenhagen—and this I have kept—fully! Five times we have been there. Five [*holding up the five fingers of the left hand.*] Have you been in Copenhagen?

CURT. [*Smiling.*] No, I have mostly been in America.

CAPTAIN. America? Isn't that a rotten sort of a country?

CURT. [*Unpleasantly impressed.*] It is not Copenhagen.

ALICE. Have you—heard anything—from your children?

CURT. No.

ALICE. I hope you pardon me—but was it not rather inconsiderate to leave them like that——

CURT. I didn't leave them, but the court gave them to the mother.

CAPTAIN. Don't let us talk of that now. I for my part think it was lucky for you to get out of that mess.

CURT. [*To* ALICE.] How are your children?

ALICE. Well, thank you. They are at school in the city and will soon be grown up.

CAPTAIN. Yes, they're splendid kids, and the boy has a brilliant head—brilliant! He is going to join the General Staff——

ALICE. If they accept him!

CAPTAIN. Him? Who has the making of a War Minister in him!

CURT. From one thing to another. There is to be a quarantine station here—against plague, cholera, and that sort of thing. And the doctor will be my superior, as you know—what sort of man is he?

CAPTAIN. Man? He is no man! He's an ignorant rascal!

CURT. [*To* ALICE.] That is very unpleasant for me.

ALICE. Oh, it is not quite as bad as Edgar makes it out, but I must admit that I have small sympathy for the man——

CAPTAIN. A rascal, that's what he is. And that's what the others are, too—the Collector of Customs, the Postmaster, the telephone girl, the druggist, the pilot—what is it they call him now?—the Pilot Master—rascals one and all—and that's why I don't associate with them.

CURT. Are you on bad terms with all of them?

CAPTAIN. Every one!

ALICE. Yes, it is true that intercourse with those people is out of the question.

CAPTAIN. It is as if all the tyrants of the country had been sent to this island for safe-keeping.

ALICE. [*Ironically.*] Exactly!

CAPTAIN. [*Good-naturedly.*] Hm! Is that meant for me? I am no tyrant—not in my own house at least.

ALICE. You know better!

CAPTAIN. [*To* CURT.] Don't believe her! I am a very reasonable husband, and the old lady is the best wife in the world.

ALICE. Would you like something to drink, Curt?

CURT. No, thank you, not now.

CAPTAIN. Have you turned——

CURT. A little moderate only——

CAPTAIN. Is that American?

CURT. Yes.

CAPTAIN. No moderation for me, or I don't care at all. A man should stand his liquor.

CURT. Returning to our neighbours on the island—my position will put me in touch with all of them—and it is not easy to steer clear of everything, for no matter how little you care to get mixed up in other people's intrigues, you are drawn into them just the same.

ALICE. You had better take up with them—in the end you will return to us, for here you find your true friends.

CURT. Is it not dreadful to be alone among a lot of enemies as you are?

ALICE. It is not pleasant.

CAPTAIN. It isn't dreadful at all. I have never had anything but enemies all my life, and they have helped me on instead of doing me harm. And when my time to die comes, I may say that I owe nothing to anybody, and that I have never got a thing for nothing. Every particle of what I own I have had to fight for.

ALICE. Yes, Edgar's path has not been strewn with roses——

CAPTAIN. No, with thorns and stones—pieces of flint—but a man's own strength: do you know what that means?

CURT. [*Simply.*]   Yes, I learned to recognise its insufficiency about ten years ago.

CAPTAIN.   Then you are no good!

ALICE. [*To the* CAPTAIN.]   Edgar!

CAPTAIN.   He is no good, I say, if he does not have the strength within himself.   Of course it is true that when the mechanism goes to pieces there is nothing left but a barrowful to chuck out on the garden beds; but as long as the mechanism holds together the thing to do is to kick and fight, with hands and feet, until there is nothing left.   That is my philosophy.

CURT. [*Smiling.*]   It is fun to listen to you.

CAPTAIN.   But you don't think it's true?

CURT.   No, I don't.

CAPTAIN.   But true it is, for all that.

During the preceding scene the wind has begun to blow hard, and now one of the big doors is closed with a bang.

CAPTAIN. [*Rising.*]   It's blowing.   I could just feel it coming.

Goes back and closes both doors.   Knocks on the barometer.

ALICE. [*To* CURT.]   You will stay for supper?

CURT.   Thank you.

ALICE.   But it will be very simple, as our housemaid has just left us.

CURT.   Oh, it will do for me, I am sure.

ALICE.   You ask for so little, dear Curt.

CAPTAIN. [*At the barometer.*]   If you could only see how the mercury is dropping!   Oh, I felt it coming!

ALICE. [*Secretly to* CURT.]   He is nervous.

CAPTAIN.   We ought to have supper soon.

ALICE. [*Rising.*]   I am going to see about it now.   You can sit here and philosophise—[*secretly to* CURT], but don't contradict him, for then he gets into bad humour.   And don't ask him why he was not made a major.

CURT *nods assent.*   ALICE *goes towards the right.*

CAPTAIN.   See that we get something nice now, old lady!

ALICE.   You give me money, and you'll get what you want.

CAPTAIN.   Always money!   [ALICE *goes out.*

CAPTAIN. [*To* CURT.]   Money, money, money!   All day

long I have to stand ready with the purse, until at last I have come to feel as if I myself were nothing but a purse. Are you familiar with that kind of thing?

CURT. Oh, yes—with the difference that I took myself for a pocket-book.

CAPTAIN. Ha-ha. So you know the flavour of the brand! Oh, the ladies! Ha-ha! And you had one of the proper kind!

CURT. [*Patiently.*] Let that be buried now.

CAPTAIN. She was a jewel! Then I have after all—in spite of everything—one that's pretty decent. For she is straight, in spite of everything.

CURT. [*Smiling good-humouredly.*] In spite of everything.

CAPTAIN. Don't you laugh!

CURT. [*As before.*] In spite of everything!

CAPTAIN. Yes, she has been a faithful mate, a splendid mother—excellent—but [*with a glance at the door on the right*] she has a devilish temper. Do you know, there have been moments when I cursed you for saddling me with her.

CURT. [*Good-naturedly.*] But I didn't. Listen, man——

CAPTAIN. Yah, yah, yah! You talk nonsense and forget things that are not pleasant to remember. Don't take it badly, please—— I am accustomed to command and raise Cain, you see, but you know me, and don't get angry!

CURT. Not at all. But I have not provided you with a wife —on the contrary.

CAPTAIN. [*Without letting his flow of words be checked.*] Don't you think life is queer anyhow?

CURT. I suppose so.

CAPTAIN. And to grow old—it is no fun, but it is interesting. Well, my age is nothing to speak of, but it does begin to make itself felt. All your friends die off, and then you become so lonely.

CURT. Lucky the man who can grow old in company with a wife.

CAPTAIN. Lucky? Well, it is luck, for the children go their way, too. You ought not to have left yours.

CURT. Well, I didn't. They were taken away from me——

CAPTAIN. Don't get mad now, because I tell you——

CURT. But it was not so.

CAPTAIN. Well, whichever way it was, it has now become forgotten—but you are alone!

CURT. You get accustomed to everything.

CAPTAIN. Do you—is it possible to get accustomed—to being quite alone also?

CURT. Here am I!

CAPTAIN. What have you been doing these fifteen years?

CURT. What a question! These fifteen years!

CAPTAIN. They say you have got hold of money and grown rich.

CURT. I can hardly be called rich——

CAPTAIN. I am not going to ask for a loan.

CURT. If you were, you would find me ready.

CAPTAIN. Many thanks, but I have my bank account. You see [*with a glance towards the door on the right*], nothing must be lacking in this house; and the day I had no more money—she would leave me!

CURT. Oh, no!

CAPTAIN. No? Well, I know better. Think of it, she makes a point of asking me when I happen to be short, just for the pleasure of showing me that I am not supporting my family.

CURT. But I heard you say that you have a large income.

CAPTAIN. Of course, I have a large income—but it is not enough.

CURT. Then it is not large, as such things are reckoned——

CAPTAIN. Life is queer, and we as well!

The telegraph receiver begins to click.

CURT. What is that?

CAPTAIN. Nothing but a time correction.

CURT. Have you no telephone?

CAPTAIN. Yes, in the kitchen. But we use the telegraph because the girls at the central report everything we say.

CURT. Social conditions out here by the sea must be frightful!

CAPTAIN. They are simply horrible! But all life is horrible. And you, who believe in a sequel, do you think there will be any peace further on?

CURT. I presume there will be storms and battles there also.

CAPTAIN. There also—if there be any "there"; I prefer annihilation!

CURT. Are you sure that annihilation will come without pain?

CAPTAIN. I am going to die all of a sudden, without pain.

CURT. So you know that?

CAPTAIN. Yes, I know it.

CURT. You don't appear satisfied with your life?

CAPTAIN. [*Sighing.*] Satisfied? The day I could die, I should be satisfied.

CURT. [*Rising.*] That you don't know! But tell me: what is going on in this house? What is happening here? There is a smell as of poisonous wall-paper, and one feels sick the moment one enters. I should prefer to get away from here, had I not promised Alice to stay. There are dead bodies beneath the flooring, and the place is so filled with hatred that one can hardly breathe. [*The* CAPTAIN *sinks together and sits staring into vacancy.*] What is the matter with you? Edgar! [*The* CAPTAIN *does not move. Slaps the* CAPTAIN *on the shoulder.*] Edgar!

CAPTAIN. [*Recovering consciousness.*] Did you say anything? [*Looks around.*] I thought it was—Alice!— Oh, is that you?— Say—— [*Relapses into apathy.*

CURT. This is horrible! [*Goes over to the door on the right and opens it.*] Alice!

ALICE. [*Enters, wearing a kitchen apron.*] What is it?

CURT. I don't know. Look at him.

ALICE. [*Calmly.*] He goes off like that at times— I'll play and then he will wake up.

CURT. No, don't! Not that way! Leave it to me— Does he hear? Or see?

ALICE. Just now he neither hears nor sees.

CURT. And you can speak of that with such calm? Alice, what is going on in this house?

ALICE. Ask him there.

CURT. Him there? But he is your husband!

ALICE. A stranger to me—as strange as he was twenty-five

years ago. I know nothing at all about that man—nothing but——

CURT. Stop! He may overhear you.

ALICE. Now he cannot hear anything.

A trumpet signal is sounded outside.

CAPTAIN. [*Leaps to his feet and grabs sabre and cap.*] Pardon me. I have to inspect the sentries.

[*Goes out through the door in the background.*

CURT. Is he ill?

ALICE. I don't know.

CURT. Has he lost his reason?

ALICE. I don't know.

CURT. Does he drink?

ALICE. He boasts more of it than he really drinks.

CURT. Sit down and talk—but calmly and truthfully.

ALICE. [*Sitting down.*] What am I to talk about? That I have spent a lifetime in this tower, locked up, guarded by a man whom I have always hated, and whom I now hate so, beyond all bounds, that the day he died I should be laughing until the air shook.

CURT. Why have you not parted?

ALICE. You may well ask! While still engaged, we parted twice; since then we have been trying to part every single day— but we are chained together and cannot break away. Once we were separated—within the same house—for five whole years. Now nothing but death can part us. This we know, and for that reason we are waiting for him as a liberator.

CURT. Why are you so lonely?

ALICE. Because he isolates me. First he " exterminated " all my brothers and sisters from our home—he speaks of it himself as " extermination "—and then my girl friends and everybody else.

CURT. But *his* relatives? He has not " exterminated " them?

ALICE. Yes, for they came near taking my life, after having taken my honour and good name. Finally I became forced to keep up my connection with the world and with other human beings by means of that telegraph—for the telephone was watched by the operators. I have taught myself telegraphy, and he doesn't know it. You must not tell him, for then he would kill me.

CURT. Frightful! Frightful!— But why does he hold me responsible for your marriage? Let me tell you now how it was. Edgar was my childhood friend. When he saw you he fell in love at once. He came to me and asked me to plead his cause. I said no at once—and, my dear Alice, I knew your tyrannical and cruel temperament. For that reason I warned him—and when he persisted, I sent him to get your brother for his spokesman.

ALICE. I believe what you say. But he has been deceiving himself all these years, so that now you can never get him to believe anything else.

CURT. Well, let him put the blame on me if that can relieve his sufferings.

ALICE. But that is too much——

CURT. I am used to it. But what does hurt me is his unjust charge that I have deserted my children——

ALICE. That's the manner of man he is. He says what suits him, and then he believes it. But he seems to be fond of you, principally because you don't contradict him. Try not to grow tired of us now. I believe you have come in what was to us a fortunate moment; I think it was even providential—Curt, you must not grow tired of us, for we are undoubtedly the most unhappy creatures in the whole world! [*She weeps.*

CURT. I have seen *one* marriage at close quarters, and it was dreadful—but this is almost worse!

ALICE. Do you think so?

CURT. Yes.

ALICE. Whose fault is it?

CURT. The moment you quit asking whose fault it is, Alice, you will feel a relief. Try to regard it as a fact, a trial that has to be borne——

ALICE. I cannot do it! It is too much! [*Rising.*] It is beyond help!

CURT. I pity both of you!— Do you know why you are hating each other?

ALICE. No, it is the most unreasoning hatred, without cause, without purpose, but also without end. And can you imagine why he is principally afraid of death? He fears that I may marry again.

CURT. Then he loves you.

ALICE. Probably. But that does not prevent him from hating me.

CURT. [*As if to himself.*] It is called love-hatred, and it hails from the pit!— Does he like you to play for him?

ALICE. Yes, but only horrid melodies—for instance, that awful "The Entry of the Boyars." When he hears it he loses his head and wants to dance.

CURT. Does he dance?

ALICE. Oh, he is very funny at times.

CURT. One thing—pardon me for asking. Where are the children?

ALICE. Perhaps you don't know that two of them are dead?

CURT. So you have had that to face also?

ALICE. What is there I have not faced?

CURT. But the other two?

ALICE. In the city. They couldn't stay at home. For he set them against me.

CURT. And you set them against him?

ALICE. Of course. And then parties were formed, votes bought, bribes given—and in order not to spoil the children completely we had to part from them. What should have been the uniting link became the seed of dissension; what is held the blessing of the home turned into a curse—well, I believe sometimes that we belong to a cursed race!

CURT. Yes, is it not so—ever since the Fall?

ALICE. [*With a venomous glance and sharp voice.*] What fall?

CURT. That of our first parents.

ALICE. Oh, I thought you meant something else!

Embarrassed silence.

ALICE. [*With folded hands.*] Curt, my kinsman, my childhood friend—I have not always acted towards you as I should. But now I am being punished, and you are having your revenge.

CURT.   No revenge!   Nothing of that kind here!   Hush!

ALICE.   Do you recall one Sunday while you were engaged—
and I had invited you for dinner——

CURT.   Never mind!

ALICE.   I must speak!   Have pity on me!   When you came
to dinner, we had gone away, and you had to leave again.

CURT.   You had received an invitation yourselves—what is
that to speak of!

ALICE.   Curt, when to-day, a little while ago, I asked you to
stay for supper, I thought we had something left in the pantry.
[*Hiding her face in her hands.*]   And there is not a thing, not
even a piece of bread——

CURT.   [*Weeping.*]   Alice—poor Alice!

ALICE.   But when he comes home and wants something to
eat, and there is nothing—then he gets angry.   You have never
seen him angry!   O, God, what humiliation!

CURT.   Will you not let me go out and arrange for something?

ALICE.   There is nothing to be had on this island.

CURT.   Not for my sake, but for his and yours—let me think
up something—something.   We must make the whole thing
seem laughable when he comes.   I'll propose that we have a
drink, and in the meantime I'll think of something.   Put him in
good humour; play for him, any old nonsense.   Sit down at the
piano and make yourself ready——

ALICE. Look at my hands—are they fit to play with? I have to
wipe glasses and polish brass, sweep floors and make fires——

CURT.   But you have two servants?

ALICE.   So we have to pretend because he is an officer—but
the servants are leaving us all the time, so that often we have none
at all—most of the time, in fact.   How am I to get out of this—
this about supper?   Oh, if only fire would break out in this
house!

CURT.   Don't, Alice, don't!

ALICE.   If the sea would rise and take us away!

CURT.   No, no, no, I cannot listen to you!

ALICE.   What will he say, what will he say—   Don't go,
Curt, don't go away from me!

Curt.   No, dear Alice— I shall not go.
Alice.   Yes, but when you are gone——
Curt.   Has he ever laid hands on you?
Alice.   On me? Oh, no, for he knew that then I should
have left him.   One has to preserve some pride.
    From without is heard: " Who goes there?— Friend."
Curt.   [*Rising.*] Is he coming?
Alice.   [*Frightened.*] Yes, that's he.   [*Pause.*
Curt.   What in the world are we to do?
Alice.   I don't know, I don't know!
Captain.   [*Enters from the background, cheerful.*] There!
Leisure now!   Well, has she had time to make her complaints?
Is she not unhappy—hey?
Curt.   How's the weather outside?
Captain.   Half storm— [*Facetiously; opening one of the
doors ajar.*] Sir Bluebeard with the maiden in the tower; and
outside stands the sentry with drawn sabre to guard the pretty
maiden—and then come the brothers, but the sentry is there.
Look at him.   Hip-hip!   That's a fine sentry.   Look at him.
Malbrough s'en va-t-en guerre!   Let us dance the sword dance!
Curt ought to see it!
Curt.   No, let us have " The Entry of the Boyars " instead!
Captain.   Oh, you know that one, do you?— Alice in the
kitchen apron, come and play.   Come, I tell you!
                    [Alice *goes reluctantly to the piano.*
Captain.   [*Pinching her arm.*] Now you have been black-
guarding me!
Alice.   I?
Curt *turns away from them.* Alice *plays the " Entry of the
    Boyars." The* Captain *performs some kind of Hungarian
    dance step behind the writing-table so that his spurs are set
    jingling.   Then he sinks down on the floor without being
    noticed by* Curt *and* Alice, *and the latter goes on playing
    the piece to the end.*
Alice.   [*Without turning around.*] Shall we have it again?
[*Silence.   Turns around and becomes aware of the* Captain,
*who is lying unconscious on the floor in such a way that he is
hidden from the public by the writing-table.*] Lord Jesus!

*She stands still, with arms crossed over her breast, and gives
    vent to a sigh as of gratitude and relief.*

CURT. [*Turns around; hurries over to the* CAPTAIN.] What
is it?   What is it?

ALICE. [*In a high state of tension.*]   Is he dead?

CURT. I don't know.   Come and help me.

ALICE. [*Remains still.*]   I cannot touch him—is he dead?

CURT. No—he lives.

ALICE *sighs.* CURT *helps the* CAPTAIN *to his feet and places
    him in a chair.*

CAPTAIN. What was it?   [*Silence.*]   What was it?

CURT. You fell down.

CAPTAIN. Did anything happen?

CURT. You fell on the floor.   What is the matter with you?

CAPTAIN. With me?   Nothing at all.   I don't know of
anything.   What are you staring at me for?

CURT. You are ill.

CAPTAIN. What nonsense is that?   You go on playing,
Alice—   Oh, now it's back again!

[*Puts both hands up to his head.*

ALICE. Can't you see that you are ill?

CAPTAIN. Don't shriek!   It is only a fainting spell.

CURT. We must call a doctor—   I'll use your telephone——

CAPTAIN. I don't want any doctor.

CURT. You must!   We have to call him for our own sake
—otherwise we shall be held responsible——

CAPTAIN. I'll show him the door if he comes here.   I'll
shoot him.   Oh, now it's there again!

[*Takes hold of his head.*

CURT. [*Goes towards the door on the right.*]   Now I am
going to telephone!   [*Goes out.*

ALICE *takes off her apron.*

CAPTAIN. Will you give me a glass of water?

ALICE. I suppose I have to!   [*Gives him a glass of water.*

CAPTAIN. How amiable!

ALICE. Are you ill?

CAPTAIN. Please pardon me for not being well.

ALICE. Will you take care of yourself then?

CAPTAIN.   *You* won't do it, I suppose?

ALICE.   No, of that you may be sure!

CAPTAIN.   The hour is come for which you have been waiting so long.

ALICE.   The hour you believed would never come.

CAPTAIN.   Don't be angry with me!

CURT.   [*Enters from the right.*]   Oh, it's too bad――――

ALICE.   What did he say?

CURT.   He rang off without a word.

ALICE.   [*To the* CAPTAIN.]   There is the result of your limitless arrogance!

CAPTAIN.   I think I am growing worse― Try to get a doctor from the city.

ALICE.   [*Goes to the telegraph instrument.*]   We shall have to use the telegraph then.

CAPTAIN.   [*Rising half-way from the chair; startled.*]   Do you―know―how to use it?

ALICE.   [*Working the key.*]   Yes, I do.

CAPTAIN.   So-o!   Well, go on then―But isn't she treacherous!   [*To* CURT.]   Come over here and sit by me.   [CURT *sits down beside the* CAPTAIN.]   Take my hand.   I sit here and fall―can you make it out?   Down something―such a queer feeling.

CURT.   Have you had any attack like this before?

CAPTAIN.   Never――――

CURT.   While you are waiting for an answer from the city, I'll go over to the doctor and have a talk with him.   Has he attended you before?

CAPTAIN.   He has.

CURT.   Then he knows your case.   [*Goes towards the left.*

ALICE.   There will be an answer shortly.   It is very kind of you, Curt.   But come back soon.

CURT.   As soon as I can.   [*Goes out.*

CAPTAIN.   Curt *is* kind!   And how he has changed.

ALICE.   Yes, and for the better.   It is too bad, however, that he must be dragged into our misery just now.

CAPTAIN.   But good for us― I wonder just how he stands. Did you notice that he wouldn't speak of his own affairs?

ALICE.   I did notice it, but then I don't think anybody asked him.

CAPTAIN.   Think, what a life!   And ours!   I wonder if it is the same for all people?

ALICE.   Perhaps, although they don't speak of it as we do.

CAPTAIN.   At times I have thought that misery draws misery, and that those who are happy shun the unhappy.   That is the reason why we see nothing but misery.

ALICE.   Have you known anybody who was happy?

CAPTAIN.   Let me see!   No—   Yes—the Ekmarks.

ALICE.   You don't mean it.   She had to have an operation last year——

CAPTAIN.   That's right.   Well, then I don't know—yes, the Von Kraffts.

ALICE.   Yes, the whole family lived an idyllic life, well off, respected by everybody, nice children, good marriages—right along until they were fifty.   Then that cousin of theirs committed a crime that led to a prison term and all sorts of after-effects. And that was the end of their peace.   The family name was dragged in the mud by all the newspapers.   The Krafft murder case made it impossible for the family to appear anywhere, after having been so much thought of.   The children had to be taken out of school.   Oh, heavens!

CAPTAIN.   I wonder what my trouble is?

ALICE.   What do you think?

CAPTAIN.   Heart or head.   It is as if the soul wanted to fly off and turn into smoke.

ALICE.   Have you any appetite?

CAPTAIN.   Yes, how about the supper?

ALICE.   [Crosses the stage, disturbed.]   I'll ask Jenny.

CAPTAIN.   Why, she's gone!

ALICE.   Yes, yes, yes!

CAPTAIN.   Ring for Christine so that I can get some fresh water.

ALICE.   [Rings.]   I wonder—   [Rings again.]   She doesn't hear.

CAPTAIN.   Go and look—just think, if she should have left also!

ALICE. [*Goes over to the door on the left and opens it.*]
What is this? Her trunk is in the hallway—packed.

CAPTAIN. Then she has gone.

ALICE. This is hell!

Begins to cry, falls on her knees, and puts her head on a chair, sobbing.

CAPTAIN. And everything at once! And then Curt had to turn up just in time to get a look into this mess of ours! If there be any further humiliation in store, let it come this moment!

ALICE. Do you know what I suspect? Curt went away and will not come back.

CAPTAIN. I believe it of him.

ALICE. Yes, we are cursed——

CAPTAIN. What are you talking of?

ALICE. Don't you see how everybody shuns us?

CAPTAIN. I don't mind! [*The telegraph receiver clicks.*] There is the answer. Hush, I can hear it— Nobody can spare the time. Evasions! The rabble!

ALICE. That's what you get because you have despised your physicians—and failed to pay them.

CAPTAIN. That is not so!

ALICE. Even when you could, you didn't care to pay their bills because you looked down upon their work, just as you have looked down upon mine and everybody else's. They don't want to come. And the telephone is cut off because you didn't think that good for anything either. Nothing is good for anything but your rifles and guns!

CAPTAIN. Don't stand there and talk nonsense——

ALICE. Everything comes back.

CAPTAIN. What sort of superstition is that? Talk for old women!

ALICE. You will see! Do you know that we owe Christine six months' wages?

CAPTAIN. Well, she has stolen that much.

ALICE. But I have also had to borrow money from her.

CAPTAIN. I think you capable of it.

ALICE. What an ingrate you are! You know I borrowed that money for the children to get into the city.

CAPTAIN. Curt had a fine way of coming back! A rascal, that one, too! And a coward! He didn't dare to say he had had enough, and that he found the doctor's party more pleasant—— He's the same rapscallion as ever!

CURT. [*Enters quickly from the left.*] Well, my dear Edgar, this is how the matter stands—the doctor knows everything about your heart——

CAPTAIN. My heart?

CURT. You have long been suffering from calcification of the heart——

CAPTAIN. Stone heart?

CURT. And——

CAPTAIN. Is it serious?

CURT. Well, that is to say——

CAPTAIN. It is serious.

CURT. Yes.

CAPTAIN. Fatal?

CURT. You must be very careful. First of all: the cigar must go. [*The* CAPTAIN *throws away his cigar.*] And next: no more whisky! Then, to bed!

CAPTAIN. [*Scared.*] No, I don't want *that*! Not to bed! That's the end! Then you never get up again. I shall sleep on the couch to-night. What more did he say?

CURT. He was very nice about it and will come at once if you call him.

CAPTAIN. Was he nice, the hypocrite? I don't want to see him! I can at least eat?

CURT. Not to-night. And during the next few days nothing but milk.

CAPTAIN. Milk! I cannot take that stuff into my mouth.

CURT. Better learn how!

CAPTAIN. I am too old to learn. [*Puts his hand up to his head.*] Oh, there it is again now!

[*He sits perfectly still, staring straight ahead.*

ALICE. [*To* CURT.] What did the doctor tell you?

CURT. That he *may* die.

ALICE. Thank God!

CURT. Take care, Alice, take care! And now, go and get

a pillow and a blanket and I'll put him here on the couch. Then I'll sit on the chair here all night.

ALICE. And I?

CURT. You go to bed. Your presence seems only to make him worse.

ALICE. Command! I shall obey, for you seem to mean well towards both of us. [*Goes out to the left.*

CURT. Mark you—towards both of you! And I shall not mix in any partisan squabbles.

CURT *takes the water bottle and goes out to the right. The noise of the wind outside is clearly heard. Then one of the doors is blown open and an old woman of shabby, unprepossessing appearance peeps into the room.*

CAPTAIN. [*Wakes up, rises, and looks around.*] So, they have left me, the rascals! [*Catches sight of the old woman and is frightened by her.*] Who is it? What do you want?

OLD WOMAN. I just wanted to close the door, sir.

CAPTAIN. Why should you? Why should you?

OLD WOMAN. Because it blew open just as I passed by.

CAPTAIN. Wanted to steal, did you?

OLD WOMAN. Not much here to take away, Christine said.

CAPTAIN. Christine?

OLD WOMAN. Good night, sir, and sleep well!

[*Closes the door and disappears.*

ALICE *comes in from the left with pillows and a blanket.*

CAPTAIN. Who was that at the door? Anybody?

ALICE. Why, it was old Mary from the poorhouse who just went by.

CAPTAIN. Are you sure?

ALICE. Are you afraid?

CAPTAIN. I, afraid? Oh, no!

ALICE. As you don't want to go to bed, you can lie here.

CAPTAIN. [*Goes over to the couch and lies down.*] I'll lie here. [*Tries to take* ALICE'S *hand, but she pulls it away.*]

CURT *comes in with the water bottle.*

CAPTAIN. Curt, don't go away from me!

CURT. I am going to stay up with you all night. Alice is going to bed.

CAPTAIN.   Good night then, Alice.

ALICE.   [*To* CURT.]   Good night, Curt.

CURT.   Good night.   [ALICE *goes out.*

CURT.   [*Takes a chair and sits down beside the couch.*] Don't you want to take off your boots?

CAPTAIN.   No, a warrior should always be armed.

CURT.   Are you expecting a battle then?

CAPTAIN.   Perhaps!   [*Rising up in bed.*]   Curt, you are the only human being to whom I ever disclosed anything of myself.   Listen to me!——   If I die to-night—look after my children!

CURT.   I will do so.

CAPTAIN.   Thank you—I trust in you!

CURT.   Can you explain why you trust me?

CAPTAIN.   We have not been friends, for friendship is something I don't believe in, and our families were born enemies and have always been at war——

CURT.   And yet you trust me?

CAPTAIN.   Yes, and I don't know why.   [*Silence.*]   Do you think I am going to die?

CURT.   You as well as everybody.   There will be no exception made in your case.

CAPTAIN.   Are you bitter?

CURT.   Yes—are you afraid of death?   Of the wheelbarrow and the garden bed?

CAPTAIN.   Think, if it were not the end!

CURT.   That's what a great many think!

CAPTAIN.   And then?

CURT.   Nothing but surprises, I suppose.

CAPTAIN.   But nothing at all is known with certainty?

CURT.   No, that's just it!   That is why you must be prepared for everything.

CAPTAIN.   You are not childish enough to believe in a hell?

CURT.   Do you not believe in it—you, who are right in it?

CAPTAIN.   That is metaphorical only.

CURT.   The realism with which you have described yours seems to preclude all thought of metaphors, poetical or otherwise.

[*Silence,*

CAPTAIN. If you only knew what pangs I suffer!

CURT. Of the body?

CAPTAIN. No, not of the body.

CURT. Then it must be of the spirit, for no other alternative exists.   [*Pause.*

CAPTAIN. [*Rising up in bed.*] I don't want to die!

CURT. Not long ago you wished for annihilation.

CAPTAIN. Yes, if it be painless.

CURT. Apparently it is not!

CAPTAIN. Is this annihilation then?

CURT. The beginning of it.

CAPTAIN. Good night.

CURT. Good night.

Curtain.

The same setting, but now the lamp is at the point of going out. Through the windows and the glass panes of the doors a grey morning is visible. The sea is stirring. The sentry is on the battery as before.

The CAPTAIN *is lying on the couch, asleep.* CURT *sits on a chair beside him, looking pale and wearied from his watch.*

ALICE. [*Enters from the left.*] Is he asleep?

CURT. Yes, since the time when the sun should have risen.

ALICE. What kind of night did he have?

CURT. He slept now and then, but he talked a good deal.

ALICE. Of what?

CURT. He argued about religion like a schoolboy, but with a pretension of having solved all the world's riddles. Finally, towards morning, he invented the immortality of the soul.

ALICE. For his own glory.

CURT. Exactly! He is actually the most conceited person I have ever met. " I am; consequently, God must be."

ALICE. You have become aware of it? Look at those boots. With those he would have trampled the earth flat, had he been allowed to do so. With those he has trampled down other people's fields and gardens. With those he has trampled on some people's toes and other people's heads— Man-eater, you have got your bullet at last!

CURT. He would be comical were he not so tragical; and there are traces of greatness in all his narrow-mindedness— Have you not a single good word to say about him?

ALICE. [*Sitting down.*] Yes, if he only does not hear it; for if he hears a single word of praise he develops megalomania on the spot.

CURT. He can hear nothing now, for he has had a dose of morphine.

ALICE. Born in a poor home, with many brothers and sisters, Edgar very early had to support the family by giving lessons, as the father was a ne'er-do-well, if nothing worse. It must be hard for a young man to give up all the pleasures of youth in order to slave for a bunch of thankless children whom he has not brought into the world. I was a little girl when I saw him, as a young man, going without an overcoat in the winter while the mercury stood at fifteen below zero—his little sisters wore kersey coats—it was fine, and I admired him, but his ugliness repelled me. Is he not unusually ugly?

CURT. Yes, and his ugliness has a touch of the monstrous at times. Whenever we fell out, I noticed it particularly. And when, at such times, he went away, his image assumed enormous forms and proportions, and he literally haunted me.

ALICE. Think of me then! However, his earlier years as an officer were undoubtedly a martyrdom. But now and then he was helped by rich people. This he will never admit, and whatever has come to him in that way he has accepted as a due tribute, without giving thanks for it.

CURT. We were to speak well of him.

ALICE. Yes—after he is dead. But then I recall nothing more.

CURT. Have you found him cruel?

ALICE. Yes—and yet he can show himself both kind and susceptible to sentiment. As an enemy he is simply horrible.

CURT. Why did he not get the rank of major?

ALICE. Oh, you ought to understand that! They didn't

want to raise a man above themselves who had already proved himself a tyrant as an inferior. But you must never let on that you know this. He says himself that he did not want promotion — Did he speak of the children?

CURT. Yes, he was longing for Judith.

ALICE. I thought so— Oh! Do you know what Judith is? His own image, whom he has trained for use against me. Think only, that my own daughter—has raised her hand against me!

CURT. That is too much!

ALICE. Hush! He is moving— Think if he overheard us! He is full of trickery also.

CURT. He is actually waking up.

ALICE. Does he not look like an ogre? I am afraid of him!
[*Silence.*

CAPTAIN. [*Stirs, wakes up, rises in bed, and looks around.*] It is morning—at last!

CURT. How are you feeling?

CAPTAIN. Not so very bad.

CURT. Do you want a doctor?

CAPTAIN. No—I want to see Judith—my child!

CURT. Would it not be wise to set your house in order before—or if something should happen?

CAPTAIN. What do you mean? What could happen?

CURT. What may happen to all of us.

CAPTAIN. Oh, nonsense! Don't you believe that I die so easily! And don't rejoice prematurely, Alice!

CURT. Think of your children. Make your will so that your wife at least may keep the household goods.

CAPTAIN. Is she going to inherit from me while I am still alive?

CURT. No, but if something happens she ought not to be turned into the street. One who has dusted and polished and looked after these things for twenty-five years should have some right to remain in possession of them. May I send word to the regimental lawyer?

CAPTAIN. No!

CURT. You are a cruel man—more cruel than I thought you!

CAPTAIN.   Now it is back again!

> [*Falls back on the bed, unconscious.*

ALICE.   [*Goes towards the right.*]   There are some people in the kitchen—   I have to go down there.

CURT.   Yes, go.   Here is not much to be done.

> [ALICE *goes out.*

CAPTAIN.   [*Recovers.*]   Well, Curt, what are you going to do about your quarantine?

CURT.   Oh, that will be all right.

CAPTAIN.   No; I am in command on this island, so you will have to deal with me—don't forget that!

CURT.   Have you ever seen a quarantine station?

CAPTAIN.   Have I?   Before you were born.   And I'll give you a piece of advice: don't place your disinfection plant too close to the shore.

CURT.   I was thinking that the nearer I could get to the water the better——

CAPTAIN.   That shows how much you know of your business. Water, don't you see, is the element of the bacilli, their life element?

CURT.   But the salt water of the sea is needed to wash away all the impurity.

CAPTAIN.   Idiot!   Well, now, when you get a house for yourself, I suppose you'll bring home your children?

CURT.   Do you think they will let themselves be brought?

CAPTAIN.   Of course, if you have got any backbone!   It would make a good impression on the people if you fulfilled your duties in that respect also—

CURT.   I have always fulfilled my duties in that respect.

CAPTAIN.   [*Raising his voice*]   —in the one respect where you have proved yourself most remiss—

CURT.   Have I not told you—

CAPTAIN.   [*Paying no attention*]   —for one does not desert one's children like that——

CURT.   Go right on!

CAPTAIN.   As your relative—a relative older than yourself—I feel entitled to tell you the truth, even if it should prove bitter—and you should not take it badly——

CURT. Are you hungry?

CAPTAIN. Yes, I am.

CURT. Do you want something light?

CAPTAIN. No, something solid.

CURT. Then you would be done for.

CAPTAIN. Is it not enough to be sick, but one must starve also?

CURT. That's how the land lies.

CAPTAIN. And neither drink nor smoke? Then life is not worth much!

CURT. Death demands sacrifices, or it comes at once.

ALICE. [*Enters with several bunches of flowers and some telegrams and letters.*] These are for you.

[*Throws the flowers on the writing-table.*

CAPTAIN. [*Flattered.*] For me! Will you please let me look?

ALICE. Oh, they are only from the non-commissioned officers, the bandmen, and the gunners.

CAPTAIN. You are jealous.

ALICE. Oh, no. If it were laurel wreaths, that would be another matter—but those you can never get.

CAPTAIN. Hm!— Here's a telegram from the Colonel— read it, Curt. The Colonel is a gentleman after all—though he is something of an idiot. And this is from—what does it say? It is from Judith! Please telegraph her to come with the next boat. And here—yes, one is not quite without friends after all, and it is fine to see them take thought of a sick man, who is also a man of deserts above his rank, and a man free of fear or blemish.

ALICE. I don't quite understand—are they congratulating you because you are sick?

CAPTAIN. Hyena!

ALICE. Yes, we had a doctor here on the island who was so hated that when he left they gave a banquet—after him, and not for him!

CAPTAIN. Put the flowers in water—I am not easily caught, and all people are a lot of rabble, but, by heavens, these simple tributes are genuine—they cannot be anything but genuine!

ALICE. Fool!

CURT. [*Reading the telegram.*]   Judith says she cannot come because the steamer is held back by the storm.

CAPTAIN.   Is that all?

CURT.   No-o—there is a postscript.

CAPTAIN.   Out with it!

CURT.   Well, she asks her father not to drink so much.

CAPTAIN.   Impudence!   That's like children!   That's my only beloved daughter—my Judith—my idol!

ALICE.   And your image!

CAPTAIN.   Such is life.   Such are its best joys—   Hell!

ALICE.   Now you get the harvest of your sowing.   You have set her against her own mother and now she turns against the father.   Tell me, then, that there is no God!

CAPTAIN.   [*To* CURT.]   What does the Colonel say?

CURT.   He grants leave of absence without any comment.

CAPTAIN.   Leave of absence?   I have not asked for it.

ALICE.   No, but I have asked for it.

CAPTAIN.   I don't accept it.

ALICE.   Order has already been issued.

CAPTAIN.   That's none of my concern!

ALICE.   Do you see, Curt, that for this man exist no laws, no constitutions, no prescribed human order?   He stands above everything and everybody.   The universe is created for his private use.   The sun and the moon pursue their courses in order to spread his glory among the stars.   Such is this man: this insignificant captain, who could not even reach the rank of major, and at whose strutting everybody laughs, while he thinks himself feared; this poor wretch who is afraid in the dark and believes in barometers: and all this in conjunction with and having for its climax—a barrowful of manure that is not even prime quality!

CAPTAIN.   [*Fanning himself with a bunch of flowers, conceitedly, without listening to* ALICE.]   Have you asked Curt to breakfast?

ALICE.   No.

CAPTAIN.   Get us, then, at once, two nice tender loin steaks.

ALICE.   Two?

CAPTAIN. I am going to have one myself.

ALICE. But we are three here.

CAPTAIN. Oh, you want one also? Well, make it three then.

ALICE. Where am I to get them? Last night you asked Curt to supper, and there was not a crust of bread in the house. Curt has been awake all night without anything to eat, and he has had no coffee because there is none in the house and the credit is gone.

CAPTAIN. She is angry at me for not dying yesterday.

ALICE. No, for not dying twenty-five years ago—for not dying before you were born!

CAPTAIN. [*To* CURT.] Listen to her! That's what happens when you institute a marriage, my dear Curt. And it is perfectly clear that it was not instituted in heaven.

[ALICE *and* CURT *look at each other meaningly.*

CAPTAIN. [*Rises and goes towards the door.*] However, say what you will, now I am going on duty. [*Puts on an old-fashioned helmet with a brush crest, girds on the sabre, and shoulders his cloak.*] If anybody calls for me, I am at the battery. [ALICE *and* CURT *try vainly to hold him back.*] Stand aside! [*Goes out.*

ALICE. Yes, go! You always go, always show your back, whenever the fight becomes too much for you. And then you let your wife cover the retreat—you hero of the bottle, you arch-braggart, you arch-liar! Fie on you!

CURT. This is bottomless!

ALICE. And you don't know everything yet.

CURT. Is there anything more——

ALICE. But I am ashamed——

CURT. Where is he going now? And where does he get the strength?

ALICE. Yes, you may well ask! Now he goes down to the non-commissioned officers and thanks them for the flowers—and then he eats and drinks with them. And then he speaks ill of all the other officers— If you only knew how many times he has been threatened with discharge! Nothing but sympathy for his family has saved him. And this he takes for fear of his superiority.   And he hates and maligns the very women—wives of other officers—who have been pleading our cause.

CURT.   I have to confess that I applied for this position in order to find peace by the sea—and of your circumstances I knew nothing at all.

ALICE.   Poor Curt!   And how will he get something to eat?

CURT.   Oh, I can go over to the doctor's—but you.   Will you not permit me to arrange this for you?

ALICE.   If only he does not learn of it, for then he would kill me.

CURT.   [*Looking out through the window.*]   Look, he stands right in the wind out there on the rampart.

ALICE.   He is to be pitied—for being what he is!

CURT.   Both of you are to be pitied!   But what can be done?

ALICE.   I don't know—   The mail brought a batch of unpaid bills also, and those he did not see.

CURT.   It may be fortunate to escape seeing things at times.

ALICE.   [*At the window.*]   He has unbuttoned his cloak and let the wind strike his chest.   Now he wants to die!

CURT.   That is not what he wants, I think, for a while ago, when he felt his life slipping away, he grabbed hold of mine and began to stir in my affairs as if he wanted to crawl into me and live my life.

ALICE.   That is just his vampire nature—to interefere with other people's destinies, to suck interest out of other existences, to regulate and arrange the doings of others, since he can find no interest whatever in his own life.   And remember, Curt, don't ever admit him into your family life, don't ever make him acquainted with your friends, for he will take them away from you and make them his own.   He is a perfect magician in this respect.   Were he to meet your children, you would soon find them intimate with *him,* and he would be advising them and educating them to suit himself—but principally in opposition to *your* wishes.

CURT.   Alice, was it not he who took my children away from me at the time of the divorce?

ALICE.   Since it is all over now—yes, it was he.

CURT. I have suspected it, but never had any certainty. It was he!

ALICE. When you placed your full trust in my husband and sent him to make peace between yourself and your wife, he made love to her instead, and taught her the trick that gave her the children.

CURT. Oh, God! God in heaven!

ALICE. There you have another side of him. [*Silence.*

CURT. Do you know, last night—when he thought himself dying—then—he made me promise that I should look after his children!

ALICE. But you don't want to revenge yourself on my children?

CURT. Yes—by keeping my promise. I shall look after your children.

ALICE. You could take no worse revenge, for there is nothing he hates so much as generosity.

CURT. Then I may consider myself revenged—without any revenge.

ALICE. I love revenge as a form of justice, and I am yearning to see evil get its punishment.

CURT. You still remain at that point?

ALICE. There I shall always remain, and the day I forgave or loved an enemy I should be a hypocrite.

CURT. It may be a duty not to say everything, Alice, not to see everything. It is called forbearance, and all of us need it.

ALICE. Not I! My life lies clear and open, and I have always played my cards straight.

CURT. That is saying a good deal.

ALICE. No, it is not saying enough. Because what I have suffered innocently for the sake of this man, whom I never loved——

CURT. Why did you marry?

ALICE. Who can tell? Because he took me, seduced me! I don't know. And then I was longing to get up on the heights——

CURT. And deserted your art?

ALICE. Which was despised! But you know, he cheated

me! He held out hopes of a pleasant life, a handsome home—
and there was nothing but debts; no gold except on the uniform
—and even that was not real gold. He cheated me!

CURT. Wait a moment! When a young man falls in love,
he sees the future in a hopeful light: that his hopes are not always
realised, one must pardon. I have the same kind of deceit on
my own conscience without thinking myself dishonest— What
is it you see on the rampart?

ALICE. I want to see if he has fallen down.

CURT. Has he?

ALICE. No—worse luck! He is cheating me all the time.

CURT. Then I shall call on the doctor and the lawyer.

ALICE. [*Sitting down at the window.*] Yes, dear Curt, go.
I shall sit here and wait. And I have learned how to wait!

Curtain.

*Same setting in full daylight. The sentry is pacing back and
forth on the battery as before.*

ALICE *sits in the right-hand easy-chair. Her hair is now grey.*

CURT. [*Enters from the left, after having knocked.*] Good
day, Alice.

ALICE. Good day, Curt. Sit down.

CURT. [*Sits down in the left-hand easy-chair.*] The
steamer is just coming in.

ALICE. Then I know what's in store, for he is on board.

CURT. Yes, he is, for I caught the glitter of his helmet—
What has he been doing in the city?

ALICE. Oh, I can figure it out. He dressed for parade,
which means that he saw the Colonel, and he put on white gloves,
which means that he made some calls.

CURT. Did you notice his quiet manner yesterday? Since
he has quit drinking and become temperate, he is another man:
calm, reserved, considerate——

ALICE. I know it, and if that man had always kept sober he
would have been a menace to humanity. It is perhaps fortunate

for the rest of mankind that he made himself ridiculous and harmless through his whisky.

CURT. The spirit in the bottle has chastised him— But have you noticed since death put its mark on him that he has developed a dignity which elevates? And is it not possible that with this new idea of immortality may have come a new outlook upon life?

ALICE. You are deceiving yourself. He is conjuring up something evil. And don't you believe what he says, for he lies with premeditation, and he knows the art of intriguing as no one else——

CURT. [*Watching* ALICE.] Why, Alice, what does this mean? Your hair has turned grey in these two nights!

ALICE. No, my friend, it has long been grey, and I have simply neglected to darken it since my husband is as good as dead. Twenty-five years in prison—do you know that this place served as a prison in the old days?

CURT. Prison—well, the walls show it.

ALICE. And my complexion! Even the children took on prison colour in here.

CURT. I find it hard to imagine children prattling within these walls.

ALICE. There was not much prattling done either. And those two that died perished merely from lack of light.

CURT. What do you think is coming next?

ALICE. The decisive blow at us two. I caught a familiar glimmer in his eye when you read out that telegram from Judith. It ought, of course, to have been directed against her, but she, you know, is inviolate, and so his hatred sought you.

CURT. What are his intentions in regard to me, do you think?

ALICE. Hard to tell, but he possesses a marvellous skill in nosing out other people's secrets—and did you notice how, all day yesterday, he seemed to be living in your quarantine; how he drank a life-interest out of your existence; how he ate your children alive? A cannibal, I tell you—for I know him. His own life is going, or has gone——

CURT. I also have that impression of his being already on the other side. His face seems to phosphoresce, as if he were in a state of decay—and his eyes flash like will-o'-the-wisps over graves or morasses— Here he comes! Tell him you thought it possible he might be jealous.

ALICE. No, he is too self-conceited. " Show me the man of whom I need to be jealous! " Those are his own words.

CURT. So much the better, for even his faults carry with them a certain merit— Shall I get up and meet him anyhow?

ALICE. No, be impolite, or he will think you false. And if he begins to lie, pretend to believe him. I know perfectly how to translate his lies, and get always at the truth with the help of my dictionary. I foresee something dreadful—but, Curt, don't lose your self-control! My own advantage in our own long struggle has been that I was always sober, and, for that reason, in full control of myself. He was always tripped by his whisky— Now we shall see!

CAPTAIN. [*Enters from the left in full uniform, with helmet, cloak, and white gloves. Calm, dignified, but pale and hollow-eyed. Moves forward with a tottering step and sinks down, his helmet and cloak still on, in a chair at the right of the stage, far from* CURT *and* ALICE.] Good day. Pardon me for sitting down like this, but I feel a little tired.

ALICE *and* CURT. Good day. Welcome home.

ALICE. How are you feeling?

CAPTAIN. Splendid! Only a little tired——

ALICE. What news from the city?

CAPTAIN. Oh, a little of everything. I saw the doctor, among other things, and he said it was nothing at all—that I might live twenty years, if I took care of myself.

ALICE. [*To* CURT.] Now he is lying. [*To the* CAPTAIN.] Why, that's fine, my dear.

CAPTAIN. So much for that.

Silence, during which the CAPTAIN *is looking at* ALICE *and* CURT *as if expecting them to speak.*

ALICE. [*To* CURT.] Don't say a word, but let him begin —then he will show his cards.

CAPTAIN. [*To* ALICE.] Did you say anything?

ALICE. No, not a word.

CAPTAIN. [*Dragging on the words.*] Well, Curt!

THE DANCE OF DEATH   363

ALICE. [*To* CURT.] There—now he is coming out.

CAPTAIN. Well, I went to the city, as you know. [CURT *nods assent.*] Mm-mm, I picked up acquaintances—and among others—a young cadet [*dragging*] in the artillery. [*Pause, during which* CURT *shows some agitation.*] As—we are in need of cadets right here, I arranged with the Colonel to let him come here. This ought to please you, especially when I inform you that—he is—your own son!

ALICE. [*To* CURT.] The vampire—don't you see?

CURT. Under ordinary circumstances that ought to please a father, but in my case it will merely be painful.

CAPTAIN. I don't see why it should!

CURT. You don't need to—it is enough that I don't want it.

CAPTAIN. Oh, you think so? Well, then, you ought to know that the young man has been ordered to report here, and that from now on he has to obey me.

CURT. Then I shall force him to seek transfer to another regiment.

CAPTAIN. You cannot do it, as you have no rights over your son.

CURT. No?

CAPTAIN. No, for the court gave those rights to the mother.

CURT. Then I shall communicate with the mother.

CAPTAIN. You don't need to.

CURT. Don't need to?

CAPTAIN. No, for I have already done so. Yah!

[CURT *rises but sinks back again.*

ALICE. [*To* CURT.] Now he must die!

CURT. Why, he *is* a cannibal!

CAPTAIN. So much for that! [*Straight to* ALICE *and* CURT.] Did you say anything?

ALICE. No—have you grown hard of hearing?

CAPTAIN. Yes, a little—but if you come nearer to me I can tell you something between ourselves.

ALICE. That is not necessary—and a witness is sometimes good to have for both parties.

CAPTAIN. You are right; witnesses are sometimes good to have! But, first of all, did you get that will?

ALICE. [*Hands him a document.*]   The regimental lawyer drew it up himself.

CAPTAIN.   In your favour—good!   [*Reads the document, and then tears it carefully into strips which he throws on the floor.*]   So much for that!   Yah!

ALICE. [*To* CURT.]   Did you ever see such a man?

CURT.   That is no man!

CAPTAIN.   Well, Alice, this was what I wanted to say——

ALICE. [*Alarmed.*]   Go on, please.

CAPTAIN. [*Calmly as before.*]   On account of your long-cherished desire to quit this miserable existence in an unhappy marriage; on account of the lack of feeling with which you have treated your husband and children, and on account of the carelessness you have shown in the handling of our domestic economy, I have, during this trip to the city, filed an application for divorce in the City Court.

ALICE.   Oh—and your grounds?

CAPTAIN. [*Calmly as before.*]   Besides the grounds already mentioned, I have others of a purely personal nature.   As it has been found that I may live another twenty years, I am contemplating a change from this unhappy marital union to one that suits me better, and I mean to join my fate to that of some woman capable of devotion to her husband, and who also may bring into the home not only youth, but—let us say—a little beauty!

ALICE. [*Takes the wedding-ring from her finger and throws it at the* CAPTAIN.]   You are welcome!

CAPTAIN. [*Picks up the ring and puts it in his vest pocket.*] She throws away the ring.   The witness will please take notice.

ALICE. [*Rises in great agitation.*]   And you intend to turn me out in order to put another woman into my home?

CAPTAIN.   Yah!

ALICE.   Well, then, we'll speak plain language!   Cousin Curt, that man is guilty of an attempt to murder his wife.

CURT.   An attempt to murder?

ALICE.   Yes, he pushed me into the water.

CAPTAIN.   Without witnesses!

ALICE.   He lies again—Judith saw it!

CAPTAIN. Well, what of it?

ALICE. She can testify to it.

CAPTAIN. No, she cannot, for she says that she didn't see anything.

ALICE. You have taught the child to lie!

CAPTAIN. I didn't need to, for you had taught her already.

ALICE. You have met Judith?

CAPTAIN. Yah!

ALICE. Oh, God! Oh, God!

CAPTAIN. The fortress has surrendered. The enemy will be permitted to depart in safety on ten minutes' notice. [*Places his watch on the table.*] Ten minutes—watch on the table!
[*Stops and puts one hand up to his heart.*

ALICE. [*Goes over to the* CAPTAIN *and takes his arm.*] What is it?

CAPTAIN. I don't know.

ALICE. Do you want anything—a drink?

CAPTAIN. Whisky? No, I don't want to die—You! [*Straightening himself up.*] Don't touch me! Ten minutes, or the garrison will be massacred. [*Pulls the sabre partly from the scabbard.*] Ten minutes!
[*Goes out through the background.*

CURT. What kind of man is this?

ALICE. He is a demon, and no man!

CURT. What does he want with my son?

ALICE. He wants him as hostage in order to be your master —he wants to isolate you from the authorities of the island— Do you know that the people around here have named this island " Little Hell "?

CURT. I didn't know that— Alice, you are the first woman who ever inspired me with compassion—all others have seemed to me to deserve their fate.

ALICE. Don't desert me now! Don't leave me, for he will beat me—he has been doing so all these twenty-five years—in the presence of the children—and he has pushed me into the water——

CURT. Having heard this, I place myself absolutely against him. I came here without an angry thought, without memory of his former slanders and attempts to humiliate me.   I forgave him even when you told me that he was the man who had parted me from my children—for he was ill and dying—but now, when he wants to steal my son, he must die—he or I!

ALICE.   Good!   No surrender of the fortress!   But blow it up instead, with him in it, even if we have to keep him company! I am in charge of the powder!

CURT.   There was no malice in me when I came here, and I wanted to run away when I felt myself infected with your hatred, but now I am moved by an irresistible impulse to hate this man, as I hate everything that is evil.   What can be done?

ALICE.   I have learned the tactics from him.   Drum up his enemies and seek allies.

CURT.   Just think—that he should get hold of my wife! Why didn't those two meet a life-time ago?   Then there would have been a battle-royal that had set the earth quaking.

ALICE.   But now these souls have spied each other—and yet they must part.   I guess what is his most vulnerable spot—   I have long suspected it——

CURT.   Who is his most faithful enemy on the island?

ALICE.   The Quartermaster.

CURT.   Is he an honest man?

ALICE.   He is.   And he knows what I—I know, too—he knows what the Sergeant-Major and the Captain have been up to.

CURT.   What have they been up to?   You don't mean——

ALICE.   Defalcations!

CURT.   This is terrible!   No, I don't want to have any finger in that mess!

ALICE.   Ha-ha!   You cannot hit an enemy.

CURT.   Formerly I could, but I can do so no longer.

ALICE.   Why?

CURT.   Because I have discovered—that justice is done anyhow.

ALICE.   And you could wait for that?   Then your son would already have been taken away from you.   Look at my grey hairs—just feel how thick it still is, for that matter—   He intends to marry again, and then I shall be free—to do the same — I am free!   And in ten minutes he will be under arrest

down below, right under us—[*stamps her foot on the floor*]
right under us—and I shall dance above his head—I shall dance
"The Entry of the Boyars"—[*makes a few steps with her arms
akimbo*] ha-ha-ha-ha!   And I shall play on the piano so that he
can hear it.   [*Hammering on the piano.*]   Oh, the tower is
opening its gates, and the sentry with the drawn sabre will no
longer be guarding me, but him—*Malbrough s'en va-t-en guerre!*
Him, him, him, the sentry is going to guard!

CURT.   [*Has been watching her with an intoxicated look in
his eyes.*]   Alice, are you, too, a devil?

ALICE.   [*Jumps up on a chair and pulls down the wreaths.*]
These we will take along when we depart—the laurels of triumph!   And fluttering ribbons!   A little dusty, but eternally
green—like my youth—   I am not old, Curt?

CURT.   [*With shining eyes.*]   You are a devil!

ALICE.   In "Little Hell"—   Listen!   Now I shall fix my
hair—[*loosens her hair*], dress in two minutes—go to the Quartermaster in two minutes—and then, up in the air with the
fortress!

CURT.   [*As before.*]   You are a devil!

ALICE.   That's what you always used to say when we were
children.   Do you remember when we were small and became
engaged to each other?   Ha-ha!   You were bashful, of course

CURT.   [*Seriously.*]   Alice!

ALICE.   Yes, you were!   And it was becoming to you.   Do
you know there are gross women who like modest men.   And
there are said to be modest men who like gross women—   You
liked me a little bit, didn't you?

CURT.   I don't know where I am!

ALICE.   With an actress whose manners are free, but who is
an excellent lady otherwise.   Yes!   But now I am free, free,
free!   Turn away and I'll change my waist!

She opens her waist.   CURT *rushes up to her, grabs her in his
arms, lifts her high up, and bites her throat so that she cries
out.   Then he drops her on the couch and runs out to the
left.*

Curtain and intermission.

Same stage setting in early evening light. The sentry on the battery is still visible through the windows in the background. The laurel wreaths are hung over the arms of an easy-chair. The hanging lamp is lit. Faint music.

The CAPTAIN, *pale and hollow-eyed, his hair showing touches of grey, dressed in a worn undress uniform, with riding-boots, sits at the writing-table and plays solitaire. He wears his spectacles. The entr'acte music continues after the curtain has been raised and until another person enters.*

The CAPTAIN *plays away at his solitaire, but with a sudden start now and then, when he looks up and listens with evident alarm.*

He does not seem able to make the solitaire come out, so he becomes impatient and gathers up the cards. Then he goes to the left-hand window, opens it, and throws out the cards. The window (of the French type) remains open, rattling on its hinges.

He goes over to the buffet, but is frightened by the noise made by the window, so he turns around to see what it is. Takes out three dark-coloured square whisky bottles, examines them carefully—and throws them out of the window. Takes out some boxes of cigars, smells at one, and throws them out of the window.

Next he takes off his spectacles, cleans them carefully, and tries how far he can see with them. Then he throws them out of the window, stumbles against the furniture, as if he could not see, and lights six candles in a candelabrum on the chiffonier. Catches sight of the laurel wreaths, picks them up, and goes towards the window, but turns back. Folds the wreaths carefully in the piano cover, fastens the corners together with pins taken from the writing-table, and puts the bundle on a chair. Goes to the piano, strikes the keyboard with his fists, locks the piano, and throws the key out through the window. Then he lights the candles on the piano. Goes to the whatnot, takes his wife's picture from it, looks at this and tears it to pieces, dropping the pieces on the floor. The window rattles on its hinges, and again he becomes frightened.

Then, after having calmed himself, he takes the pictures of his son and daughter, kisses them in an off-hand way, and puts them into his pocket. All the rest of the pictures he sweeps down with his elbow and pokes together into a heap with his foot.

Then he sits down at the writing-table, tired out, and puts a hand up to his heart. Lights the candle on the table and sighs; stares in front of himself as if confronted with unpleasant visions. Rises and goes over to the chiffonier, opens the lid, takes out a bundle of letters tied together with a blue silk ribbon, and throws the bundle into the fireplace of the glazed-brick oven. Closes the chiffonier. The telegraph receiver sounds a single click. The CAPTAIN *shrinks together in deadly fear, and stands fixed to the spot, listening. But hearing nothing more from the instrument, he turns to listen in the direction of the door on the left. Goes over and opens it, takes a step inside the doorway, and returns, carrying on his arm a cat whose back he strokes. Then he goes out to the right. Now the music ceases.*

ALICE *enters from the background, dressed in a walking suit, with gloves and hat on; her hair is black; she looks around with surprise at the many lighted candles.* CURT *enters from the left, nervous.*

ALICE. It looks like Christmas Eve here.

CURT. Well?

ALICE. [*Holds out her hand for him to kiss.*] Thank me! [CURT *kisses her hand unwillingly.*] Six witnesses, and four of them solid as rock. The report has been made, and the answer will come here by telegraph—right here, into the heart of the fortress.

CURT. So!

ALICE. You should say " thanks " instead of " so."

CURT. Why has he lit so many candles?

ALICE. Because he is afraid of the dark, of course. Look at the telegraph key—does it not look like the handle of a coffee mill? I grind, I grind, and the beans crack as when you pull teeth——

CURT. What has he been doing in the room here?

ALICE. It looks as if he intended to move. Down below, that's where you are going to move!

CURT. Don't, Alice—I think it's distressing! He was the friend of my youth, and he showed me kindness many times when I was in difficulty—— He should be pitied!

ALICE. And how about me, who have done nothing wrong, and who have had to sacrifice my career to that monster?

CURT. How about that career? Was it so very brilliant?

ALICE. [*Enraged.*] What are you saying? Do you know who I am, what I have been?

CURT. Now, now!

ALICE. Are you beginning already?

CURT. Already?

ALICE *throws her arms around* CURT'S *neck and kisses him.* CURT *takes her by the arms and bites her neck so that she screams.*

ALICE. You bite me!

CURT. [*Beyond himself.*] Yes, I want to bite your throat and suck your blood like a lynx. You have aroused the wild beast in me—that beast which I have tried for years to kill by privation and self-inflicted tortures. I came here believing myself a little better than you two, and now I am the vilest of all. Since I first saw you—in all your odious nakedness—and since my vision became warped by passion, I have known the full strength of evil. What is ugly becomes beautiful; what is good becomes ugly and mean—— Come here and I'll choke you with a kiss!   [*He locks her in his arms.*

ALICE. [*Holds up her left hand.*] Behold the mark of the shackles that you have broken. I was a slave, and you set me free.

CURT. But I am going to bind you——

ALICE. You?

CURT. I!

ALICE. For a moment I thought you were——

CURT. Pious?

ALICE. Yes, you prated about the fall of man——

CURT. Did I?

ALICE. And I thought you had come here to preach——

CURT. You thought so? In an hour we shall be in the city, and then you shall see what I am——

ALICE. Then we will go to the theatre to-night, just to show ourselves. The shame will be his if I run away, don't you see!

CURT. I begin to understand that prison is not enough——

ALICE. No, it is not—there must be shame also.

CURT. A strange world! You commit a shameful act, and the shame falls on him.

ALICE. Well, if the world be so stupid——

CURT. It is as if these prison walls had absorbed all the corruption of the criminals, and it gets into you if you merely breathe this air. You were thinking of the theatre and the supper, I suppose. I was thinking of my son.

ALICE. [Strikes him on the mouth with her glove.] Fogey!
[CURT lifts his hand as if to strike her.

ALICE. [Drawing back.] Tout beau!

CURT. Forgive me!

ALICE. Yes—on your knees! [CURT kneels down.] Down on your face! [CURT touches the ground with his forehead.] Kiss my foot! [CURT kisses her foot.] And don't you ever do it again! Get up!

CURT. [Rising.] Where have I landed? Where am I?

ALICE. Oh, you know!

CURT. [Looking around with horror.] I believe almost——

CAPTAIN. [Enters from the right, looking wretched, leaning on a cane.] Curt, may I have a talk with you—alone?

ALICE. Is it about that departure in safety?

CAPTAIN. [Sits down at the sewing-table.] Curt, will you kindly sit down here by me a little while? And, Alice, will you please grant me a moment—of peace!

ALICE. What is up now? New signals! [To CURT.] Please be seated. [CURT sits down reluctantly.] And listen to the words of age and wisdom— And if a telegram should come ——tip me off! [Goes out to the left.

CAPTAIN. [With dignity, after a pause.] Can you explain a fate like mine, like ours?

CURT.   No more than I can explain my own!

CAPTAIN.   What can be the meaning of this jumble?

CURT.   In my better moments I have believed that just this was the meaning—that we should not be able to catch a meaning, and yet submit——

CAPTAIN.   Submit?   Without a fixed point outside myself I cannot submit.

CURT.   Quite right, but as a mathematician you should be able to seek that unknown point when several known ones are given——

CAPTAIN.   I have sought it, and—I have not found it!

CURT.   Then you have made some mistake in your calculations—do it all over again!

CAPTAIN.·   I should do it over again?   Tell me, where did you get your resignation?

CURT.   I have none left.   Don't overestimate me.

CAPTAIN.   As you may have noticed, my understanding of the art of living has been—elimination!   That means: wipe out and pass on!   Very early in life I made myself a bag into which I chucked my humiliations, and when it was full I dropped it into the sea.   I don't think any man ever suffered so many humiliations as I have.   But when I wiped them out and passed on they ceased to exist.

CURT.   I have noticed that you have wrought both your life and your environment out of your poetical imagination.

CAPTAIN.   How could I have lived otherwise?   How could I have endured?   [*Puts his hand over his heart.*

CURT.   How are you doing?

CAPTAIN.   Poorly.   [*Pause.*]   Then comes a moment when the faculty for what you call poetical imagination gives out.   And then reality leaps forth in all its nakedness——   It is frightful! [*He is now speaking in a voice of lachrymose senility, and with his lower jaw drooping.*]   Look here, my dear friend—[*controls himself and speaks in his usual voice*] forgive me!——   When I was in the city and consulted the doctor [*now the tearful voice returns*] he said that I was played out—[*in his usual voice*] and that I couldn't live much longer.

CURT.   Was *that* what he said?

CAPTAIN [*With tearful voice.*] That's what he said!

CURT. So it was not true?

CAPTAIN. What? Oh—no, that was not true. [*Pause.*

CURT. Was the rest of it not true either?

CAPTAIN. What do you mean?

CURT. That my son was ordered to report here as cadet?

CAPTAIN. I never heard of it.

CURT. Do you know—your ability to wipe out your own misdeeds is miraculous!

CAPTAIN. I don't understand what you are talking of.

CURT. Then you have come to the end!

CAPTAIN. Well, there is not much left!

CURT. Tell me, perhaps you never applied for that divorce which would bring your wife into disgrace?

CAPTAIN. Divorce? No, I have not heard of it.

CURT. [*Rising.*] Will you admit, then, that you have been lying?

CAPTAIN. You employ such strong words, my friend. All of us need forbearance.

CURT. Oh, you have come to see that?

CAPTAIN. [*Firmly, with clear voice.*] Yes, I have come to see that— And for this reason, Curt, please forgive me! Forgive everything!

CURT. That was a manly word! But I have nothing to forgive you. And I am not the man you believe me to be. No longer now! Least of all one worthy of receiving your confessions!

CAPTAIN. [*With clear voice.*] Life seemed so peculiar— so contrary, so malignant—ever since my childhood—and people seemed so bad that I grew bad also——

CURT. [*On his feet, perturbed, and glancing at the telegraph instrument.*] Is it possible to close off an instrument like that?

CAPTAIN. Hardly.

CURT. [*With increasing alarm.*] Who is Sergeant-Major Östberg?

CAPTAIN. An honest fellow, but something of a busybody, I should say.

CURT.   And who is the Quartermaster?

CAPTAIN.   He is my enemy, of course, but I have nothing bad to say of him.

CURT.   [*Looking out through the window, where a lantern is seen moving to and fro.*]   What are they doing with the lantern out on the battery?

CAPTAIN.   Do you see a lantern?

CURT.   Yes, and people moving about.

CAPTAIN.   I suppose it is what we call a service squad.

CURT.   What is that?

CAPTAIN.   A few men and a corporal.   Probably some poor wretch that has to be locked up.

CURT.   Oh!   [*Pause.*

CAPTAIN.   Now, when you know Alice, how do you like her?

CURT.   I cannot tell—   I have no understanding of people at all.   She is as inexplicable to me as you are, or as I am myself.   For I am reaching the age when wisdom makes this acknowledgement: I know nothing, I understand nothing!   But when I observe an action, I like to get at the motive behind it.   Why did you push her into the water?

CAPTAIN.   I don't know.   It merely seemed quite natural to me, as she was standing on the pier, that she ought to be in the water.

CURT.   Have you ever regretted it?

CAPTAIN.   Never!

CURT.   That's strange!

CAPTAIN.   Of course, it is!   So strange that I cannot realise that I am the man who has been guilty of such a mean act.

CURT.   Have you not expected her to take some revenge?

CAPTAIN.   Well, she seems to have taken it in full measure; and that, too, seems no less natural to me.

CURT.   What has so suddenly brought you to this cynical resignation?

CAPTAIN.   Since I looked death in the face, life has presented itself from a different viewpoint.   Tell me, if you were to judge between Alice and myself, whom would you place in the right?

CURT.   Neither of you.   But to both of you I should give endless compassion—perhaps a little more of it to you!

CAPTAIN. Give me your hand, Curt!

CURT. [*Gives him one hand and puts the other one on the* CAPTAIN's *shoulder.*] Old boy!

ALICE. [*Enters from the left, carrying a sunshade.*] Well, how harmonious! Oh, friendship! Has there been no telegram yet?

CURT. [*Coldly.*] No.

ALICE. This delay makes me impatient, and when I grow impatient I push matters along— Look, Curt, how I give him the final bullet. And now he'll bite the grass! First, I load— I know all about rifle practice, the famous rifle practice of which less than 5,000 copies were sold—and then I aim—fire! [*She takes aim with her sunshade.*] How is your new wife? The young, beautiful, unknown one? You don't know! But I know how my lover is doing. [*Puts her arms around the neck of* CURT *and kisses him; he thrusts her away from himself.*] He is well, although still a little bashful! You wretch, whom I have never loved—you, who were too conceited to be jealous— you never saw how I was leading you by the nose!

The CAPTAIN *draws the sabre and makes a leap at her, aiming at her several futile blows that only hit the furniture.*

ALICE. Help! Help! [CURT *does not move.*

CAPTAIN. [*Falls·with the sabre in his hand.*] Judith, avenge me!

ALICE. Hooray! He's dead!

[CURT *withdraws towards the door in the background.*

CAPTAIN. [*Gets on his feet.*] Not yet! [*Sheathes the sabre and sits down in the easy-chair by the sewing-table.*] Judith! Judith!

ALICE. [*Drawing nearer to* CURT.] Now I go—with you!

CURT. [*Pushes her back with such force that she sinks to her knees.*] Go back to the hell whence you came! Good-bye for ever! [*Goes to the door.*

CAPTAIN. Don't leave me, Curt; she will kill me!

ALICE. Don't desert me, Curt—don't desert us!

CURT. Good-bye! [*Goes out.*

ALICE. [*With a sudden change of attitude.*] The wretch! That's a friend for you!

CAPTAIN. [*Softly.*] Forgive me, Alice, and come here—come quick!

ALICE. [*Over to the* CAPTAIN.] That's the worst rascal and hypocrite I have met in my life! Do you know, you are a man after all!

CAPTAIN. Listen, Alice! I cannot live much longer.

ALICE. Is that so?

CAPTAIN. The doctor has said so.

ALICE. Then there was no truth in the rest either?

CAPTAIN. No.

ALICE. [*In despair.*] Oh, what have I done!

CAPTAIN. There is help for everything.

ALICE. No, this is beyond helping!

CAPTAIN. Nothing is beyond helping, if you only wipe it out and pass on.

ALICE. But the telegram—the telegram!

CAPTAIN. Which telegram?

ALICE. [*On her knees beside the* CAPTAIN.] Are we then cast out? Must this happen? I have sprung a mine under myself, under us. Why did you have to tell untruths? And why should that man come here to tempt me? We are lost! Your magnanimity might have helped everything, forgiven everything!

CAPTAIN. What is it that cannot be forgiven? What is it that I have not already forgiven you?

ALICE. You are right—but there is no help for this.

CAPTAIN. I cannot guess, although I know your ingenuity when it comes to villainies——

ALICE. Oh, if I could only get out of this, I should care for you— I should love you, Edgar!

CAPTAIN. Listen to me! Where do I stand?

ALICE. Don't you think anybody can help us—well, no man can!

CAPTAIN. Who could then help?

ALICE. [*Looking the* CAPTAIN *straight in the eye.*] I don't know— Think of it, what is to become of the children with their name dishonoured——?

CAPTAIN. Have you dishonoured that name?

ALICE. Not I! Not I! And then they must leave school!

And as they go out into the world, they will be as lonely as we, and cruel as we— Then you didn't meet Judith either, I understand now?

CAPTAIN. No, but wipe it out!

The telegraph receiver clicks. ALICE *flies up.*

ALICE. [*Screams.*] Now ruin is overtaking us! [*To the* CAPTAIN.] Don't listen!

CAPTAIN. [*Quietly.*] I am not going to listen, dear child —just calm yourself!

ALICE. [*Standing by the instrument, raises herself on tiptoe in order to look out through the window.*] Don't listen! Don't listen!

CAPTAIN. [*Holding his hands over his ears.*] Lisa, child, I am stopping up my ears.

ALICE. [*On her knees, with lifted hands.*] God, help us! The squad is coming— [*Weeping and sobbing.*] God in heaven!

She appears to be moving her lips as if in silent prayer.

The telegraph receiver continues to click for a while and a long white strip of paper seems to crawl out of the instrument. Then complete silence prevails once more.

ALICE. [*Rises, tears off the paper strip, and reads it in silence. Then she turns her eyes upwards for a moment. Goes over to the* CAPTAIN *and kisses him on the forehead.*] That is over now! It was nothing!

Sits down in the other chair, puts her handkerchief to her face, and breaks into a violent spell of weeping.

CAPTAIN. What kind of secrets are these?

ALICE. Don't ask! It is over now!

CAPTAIN. As you please, child.

ALICE. You would not have spoken like that three days ago —what has done it?

CAPTAIN. Well, dear, when I fell down that first time, I went a little way on the other side of the grave. What I saw has been forgotten, but the impression of it still remains.

ALICE. And it was?

CAPTAIN. A hope—for something better!

ALICE. Something better?

CAPTAIN. Yes. That this could be the real life, I have, in fact, never believed: it is death—or something still worse!

ALICE. And we——

CAPTAIN. Have probably been set to torment each other—so it seems at least!

ALICE. Have we tormented each other enough?

CAPTAIN. Yes, I think so! And upset things! [*Looks around.*] Suppose we put things to rights? And clean house?

ALICE. Yes, if it can be done.

CAPTAIN. [*Gets up to survey the room.*] It can't be done in one day—no, it can't!

ALICE. In two, then! Many days!

CAPTAIN. Let us hope so! [*Pause. Sits down again.*] So you didn't get free this time after all! But then, you didn't get me locked up either! [ALICE *looks staggered.*] Yes, I know you wanted to put me in prison, but I wipe it out. I suppose you have done worse than that— [ALICE *is speechless.*] And I was innocent of those defalcations.

ALICE. And now you intend me to become your nurse?

CAPTAIN. If you are willing!

ALICE. What else could I do?

CAPTAIN. I don't know!

ALICE. [*Sits down, numbed and crushed.*] These are the eternal torments! Is there, then, no end to them?

CAPTAIN. Yes, if we are patient. Perhaps life begins when death comes.

ALICE. If it were so!   [*Pause.*

CAPTAIN. You think Curt a hypocrite?

ALICE. Of course I do!

CAPTAIN. And I don't! But all who come near us turn evil and go their way. Curt was weak, and the evil is strong! [*Pause.*] How commonplace life has become! Formerly blows were struck; now you shake your fist at the most! I am fairly certain that, three months from now, we shall celebrate our silver wedding—with Curt as best man—and with the Doctor and Gerda among the guests. The Quartermaster will make the speech and the Sergeant-Major will lead the cheering. And if I know the Colonel right, he will come on his own invitation— Yes, you may laugh! But do you recall the silver wedding of Adolph—in the Fusiliers? The bride had to carry her wedding ring on the right hand, because the groom in a tender moment had chopped off her left ring finger with his dirk. [ALICE *puts her handkerchief to her mouth in order to repress her laughter.*] Are you crying? No, I believe you are laughing! Yes, child, partly we weep and partly we laugh. Which is the right thing to do?—Don't ask me! The other day I read in a newspaper that a man had been divorced seven times— which means that he had been married seven times—and finally, at the age of ninety-eight, he ran away with his first wife and married her again. Such is love! If life be serious, or merely a joke, is more than I can decide. Often it is most painful when a joke, and its seriousness is after all more agreeable and peaceful. But when at last you try to be serious, somebody comes and plays a joke on you—as Curt, for instance! Do you want a silver wedding? [ALICE *remains silent.*] Oh, say yes! They will laugh at us, but what does it matter? We may laugh also, or keep serious, as the occasion may require.

ALICE. Well, all right!

CAPTAIN. Silver wedding, then! [*Rising.*] Wipe out and pass on! Therefore, let us pass on!

Curtain.

THE DANCE OF DEATH
Part II

CHARACTERS

EDGAR
ALICE
CURT
ALLAN, *the son of* CURT
JUDITH, *the daughter of* EDGAR
THE LIEUTENANT

THE DANCE OF DEATH

PART II

*A rectangular drawing-room in white and gold. The rear wall
is broken by several french-windows reaching down to the
floor. These stand open, revealing a garden terrace outside.
Along this terrace, serving as a public promenade, runs a stone
balustrade, on which are ranged pots of blue and white faïence,
with petunias and scarlet geraniums in them. Beyond, in the
background, can be seen the shore battery with a sentry pacing
back and forth. In the far distance, the open sea.*

*At the left of the drawing-room stands a sofa with gilded wood-
work. In front of it are a table and chairs. At the right is
a grand piano, a writing-table, and an open fireplace.*

In the foreground, an American easy-chair.

*By the writing-table is a standing lamp of copper with a table
attached to it.*

On the walls are several old-fashioned oil paintings.

ALLAN *is sitting at the writing-table, engrossed in some mathe-
matical problem.* JUDITH *enters from the background, in
summer dress, short skirt, hair in a braid down her back, hat
in one hand, and tennis racket in the other. She stops in the
doorway.* ALLAN *rises, serious and respectful.*

JUDITH. [*In serious but friendly tone.*] Why don't you
come and play tennis?

ALLAN. [*Bashful, struggling with his emotion.*] I am
very busy——

JUDITH. Didn't you see that I had made my bicycle point
towards the oak, and not away from it?

ALLAN. Yes, I saw it.

JUDITH. Well, what does it mean?

ALLAN. It means—that you want to come and play tennis—

383

but my duty—I have some problems to work out—and your father is a rather exacting teacher——

JUDITH. Do you like him?

ALLAN. Yes, I do. He takes such interest in all his pupils——

JUDITH. He takes an interest in everything and everybody. Won't you come?

ALLAN. You know I should like to—but I must not!

JUDITH. I'll ask papa to give you leave.

ALLAN. Don't do that. It will only cause talk.

JUDITH. Don't you think I can manage him? He wants what I want.

ALLAN. I suppose that is because you are so hard.

JUDITH. You should be hard also.

ALLAN. I don't belong to the wolf family.

JUDITH. Then you are a sheep.

ALLAN. Rather that.

JUDITH. Tell me why you don't want to come and play tennis?

ALLAN. You know it.

JUDITH. Tell me anyhow. The Lieutenant——

ALLAN. Yes, you don't care for me at all, but you cannot enjoy yourself with the Lieutenant unless I am present, so you can see me suffer.

JUDITH. Am I as cruel as that? I didn't know it.

ALLAN. Well, now you know it.

JUDITH. Then I shall do better hereafter, for I don't want to be cruel, I don't want to be bad—in your eyes.

ALLAN. You say this only to fasten your hold on me. I am already your slave, but it does not satisfy you. The slave must be tortured and thrown to the wild beasts. You have already that other fellow in your clutches—what do you want with me then? Let me go my own way, and you can go yours.

JUDITH. Do you send me away? [ALLAN *does not answer.*] Then I go! As second cousins, we shall have to meet now and then, but I am not going to bother you any longer.

ALLAN *sits down at the table and returns to his problem.*

JUDITH. [*Instead of going away, comes down the stage and approaches gradually the table where* ALLAN *is sitting.*] Don't be afraid, I am going at once— I wanted only to see how the Master of Quarantine lives— [*Looks around.*] White and gold—a Bechstein grand—well, well! We are still in the fort since papa was pensioned—in the tower where mamma has been kept twenty-five years—and we are there on sufferance at that. You—you are rich——

ALLAN. [*Calmly.*] We are not rich.

JUDITH. So you say, but you are always wearing fine clothes —but whatever you wear, for that matter, is becoming to you. Do you hear what I say? [*Drawing nearer.*

ALLAN. [*Submissively.*] I do.

JUDITH. How can you hear when you keep on figuring, or whatever you are doing?

ALLAN. I don't use my eyes to listen with.

JUDITH. Your eyes—have you ever looked at them in the mirror?

ALLAN. Go away!

JUDITH. You despise me, do you?

ALLAN. Why, girl, I am not thinking of you at all.

JUDITH. [*Still nearer.*] Archimedes is deep in his figures when the soldier comes and cuts him down.

[*Stirs his papers about with the racket.*

ALLAN. Don't touch my papers!

JUDITH. That's what Archimedes said also. Now you are thinking something foolish—you are thinking that I cannot live without you——

ALLAN. Why can't you leave me alone?

JUDITH. Be courteous, and I'll help you with your examinations——

ALLAN. You?

JUDITH. Yes, I know the examiners——

ALLAN. [*Sternly.*] And what of it?

JUDITH. Don't you know that one should stand well with the teachers?

ALLAN. Do you mean your father and the Lieutenant?

JUDITH. And the Colonel!

ALLAN.   And then you mean that your protection would enable me to shirk my work?

JUDITH.   You are a bad translator——

ALLAN.   Of a bad original——

JUDITH.   Be ashamed!

ALLAN.   So I am—both on your behalf and my own!   I am ashamed of having listened to you——   Why don't you go?

JUDITH.   Because I know you appreciate my company— Yes, you manage always to pass by my window.   You have always some errand that brings you into the city with the same boat that I take.   You cannot go for a sail without having me to look after the jib.

ALLAN.   But a young girl shouldn't say that kind of thing!

JUDITH.   Do you mean to say that I am a child?

ALLAN.   Sometimes you are a good child, and sometimes a bad woman.   Me you seem to have picked to be your sheep.

JUDITH.   You are a sheep, and that's why I am going to protect you.

ALLAN.   [*Rising.*]   The wolf makes a poor shepherd!   You want to eat me—that is the secret of it, I suppose.   You want to put your beautiful eyes in pawn to get possession of my head.

JUDITH.   Oh, you have been looking at my eyes?   I didn't expect that much courage of you.

ALLAN *collects his papers and starts to go out towards the right.* JUDITH *places herself in front of the door.*

ALLAN.   Get out of my way, or——

JUDITH.   Or?

ALLAN.   If you were a boy—bah!   But you are a girl.

JUDITH.   And then?

ALLAN.   If you had any pride at all, you would be gone, as you may regard yourself as shown the door.

JUDITH.   I'll get back at you for that!

ALLAN.   I don't doubt it!

JUDITH.   [*Goes enraged towards the background.*]   I— shall—get—back—at you for that!   [*Goes out.*

CURT.   [*Enters from the left.*]   Where are you going, Allan?

ALLAN. Oh, is that you?

CURT. Who was it that left in such hurry—so that the bushes shook?

ALLAN. It was Judith.

CURT. She is a little impetuous, but a fine girl.

ALLAN. When a girl is cruel and rude, she is always said to be a fine girl.

CURT. Don't be so severe, Allan! Are you not satisfied with your new relatives?

ALLAN. I like Uncle Edgar——

CURT. Yes, he has many good sides. How about your other teachers—the Lieutenant, for instance?

ALLAN. He's so uncertain. Sometimes he seems to have a grudge against me.

CURT. Oh, no! You just go here and make people " seem " this or that. Don't brood, but look after your own affairs, do what is proper, and leave others to their own concerns.

ALLAN. So I do, but—they won't leave me alone. They pull you in—as the cuttlefish down at the landing—they don't bite, but they stir up vortices that suck——

CURT. You have some tendency to melancholia, I think. Don't you feel at home here with me? Is there anything you miss?

ALLAN. I have never been better off, but—there is something here that smothers me.

CURT. Here by the sea? Are you not fond of the sea?

ALLAN. Yes, the open sea. But along the shores you find eelgrass, cuttlefish, jellyfish, sea-nettles, or whatever they are called.

CURT. You shouldn't stay indoors so much. Go out and play tennis.

ALLAN. Oh, that's no fun!

CURT. You are angry with Judith, I guess?

ALLAN. Judith?

CURT. You are so exacting towards people—it is not wise, for then you become isolated.

ALLAN. I am not exacting, but— It feels as if I were lying at the bottom of a pile of wood and had to wait my turn to get into the fire—and it weighs on me—all that is above weighs me down.

Curt. Bide your turn. The pile grows smaller——

Allan. Yes, but so slowly, so slowly. And in the meantime I lie here and grow mouldy.

Curt. It is not pleasant to be young. And yet you young ones are envied.

Allan. Are we? Would you change?

Curt. No, thanks!

Allan. Do you know what is worse than anything else? It is to sit still and keep silent while the old ones talk nonsense—I know that I am better informed than they on some matters—and yet I must keep silent. Well, pardon me, I am not counting you among the old.

Curt. Why not?

Allan. Perhaps because we have only just now become acquainted——

Curt. And because—your ideas of me have undergone a change?

Allan. Yes.

Curt. During the years we were separated, I suppose you didn't always think of me in a friendly way?

Allan. No.

Curt. Did you ever see a picture of me?

Allan. One, and it was very unfavourable.

Curt. And old-looking?

Allan. Yes.

Curt. Ten years ago my hair turned grey in a single night —it has since then resumed its natural colour without my doing anything for it— Let us talk of something else! There comes your aunt—my cousin. How do you like her?

Allan. I don't want to tell!

Curt. Then I shall not ask you.

Alice. [*Enters dressed in a very light-coloured walking-suit and carrying a sunshade.*] Good morning, Curt.

Gives him a glance signifying that Allan *should leave.*

Curt. [*To* Allan.] Leave us, please.

[Allan *goes out to the right.*

ALICE *takes a seat on the sofa to the left.* CURT *sits down on a chair near her.*

ALICE. [*In some confusion.*] He will be here in a moment, so you need not feel embarrassed.

CURT. And why should I?

ALICE. You, with your strictness——

CURT. Towards myself, yes——

ALICE. Of course—— Once I forgot myself, when in you I saw the liberator, but you kept your self-control—and for that reason we have a right to forget—what has never been.

CURT. Forget it then!

ALICE. However—— I don't think *he* has forgotten——

CURT. You are thinking of that night when his heart gave out and he fell on the floor—and when you rejoiced too quickly, thinking him already dead?

ALICE. Yes. Since then he has recovered; but when he gave up drinking, he learned to keep silent, and now he is terrible. He is up to something that I cannot make out——

CURT. Your husband, Alice, is a harmless fool who has shown me all sorts of kindnesses——

ALICE. Beware of his kindnesses. I know them.

CURT. Well, well——

ALICE. He has then blinded you also? Can you not see the danger? Don't you notice the snares?

CURT. No.

ALICE. Then your ruin is certain.

CURT. Oh, mercy!

ALICE. Think only, I have to sit here and see disaster stalking you like a cat—I point at it, but you cannot see it.

CURT. Allan, with his unspoiled vision, cannot see it either. He sees nothing but Judith, for that matter, and this seems to me a safeguard of our good relationship.

ALICE. Do you know Judith?

CURT. A flirtatious little thing, with a braid down her back and rather too short skirts——

ALICE. Exactly! But the other day I saw her dressed up in long skirts—and then she was a young lady—and not so very young either, when her hair was put up.

CURT. She is somewhat precocious, I admit.

ALICE. And she is playing with Allan.

CURT. That's all right, so long as it remains play.

ALICE. So *that* is all right?—   Now Edgar will be here soon, and he will take the easy-chair—he loves it with such passion that he could steal it.

CURT. Why, he can have it!

ALICE. Let him sit over there, and we'll stay here. And when he talks—he is always talkative in the morning—when he talks of insignificant things, I'll translate them for you——

CURT. Oh, my dear Alice, you are too deep, far too deep. What could I have to fear as long as I look after my quarantine properly and otherwise behave decently?

ALICE. You believe in justice and honour and all that sort of thing.

CURT. Yes, and it is what experience has taught me. Once I believed the very opposite—and paid dearly for it!

ALICE. Now he's coming!

CURT. I have never seen you so frightened before.

ALICE. My bravery was nothing but ignorance of the danger.

CURT. Danger? Soon you'll have me frightened, too!

ALICE. Oh, if I only could— There!

The CAPTAIN *enters from the background, in civilian dress, black Prince Albert buttoned all the way, military cap, and a cane with silver handle. He greets them with a nod and goes straight to the easy-chair, where he sits down.*

ALICE. [*To* CURT.] Let him speak first.

CAPTAIN. This is a splendid chair you have here, dear Curt; perfectly splendid.

CURT. I'll give it to you, if you will accept it.

CAPTAIN. That was not what I meant——

CURT. But I mean it seriously. How much have I not received from you?

CAPTAIN. [*Garrulously.*] Oh, nonsense! And when I sit here, I can overlook the whole island, all the walks; I can see all the people on their verandahs, all the ships on the sea, that are coming in and going out. You have really happened on the best piece of this island, which is certainly not an island of the blessed.

Or what do you say, Alice? Yes, they call it "Little Hell," and here Curt has built himself a paradise, but without an Eve, of course, for when she appeared, then the paradise came to an end. I say—do you know that this was a royal hunting lodge?

CURT. So I have heard.

CAPTAIN. You live royally, you, but if I may say so myself, you have me to thank for it.

ALICE. [To CURT.] There—now he wants to steal you.

CURT. I have to thank you for a good deal.

CAPTAIN. Fudge; Tell me, did you get the wine cases?

CURT. Yes.

CAPTAIN. And you are satisfied?

CURT. Quite satisfied, and you may tell your dealer so.

CAPTAIN. His goods are always prime quality——

ALICE. [To CURT.] At second-rate prices, and you have to pay the difference.

CAPTAIN. What did you say, Alice?

ALICE. I? Nothing!

CAPTAIN. Well, when this quarantine station was about to be established, I had in mind applying for the position—and so I made a study of quarantine methods.

ALICE. [To CURT.] Now he's lying!

CAPTAIN. [Boastfully.] And I did not share the antiquated ideas concerning disinfection which were then accepted by the government. For I placed myself on the side of the Neptunists —so called because they emphasise the use of water——

CURT. Beg your pardon, but I remember distinctly that it was I who preached water, and you fire, at that time.

CAPTAIN. I? Nonsense!

ALICE. [Aloud.] Yes, I remember that, too.

CAPTAIN. You?

CURT. I remember it so much the better because——

CAPTAIN. [Cutting him short.] Well, it's possible, but it does not matter. [Raising his voice.] However—we have now reached a point where a new state of affairs—[To CURT, who wants to interrupt] just a moment!—has begun to prevail—and when the methods of quarantining are about to become revolutionised.

CURT.   By the by, do you know who is writing those stupid articles in that periodical?

CAPTAIN.   [*Flushing.*]   No, I don't know, but why do you call them stupid?

ALICE.   [*To* CURT.]   Look out! It is he who writes them.

CURT.   He?—   [*To the* CAPTAIN.]   Not very well advised, at least.

CAPTAIN.   Well, are you the man to judge of that?

ALICE.   Are we going to have a quarrel?

CURT.   Not at all.

CAPTAIN.   It is hard to keep peace on this island, but we ought to set a good example——

CURT.   Yes, can you explain this to me?   When I came here I made friends with all the officials and became especially intimate with the regimental auditor—as intimate as men are likely to become at our age.   And then, in a little while—it was shortly after your recovery—one after another began to grow cold towards me—and yesterday the auditor avoided me on the promenade. I cannot tell you how it hurt me! [*The* CAPTAIN *remains silent.*]   Have you noticed any ill-feeling towards yourself?

CAPTAIN.   No, on the contrary.

ALICE.   [*To* CURT.]   Don't you understand that he has been stealing your friends?

CURT.   [*To the* CAPTAIN.]   I wondered whether it might have anything to do with this new stock issue to which I refused to subscribe.

CAPTAIN.   No, no—   But can you tell me why you didn't subscribe?

CURT.   Because I have already put my small savings into your soda factory.   And also because a new issue means that the old stock is shaky.

CAPTAIN.   [*Preoccupied.*]   That's a splendid lamp you have.   Where did you get it?

CURT.   In the city, of course.

ALICE.   [*To* CURT.]   Look out for your lamp!

CURT.   [*To the* CAPTAIN.]   You must not think that I am ungrateful or distrustful, Edgar.

CAPTAIN. No, but it shows small confidence to withdraw from an undertaking which you have helped to start.

CURT. Why, ordinary prudence bids everybody save himself and what is his.

CAPTAIN. Save? Is there any danger then? Do you think anybody wants to rob you?

CURT. Why such sharp words?

CAPTAIN. Were you not satisfied when I helped you to place your money at six per cent.?

CURT. Yes, and even grateful.

CAPTAIN. You are not grateful—it is not in your nature, but this you cannot help.

ALICE. [To CURT.] Listen to him!

CURT. My nature has shortcomings enough, and my struggle against them has not been very successful, but I do recognise obligations——

CAPTAIN. Show it then! [Reaches out his hand to pick up a newspaper.] Why, what is this? A death notice? [Reads.] The Health Commissioner is dead.

ALICE. [To CURT.] Now he is speculating in the corpse

——

CAPTAIN. [As if to himself.] This is going to bring about certain—changes——

CURT. In what respect?

CAPTAIN. [Rising.] That remains to be seen.

ALICE. [To the CAPTAIN.] Where are you going?

CAPTAIN. I think I'll have to go to the city— [Catches sight of a letter on the writing-table, picks it up as if unconsciously, reads the address, and puts it back.] Oh, I hope you will pardon my absent-mindedness.

CURT. No harm done.

CAPTAIN. Why, that's Allan's drawing case. Where is the boy?

CURT. He is out playing with the girls.

CAPTAIN. That big boy? I don't like it. And Judith must not be running about like that. You had better keep an eye on your young gentleman, and I'll look after my young lady. [Goes over to the piano and strikes a few notes.] Splendid tone in this instrument. A Steinbech, isn't it?

CURT. A Bechstein.

CAPTAIN. Yes, you are well fixed. Thank me for bringing you here.

ALICE. [*To* CURT.] He lies, for he tried to keep you away.

CAPTAIN. Well, good-bye for a while. I am going to take the next boat.

[*Scrutinises the paintings on the walls as he goes out.*

ALICE. Well?

CURT. Well?

ALICE. I can't see through his plans yet. But—tell me one thing. This envelope he looked at—from whom is the letter?

CURT. I am sorry to admit—it was my one secret.

ALICE. And he ferreted it out. Can you see that he knows witchery, as I have told you before? Is there anything printed on the envelope?

CURT. Yes—" The Citizens' Union."

ALICE. Then he has guessed your secret. You want to get into the Riksdag, I suppose. And now you'll see that he goes there instead of you.

CURT. Has he ever thought of it?

ALICE. No, but he is thinking of it now. I read it on his face while he was looking at the envelope.

CURT. That's why he has to go to the city?

ALICE. No, he made up his mind to go when he read the death notice.

CURT. What has he to gain by the death of the Health Commissioner?

ALICE. Hard to tell! Perhaps the man was an enemy who had stood in the way of his plans.

CURT. If he be as terrible as you say, then there is reason to fear him.

ALICE. Didn't you hear how he wanted to steal you, to tie your hands by means of pretended obligations that do not exist? For instance, he has done nothing to get you this position, but has, on the contrary, tried to keep you out of it. He is a man-thief, an insect, one of those wood-borers that eat up your insides so that one day you find yourself as hollow as a dying pine tree.

He hates you, although he is bound to you by the memory of your youthful friendship——

CURT.   How keen-witted we are made by our hatreds!

ALICE.   And stupid by our loves—blind and stupid!

CURT.   Oh, no, don't say that!

ALICE.   Do you know what is meant by a vampire?   They say it is the soul of a dead person seeking a body in which it may live as a parasite.   Edgar is dead—ever since he fell down on the floor that time.   You see, he has no interests of his own, no personality, no initiative.   But if he can only get hold of some other person he hangs on to him, sends down roots into him, and begins to flourish and blossom.   Now he has fastened himself on you.

CURT.   If he comes too close I'll shake him off.

ALICE.   Try to shake off a burr!   Listen: do you know why he does not want Judith and Allan to play?

CURT.   I suppose he is concerned about their feelings.

ALICE.   Not at all.   He wants to marry Judith to—the Colonel!

CURT.   [Shocked.]   That old widower!

ALICE.   Yes.

CURT.   Horrible!   And Judith?

ALICE.   If she could get the General, who is eighty, she would take him in order to bully the Colonel, who is sixty.   To bully, you know, that's the aim of her life.   To trample down and bully—there you have the motto of *that* family.

CURT.   Can this be Judith.   That maiden fair and proud and splendid?

ALICE.   Oh, I know all about that!   May I sit here and write a letter?

CURT.   [Puts the writing-table in order.]   With pleasure.

ALICE.   [Takes off her gloves and sits down at the writing-table.]   Now we'll try our hand at the art of war.   I failed once when I tried to slay my dragon.   But now I have mastered the trade.

CURT.   Do you know that it is necessary to load before you fire?

ALICE.   Yes, and with ball cartridges at that!

[CURT withdraws to the right.

ALICE *ponders and writes.* ALLAN *comes rushing in without
noticing* ALICE *and throws himself face downwards on the
sofa.   He is weeping convulsively into a lace handkerchief.*

ALICE.   [*Watches him for a while.   Then she rises and goes
over to the sofa.   Speaks in a tender voice.*]   Allan!

ALLAN *sits up disconcertedly and hides the handkerchief behind his back.*

ALICE.   [*Tenderly, womanly, and with true emotion.*]   You
should not be afraid of me, Allan——   I am not dangerous to
you——   What is wrong?   Are you sick?

ALLAN.   Yes.

ALICE.   In what way?

ALLAN.   I don't know.

ALICE.   Have you a headache?

ALLAN.   No.

ALICE.   And your chest?   Pain?

ALLAN.   Yes.

ALICE.   Pain—pain—as if your heart wanted to melt away.
And it pulls, pulls——

ALLAN.   How do you know?

ALICE.   And then you wish to die—that you were already
dead—and everything seems so hard.   And you can only think
of one thing—always the same—but if two are thinking of the
same thing, then sorrow falls heavily on one of them.   [ALLAN
forgets himself and begins to pick at the handkerchief.]   That's
the sickness which no one can cure.   You cannot eat and you
cannot drink; you want only to weep, and you weep so bitterly—
especially out in the woods where nobody can see you, for at that
kind of sorrow all men laugh—men who are so cruel!   Dear
me!   What do you want of her?   Nothing!   You don't want
to kiss her mouth, for you feel that you would die if you did.
When your thoughts run to her, you feel as if death were approaching.   And it is death, child—that sort of death—which
brings life.   But you don't understand it yet!   I smell violets—
it is herself.   [*Steps closer to* ALLAN *and takes the handkerchief
gently away from him.*]   It is she, it is she everywhere, none
but she!   Oh, oh, oh!   [ALLAN *cannot help burying his face in*
ALICE's *bosom.*]   Poor boy!   Poor boy!   Oh, how it hurts,

how it hurts! [*Wipes off his tears with the handkerchief.*]
There, there! Cry—cry to your heart's content. There now!
Then the heart grows lighter— But now, Allan, rise up and
be a man, or she will not look at you—she, the cruel one, who is
not cruel. Has she tormented you? With the Lieutenant?
You must make friends with the Lieutenant, so that you two can
talk of her. That gives a little ease also.

ALLAN. I don't want to see the Lieutenant!

ALICE. Now. Look here, little boy, it won't be long before
the Lieutenant seeks you out in order to get a chance to talk of
her. For— [ALLAN *looks up with a ray of hope on his face.*]
Well, shall I be nice and tell you? [ALLAN *droops his head.*]
He is just as unhappy as you are.

ALLAN. [*Happy.*] No?

ALICE. Yes, indeed, and he needs somebody to whom he
may unburden his heart when Judith has wounded him. You
seem to rejoice in advance?

ALLAN. Does she not want the Lieutenant?

ALICE. She does not want you either, dear boy, for she
wants the Colonel. [ALLAN *is saddened again.*] Is it raining
again? Well, the handkerchief you cannot have, for Judith is
careful about her belongings and wants her dozen complete.
[ALLAN *looks dashed.*] Yes, my boy, such is Judith. Sit over
there now, while I write another letter, and then you may do
an errand for me.

Sits down at the writing-table and begins to write again.

LIEUTENANT. [*Enters from the background, with a melan-
choly face, but without being ridiculous. Without noticing*
ALICE *he makes straight for* ALLAN.] I say, Cadet— [ALLAN
rises and stands at attention.] Please be seated.

ALICE *watches them. The* LIEUTENANT *goes up to* ALLAN
*and sits down beside him. Sighs, takes out a lace handker-
chief just like the other one, and wipes his forehead with it.*
ALLAN *stares greedily at the handkerchief. The* LIEU-
TENANT *looks sadly at* ALLAN. ALICE *coughs. The*
LIEUTENANT *jumps up and stands at attention.*

ALICE. Please be seated.

LIEUTENANT. I beg your pardon, madam——

ALICE. Never mind! Please sit down and keep the Cadet company—he is feeling a little lonely here on the island.

[*Writes.*

LIEUTENANT. [*Conversing with* ALLAN *in low tone and uneasily.*] It is awfully hot.

ALLAN. Rather.

LIEUTENANT. Have you finished the sixth book yet?

ALLAN. I have just got to the last proposition.

LIEUTENANT. That's a tough one. [*Silence.*] Have you —[*seeking for words*] played tennis to-day?

ALLAN. No-o—the sun was too hot.

LIEUTENANT. [*In despair, but without comical effect.*] Yes, it's awfully hot to-day!

ALLAN. [*In a whisper.*] Yes, it is very hot.   [*Silence.*

LIEUTENANT. Have you—been out sailing to-day?

ALLAN. No-o, I couldn't get anybody to tend the jib.

LIEUTENANT. Could you—trust me sufficiently to let me tend the jib?

ALLAN. [*Respectfully as before.*] That would be too great an honour for me, Lieutenant.

LIEUTENANT. Not at all, not at all! Do you think—the wind might be good enough to-day—about dinner-time, say, for that's the only time I am free?

ALLAN. [*Slyly.*] It always calms down about dinner-time, and—that's the time Miss Judith has her lesson.

LIEUTENANT. [*Sadly.*] Oh, yes, yes! Hm! Do you think——

ALICE. Would one of you young gentlemen care to deliver a letter for me? [ALLAN *and the* LIEUTENANT *exchange glances of mutual distrust*]—to Miss Judith? [ALLAN *and the* LIEUTENANT *jump up and hasten over to* ALICE, *but not without a certain dignity meant to disguise their emotion.*] Both of you? Well, the more safely my errand will be attended to. [*Hands the letter to the* LIEUTENANT.] If you please, Lieutenant, I should like to have that handkerchief. My daughter is very careful about her things—there is a touch of pettiness in her nature— Give me that handkerchief! I don't wish to laugh at you, but you must not make yourself ridiculous—needlessly.

And the Colonel does not like to play the part of an Othello. [*Takes the handkerchief.*] Away with you now, young men, and try to hide your feelings as much as you can.

[*The* LIEUTENANT *bows and goes out, followed closely by* ALLAN.

ALICE. [*Calls out.*] Allan!

ALLAN. [*Stops unwillingly in the doorway*]. Yes, Aunt.

ALICE. Stay here, unless you want to inflict more suffering on yourself than you can bear.

ALLAN. But he is going!

ALICE. Let him burn himself. But take care of yourself.

ALLAN. I don't want to take care of myself.

ALICE. And then you cry afterwards. And so I get the trouble of consoling you.

ALLAN. I want to go!

ALICE. Go then! But come back here, young madcap, and I'll have the right to laugh at you.

[ALLAN *runs after the* LIEUTENANT.
ALICE *writes again.*

CURT. [*Enters.*] Alice, I have received an anonymous letter that is bothering me.

ALICE. Have you noticed that Edgar has become another person since he put off the uniform? I could never have believed that a coat might make such a difference.

CURT. You didn't answer my question.

ALICE. It was no question. It was a piece of information. What do you fear?

CURT. Everything!

ALICE. He went to the city. And his trips to the city are always followed by something dreadful.

CURT. But I can do nothing because I don't know from which quarter the attack will begin.

ALICE. [*Folding the letter.*] We'll see whether I have guessed it.

CURT. Will you help me then?

ALICE. Yes—but no further than my own interests permit. My own—that is my children's.

CURT. I understand that! Do you hear how silent everything is—here on land, out on the sea, everywhere?

ALICE. But behind the silence I hear voices—mutterings, cries!

CURT. Hush! I hear something, too—no, it was only the gulls.

ALICE. But I hear something else! And now I am going to the post-office—with this letter!

Curtain.

Same stage setting. ALLAN *is sitting at the writing-table studying.* JUDITH *is standing in the doorway. She wears a tennis hat and carries the handle-bars of a bicycle.*

JUDITH. Can I borrow your wrench?

ALLAN. [*Without looking up.*] No, you cannot.

JUDITH. You are discourteous now, because you think I am running after you.

ALLAN. [*Without crossness.*] I am nothing at all, but I ask merely to be left alone.

JUDITH. [*Comes nearer.*] Allan!

ALLAN. Yes, what is it?

JUDITH. You mustn't be angry with me!

ALLAN. I am not.

JUDITH. Will you give me your hand on that?

ALLAN. [*Kindly.*] I don't want to shake hands with you, but I am not angry—— What do you want with me anyhow?

JUDITH. Oh, but you're stupid!

ALLAN. Well, let it go at that.

JUDITH. You think me cruel, and nothing else.

ALLAN. No, for I know that you are kind, too—you *can* be kind!

JUDITH. Well—how can I help—that you and the Lieutenant run around and weep in the woods? Tell me, why do you weep? [ALLAN *is embarrassed.*] Tell me now—— I never weep. And why have you become such good friends? Of what do you talk while you are walking about arm in arm? [ALLAN *cannot answer.*] Allan, you'll soon see what kind I am and whether I can strike a blow for one I like. And I want to give you a piece of advice—although I have no use for tale-bearing. Be prepared!

ALLAN. For what?

JUDITH. Trouble.

ALLAN. From what quarter?

JUDITH. From the quarter where you least expect it.

ALLAN. I am rather used to disappointment, and life has not brought me much that was pleasant. What's in store now?

JUDITH. [*Pensively.*] You poor boy—give me your hand! [ALLAN *gives her his hand.*] Look at me! Don't you dare to look at me?

[ALLAN *rushes out to the left in order to hide his emotion.*

LIEUTENANT. [*In from the background.*] I beg your pardon! I thought that——

JUDITH. Tell me, Lieutenant, will you be my friend and ally?

LIEUTENANT. If you'll do me the honour——

JUDITH. Yes—a word only—don't desert Allan when disaster overtakes him.

LIEUTENANT. What disaster?

JUDITH. You'll soon see—this very day perhaps. Do you like Allan?

LIEUTENANT. The young man is my best pupil, and I value him personally also on account of his strength of character— Yes, life has moments when strength is required [*with emphasis*] to bear up, to endure, to suffer, in a word!

JUDITH. That was more than one word, I should say. However, you like Allan?

LIEUTENANT. Yes.

JUDITH. Look him up then, and keep him company.

LIEUTENANT. It was for that purpose I came here—for that and no other. I had no other object in my visit.

JUDITH. I had not supposed anything of that kind—of the kind you mean! Allan went that way. [*Pointing to the left.*

LIEUTENANT. [*Goes reluctantly to the left.*] Yes—I'll do what you ask.

JUDITH. Do, please.

ALICE. [*In from the background.*] What are you doing here?

JUDITH. I wanted to borrow a wrench.

ALICE. Will you listen to me a moment?

JUDITH. Of course I will.

ALICE sits down on the sofa.

JUDITH. [*Remains standing.*] But tell me quickly what you want to say. I don't like long lectures.

ALICE. Lectures? Well, then—put up your hair and put on a long dress.

JUDITH. Why?

ALICE. Because you are no longer a child. And you are young enough to need no coquetry about your age.

JUDITH. What does that mean?

ALICE. That you have reached marriageable age. . And your way of dressing is causing scandal.

JUDITH. Then I shall do what you say.

ALICE. You have understood then?

JUDITH. Oh, yes.

ALICE. And we are agreed?

JUDITH. Perfectly.

ALICE. On all points?

JUDITH. Even the tenderest!

ALICE. Will you at the same time cease playing—with Allan?

JUDITH. It is going to be serious then?

ALICE. Yes.

JUDITH. Then we may just as well begin at once.

She has already laid aside the handle-bars. Now she lets down the bicycle skirt and twists her braid into a knot which she fastens on top of her head with a hairpin taken out of her mother's hair.

ALICE. It is not proper to make your toilet in a strange place.

JUDITH. Am I all right this way? Then I am ready. Come now who dares!

ALICE. Now at last you look decent. And leave Allan in peace after this.

JUDITH. I don't understand what you mean?

ALICE. Can't you see that he is suffering?

JUDITH. Yes, I think I have noticed it, but I don't know why. I don't suffer!

ALICE. That is *your* strength. But the day will come—oh, yes, you shall know what it means. Go home now, and don't forget—that you are wearing a long skirt.

JUDITH. Must you walk differently then?

ALICE. Just try.

JUDITH. [*Tries to walk like a lady.*] Oh, my feet are tied; I am caught, I cannot run any longer!

ALICE. Yes, child, now the walking begins, along the slow road towards the unknown, which you know already, but most pretend to ignore. Shorter steps, and much slower—much slower! The low shoes of childhood must go, Judith, and you have to wear boots. You don't remember when you laid aside baby socks and put on shoes, but I do!

JUDITH. I can never stand this!

ALICE. And yet you must—must!

JUDITH. [*Goes over to her mother and kisses her lightly on the cheek; then walks out with the dignified bearing of a lady, but forgetting the handle-bars.*] Good-bye then!

CURT. [*Enters from the right.*] So you're already here?

ALICE. Yes.

CURT. Has *he* come back?

ALICE. Yes.

CURT. How did he appear?

ALICE. In full dress—so he has called on the Colonel. And he wore two orders.

CURT. Two? I knew he was to receive the Order of the Sword on his retirement. But what can the other one be?

ALICE. I am not very familiar with those things, but there was a white cross within a red one.

CURT. It is a Portuguese order then. Let me see—tell me, didn't his articles in that periodical deal with quarantine stations in Portuguese harbours?

ALICE.   Yes, as far as I can recall.

CURT.   And he has never been in Portugal?

ALICE.   Never.

CURT.   But I have been there.

ALICE.   You shouldn't be so communicative.   His ears and his memory are so good.

CURT.   Don't you think Judith may have helped him to this honour?

ALICE.   Well, I declare!   There are limits—[*rising*] and you have passed them.

CURT.   Are we to quarrel now?

ALICE.   That depends on you.   Don't meddle with my interests.

CURT.   If they cross my own, I have to meddle with them, although with a careful hand.   Here he comes!

ALICE.   And now it is going to happen.

CURT.   What is—going to happen?

ALICE.   We shall see!

CURT.   Let it come to open attack then, for this state of siege is getting on my nerves.   I have not a friend left on the island.

ALICE.   Wait a minute!   You sit on this side—he must have the easy-chair, of course—and then I can prompt you.

CAPTAIN.   [*Enters from the background, in full dress uniform, wearing the Order of the Sword and the Portuguese Order of Christ.*]   Good day!   Here's the meeting place.

ALICE.   You are tired—sit down.   [*The* CAPTAIN, *contrary to expectation, takes a seat on the sofa to the left.*]   Make yourself comfortable.

CAPTAIN.   This is all right.   You're too kind.

ALICE.   [*To* CURT.]   Be careful—he's suspicious of us.

CAPTAIN.   [*Crossly.*]   What was that you said?

ALICE.   [*To* CURT.]   He must have been drinking.

CAPTAIN.   [*Rudely.*]   No-o, he has not.   [*Silence.*]   Well —how have you been amusing yourselves?

ALICE.   And you?

CAPTAIN.   Are you looking at my orders?

ALICE.   No-o!

CAPTAIN.   I guess not, because you are jealous—   Otherwise it is customary to offer congratulations to the recipient of honours.

ALICE. We congratulate you.

CAPTAIN. We get things like these instead of laurel wreaths, such as they give to actresses.

ALICE. That's for the wreaths at home on the walls of the tower——

CAPTAIN. Which your brother gave you——

ALICE. Oh, how you talk!

CAPTAIN. Before which I have had to bow down these twenty-five years—and which it has taken me twenty-five years to expose.

ALICE. You have seen my brother?

CAPTAIN. Rather! [ALICE *is crushed.* *Silence.*] And you, Curt—you don't say anything, do you?

CURT. I am waiting.

CAPTAIN. Well, I suppose you know the big news?

CURT. No.

CAPTAIN. It is not exactly agreeable for me to be the one who——

CURT. Oh, speak up!

CAPTAIN. The soda factory has gone to the wall——

CURT. That's decidedly unpleasant! Where does that leave you?

CAPTAIN. I am all right, as I sold out in time.

CURT. That was sensible.

CAPTAIN. But how about you?

CURT. Done for!

CAPTAIN. It's your own fault. You should have sold out in time, or taken new stock.

CURT. So that I could lose that, too.

CAPTAIN. No, for then the company would have been all right.

CURT. Not the company, but the directors, for in my mind that new subscription was simply a collection for the benefit of the board.

CAPTAIN. And now I ask whether such a view of the matter will save your money?

Curt.   No, I shall have to give up everything.

Captain.   Everything?

Curt.   Even my home, the furniture——

Captain.   But that's dreadful!

Curt.   I have experienced worse things.   [*Silence.*

Captain.   That's what happens when amateurs want to speculate.

Curt.   You surprise me, for you know very well that if I had not subscribed, I should have been boycotted.   The supplementary livelihood of the coast population, toilers of the sea, inexhaustible capital, inexhaustible as the sea itself—philanthropy and national prosperity—   Thus you wrote and printed——   And now you speak of it as speculation!

Captain.   [*Unmoved.*]   What are you going to do now?

Curt.   Have an auction, I suppose.

Captain.   You had better.

Curt.   What do you mean?

Captain.   What I said!   For there are going to be some changes——

Curt.   On the island?

Captain.   Yes—as, for instance—your quarters are going to be exchanged for somewhat simpler ones.

Curt.   Well, well.

Captain.   Yes, the plan is to place the quarantine station on the outside shore near the water.

Curt.   My original idea!

Captain.   [*Dryly.*]   I don't know about that—for I am not familiar with your ideas on the subject.   However—it seems then quite natural that you dispose of the furniture, and it will attract much less notice—the scandal!

Curt.   What?

Captain.   The scandal!   [*Egging himself on.*]   For it is a scandal to come to a new place and immediately get into financial troubles which must result in a lot of annoyance to the relatives—particularly to the relatives.

Curt.   Oh, I guess I'll have to bear the worst of it.

Captain.   I'll tell you one thing, my dear Curt: if I had not stood by you in this matter, you would have lost your position.

CURT. That, too?

CAPTAIN. It comes rather hard for you to keep things in order—complaints have been made against your work.

CURT. Warranted complaints?

CAPTAIN. Yah! For you are—in spite of your other respectable qualities—a careless fellow— Don't interrupt me!— You are a very careless fellow!

CURT. How strange!

CAPTAIN. However—the suggested change is going to take place very soon. And I should advise you to hold the auction at once or sell privately.

CURT. Privately? And where could I find a buyer in this place?

CAPTAIN. Well, I hope you don't expect me to settle down in the midst of your things? That would make a fine story— [*staccato*] hm!—especially when I—think of what happened—once upon a time——

CURT. What was that? Are you referring to what did *not* happen?

CAPTAIN. [*Turning about.*] You are so silent, Alice? What is the matter, old girl? Not blue, I hope?

ALICE. I sit here and think——

CAPTAIN. Goodness! Are you thinking? But you have to think quickly, keenly, and correctly, if it is to be of any help! So do your thinking now—one, two, three! Ha-ha! You can't! Well, then, I must try— Where is Judith?

ALICE. Somewhere.

CAPTAIN. Where is Allan? [ALICE *remains silent.*] Where is the Lieutenant? [ALICE *as before.*] I say, Curt— what are you going to do with Allan now?

CURT. Do with him?

CAPTAIN. Yes, you cannot afford to keep him in the artillery now.

CURT. Perhaps not.

CAPTAIN. You had better get him into some cheap infantry regiment—up in Norrland, or somewhere.

CURT. In Norrland?

CAPTAIN. Yes, or suppose you turned him into something

practical at once? If I were in your place, I should get him into some business office—why not? [CURT *is silent.*] In these enlightened times—yah! Alice is so *uncommonly* silent! Yes, children, this is the seesawing seesaw board of life—one moment high up, looking boldly around, and the next way down, and then upward again, and so on—— So much for that—— [*To* ALICE.] Did you say anything? [ALICE *shakes her head.*] We may expect company here in a few days.

ALICE. Were you speaking to me?

CAPTAIN. We may expect company in a few days—notable company!

ALICE. Who?

CAPTAIN. Behold—you're interested! Now you can sit there and guess who is coming, and between guesses you may read this letter over again.   [*Hands her an opened letter.*

ALICE. My letter? Opened? Back from the mail?

CAPTAIN. [*Rising.*] Yes, as the head of the family and your guardian, I look after the sacred interests of the family, and with iron hand I shall cut short every effort to break the family ties by means of criminal correspondence. Yah! [ALICE *is crushed.*] I am not dead, you know, but don't take offence now because I am going to raise us all out of undeserved humility—undeserved on my own part, at least!

ALICE. Judith! Judith!

CAPTAIN. And Holofernes? I, perhaps? Pooh!
                            [*Goes out through the background.*

CURT. Who is that man?

ALICE. How can I tell?

CURT. We are beaten.

ALICE. Yes—beyond a doubt.

CURT. He has stripped me of everything, but so cleverly that I can accuse him of nothing.

ALICE. Why, no—you owe him a debt of gratitude instead!

CURT. Does he know what he is doing?

ALICE. No, I don't think so. He follows his nature and his instincts, and just now he seems to be in favour where fortune and misfortune are being meted out.

CURT. I suppose it's the Colonel who is to come here.

ALICE. Probably. And that is why Allan must go.

CURT. And you find that right?

ALICE. Yes.

CURT. Then our ways part.

ALICE. [*Ready to go.*] A little—but we shall come together again.

CURT. Probably.

ALICE. And do you know where?

CURT. Here.

ALICE. You guess it?

CURT. That's easy! He takes the house and buys the furniture.

ALICE. I think so, too. But don't desert me!

CURT. Not for a little thing like that.

ALICE. Good-bye. [*Goes.*

CURT. Good-bye.

Curtain.

Same stage setting, but the day is cloudy and it is raining outside.

ALICE *and* CURT *enter from the background, wearing raincoats and carrying umbrellas.*

ALICE. At last I have got you to come here! But, I cannot be so cruel as to wish you welcome to your own home——

CURT. Oh, why not? I have passed through three forced sales—and worse than that—— It doesn't matter to me.

ALICE. Did he call you?

CURT. It was a formal command, but on what basis I don't understand.

ALICE. Why, he is not your superior!

CURT. No, but he has made himself king of the island. And if there be any resistance, he has only to mention the Colonel's name, and everybody submits. Tell me, is it to-day the Colonel is coming?

ALICE. He is expected—but I know nothing with certainty — Sit down, please.

CURT. [*Sitting down.*] Nothing has been changed here.

ALICE. Don't think of it! Don't renew the pain!

CURT. The pain? I find it merely a little strange. Strange as the man himself. Do you know, when I made his acquaintance as a boy, I fled him. But he was after me. Flattered, offered services, and surrounded me with ties— I repeated my attempt at escape, but in vain— And now I am his slave!

ALICE. And why? He owes you a debt, but you appear as the debtor.

CURT. Since I lost all I had, he has offered me help in getting Allan through his examinations——

ALICE. For which you will have to pay dearly! You are still a candidate for the Riksdag?

CURT. Yes, and, so far as I can see, there is nothing in my way. [*Silence.*

ALICE. Is Allan really going to leave to-day?

CURT. Yes, if I cannot prevent it.

ALICE. That was a short-lived happiness.

CURT. Short-lived as everything but life itself, which lasts all too long.

ALICE. Too long, indeed!— Won't you come in and wait in the sitting-room? Even if it does not trouble you, it troubles me—these surroundings!

CURT. If you wish it——

ALICE. I feel ashamed, so ashamed that I could wish to die —but I can alter nothing!

CURT. Let us go then—as you wish it.

ALICE. And somebody is coming, too.

[*They go out to the left.*

The CAPTAIN *and* ALLAN *enter from the background, both in uniform and wearing cloaks.*

CAPTAIN. Sit down, my boy, and let me have a talk with you. [*Sits down in the easy-chair.*

ALLAN *sits down on the chair to the left.*

CAPTAIN. It's raining to-day—otherwise I could sit here comfortably and look at the sea. [*Silence.*] Well?— You don't like to go, do you?

ALLAN. I don't like to leave my father.

CAPTAIN. Yes, your father—he is rather an unfortunate man. [*Silence.*] And parents rarely understand the true welfare of their children. That is to say—there are exceptions, of course. Hm! Tell me, Allan, have you any communication with your mother?

ALLAN. Yes, she writes now and then.

CAPTAIN. Do you know that she is your guardian?

ALLAN. Yes.

CAPTAIN. Now, Allan, do you know that your mother has authorised me to act in her place?

ALLAN. I didn't know that!

CAPTAIN. Well, you know it now. And, therefore, all discussions concerning your career are done with— And you are going to Norrland.

ALLAN. But I have no money.

CAPTAIN. I have arranged for what you need.

ALLAN. All I can do then is to thank you, Uncle.

CAPTAIN. Yes, *you* are grateful—which everybody is not. Hm!—[*Raising his voice.*] The Colonel—do you know the Colonel?

ALLAN. [*Embarrassed.*] No, I don't.

CAPTAIN. [*With emphasis.*] The Colonel—is my special friend—[*a little more hurriedly*] as you know, perhaps. Hm! The Colonel has wished to show his interest in my family, including my wife's relatives. Through his intercession, the Colonel has been able to provide the means needed for the completion of your course. Now you understand the obligation under which you and your father are placed towards the Colonel. Have I spoken with sufficient plainness? [ALLAN *bows.*] Go and pack your things now. The money will be handed to you at the landing. And now good-bye, my boy. [*Holds out a finger to* ALLAN.] Good-bye then. [*Rises and goes out to the right.*

ALLAN, *alone, stands still, looking sadly around the room.*

JUDITH. [*Enters from the background, wearing a hooded rain coat and carrying an umbrella; otherwise exquisitely dressed, in long skirt and with her hair put up.*] Is that you, Allan!

ALLAN. [*Turning around, surveys* JUDITH *carefully.*] Is that you, Judith?

JUDITH.   You don't know me any longer?   Where have you been all this time?   What are you looking at?   My long dress—and my hair——   You have not seen me like this before?

ALLAN.   No-o——

JUDITH.   Do I look like a married woman?

ALLAN *turns away from her.*

JUDITH.   [*Earnestly.*]   What are you doing here?

ALLAN.   I am saying good-bye.

JUDITH.   What?   You are going—away?

ALLAN.   I am transferred to Norrland.

JUDITH.   [*Dumfounded.*]   To Norrland?   When are you going?

ALLAN.   To-day.

JUDITH.   Whose doing is this?

ALLAN.   Your father's.

JUDITH.   That's what I thought!   [*Walks up and down the floor, stamping her feet.*]   I wish you had stayed over to-day.

ALLAN.   In order to meet the Colonel?

JUDITH.   What do you know about the Colonel?——   Is it certain that you are going?

ALLAN.   There is no other choice.   And now I want it myself.   [*Silence.*

JUDITH.   Why do you want it now?

ALLAN.   I want to get away from here—out into the world!

JUDITH.   It's too close here?   Yes, Allan, I understand you —it's unbearable here—here, where they speculate—in soda and human beings!   [*Silence.*

JUDITH.   [*With genuine emotion.*]   As you know, Allan, I possess that fortunate nature which cannot suffer—but—now I am learning!

ALLAN.   You?

JUDITH.   Yes—now it's the beginning!   [*She presses both hands to her breast.*]   Oh, how it hurts—oh!

ALLAN.   What is it?

JUDITH.   I don't know—I choke—I think I'm going to die!

ALLAN.   Judith?

JUDITH.   [*Crying out.*]   Oh!   Is this the way it feels?   Is this the way—poor boys!

ALLAN. I should smile, if I were as cruel as you are.

JUDITH. I am not cruel, but I didn't know better— You must not go!

ALLAN. I have to!

JUDITH. Go then—but give me a keepsake!

ALLAN. What have I to give you?

JUDITH. [*With all the seriousness of deepest suffering.*] You!— No, I can never live through this! [*Cries out, pressing her breast with both hands.*] I suffer, I suffer— What have you done to me? I don't want to live any longer! Allan, don't go—not alone! Let us go together—we'll take the small boat, the little white one—and we'll sail far out, with the main sheet made fast—the wind is high—and we'll sail till we founder —out there, way out, where there is no eelgrass and no jellyfish— What do you say?— But we should have washed the sails yesterday—they should be as white as snow—for I want to see white in that moment—and you swim with your arm about me until you grow tired—and then we sink— [*Turning around.*] There would be style in that, a good deal more style than in going about here lamenting and smuggling letters that will be opened and jeered at by father— Allan! [*She takes hold of both his arms and shakes him.*] Do you hear?

ALLAN. [*Who has been watching her with shining eyes.*] Judith! Judith! Why were you not like this before?

JUDITH. I didn't know—how could I tell what I didn't know?

ALLAN. And now I must go away from you! But I suppose it is the better, the only thing! I cannot compete with a man—like——

JUDITH. Don't speak of the Colonel!

ALLAN. Is it not true?

JUDITH. It is true—and it is not true.

ALLAN. Can it become wholly untrue?

JUDITH. Yes, so it shall—within an hour!

ALLAN. And you keep your word? I can wait, I can suffer, I can work—Judith!

JUDITH. Don't go yet! How long must I wait?

ALLAN. A year.

JUDITH. [*Exultantly.*] One? I shall wait a thousand years, and if you do not come then, I shall turn the dome of heaven upside down and make the sun rise in the west— Hush, somebody is coming! Allan, we must part—take me into your arms! [*They embrace each other.*] But you must not kiss me. [*Turns her head away.*] There, go now! Go now!

ALLAN *goes towards the background and puts on his cloak. Then they rush into each other's arms so that* JUDITH *disappears beneath the cloak, and for a moment they exchange kisses.* ALLAN *rushes out.* JUDITH *throws herself face downward on the sofa and sobs.*

ALLAN. [*Comes back and kneels beside the sofa.*] No, I cannot go! I cannot go away from you—not now!

JUDITH. [*Rising.*] If you could only see how beautiful you are now! If you could only see yourself!

ALLAN. Oh, no, a man cannot be beautiful. But you, Judith! You—that you—oh, I saw that, when you were kind, another Judith appeared—and she's mine!— But if you don't keep faith with me now, then I shall die!

JUDITH. I think I am dying even now— Oh, that I might die now, just now, when I am so happy——

ALLAN. Somebody is coming!

JUDITH. Let them come! I fear nothing in the world hereafter. But I wish you could take me along under your cloak. [*She hides herself in play under his cloak.*] And then I should fly with you to Norrland. What are we to do in Norrland? Become a Fusilier—one of those that wear plumes on their hats? There's style in that, and it will be becoming to you.

[*Plays with his hair.*

ALLAN *kisses the tips of her fingers, one by one—and then he kisses her shoe.*

JUDITH. What are you doing, Mr. Madcap? Your lips will get black. [*Rising impetuously.*] And then I cannot kiss you when you go! Come, and I'll go with you!

ALLAN. No, then I should be placed under arrest.

JUDITH. I'll go with you to the guard-room.

ALLAN. They wouldn't let you! We must part now!

JUDITH. I am going to swim after the steamer—and then

you jump in and save me—and it gets into the newspapers, and we become engaged. Shall we do that?

ALLAN. You can still jest?

JUDITH. There will always be time for tears— Say good-bye now!——

They rush into each other's arms; then ALLAN *withdraws slowly through the door in the background,* JUDITH *following him; the door remains open after them; they embrace again outside, in the rain.*

ALLAN. You'll get wet, Judith.

JUDITH. What do I care!

They tear themselves away from each other. ALLAN *leaves.* JUDITH *remains behind, exposing herself to the rain and to the wind, which strains at her hair and her clothes while she is waving her handkerchief. Then* JUDITH *runs back into the room and throws herself on the sofa, with her face buried in her hands.*

ALICE. [*Enters and goes over to* JUDITH.] What is this? Get up and let me look at you.   [JUDITH *sits up.*

ALICE. [*Scrutinising her.*] You are not sick— And I am not going to console you.   [*Goes out to the right.*

The LIEUTENANT *enters from the background.*

JUDITH. [*Gets up and puts on the hooded coat.*] Come along to the telegraph office, Lieutenant.

LIEUTENANT. If I can be of any service—but I don't think it's quite proper——

JUDITH. So much the better! I want you to compromise me—but without any illusions on your part— Go ahead, please!   [*They go out through the background.*

The CAPTAIN *and* ALICE *enter from the right; he is in undress uniform.*

CAPTAIN. [*Sits down in the easy-chair.*] Let him come in.

ALICE *goes over to the door on the left and opens it, whereupon she sits down on the sofa.*

CURT. [*Enters from the left.*] You want to speak to me?

CAPTAIN. [*Pleasantly, but somewhat condescendingly.*] Yes, I have quite a number of important things to tell you. Sit down.

CURT. [*Sits down on the chair to the left.*] I am all ears.

CAPTAIN. Well, then!— [*Bumptiously.*] You know that our quarantine system has been neglected during nearly a century—hm!

ALICE. [*To* CURT.] That's the candidate for the Riksdag who speaks now.

CAPTAIN. But with the tremendous development witnessed by our own day in—

ALICE. [*To* CURT.] The communications, of course!

CAPTAIN. —all kinds of ways the government has begun to consider improvements. And for this purpose the Board of Health has appointed inspectors—hm!

ALICE. [*To* CURT.] He's giving dictation.

CAPTAIN. You may as well learn it now as later—I have been appointed an inspector of quarantines.   [*Silence.*

CURT. I congratulate—and pay my respects to my superior at the same time.

CAPTAIN. On account of ties of kinship our personal relations will remain unchanged. However—to speak of other things— At my request, your son Allan has been transferred to an infantry regiment in Norrland.

CURT. But I don't want it.

CAPTAIN. Your will in this case is subordinate to the mother's wishes—and as the mother has authorised me to decide, I have formed this decision.

CURT. I admire you!

CAPTAIN. Is that the only feeling you experience at this moment when you are to part from your son? Have you no other purely human feelings?

CURT. You mean that I ought to be suffering?

CAPTAIN. Yes.

CURT. It would please you if I suffered. You wish me to suffer.

CAPTAIN. *You* suffer?— Once I was taken sick—you were present and I can still remember that your face expressed nothing but undisguised pleasure.

ALICE. That is not true! Curt sat beside your bed all night and calmed you down when your qualms of conscience became too violent—but when you recovered you ceased to be thankful for it——

CAPTAIN. [*Pretending not to hear* ALICE.] Consequently Allan will have to leave us.

CURT. And who is going to pay for it?

CAPTAIN. I have done so already—that is to say, we—a syndicate of people interested in the young man's future.

CURT. A syndicate?

CAPTAIN. Yes—and to make sure that everything is all right you can look over these subscription lists.

[*Hands him some papers.*

CURT. Lists? [*Reading the papers.*] These are begging letters?

CAPTAIN. Call them what you please.

CURT. Have you gone begging on behalf of my son?

CAPTAIN. Are you ungrateful again? An ungrateful man is the heaviest burden borne by the earth.

CURT. Then I am dead socially! And my candidacy is done for!

CAPTAIN. What candidacy?

CURT. For the Riksdag, of course.

CAPTAIN. I hope you never had any such notions—particularly as you might have guessed that I, as an older resident, intended to offer my own services, which you seem to underestimate.

CURT. Oh, well, then that's gone, too!

CAPTAIN. It doesn't seem to trouble you very much.

CURT. Now you have taken everything—do you want more?

CAPTAIN. Have you anything more? And have you anything to reproach me with? Consider carefully if you have anything to reproach me with.

CURT. Strictly speaking, no! Everything has been correct and legal as it should be between honest citizens in the course of daily life——

CAPTAIN. You say this with a resignation which I would call cynical. But your entire nature has a cynical bent, my dear Curt, and there are moments when I feel tempted to share Alice's opinion of you—that you are a hypocrite, a hypocrite of the first water.

CURT. [*Calmly.*] So that's Alice's opinion?

ALICE. [*To* CURT.] It was—once. But not now, for it takes true heroism to bear what you have borne—or it takes something else!

CAPTAIN. Now I think the discussion may be regarded as closed. You, Curt, had better go and say good-bye to Allan, who is leaving with the next boat.

CURT. [*Rising.*] So soon? Well, I have gone through worse things than that.

CAPTAIN. You say that so often that I am beginning to wonder what you went through in America?

CURT. What I went through? I went through misfortunes. And it is the unmistakable right of every human being to suffer misfortune.

CAPTAIN. [*Sharply.*] There are self-inflicted misfortunes —were yours of that kind?

CURT. Is not this a question of conscience?

CAPTAIN. [*Brusquely.*] Do you mean to say you have a conscience?

CURT. There are wolves and there are sheep, and no human being is honoured by being a sheep. But I'd rather be that than a wolf!

CAPTAIN. You don't recognise the old truth, that everybody is the maker of his own fortune?

CURT. Is *that* a truth?

CAPTAIN. And you don't know that a man's own strength

———

CURT. Yes, I know that from the night when your own strength failed you, and you lay flat on the floor.

CAPTAIN. [*Raising his voice.*] A deserving man like myself—yes, look at me—— For fifty years I have fought—against a world—but at last I have won the game, by perseverance, loyalty, energy, and—integrity!

ALICE. You should leave that to be said by others!

CAPTAIN. The others won't say it because they are jealous. However—we are expecting company—my daughter Judith will to-day meet her intended—— Where is Judith?

ALICE. She is out.

CAPTAIN. In the rain? Send for her.

CURT. Perhaps I may go now?

CAPTAIN. No, you had better stay. Is Judith dressed—Properly?

ALICE. Oh, so-so— Have you definite word from the Colonel that he is coming?

CAPTAIN. [*Rising.*] Yes—that is to say, he will take us by surprise, as it is termed. And I am expecting a telegram from him—any moment. [*Goes to the right.*] I'll be back at once.

ALICE. There you see him as he is! Can he be called human?

CURT. When you asked that question once before, I answered no. Now I believe him to be the commonest kind of human being of the sort that possess the earth. Perhaps we, too, are of the same kind—making use of other people and of favourable opportunities?

ALICE. He has eaten you and yours alive—and you defend him?

CURT. I have suffered worse things. And this man-eater has left my soul unharmed—*that* he couldn't swallow!

ALICE. What " worse " have you suffered?

CURT. And *you* ask that?

ALICE. Do you wish to be rude?

CURT. No, I don't wish to—and therefore—don't ask again!

CAPTAIN. [*Enters from the right.*] The telegram was already there, however— Please read it, Alice, for I cannot see— [*Seats himself pompously in the easy-chair.*] Read it! You need not go, Curt.

ALICE *glances through the telegram quickly and looks perplexed.*

CAPTAIN. Well? Don't you find it pleasing?

ALICE *stares in silence at the* CAPTAIN.

CAPTAIN. [*Ironically.*] Who is it from?

ALICE. From the Colonel.

CAPTAIN. [*With self-satisfaction.*] So I thought—and what does the Colonel say?

ALICE. This is what he says: " On account of Miss Judith's

impertinent communication over the telephone, I consider the relationship ended—for ever! " [*Looks intently at the* CAPTAIN.

CAPTAIN. Once more, if you please.

ALICE. [*Reads rapidly.*] "On account of Miss Judith's
impertinent communication over the telephone, I consider the
relationship ended—for ever! "

CAPTAIN. [*Turns pale.*] It is Judith!

ALICE. And there is Holofernes!

CAPTAIN. And what are you?

ALICE. Soon you will see!

CAPTAIN. This is your doing!

ALICE. No!

CAPTAIN. [*In a rage.*] This is your doing!

ALICE. No! [*The* CAPTAIN *tries to rise and draw his
sabre, but falls back, touched by an apoplectic stroke.*] There
you got what was coming to you!

CAPTAIN. [*With senile tears in his voice.*] Don't be angry
at me— I am very sick——

ALICE. Are you? I am glad to hear it.

CURT. Let us put him to bed.

ALICE. No, I don't want to touch him.   [*Rings.*

CAPTAIN. [*As before.*] You must not be angry at me!
[*To* CURT.] Look after my children!

CURT. This is sublime! I am to look after his children,
and he has stolen mine!

ALICE. Always the same self-deception!

CAPTAIN. Look after my children! [*Continues to mumble
unintelligibly.*] Blub-blub-blub-blub.

ALICE. At last that tongue is checked! Can brag no more,
lie no more, wound no more! You, Curt, who believe in God,
give Him thanks on my behalf. Thank Him for my liberation
from the tower, from the wolf, from the vampire!

CURT. Not that way, Alice!

ALICE. [*With her face close to the* CAPTAIN's.] Where is
your own strength now? Tell me? Where is your energy?
[*The* CAPTAIN, *speechless, spits in her face.*] Oh, you can still
squirt venom, you viper—then I'll tear the tongue out of your
throat! [*Cuffs him on the ear.*] The head is off, but still it

blushes!— Oh, Judith, glorious girl, whom I have carried like
vengeance under my heart—you, you have set us free, all of us!
— If you have more heads than one, Hydra, we'll take them!
[*Pulls his beard.*] Think only that justice exists on the earth!
Sometimes I dreamed it, but I could never believe it. Curt, ask
God to pardon me for misjudging Him. Oh, there is justice!
So I will become a sheep, too! Tell Him that, Curt! A little
success makes us better, but adversity alone turns us into wolves.

    The LIEUTENANT *enters from the background.*

ALICE. The Captain has had a stroke—will you please help
us to roll out the chair?

LIEUTENANT. Madam——

ALICE. What is it?

LIEUTENANT. Well, Miss Judith——

ALICE. Help us with this first—then you can speak of Miss
Judith afterwards.

        [*The* LIEUTENANT *rolls out the chair to the right.*

ALICE. Away with the carcass! Out with it, and let's open
the doors! The place must be aired! [*Opens the doors in the
background; the sky has cleared.*] Ugh!

CURT. Are you going to desert him?

ALICE. A wrecked ship is deserted, and the crew save their
lives—I'll not act as undertaker to a rotting beast! Drainmen
and dissectors may dispose of him! A garden bed would be too
good for that barrowful of filth! Now I am going to wash and
bathe myself in order to get rid of all this impurity—if I can
ever cleanse myself completely!

    JUDITH *is seen outside, by the balustrade, waving her handker-
chief towards the sea.*

CURT. [*Towards the background.*] Who is there? Judith!
[*Calls out.*] Judith!

JUDITH. [*Cries out as she enters.*] He is gone!

CURT. Who?

JUDITH. Allan is gone!

CURT. Without saying good-bye?

JUDITH. He did to me, and he sent his love to you, Uncle.

ALICE. Oh, that was it!

JUDITH. [*Throwing herself into* CURT'S *arms.*] He is gone!

CURT. He will come back, little girl.

ALICE. Or we will go after him!

CURT. [*With a gesture indicating the door on the right.*] And leave him? What would the world——

ALICE. The world—bah! Judith, come into my arms! [JUDITH *goes up to* ALICE, *who kisses her on the forehead.*] Do you want to go after him?

JUDITH. How can you ask?

ALICE. But your father is sick.

JUDITH. What do I care!

ALICE. This is Judith! Oh, I love you, Judith!

JUDITH. And besides, papa is never mean—and he doesn't like cuddling. There's style to papa, after all.

ALICE. Yes, in a way!

JUDITH. And I don't think he is longing for me after that telephone message—— Well, why should he pester me with an old fellow? No, Allan, Allan! [*Throws herself into* CURT's *arms.*] I want to go to Allan!

Tears herself loose again and runs out to wave her handkerchief. CURT *follows her and waves his handkerchief also.*

ALICE. Think of it, that flower can grow out of dirt!

The LIEUTENANT *enters from the right.*

ALICE. Well?

LIEUTENANT. Yes, Miss Judith——

ALICE. Is the feeling of those letters that form her name so sweet on your lips that it makes you forget him who is dying?

LIEUTENANT. Yes, but she said——

ALICE. She? Say rather Judith then! But first of all—how goes it in there?

LIEUTENANT. Oh, in there—it's all over!

ALICE. All over? Oh, God, on my behalf and that of all mankind, I thank Thee for having freed us from this evil! Your arm, if you please—I want to go outside and get a breath —breathe!

The LIEUTENANT *offers his arm.*

ALICE. [*Checks herself.*] Did he say anything before the end came?

LIEUTENANT. Miss Judith's father spoke a few words only.

ALICE.   What did he say?

LIEUTENANT.   He said: " Forgive them, for they know not what they do! "

ALICE.   Inconceivable!

LIEUTENANT.   Yes, Miss Judith's father was a good and noble man.

ALICE.   Curt!

CURT *enters.*

ALICE.   It is over!

CURT.   Oh!

ALICE.   Do you know what his last words were?   No, you can never guess it.   " Forgive them, for they know not what they do! "

CURT.   Can you translate it?

ALICE.   I suppose he meant that he had always done right and died as one that had been wronged by life.

CURT.   I am sure his funeral sermon will be fine.

ALICE.   And plenty of flowers—from the non-commissioned officers.

CURT.   Yes.

ALICE.   About a year ago he said something like this: " It looks to me as if life were a tremendous hoax played on all of us! "

CURT.   Do you mean to imply that he was playing a hoax on us up to the very moment of death?

ALICE.   No—but now, when he is dead, I feel a strange inclination to speak well of him.

CURT.   Well, let us do so!

LIEUTENANT.   Miss Judith's father was a good and noble man.

ALICE.   [*To* CURT.]   Listen to that!

CURT.   " They know not what they do."   How many times did I not ask you whether he knew what he was doing?   And you didn't think he knew.   Therefore, forgive him!

ALICE.   Riddles!   Riddles!   But do you notice that there is peace in the house now?   The wonderful peace of death.   Wonderful as the solemn anxiety that surrounds the coming of a child into the world.   I hear the silence—and on the floor I see the traces of the easy-chair that carried him away— And I feel that now my own life is ended, and I am starting on the road to dissolution!   Do you know, it's queer, but those simple words of the Lieutenant—and his is a simple mind—they pursue me, but now they have become serious.   My husband, my youth's beloved —yes, perhaps you laugh!—he *was* a good .and noble man —nevertheless!

CURT.   Nevertheless?   And a brave one—as he fought for his own and his family's existence!

ALICE.   What worries!   What humiliations!   Which he wiped out—in order to pass on!

CURT.   He was one who had been passed by!   And that is to say much!   Alice, go in there!

ALICE.   No, I cannot do it!   For while we have been talking here, the image of him as he was in his younger years has come back to me—I have seen him, I see him—now, as when he was only twenty—I must have loved that man!

CURT.   And hated him!

ALICE.   And hated!— Peace be with him.

Goes towards the right door and stops in front of it, folding her hands as if to pray.

Curtain.

THE SPOOK SONATA

CHAMBER PLAYS: OPUS III

1907

CHARACTERS

OLD HUMMEL

THE STUDENT, *named Arkenholtz*

THE MILKMAID, *an apparition*

THE JANITRESS

THE GHOST *of the Consul*

THE DARK LADY, *daughter of the Consul and the* JANITRESS

THE COLONEL

THE MUMMY, *wife of the* COLONEL

THE YOUNG LADY, *supposedly the* COLONEL'S *daughter, but in reality the daughter of* OLD HUMMEL

THE DANDY, *called Baron Skansenkorge and engaged to the* DARK LADY

JOHANSSON, *in the service of* HUMMEL

BENGTSSON, *the valet of the* COLONEL

THE FIANCÉE, *a white-haired old woman, formerly engaged to* HUMMEL

THE COOK

A SERVANT-GIRL

BEGGARS

THE SPOOK SONATA

SCENE I

*The stage shows the first and second storeys of a modern corner
house. At the left, the house continues into the wings; at
the right, it faces on a street supposed to be running at right
angles to the footlights.*

*The apartment on the ground floor ends at the corner in a round
room, above which is a balcony belonging to the apartment on
the second floor. A flagstaff is fixed to the balcony.*

*When the shades are raised in the windows of the Round Room,
a statue of a young woman in white marble becomes visible
inside, strongly illuminated by sunlight. It is surrounded by
palms. The windows on the left side of the Round Room
contain a number of flower-pots, in which grow blue, white,
and red hyacinths.*

*A bedquilt of blue silk and two pillows in white cases are hung
over the railing of the balcony on the second floor. The windows at the left of the balcony are covered with white sheets
on the inside.*

*A green bench stands on the sidewalk in front of the house. The
right corner of the foreground is occupied by a drinking fountain; the corner at the left, by an advertising column.*

*The main entrance to the house is near the left wing. Through
the open doorway appears the foot of the stairway, with steps
of white marble and a banister of mahogany with brass trimmings. On the sidewalk, flanking the entrance, stand two
laurel trees in wooden tubs.*

*At the left of the entrance, there is a window on the ground
floor, with a window-mirror outside.*

It is a bright Sunday morning.

*When the curtain rises, the bells of several churches are heard
ringing in the distance.*

*The doors of the entrance are wide open, and on the lowest
step of the stairway stands the* DARK LADY. *She does not
make the slightest movement.*

The JANITRESS *is sweeping the hallway. Then she polishes
the brass knobs on the doors. Finally, she waters the laurel
trees.*

Near the advertising column, OLD HUMMEL *is reading his
paper, seated in an invalid's chair on wheels. His hair and
beard are white, and he wears spectacles.*

The MILKMAID *enters from the side street, carrying milk-
bottles in a crate of wire-work. She wears a light dress,
brown shoes, black stockings, and a white cap.*

*She takes off her cap and hangs it on the fountain; wipes the
perspiration from her forehead; drinks out of the cup;
washes her hands in the basin, and arranges her hair, using
the water in the basin as a mirror.*

*A steamship-bell is heard outside. Then the silence is broken
fitfully by a few bass notes from the organ in the nearest
church.*

When silence reigns again, and the MILKMAID *has finished her
toilet, the* STUDENT *enters from the left, unshaved and
showing plainly that he has spent a sleepless night. He
goes straight to the fountain. A pause ensues.*

STUDENT.   Can I have the cup?
       The MILKMAID *draws back with the cup.*
STUDENT.   Are you not almost done?
       The MILKMAID *stares at him with horror.*
HUMMEL.   [*To himself.*]   With whom is he talking?   I
don't see anybody.   Wonder if he's crazy?
       He continues to look at them with evident surprise.
STUDENT.   Why do you stare at me?   Do I look so terrible?
—It is true that I haven't slept at all, and I suppose you think I
have been making a night of it. . . .
       The MILKMAID *remains as before.*
STUDENT.   You think I have been drinking, do you?   Do I
smell of liquor?
       The MILKMAID *remains as before.*

STUDENT. I haven't shaved, of course. . . . Oh, give me a drink of water, girl. I have earned it. [*Pause.*] Well? Must I then tell you myself that I have spent the night dressing wounds and nursing the injured. You see, I was present when that house collapsed last night. . . . Now you know all about it.

The MILKMAID *rinses the cup, fills it with water, and hands it to him.*

STUDENT. Thanks!

The MILKMAID *stands immovable.*

STUDENT. [*Hesitatingly.*] Would you do me a favour? [*Pause.*] My eyes are inflamed, as you can see, and my hands have touched wounds and corpses. To touch my eyes with them would be dangerous. . . . Will you take my handkerchief, which is clean, dip it in the fresh water, and bathe my poor eyes with it?—Will you do that?—Won't you play the good Samaritan?

The MILKMAID *hesitates at first, but does finally what he has asked.*

STUDENT. Thank you! [*He takes out his purse.*

The MILKMAID *makes a deprecatory gesture.*

STUDENT. Pardon my absent-mindedness. I am not awake, you see. . . . [*The* MILKMAID *disappears.*

HUMMEL. [*To the* STUDENT.] Excuse a stranger, but I heard you mention last night's accident. . . . I was just reading about it in the paper. . . .

STUDENT. Is it already in the papers?

HUMMEL. All about it. Even your portrait. They are sorry, though, that they have not been able to learn the name of the young student who did such splendid work. . . .

STUDENT. [*Glancing at the paper.*] Oh, is that me? Well!

HUMMEL. Whom were you talking to a while ago?

STUDENT. Didn't you see? [*Pause.*

HUMMEL. Would it be impertinent—to ask—your estimable name?

STUDENT. What does it matter? I don't care for publicity. Blame is always mixed into any praise you may get. The art of belittling is so highly developed. And besides, I ask no reward. . . .

HUMMEL.   Wealthy, I suppose?

STUDENT.   Not at all—on the contrary—poor as a durmouse!

HUMMEL.   Look here. . . .   It seems to me as if I recognised your voice.   When I was young, I had a friend who always said "dur" instead of door.   Until now he was the one person I had ever heard using that pronunciation.   You are the only other one. . . .   Could you possibly be a relative of the late Mr. Arkenholtz, the merchant?

STUDENT.   He was my father.

HUMMEL.   Wonderful are the ways of life. . . .   I have seen you when you were a small child, under very trying circumstances. . . .

STUDENT.   Yes, I have been told that I was born just after my father had gone bankrupt.

HUMMEL.   So you were.

STUDENT.   May I ask your name?

HUMMEL.   I am Mr. Hummel.

STUDENT.   You are?   Then I remember. . . .

HUMMEL.   Have you often heard my name ·mentioned at home?

STUDENT.   I have.

HUMMEL.   And not in a pleasant way, I suppose?

The STUDENT *remains silent.*

HUMMEL.   That's what I expected.—You were told, I suppose, that I had ruined your father?—All who are ruined by ill-advised speculations think themselves ruined by those whom they couldn't fool.   [*Pause.*]   The fact of it is, however, that your father robbed me of seventeen thousand crowns, which represented all my savings at that time.

STUDENT.   It is queer how the same story can be told in quite different ways.

HUMMEL.   You don't think that I am telling the truth?

STUDENT.   How can I tell what to think?   My father was not in the habit of lying.

HUMMEL.   No, that's right, a father never lies. . . .   But I am also a father, and for that reason . . .

STUDENT.   What are you aiming at?

HUMMEL.   I saved your father from misery, and he repaid

me with the ruthless hatred that is born out of obligation. . . .
He taught his family to speak ill of me.

STUDENT. Perhaps you made him ungrateful by poisoning
your assistance with needless humiliation.

HUMMEL. All assistance is humiliating, sir.

STUDENT. And what do you ask of me now?

HUMMEL. Not the money back. But if you will render me
a small service now and then, I shall consider myself well paid.
I am a cripple, as you see. Some people say it is my own fault.
Others lay it to my parents. I prefer to blame life itself, with
its snares. To escape one of these snares is to walk headlong into
another. As it is, I cannot climb stairways or ring door-bells,
and for that reason I ask you: will you help me a little?

STUDENT. What can I do for you?

HUMMEL. Give my chair a push, to begin with, so that I can
read the bills on that column. I wish to see what they are playing to-night.

STUDENT. [*Pushing the chair as directed.*] Have you no at-
tendant?

HUMMEL. Yes, but he is doing an errand. He'll be back
soon. Are you a medical student?

STUDENT. No, I am studying philology, but I don't know
what profession to choose. . . .

HUMMEL. Well, well! Are you good at mathematics?

STUDENT. Reasonably so.

HUMMEL. That's good! Would you care to accept a position?

STUDENT. Yes, why not?

HUMMEL. Fine! [*Studying the playbills.*] They are
playing " The Valkyr " at the matinee. . . . Then the Colonel
will be there with his daughter, and as he always has the end seat
in the sixth row, I'll put you next to him. . . . Will you please
go over to that telephone kiosk and order a ticket for seat eighty-
two, in the sixth row?

STUDENT. Must I go to the opera in the middle of the day?

HUMMEL. Yes. Obey me, and you'll prosper. I wish to
see you happy, rich, and honoured. Your début last night in the
part of the brave rescuer will have made you famous by

to-morrow, and then your name will be worth a great deal.

STUDENT. [*On his way out to telephone.*]   What a ludi-crous adventure!

HUMMEL.   Are you a sportsman?

STUDENT.   Yes, that has been my misfortune.

HUMMEL.   Then we'll turn it into good fortune.—Go and telephone now.

The STUDENT *goes out.* HUMMEL *begins to read his paper again. In the meantime the* DARK LADY *has come out on the sidewalk and stands talking to the* JANITRESS. HUM-MEL *is taking in their conversation, of which, however, nothing is audible to the public. After a while the* STUDENT *returns.*

HUMMEL.   Ready?

STUDENT.   It's done.

HUMMEL.   Have you noticed this house?

STUDENT.   Yes, I have been watching it. . . .   I happened to pass by yesterday, when the sun was making every window-pane glitter. . . .   And thinking of all the beauty and luxury that must be found within, I said to my companion: " Wouldn't it be nice to have an apartment on the fifth floor, a beautiful young wife, two pretty little children, and an income of twenty thousand crowns? ". . .

HUMMEL.   So you said that?   Did you really?   Well, well! I am very fond of this house, too. . . .

STUDENT.   Do you speculate in houses?

HUMMEL.   Mm-yah!   But not in the way you mean.

STUDENT.   Do you know the people who live here?

HUMMEL.   All of them.   A man of my age knows every-body, including their parents and grandparents, and in some manner he always finds himself related to every one else.   I am just eighty—but nobody knows *me*—not through and through. I am very much interested in human destinies.

At that moment the shades are raised in the Round Room on the ground floor, and the COLONEL *becomes visible, dressed in civilian clothes. He goes to one of the windows to study the thermometer outside. Then he turns back into the room and stops in front of the marble statue.*

HUMMEL. There's the Colonel now, who will sit next to you at the opera this afternoon.

STUDENT. Is *he*—the Colonel? I don't understand this at all, but it's like a fairy-tale.

HUMMEL. All my life has been like a collection of fairy-tales, my dear sir. Although the tales read differently, they are all strung on a common thread, and the dominant theme recurs constantly.

STUDENT. Whom does that statue represent?

HUMMEL. His wife, of course.

STUDENT. Was she very lovely?

HUMMEL. Mm-yah—well . . .

STUDENT. Speak out.

HUMMEL. Oh, we can't form any judgment about people, my dear boy. And if I told you that she left him, that he beat her, that she returned to him, that she married him a second time, and that she is living there now in the shape of a mummy, worshipping her own statue—then you would think me crazy.

STUDENT. I don't understand at all.

HUMMEL. I didn't expect you would. Then there is the window with the hyacinths. That's where his daughter lives. She is out for a ride now, but she will be home in a few moments.

STUDENT. And who is the dark lady talking to the janitress?

HUMMEL. The answer is rather complicated, but it is connected with the dead man on the second floor, where you see the white sheets.

STUDENT. Who was he?

HUMMEL. A human being like you or me, but the most conspicuous thing about him was his vanity. . . . If you were born on a Sunday, you might soon see him come down the stairway and go out on the sidewalk to make sure that the flag of the consulate is half-masted. You see, he was a consul, and he revelled in coronets and lions and plumed hats and coloured ribbons.

STUDENT. You spoke of being born on a Sunday. . . . So was I, I understand.

HUMMEL. No! Really? . . . Oh, I should have known. . . . The colour of your eyes shows it. . . . Then you can see what other people can't.   Have you noticed anything of that kind?

STUDENT.   Of course, I can't tell what other people see or don't see, but at times . . . Oh, such things you don't talk of!

HUMMEL.   I was sure of it!   And you can talk to me, because I—I understand—things of that kind. . . .

STUDENT.   Yesterday, for instance . . .   I was drawn to that little side street where the house fell down afterwards. . . . When I got there, I stopped in front of the house, which I had never seen before. . . .   Then I noticed a crack in the wall. . . . I could hear the floor beams snapping. . . .   I rushed forward and picked up a child that was walking in front of the house at the time. . . .   In another moment the house came tumbling down. . . .   I was saved, but in my arms, which I thought held the child, there was nothing at all. . . .

HUMMEL.   Well, I must say! . . .   Much as I have heard . . . Please tell me one thing: what made you act as you did by the fountain a while ago?   Why were you talking to yourself?

STUDENT.   Didn't you see the Milkmaid to whom I was talking?

HUMMEL.   [Horrified.]   A milkmaid?

STUDENT.   Yes, the girl who handed me the cup.

HUMMEL.   Oh, that's what it was. . . .   Well, I haven't that kind of sight, but there are other things. . . .

A white-haired old woman is seen at the window beside the entrance, looking into the window-mirror.

HUMMEL.   Look at that old woman in the window.   Do you see her?—Well, she was my fiancée once upon a time, sixty years ago. . . .   I was twenty at that time. . . .   Never mind, she does not recognise me.   We see each other every day, and I hardly notice her—although once we vowed to love each other eternally. . . .   Eternally!

STUDENT.   How senseless you were in those days!   We don't talk to our girls like that.

HUMMEL.   Forgive us, young man!   We didn't know better.—Can you see that she was young and pretty once?

STUDENT.   It doesn't show. . . .   Oh, yes, she has a beautiful way of looking at things, although I can't see her eyes clearly.

The JANITRESS *comes out with a basket on her arm and begins to cover the sidewalk with chopped hemlock branches, as is usual in Sweden when a funeral is to be held.*

HUMMEL. And the Janitress—hm! That Dark Lady is her daughter and the dead man's, and that's why her husband was made janitor. . . . But the Dark Lady has a lover, who is a dandy with great expectations. He is now getting a divorce from his present wife, who is giving him an apartment-house to get rid of him. This elegant lover is the son-in-law of the dead man, and you can see his bedclothes being aired on the balcony up there. . . . That's a bit complicated, I should say!

STUDENT. Yes, it's fearfully complicated.

HUMMEL. It certainly is, inside and outside, no matter how simple it may look.

STUDENT. But who was the dead man?

HUMMEL. So you asked me a while ago, and I answered you. If you could look around the corner, where the servants' entrance is, you would see a lot of poor people whom he used to help— when he was in the mood. . . .

STUDENT. He was a kindly man, then?

HUMMEL. Yes—at times.

STUDENT. Not always?

HUMMEL. No-o. . . . People are like that!—Will you please move the chair a little, so that I get into the sunlight? I am always cold. You see, the blood congeals when you can't move about. . . . Death isn't far away from me, I know, but I have a few things to do before it comes. . . . Just take hold of my hand and feel how cold I am.

STUDENT. [*Taking his hand.*] I should say so!

He shrinks back.

HUMMEL. Don't leave me! I am tired now, and lonely, but I haven't always been like this, you know. I have an endlessly long life behind—enormously long. . . . I have made people unhappy, and other people have made me unhappy, and one thing has to be put against the other, but before I die, I wish to see you happy. . . . Our destinies have become intertwined, thanks to your father—and many other things. . . .

STUDENT. Let go my hand! You are taking all my

strength! You are freezing me! What do you want of me?

HUMMEL. Patience, and you'll see, and understand. . . . There comes the Young Lady now. . . .

STUDENT. The Colonel's daughter?

HUMMEL. His daughter—yes! Look at her!—Did you ever see such a masterpiece?

STUDENT. She resembles the marble statue in there.

HUMMEL. It's her mother.

STUDENT. You are right. . . . Never did I see such a woman of woman born!—Happy the man who may lead her to the altar and to his home!

HUMMEL. You see it, then? Her beauty is not discovered by everybody. . . . Then it is written in the book of life!

The YOUNG LADY *enters from the left, wearing a close-fitting English riding-suit. Without looking at anyone, she walks slowly to the entrance, where she stops and exchanges a few words with the* JANITRESS. *Then she disappears into the house. The* STUDENT *covers his eyes with his hand.*

HUMMEL. Are you crying?

STUDENT. Can you meet what is hopeless with anything but despair?

HUMMEL. I have the power of opening doors and hearts, if I can only find an arm to do my will. . . . Serve me, and you shall also have power. . . .

STUDENT. Is it to be a bargain? Do you want me to sell my soul?

HUMMEL. Don't sell anything! . . . You see, all my life I have been used to *take*. Now I have a craving to give—to give! But no one will accept. . . . I am rich, very rich, but have no heirs except a scamp who is tormenting the life out of me. . . . Become my son! Inherit me while I am still alive! Enjoy life, and let me look on—from a distance, at least!

STUDENT. What am I to do?

HUMMEL. Go and hear " The Valkyr " first of all.

STUDENT. That's settled—but what more?

HUMMEL. This evening you shall be in the Round Room.

STUDENT. How am I to get there?

HUMMEL. Through " The Valkyr."

STUDENT. Why have you picked me to be your instrument? Did you know me before?

HUMMEL. Of course, I did! I have had my eyes on you for a long time. . . . Look at the balcony now, where the Maid is raising the flag at half-mast in honour of the consul. . . . And then she turns the bedclothes. . . . Do you notice that blue quilt? It was made to cover two, and now it is only covering one. . . . [*The* YOUNG LADY *appears at her window, having changed dress in the meantime; she waters the hyacinths.*] There is my litle girl now. Look at her—look! She is talking to her flowers, and she herself looks like a blue hyacinth. She slakes their thirst—with pure water only—and they transform the water into colour and fragrance. . . . There comes the Colonel with the newspaper! He shows her the story about the house that fell down—and he points at your portrait! She is not indifferent! She is not indifferent—she reads of your deeds. . . . It's clouding up, I think. . . . I wonder if it's going to rain? Then I shall be in a nice fix, unless Johansson comes back soon. . . . [*The sun has disappeared, and now the stage is growing darker; the white-haired old woman closes her window.*] Now my fiancée is closing her window. . . . She is seventy-nine— and the only mirror she uses is the window-mirror, because there she sees not herself, but the world around her—and she sees it from two sides—but it has not occurred to her that she can be seen by the world, too. . . . A handsome old lady, after all. . . .

Now the GHOST, *wrapped in winding sheets, comes out of the entrance.*

STUDENT. Good God, what is that I see?

HUMMEL. What *do* you see?

STUDENT. Don't *you* see? . . . There, at the entrance. . . . The dead man?

HUMMEL. I see nothing at all, but that was what I expected. Tell me . . .

STUDENT. He comes out in the street. . . . [*Pause.*] Now he turns his head to look at the flag.

HUMMEL. What did I tell you? And you may be sure that he will count the wreaths and study the visiting-cards attached to them. . . . And I pity anybody that is missing!

STUDENT.   Now he goes around the corner. . . .

HUMMEL.   He wants to count the poor at the other entrance.
. . .   The poor are so decorative, you know. . . .   " Followed
by the blessings of many." . . .   But he won't get any blessing
from me!—Between us, he was a big rascal!

STUDENT.   But charitable. . . .

HUMMEL.   A charitable rascal, who always had in mind the
splendid funeral he expected to get. . . .   When he knew that
his end was near, he cheated the state out of fifty thousand
crowns. . . .   And now his daughter goes about with another
woman's husband, and wonders what is in his will. . . .   Yes, the
rascal can hear every word we say, and he is welcome to it!—
There comes Johansson now.

> JOHANSSON *enters from the left.*

HUMMEL.   Report!

JOHANSSON *can be seen speaking, but not a word of what he
says is heard.*

HUMMEL.   Not at home, you say?   Oh, you are no good!
—Any telegram?—Not a thing. . . .   Go on!—Six o'clock to-
night?—That's fine!—An extra, you say?—With his full
name?—Arkenholtz, a student, yes. . . .   Born . . . Parents . . .
That's splendid! . . .   I think it's beginning to rain. . . .
What did he say?—Is that so?—He won't?—Well, then he
must!—Here comes the Dandy. . . .   Push me around the
corner, Johansson, so I can hear what the poor people have to
say. . . .   [*To the* STUDENT.]   And you had better wait for me
here, Arkenholtz. . . .   Do you understand?—[*To* JOHANSSON.]
Hurry up now, hurry up!

> JOHANSSON *pushes the chair into the side street and out of sight.
> The* STUDENT *remains on the same spot, looking at the
> YOUNG LADY, who is using a small rake to loosen up the
> earth in her pots.   The* DANDY *enters and joins the* DARK
> LADY, *who has been walking back and forth on the side-
> walk.   He is in mourning.*

DANDY.   Well, what is there to do about it?   We simply
have to wait.

DARK LADY.   But I can't wait!

DANDY.   Is that so?   Then you'll have to go to the country.

DARK LADY. I don't want to!

DANDY. Come this way, or they'll hear what we are saying. *They go towards the advertising column and continue their talk inaudibly.*

JOHANSSON. [*Entering from the right; to the* STUDENT.] My master asks you not to forget that other thing.

STUDENT. [*Dragging his words.*] Look here.... Tell me, please . . . Who *is* your master?

JOHANSSON. Oh, he's so many things, and he has been everything. . . .

STUDENT. Is he in his right mind?

JOHANSSON. Who can tell?—All his life he has been looking for one born on Sunday, he says—which does not mean that it must be true. . . .

STUDENT. What is he after? Is he a miser?

JOHANSSON. He wants to rule. . . . The whole day long he travels about in his chair like the god of thunder himself. . . . He looks at houses, tears them down, opens up new streets, fills the squares with buildings. . . . At the same time he breaks into houses, sneaks through open windows, plays havoc with human destinies, kills his enemies, and refuses to forgive anything. . . . Can you imagine that a cripple like him has been a Don Juan— but one who has always lost the women he loved?

STUDENT. How can you make those things go together?

JOHANSSON. He is so full of guile that he can make the women leave him when he is tired of them. . . . Just now he is like a horse thief practising at a slave-market. . . . He steals human beings, and in all sorts of ways. . . . He has literally stolen me out of the hands of the law. . . . Hm . . . yes. . . . I had been guilty of a slip. And no one but he knew of it. Instead of putting me in jail, he made a slave of me. All I get for my slavery is the food I eat, which might be better at that. . . .

STUDENT. And what does he wish to do in this house here?

JOHANSSON. No, I don't want to tell! It's too complicated. . . .

STUDENT. I think I'll run away from the whole story. . . .

The YOUNG LADY *drops a bracelet out of the window so that it falls on the sidewalk.*

JOHANSSON. Did you see the Young Lady drop her bracelet out of the window?

Without haste, the STUDENT *picks up the bracelet and hands it to the* YOUNG LADY, *who thanks him rather stiffly; then he returns to* JOHANSSON.

JOHANSSON. So you want to run away? That is more easily said than done when he has got you in his net. . . . And he fears nothing between heaven and earth . . . except one thing . . . or one person rather. . . .

STUDENT. Wait—I think I know!

JOHANSSON. How could you?

STUDENT. I can guess! Is it not—a little milkmaid that he fears?

JOHANSSON. He turns his head away whenever he meets a milk wagon. . . . And at times he talks in his sleep. . . . He must have been in Hamburg at one time, I think. . . .

STUDENT. Is this man to be trusted?

JOHANSSON. You may trust him—to do anything!

STUDENT. What is he doing around the corner now?

JOHANSSON. Watching the poor . . . dropping a word here and a word there . . . loosening a stone at a time . . . until the whole house comes tumbling down, metaphorically speaking. . . . You see, I am an educated man, and I used to be a book dealer. . . . Are you going now?

STUDENT. I find it hard to be ungrateful. . . . Once upon a time he saved my father, and now he asks a small service in return.

JOHANSSON. What is it?

STUDENT. To go and see " The Valkyr." . . .

JOHANSSON. That's beyond me. . . . But he is always up to new tricks. . . . Look at him now, talking to the policeman! He is always thick with the police. He uses them. He snares them in their own interests. He ties their hands by arousing their expectations with false promises—while all the time he is pumping them. . . . You'll see that he is received in the Round Room before the day is over!

STUDENT. What does he want there? What has he to do with the Colonel?

JOHANSSON. I think I can guess, but know nothing with certainty. But you'll see for yourself when you get there!

STUDENT. I'll never get there. . . .

JOHANSSON. That depends on yourself!—Go to "The Valkyr."

STUDENT. Is that the road?

JOHANSSON. Yes, if he has said so—Look at him there—look at him in his war chariot, drawn in triumph by the Beggars, who get nothing for their pains but a hint of a great treat to be had at his funeral.

OLD HUMMEL appears standing in his invalid's chair, which is drawn by one of the BEGGARS, *and followed by the rest.*

HUMMEL. Give honour to the noble youth who, at the risk of his own, saved so many lives in yesterday's accident! Three cheers for Arkenholtz!

The BEGGARS *bare their heads, but do not cheer. The* YOUNG LADY *appears at her window, waving her handkerchief. The* COLONEL *gazes at the scene from a window in the Round Room. The* FIANCÉE *rises at her window. The* MAID *appears on the balcony and hoists the flag to the top.*

HUMMEL. Applaud, citizens! It is Sunday, of course, but the ass in the pit and the ear in the field will absolve us. Although I was not born on a Sunday, I have the gift of prophecy and of healing, and on one occasion I brought a drowned person back to life. . . . That happened in Hamburg on a Sunday morning just like this. . . .

The MILKMAID *enters, seen only by the* STUDENT *and* HUMMEL. *She raises her arms with the movement of a drowning person, while gazing fixedly at* HUMMEL.

HUMMEL. [*Sits down; then he crumbles in a heap, stricken with horror.*] Get me out of here, Johansson! Quick!—Arkenholtz, don't forget "The Valkyr!"

STUDENT. What is the meaning of all this?

JOHANSSON. We'll see! We'll see!

Curtain.

SCENE II

In the Round Room.   An oven of white, glazed bricks occu-
pies the centre of the background.   The mantelpiece is
covered by a large mirror.   An ornamental clock and
candelabra stand on the mantelshelf.

At the right of the mantelpiece is a door leading into a hallway,
behind which may be seen a room papered in green, with
mahogany furniture.   The COLONEL *is seated at a writing-*
desk, so that only his back is visible to the public.

The statue stands at the left, surrounded by palms and with
draperies arranged so that it can be hidden entirely.

A door at the left of the mantelpiece opens on the Hyacinth
Room, where the YOUNG LADY *is seen reading a book.*

BENGTSSON, *the valet, enters from the hallway, dressed in*
livery.   He is followed by JOHANSSON *in evening dress*
with white tie.

BENGTSSON.   Now you'll have to do the waiting, Johansson,
while I take the overclothes.   Do you know how to do it?

JOHANSSON.   Although I am pushing a war chariot in the day-
time, as you know, I wait in private houses at night, and I have
always dreamt of getting into this place.... Queer sort of
people, hm?

BENGTSSON.   Yes, a little out of the ordinary, one might
say.

JOHANSSON.   Is it a musicale, or what is it?

BENGTSSON.   The usual spook supper, as we call it.   They
drink tea and don't say a word, or else the Colonel does all the
talking.   And then they munch their biscuits, all at the same
time, so that it sounds like the gnawing of a lot of rats in an attic.

JOHANSSON.   Why do you call it a spook supper?

BENGTSSON.   Because they look like spooks.... And they
have kept this up for twenty years—always the same people, saying the same things or keeping silent entirely, lest they be put to
shame.

JOHANSSON.   Is there not a lady in the house, too?

BENGTSSON.   Yes, but she is a little cracked.   She sits all the time in a closet, because her eyes can't bear the light. [*He points at a papered door.*] She is in there now.

JOHANSSON. In there, you say?

BENGTSSON. I told you they were a little out of the ordinary. . . .

JOHANSSON. How does she look?

BENGTSSON. Like a mummy. . . . Would you care to look at her? [*He opens the papered door.*] There she is now!

JOHANSSON. Mercy!

MUMMY. [*Talking baby talk.*] Why does he open the door? Haven't I told him to keep it closed?

BENGTSSON. [*In the same way.*] Ta-ta-ta-ta! Polly must be nice now. Then she'll get something good. Pretty polly!

MUMMY. [*Imitating a parrot.*] Pretty polly! Are you there, Jacob? Currrrr!

BENGTSSON. She thinks herself a parrot, and maybe she's right. . . . [*To the* MUMMY.] Whistle for us, Polly.

The MUMMY *whistles.*

JOHANSSON. Much I have seen, but never the like of it!

BENGTSSON. Well, you see, a house gets mouldy when it gets old, and when people are too much together, tormenting each other all the time, they lose their reason. The lady of this house. . . . Shut up, Polly! . . . That mummy has been living here for forty years—with the same husband, the same furniture, the same relatives, the same friends. . . . [*He closes the papered door.*] And the happenings this house has witnessed! . . . Well, it's beyond me. . . . Look at that statue. That's the self-same lady in her youth.

JOHANSSON. Good Lord! Can that be the Mummy?

BENGTSSON. Yes, it's enough to make you weep!—And somehow, carried away by her own imagination, perhaps, she has developed some of the traits of the talkative parrot. . . . She can't stand cripples or sick people, for instance. . . . She can't bear the sight of her own daughter, because she is sick. . . .

JOHANSSON. Is the Young Lady sick?

BENGTSSON. Don't you know that?

JOHANSSON. No.—And the Colonel—who is he?

BENGTSSON. That remains to be seen!

JOHANSSON. [*Looking at the statue.*] It's horrible to think that.... How old is she now?

BENGTSSON. Nobody knows. But at thirty-five she is said to have looked like nineteen, and that's the age she gave to the Colonel.... In this house.... Do you know what that Japanese screen by the couch is used for? They call it the Death Screen, and it is placed in front of the bed when somebody is dying, just as they do in hospitals....

JOHANSSON. This must be an awful house! And the Student was longing for it as for paradise....

BENGTSSON. What student? Oh, I know! The young chap who is coming here to-night.... The Colonel and the Young Lady met him at the opera and took a great fancy to him at once.... Hm!... But now it's my turn to ask questions. Who's your master? The man in the invalid's chair? ...

JOHANSSON. Well, well! Is he coming here, too?

BENGTSSON. He has not been invited.

JOHANSSON. He'll come without invitation—if necessary.

OLD HUMMEL *appears in the hallway, dressed in frock coat and high hat. He uses crutches, but moves without a noise, so that he is able to listen to the two servants.*

BENGTSSON. He's a sly old guy, isn't he?

JOHANSSON. Yes, he's a good one!

BENGTSSON. He looks like the very devil.

JOHANSSON. He's a regular wizard, I think ... because he can pass through locked doors....

HUMMEL. [*Comes forward and pinches the ear of* JOHANSSON.] Look out, you scoundrel! [*To* BENGTSSON.] Tell the Colonel I am here.

BENGTSSON. We expect company....

HUMMEL. I know, but my visit is as good as expected, too, although not exactly desired, perhaps....

BENGTSSON. I see! What's the name? Mr. Hummel?

HUMMEL. That's right.

BENGTSSON *crosses the hallway to the Green Room, the door of which he closes behind him.*

HUMMEL. [*To* JOHANSSON.] Vanish!

JOHANSSON *hesitates.*

HUMMEL. Vanish, I say!

JOHANSSON *disappears through the hallway.*

HUMMEL. [*Looking around and finally stopping in front of the statue, evidently much surprised.*] Amelia!—It is she!—She!

He takes another turn about the room, picking up various objects to look at them; then he stops in front of the mirror to arrange his wig; finally he returns to the statue.

MUMMY. [*In the closet.*] Prrretty Polly!

HUMMEL. [*Startled.*] What was that? Is there a parrot in the room? I don't see it!

MUMMY. Are you there, Jacob?

HUMMEL. The place is haunted!

MUMMY. Jacob!

HUMMEL. Now I am scared! ... So that's the kind of secrets they have been keeping in this house! [*He stops in front of a picture with his back turned to the closet.*] And that's he.... He!

MUMMY. [*Comes out of the closet and pulls the wig of* HUMMEL.] Currrrr! Is that Currrrr?

HUMMEL. [*Almost lifted off his feet by fright.*] Good Lord in heaven! ... Who are you?

MUMMY. [*Speaking in a normal voice.*] Is that you, Jacob?

HUMMEL. Yes, my name is Jacob....

MUMMY. [*Deeply moved.*] And my name is Amelia!

HUMMEL. Oh, no, no, no!——Merciful heavens! ...

MUMMY. How I look! That's right!—And *have* looked like that! [*Pointing to the statue.*] Life is a pleasant thing, is it not? ... I live mostly in the closet, both in order to see nothing and not to be seen.... But, Jacob, what do you want here?

HUMMEL. My child ... our child....

MUMMY. There she sits.

HUMMEL. Where?

MUMMY. There—in the Hyacinth Room.

HUMMEL. [*Looking at the* YOUNG LADY.] Yes, that is she! [*Pause.*] And what does her father say.... I mean the Colonel ... your husband?

MUMMY.   Once, when I was angry with him, I told him everything. . . .

HUMMEL.   And? . . .

MUMMY.   He didn't believe me.   All he said was: " That's what all women say when they wish to kill their husbands."—It is a dreadful crime, nevertheless.   His whole life has been turned into a lie—his family tree, too.   Sometimes I take a look in the peerage, and then I say to myself: " Here she is going about with a false birth certificate, just like any runaway servant-girl, and for such things people are sent to the reformatory."

HUMMEL.   Well, it's quite common.   I think I recall a certain incorrectness in regard to the date of your own birth. . . .

MUMMY.   It was my mother who started that. . . .   I was not to blame for it. . . .   And it was you, after all, who had the greater share in our guilt. . . .

HUMMEL.   No, what wrong we did was provoked by your husband when he took my fiancée away from me!   I was born a man who cannot forgive until he has punished.   To punish has always seemed an imperative duty to me—and so it seems still!

MUMMY.   What are you looking for in this house?   What do you want?   How did you get in?—Does it concern my daughter?   If you touch her, you must die!

HUMMEL.   I mean well by her!

MUMMY.   And you have to spare her father!

HUMMEL.   No!

MUMMY.   Then you must die . . . in this very room . . . behind that screen. . . .

HUMMEL.   Perhaps . . . but I can't let go when I have got my teeth in a thing. . . .

MUMMY.   You wish to marry her to the Student?   Why? He is nothing and has nothing.

HUMMEL.   He will be rich, thanks to me.

MUMMY.   Have you been invited for to-night?

HUMMEL.   No, but I intend to get an invitation for your spook supper.

MUMMY.   Do you know who will be here?

HUMMEL.   Not quite.

MUMMY. The Baron—he who lives above us, and whose father-in-law was buried this afternoon. . . .

HUMMEL. The man who is getting a divorce to marry the daughter of the Janitress. . . . The man who used to be—your lover!

MUMMY. Another guest will be your former fiancée, who was seduced by my husband. . . .

HUMMEL. Very select company!

MUMMY. If the Lord would let us die! Oh, that we might only die!

HUMMEL. But why do you continue to associate?

MUMMY. Crime and guilt and secrets bind us together, don't you know? Our ties have snapped so that we have slipped apart innumerable times, but we are always drawn together again. . . .

HUMMEL. I think the Colonel is coming.

MUMMY. I'll go in to Adèle, then. . . . [*Pause.*] Consider what you do, Jacob! Spare him. . . .

[*Pause; then she goes out.*

COLONEL. [*Enters, haughty and reserved.*] Won't you be seated, please?

HUMMEL *seats himself with great deliberation; pause.*

COLONEL. [*Staring at his visitor.*] You wrote this letter, sir?

HUMMEL. I did.

COLONEL. Your name is Hummel?

HUMMEL. It is. [*Pause.*

COLONEL. As I learn that you have bought up all my unpaid and overdue notes, I conclude that I am at your mercy. What do you want?

HUMMEL. Payment—in one way or another.

COLONEL. In what way?

HUMMEL. A very simple one. Let us not talk of the money. All you have to do is to admit me as a guest. . . .

COLONEL. If a little thing like that will satisfy you. . . .

HUMMEL. I thank you.

COLONEL. Anything more?

HUMMEL. Discharge Bengtsson.

COLONEL. Why should I do so? My devoted servant, who

has been with me a lifetime, and who has the medal for long and
faithful service. . . . Why should I discharge him?

HUMMEL. Those wonderful merits exist only in your imagination. He is not the man he seems to be.

COLONEL. Who is?

HUMMEL. [*Taken aback.*] True!—But Bengtsson must
go!

COLONEL. Do you mean to order my household?

HUMMEL. I do . . . as everything visible here belongs to me
. . . furniture, draperies, dinner ware, linen . . . and other things!

COLONEL. What other things?

HUMMEL. Everything! All that is to be seen is mine! I
own it!

COLONEL. Granted! But for all that, my coat of arms and
my unspotted name belong to myself.

HUMMEL. No—not even that much! [*Pause.*] You are
not a nobleman!

COLONEL. Take care!

HUMMEL. [*Producing a document.*] If you'll read this
extract from the armorial, you will see that the family whose
name you are using has been extinct for a century.

COLONEL. [*Reading the document.*] I have heard rumours
to that effect, but the name was my father's before it was mine.
. . . [*Reading again.*] That's right! Yes, you are right—I am
not a nobleman! Not even that!—Then I may as well take off
my signet-ring. . . . Oh, I remember now . . . It belongs to
you. . . . If you please!

HUMMEL. [*Accepting the ring and putting it into his
pocket.*] We had better continue. You are no colonel, either.

COLONEL. Am I not?

HUMMEL. No, you have simply held the title of colonel in
the American volunteer service by special appointment. After
the war in Cuba and the reorganisation of the army, all titles of
that kind were abolished. . . .

COLONEL. Is that true?

HUMMEL. [*With a gesture towards his pocket.*] Do you
wish to see for yourself?

COLONEL. No, it won't be necessary.—Who are you, anyhow, and with what right are you stripping me naked in this fashion?

HUMMEL.   You'll see by and by.   As to stripping you naked —do you know who you are in reality?

COLONEL.   How dare you?

HUMMEL.   Take off that wig, and have a look at yourself in the mirror.   Take out that set of false teeth and shave off your moustache, too.   Let Bengtsson remove the iron stays—and perhaps a certain X Y Z, a lackey, may begin to recognise himself— the man who used to visit the maid's chamber in a certain house for a bite of something good. . . .

The COLONEL *makes a movement towards a table on which stands a bell, but is checked by* HUMMEL.

HUMMEL.   Don't touch that bell, and don't call Bengtsson! If you do, I'll have him arrested. . . .   Now the guests are beginning to arrive. . . .   Keep your composure, and let us continue to play our old parts for a while.

COLONEL.   Who are you?   Your eyes and your voice remind me of somebody. . . .

HUMMEL.   Don't try to find out!   Keep silent and obey!

STUDENT.   [*Enters and bows to the* COLONEL.]   Colonel!

COLONEL.   I bid you welcome to my house, young man. Your splendid behaviour in connection with that great disaster has brought your name to everybody's lips, and I count it an honour to receive you here. . . .

STUDENT.   Being a man of humble birth, Colonel . . . and considering your name and position. . . .

COLONEL.   May I introduce?—Mr. Arkenholtz—Mr. Hummel.   The ladies are in there, Mr. Arkenholtz—if you please— I have a few more things to talk over with Mr. Hummel. . . .

Guided by the COLONEL, *the* STUDENT *goes into the Hyacinth Room, where he remains visible, standing beside the* YOUNG LADY *and talking very timidly to her.*

COLONEL.   A splendid young chap—very musical—sings, and writes poetry. . . .   If he were only a nobleman—if he belonged to our class, I don't think I should object. . . .

HUMMEL.   To what?

COLONEL.   Oh, my daughter. . . .

HUMMEL. *Your* daughter, you say?—But apropos of that, why is she always sitting in that room?

COLONEL. She has to spend all her time in the Hyacinth Room when she is not out. That is a peculiarity of hers. . . . Here comes Miss Betty von Holstein-Kron—a charming woman —a Secular Canoness, with just enough money of her own to suit her birth and position. . . .

HUMMEL. [*To himself.*] My fiancée!

The FIANCÉE *enters. She is white-haired, and her looks indicate a slightly unbalanced mind.*

COLONEL. Miss von Holstein-Kron—Mr. Hummel.

The FIANCÉE *curtseys in old-fashioned manner and takes a seat. The* DANDY *enters and seats himself; he is in mourning and has a very mysterious look.*

COLONEL. Baron Skansenkorge. . . .

HUMMEL. [*Aside, without rising.*] That's the jewelry thief, I think. . . . [*To the* COLONEL.] If you bring in the Mummy, our gathering will be complete.

COLONEL. [*Going to the door of the Hyacinth Room.*] Polly!

MUMMY. [*Enters.*] Currrrr!

COLONEL. How about the young people?

HUMMEL. No, not the young people! They must be spared.

The company is seated in a circle, no one saying a word for a while.

COLONEL. Shall we order the tea now?

HUMMEL. What's the use? No one cares for tea, and I can't see the need of pretending. [*Pause.*

COLONEL. Shall we make conversation?

HUMMEL. [*Speaking slowly and with frequent pauses.*] Talk of the weather, which we know all about? Ask one another's state of health, which we know just as well? I prefer silence. Then thoughts become audible, and we can see the past. Silence can hide nothing—but words can. I read the other day that the differentiation of languages had its origin in the desire among savage peoples to keep their tribal secrets hidden from outsiders. This means that every language is a code, and he who finds the universal key can understand every language in the

world—which does not prevent the secret from becoming re-
vealed without any key at times, and especially when the fact of
paternity is to be proved—but, of course, legal proof is a different matter.   Two false witnesses suffice to prove anything
on which they agree, but you don't bring any witnesses along on
the kind of expedition I have in mind.   Nature herself has
planted in man a sense of modesty, which tends to hide that which,
should be hidden.   But we slip into situations unawares, and
now and then a favourable chance will reveal the most cherished
secret, stripping the impostor of his mask, and exposing the villain. . . .

> *Long pause during which everybody is subject to silent scrutiny
> by all the rest.*

HUMMEL.   How silent everybody is!   [*Long silence.*]
Here, for instance, in this respectable house, this attractive home,
where beauty and erudition and wealth have joined hands. . . .
[*Long silence.*]   All of us sitting here now—we know who we
are, don't we?   I don't need to tell. . . .   And all of you know
me, although you pretend ignorance. . . .   In the next room is
my daughter—*mine*, as you know perfectly well.   She has lost
the desire to live without knowing why. . . .   The fact is that she
has been pining away in this air charged with crime and deceit
and falsehood of every kind. . . .   That is the reason why I have
looked for a friend in whose company she may enjoy the light
and heat radiated by noble deeds. . . .   [*Long silence.*]   Here
is my mission in this house: to tear up the weeds, to expose the
crimes, to settle all accounts, so that those young people may start
life with a clean slate in a home that is my gift to them.   [*Long
silence.*]   Now I grant you safe retreat.   Everybody may leave
in his due turn.   Whoever stays will be arrested.   [*Long
silence.*]   Do you hear that clock ticking like the deathwatch
hidden in a wall?   Can you hear what it says?—" It's time!
It's time! "—When it strikes in a few seconds, your time will be
up, and then you can go, but not before.   You may notice, too,
that the clock shakes its fist at you before it strikes.   Listen!
There it is!   " Better beware," it says. . . .   And I can strike,
too. . . .   [*He raps the top of a table with one of his crutches.*]
Do you hear?

For a while everybody remains silent.

MUMMY. [*Goes up to the clock and stops it; then she speaks in a normal and dignified tone.*] But I can stop time in its course. I can wipe out the past and undo what is done. Bribes won't do that, nor will threats—but suffering and repentance will. . . . [*She goes to* HUMMEL.] We are miserable human creatures, and we know it. We have erred and we have sinned—we, like everybody else. We are not what we seem, but at bottom we are better than ourselves because we disapprove of our own misdeeds. And when you, Jacob Hummel, with your assumed name, propose to sit in judgment on us, you merely prove yourself worse than all the rest. You are not the one you seem to be—no more than we! You are a thief of human souls! You stole mine once upon a time by means of false promises. You killed the Consul, whom they buried this afternoon—strangling him with debts. You are now trying to steal the soul of the Student with the help of an imaginary claim against his father, who never owed you a farthing. . . .

Having vainly tried to rise and say something, HUMMEL *sinks back into his chair; as the* MUMMY *continues her speech he seems to shrink and lose volume more and more.*

MUMMY. There is one dark spot in your life concerning which I am not certain, although I have my suspicions. . . . I believe Bengtsson can throw light on it.

[*She rings the table-bell.*

HUMMEL. No! Not Bengtsson! Not him!

MUMMY. So he *does* know? [*She rings again.*

The MILKMAID *appears in the hallway, but is only seen by* HUMMEL, *who shrinks back in horror. Then* BENGTSSON *enters, and the* MILKMAID *disappears.*

MUMMY. Do you know this man, Bengtsson?

BENGTSSON. Oh yes, I know him, and he knows me. Life has its ups and downs, as you know. I have been in his service, and he has been in mine. For two years he came regularly to our kitchen to be fed by our cook. Because he had to be at work at a certain hour, she made the dinner far ahead of time, and we had to be satisfied with the warmed-up leavings of that beast. He drank the soup-stock, so that we got nothing but water. Like a vampire, he sucked the house of all nourishment, until we became reduced to mere skeletons—and he nearly got us into jail when we dared to call the cook a thief. Later I met that man in Hamburg, where he had another name. Then he was a moneylender, a regular leech. While there, he was accused of having lured a young girl out on the ice in order to drown her, because she had seen him commit a crime, and he was afraid of being exposed. . . .

MUMMY. [*Making a pass with her hand over the face of* HUMMEL *as if removing a mask.*] That's you! And now, give up the notes and the will!

> JOHANSSON *appears in the hallway and watches the scene with great interest, knowing that his slavery will now come to an end.*
>
> HUMMEL *produces a bundle of papers and throws them on the table.*

MUMMY. [*Stroking the back of* HUMMEL.] Polly! Are you there, Jacob?

HUMMEL. [*Talking like a parrot.*] Here is Jacob!— Pretty Polly! Currrrr!

MUMMY. May the clock strike?

HUMMEL. [*With a clucking noise like that of a clock preparing to strike.*] The clock may strike! [*Imitating a cuckoo-clock.*] Cuckoo, cuckoo, cuckoo. . . .

MUMMY. [*Opening the closet door.*] Now the clock has struck! Rise and enter the closet where I have spent twenty years bewailing our evil deed. There you will find a rope that may represent the one with which you strangled the Consul as well as the one with which you meant to strangle your benefactor. . . . Go!

> HUMMEL *enters the closet.*

MUMMY. [*Closes the door after him.*] Put up the screen, Bengtsson. . . . The Death Screen!

> BENGTSSON *places the screen in front of the door.*

MUMMY. It is finished! God have mercy on his soul!

ALL. Amen!

> *Long silence. Then the* YOUNG LADY *appears in the Hyacinth Room with the* STUDENT. *She seats herself at a harp*

and begins a prelude, which changes into an accompaniment
to the following recitative:
STUDENT.   [*Singing.*]

" Seeing the sun, it seemed to my fancy
    That I beheld the Spirit that's hidden.
    Man must for ever reap what he planted:
    Happy is he who has done no evil.
    Wrong that was wrought in moments of anger
    Never by added wrong can be righted.
    Kindness shown to the man whose sorrow
    Sprang from your deed, will serve you better.
    Fear and guilt have their home together:
    Happy indeed is the guiltless man! "

Curtain.

SCENE III

A room furnished in rather bizarre fashion.   The general
effect of it is Oriental.   Hyacinths of different colours are
scattered everywhere.   On the mantelshelf of the fire-
place is seen a huge, seated Buddha, in whose lap rests a
bulb.   From that bulb rises the stalk of a shallot (Allium
Ascalonicum), *spreading aloft its almost globular cluster of*
white, starlike flowers.

An open door in the rear wall, towards the right-hand side,
*leads to the Round Room, where the ·*COLONEL *and the*
MUMMY *are seated.   They don't stir and don't utter a*
word.   A part of the Death Screen is also visible.

Another door, at the left, leads to the pantry and the kitchen.
The YOUNG LADY [*Adèle*] *and the* STUDENT *are discovered*
near a table.   She is seated at her harp, and he stands be-
side her.

YOUNG LADY.   Sing to my flowers.
STUDENT.   Is this the flower of your soul?
YOUNG LADY.   The one and only.—Are you fond of the
hyacinth?

STUDENT. I love it above all other flowers. I love its virginal shape rising straight and slender out of the bulb that rests on the water and sends its pure white rootlets down into the colourless fluid. I love the colour of it, whether innocently white as snow or sweetly yellow as honey; whether youthfully pink or maturely red; but above all if blue—with the deep-eyed, faith-inspiring blue of the morning sky. I love these flowers, one and all; love them more than pearls or gold, and have loved them ever since I was a child. I have always admired them, too, because they possess every handsome quality that I lack. . . . And yet . . .

YOUNG LADY. What?

STUDENT. My love is unrequited. These beautiful blossoms hate me.

YOUNG LADY. How do you mean?

STUDENT. Their fragrance, powerful and pure as the winds of early spring, which have passed over melting snow—it seems to confuse my senses, to make me deaf and blind, to crowd me out of the room, to bombard me with poisoned arrows that hurt my heart and set my head on fire. Do you know the legend of that flower?

YOUNG LADY. Tell me about it.

STUDENT. Let us first interpret its symbolism. The bulb is the earth, resting on the water or buried in the soil. From that the stalk rises, straight as the axis of the universe. At its upper end appear the six-pointed, starlike flowers.

YOUNG LADY. Above the earth—the stars! What lofty thought! Where did you find it? How did you discover it?

STUDENT. Let me think. . . . In your eyes!—It is, therefore, an image of the Cosmos. And that is the reason why Buddha is holding the earth-bulb in his lap, brooding on it with a steady gaze, in order that he may behold it spread outward and upward as it becomes transformed into a heaven. . . . This poor earth must turn into a heaven! That is what Buddha is waiting for!

YOUNG LADY. I see now. . . . Are not the snow crystals six-pointed, too, like the hyacinth-lily?

STUDENT. You are right! Thus the snow crystal is a falling star. . . .

YOUNG LADY. And the snowdrop is a star of snow—grown out of the snow.

STUDENT. But the largest and most beautiful of all the stars in the firmament, the red and yellow Sirius, is the narcissus, with its yellow-and-red cup and its six white rays. . . .

YOUNG LADY. Have you seen the shallot bloom?

STUDENT. Indeed, I have! It hides its flowers within a ball, a globe resembling the celestial one, and strewn, like that, with white stars. . . .

YOUNG LADY. What a tremendous thought! Whose was it?

STUDENT. Yours!

YOUNG LADY. No, yours!

STUDENT. Ours, then! We have jointly given birth to something: we are wedded. . . .

YOUNG LADY. Not yet.

STUDENT. What more remains?

YOUNG LADY. To await the coming ordeal in patience!

STUDENT. I am ready for it. [*Pause.*] Tell me! Why do your parents sit there so silently, without saying a single word?

YOUNG LADY. Because they have nothing to say to each other, and because neither one believes what the other says. This is the way my father puts it: " What is the use of talking, when you can't fool each other anyhow? "

STUDENT. That's horrible. . . .

YOUNG LADY. Here comes the Cook. . . . Look! how big and fat she is! . . .

STUDENT. What does she want?

YOUNG LADY. To ask me about the dinner. . . . You see, I am looking after the house during my mother's illness.

STUDENT. Have we to bother about the kitchen, too?

YOUNG LADY. We must eat. . . . Look at that Cook. . . . I can't bear the sight of her. . . .

STUDENT. What kind of a monster is she?

YOUNG LADY. She belongs to the Hummel family of vampires. She is eating us alive.

STUDENT. Why don't you discharge her?

YOUNG LADY. Because she won't leave. We can do nothing with her, and we have got her for the sake of our sins. . . . Don't you see that we are pining and wasting away?

STUDENT. Don't you get enough to eat?

YOUNG LADY. Plenty of dishes, but with all the nourishment gone from the food. She boils the life out of the beef, and drinks the stock herself, while we get nothing but fibres and water. In the same way, when we have roast, she squeezes it dry. Then she eats the gravy and drinks the juice herself. She takes the strength and savour out of everything she touches. It is as if her eyes were leeches. When she has had coffee, we get the grounds. She drinks the wine and puts water into the bottles. . . .

STUDENT. Kick her out!

YOUNG LADY. We can't!

STUDENT. Why not?

YOUNG LADY. We don't know! But she won't leave! And nobody can do anything with her. She has taken all our strength away from us.

STUDENT. Will you let me dispose of her?

YOUNG LADY. No! It has to be as it is, I suppose.—Here she is now. She will ask me what I wish for dinner, and I tell her, and then she will make objections, and in the end she has her own way.

STUDENT. Why don't you leave it to her entirely?

YOUNG LADY. She won't let me.

STUDENT. What a strange house! It seems to be bewitched!

YOUNG LADY. It is!—Now she turned back on seeing you here.

COOK. [*Appearing suddenly in the doorway at that very moment.*] Naw, that was not the reason.

[*She grins so that every tooth can be seen.*

STUDENT. Get out of here!

COOK. When it suits me! [*Pause.*] Now it does suit me!

[*She disappears.*

YOUNG LADY. Don't lose your temper! You must practise patience. She is part of the ordeal we have to face in this house.

We have a chambermaid, too, after whom we have to put everything back where it belongs.

STUDENT. Now I am sinking! *Cor in æthere!* Music!

YOUNG LADY. Wait!

STUDENT. Music!

YOUNG LADY. Patience!—This is named the Room of Ordeal. . . . It is beautiful to look at, but is full of imperfections. . . .

STUDENT. Incredible! Yet such things have to be borne. It is very beautiful, although a little cold. Why don't you have a fire?

YOUNG LADY. Because the smoke comes into the room.

STUDENT. Have the chimney swept!

YOUNG LADY. It doesn't help—Do you see that writing-table?

STUDENT. Remarkably handsome!

YOUNG LADY. But one leg is too short. Every day I put a piece of cork under that leg. Every day the chambermaid takes it away when she sweeps the room. Every day I have to cut a new piece. Both my penholder and my inkstand are covered with ink every morning, and I have to clean them after that woman—as sure as the sun rises. [*Pause.*] What is the worst thing you can think of?

STUDENT. To count the wash. Ugh!

YOUNG LADY. That's what I have to do. Ugh!

STUDENT. Anything else?

YOUNG LADY. To be waked out of your sleep and have to get up and close the window—which the chambermaid has left unlatched.

STUDENT. Anything else?

YOUNG LADY. To get up on a ladder and tie on the cord which the chambermaid has torn from the window-shade.

STUDENT. Anything else?

YOUNG LADY. To sweep after her; to dust after her; to start the fire again, after she has merely thrown some wood into the fireplace! To watch the damper in the fireplace; to wipe every glass; to set the table over again; to open the wine-bottles; to see that the rooms are aired; to make over your bed; to rinse the water-bottle that is green with sediment; to buy matches and soap, which are always lacking; to wipe the chimneys and cut the wicks in order to keep the lamps from smoking ... and in order to keep them from going out when we have company, I have to fill them myself. . . .

STUDENT. Music!

YOUNG LADY. Wait! The labour comes first—the labour of keeping the filth of life at a distance.

STUDENT. But you are wealthy, and you have two servants?

YOUNG LADY. What does that help? What would it help to have three? It is troublesome to live, and at times I get tired. . . . Think, then, of adding a nursery!

STUDENT. The greatest of joys. . . .

YOUNG LADY. And the costliest. . . . Is life really worth so much trouble?

STUDENT. It depends on the reward you expect for your labours. . . . To win your hand I would face anything.

YOUNG LADY. Don't talk like that. You can never get me.

STUDENT. Why?

YOUNG LADY. You mustn't ask. [Pause.

STUDENT. You dropped your bracelet out of the window. . . .

YOUNG LADY. Yes, because my hand has grown too small. . . .
[Pause.

The COOK appears with a bottle of Japanese soy in her hand.

YOUNG LADY. There is the one that eats me and all the rest alive.

STUDENT. What has she in her hand?

COOK. This is my colouring bottle that has letters on it looking like scorpions. It's the soy that turns water into bouillon, and that takes the place of gravy. You can make cabbage soup out of it, or mock-turtle soup, if you prefer.

STUDENT. Out with you!

COOK. You take the sap out of us, and we out of you. We keep the blood for ourselves and leave you the water—with the colouring. It's the colour that counts! Now I shall leave, but I stay just the same—as long as I please! [She goes out.

STUDENT. Why has Bengtsson got a medal?

YOUNG LADY.   On account of his great merits.

STUDENT.   Has he no faults?

YOUNG LADY.   Yes, great ones, but faults bring you no medals, you know.   [*Both smile.*

STUDENT.   You have a lot of secrets in this house. . . .

YOUNG LADY.   As in all houses. . . . Permit us to keep ours!
                                                    [*Pause.*

STUDENT.   Do you care for frankness?

YOUNG LADY.   Within reason.

STUDENT.   At times I am seized with a passionate craving to say all I think. . . . Yet I know that the world would go to pieces if perfect frankness were the rule.   [*Pause.*]   I attended a funeral the other day—in one of the churches—and it was very solemn and beautiful.

YOUNG LADY.   That of Mr. Hummel?

STUDENT.   Yes, that of my pretended benefactor.   An elderly friend of the deceased acted as mace-bearer and stood at the head of the coffin.   I was particularly impressed by the dignified manner and moving words of the minister.   I had to cry —everybody cried. . . .   A number of us went to a restaurant afterwards, and there I learned that the man with the mace had been rather too friendly with the dead man's son. . . .

The YOUNG LADY *stares at him, trying to make out the meaning of his words.*

STUDENT.   I learned, too, that the dead man had borrowed money of his son's devoted friend. . . .   [*Pause.*]   And the next day the minister was arrested for embezzling the church funds. —Nice, isn't it?

YOUNG LADY.   Oh!   [*Pause.*

STUDENT.   Do you know what I am thinking of you now?

YOUNG LADY.   Don't tell, or I'll die!

STUDENT.   I must, lest *I* die!

YOUNG LADY.   It is only in the asylum you say all that you think. . . .

STUDENT.   Exactly!   My father died in a madhouse. . . .

YOUNG LADY.   Was he sick?

STUDENT.   No, perfectly well, and yet mad.   It broke out at last, and these were the circumstances.   Like all of us, he was

surrounded by a circle of acquaintances whom he called friends
for the sake of convenience, and they were a lot of scoundrels, of
course, as most people are. He had to have some society, however, as he couldn't sit all alone. As you know, no one tells
people what he thinks of them under ordinary circumstances, and
my father didn't do so either. He knew that they were false,
and he knew the full extent of their perfidy, but, being a wise
man and well brought up, he remained always polite. One day
he gave a big party.... It was in the evening, naturally, and
he was tired out by a hard day's work. Then the strain of keeping his thoughts to himself while talking a lot of damned rot to
his guests.... [*The* YOUNG LADY *is visibly shocked.*] Well,
while they were still at the table, he rapped for silence, raised his
glass, and began to speak.... Then something loosed the trig-
ger, and in a long speech he stripped the whole company naked,
one by one, telling them all he knew about their treacheries. At
last, when utterly tired out, he sat down on the table itself and
told them all to go to hell!

YOUNG LADY. Oh!

STUDENT. I was present, and I shall never forget what happened after that. My parents had a fight, the guests rushed for
the doors—and my father was taken to a madhouse, where he
died! [*Pause.*] To keep silent too long is like letting water
stagnate so that it rots. That is what has happened in this house.
There is something rotten here. And yet I thought it paradise
itself when I saw you enter here the first time.... It was a
Sunday morning, and I stood gazing into these rooms. Here I
saw a Colonel who was no colonel. I had a generous benefactor
who was a robber and had to hang himself. I saw a Mummy
who was not a mummy, and a maiden—how about the maiden-
hood, by the by? ... Where is beauty to be found? In nature,
and in my own mind when it has donned its Sunday clothes.
Where do we find honour and faith? In fairy-tales and childish
fancies. Where can I find anything that keeps its promise?
Only in my own imagination! ... Your flowers have poisoned
me and now I am squirting their poison back at you.... I asked
you to become my wife in a home full of poetry, and song, and
music; and then the Cook appeared.... *Sursum corda!* Try

once more to strike fire and purple out of the golden harp. . . .
Try, I ask you, I implore you on my knees. . . .   [*As she does
not move.*]   Then I must do it myself!   [*He picks up the harp,
but is unable to make its strings sound.*]   It has grown deaf and
dumb!   Only think, that the most beautiful flower of all can be
so poisonous—that it can be more poisonous than any other
one. . . .   There must be a curse on all creation and on life itself. . . . Why did you not want to become my bride? Because the
very well-spring of life within you has been sickened. . . . Now I
can feel how that vampire in the kitchen is sucking my life
juices. . . .   She must be a Lamia, one of those that suck the
blood of children.   It is always in the servants' quarters that the
seed-leaves of the children are nipped, if it has not already happened in the bedroom. . . .   There are poisons that blind you,
and others that open your eyes more widely.   I must have been
born with that second kind of poison, I fear, for I cannot regard
what is ugly as beautiful, or call evil good—I cannot!   They
say that Jesus Christ descended into hell.   It refers merely to his
wanderings on this earth—his descent into that madhouse, that
jail, the morgue, the earth.   The madmen killed him when he
wished to liberate them, but the robber was set free.   It is always
the robber who gets sympathy!   Woe!   Woe is all of us!
Saviour of the World, save us—we are perishing!

> *Towards the end of the* STUDENT's *speech, the* YOUNG LADY
> *has drooped more and more.   She seems to be dying.   At
> last she manages to reach a bell and rings for* BENGTSSON,
> *who enters shortly afterwards.*

YOUNG LADY.   Bring the screen!   Quick!   I am dying!

BENGTSSON *fetches the screen, opens it and places it so that the*
YOUNG LADY *is completely hidden behind it.*

STUDENT.   The liberator is approaching!   Be welcome, thou
pale and gentle one!—Sleep, you beauteous, unhappy and innocent creature, who have done nothing to deserve your own sufferings!   Sleep without dreaming, and when you wake again—
may you be greeted by a sun that does not burn, by a home without dust, by friends without stain, by a love without flaw! . . .
Thou wise and gentle Buddha, who sits waiting there to see a
heaven sprout from this earth, endow us with patience in the

hour of trial, and with purity of will, so that thy hope be not put
to shame!

*The strings of the harp begin to hum softly, and a white light
pours into the room.*

STUDENT. [*Singing.*]

" Seeing the sun, it seemed to my fancy
    That I beheld the Spirit that's hidden.
    Man must for ever reap what he planted:
    Happy is he who has done no evil.
    Wrong that was wrought in moments of anger
    Never by added wrong can be righted.
    Kindness shown to the man whose sorrow
    Sprang from your deed, will serve you better.
    Fear and guilt have their home together:
    Happy indeed is the guiltless man! " [1]

A faint moaning sound is heard from behind the screen.

STUDENT. You poor little child—you child of a world of
illusion, guilt, suffering, and death—a world of eternal change,
disappointment, and pain—may the Lord of Heaven deal mercifully with you on your journey!

*The whole room disappears, and in its place appears Boecklin's
    " The Island of Death." Soft music, very quiet and
    pleasantly wistful, is heard from without.*

Curtain.

[1] The lines recited by the *Student* are a paraphrase of several passages from
" The Song of the Sun " in the Poetic Edda. It is characteristic of Strindberg's
attitude during his final period that this Eddic poem, which apparently had
occupied his mind a great deal, as he has used it a number of times in " The
Bridal Crown " also, is the only one of that ancient collection which is unmis-
takably Christian in its colouring. It has a certain apocryphal reputation and is
not regarded on a par with the other contents of the Poetic Edda.